Readings in MONEY AND BANKING

Third Edition

GEORGE SELGIN, Editor

Pearson Custom Publishing

Copyright © 1992 by Ginn Press.
Copyright © 1998, 1996 by Simon & Schuster Custom Publishing.
All rights reserved.

This copyright covers material written expressly for this volume by the editor/s as well as the compilation itself. It does not cover the individual selections herein that first appeared elsewhere. Permission to reprint these has been obtained by Simon & Schuster Custom Publishing for this edition only. Further reproduction by any means, electronic or mechanical, including photocopying and recording, or by any information storage or retrieval system, must be arranged with the individual copyright holders noted.

Printed in the United States of America

10 9 8 7 6 5 4 3

Please visit our website at www.pearsoncustom.com

ISBN 0–536–01172–9

BA 990479

PEARSON CUSTOM PUBLISHING
75 Arlington Street, Boston, MA 02116
A Pearson Education Company

Copyright Acknowledgments

Grateful acknowledgment is made to the following sources for permission to reprint material copyrighted or controlled by them:

"Why Bother?" by J. Huston McCulloch, reprinted from *Money & Inflation: A Monetarist Approach,* Second Edition, 1982, Academic Press, Inc.

"B.C." (cartoon), reprinted with permission from *Creator's Syndicate.*

"Cartoon," by Booth, reprinted with permission from *The New Yorker.* Copyright © 1979, The New Yorker Magazine, Inc.

"The Theory of Money," by Carl Menger, reprinted with permission from *Principles of Economics*, 1981, The Institute for Humane Studies.

"The Evolution of a Free Banking System," by George Selgin and Lawrence White, reprinted from *Economic Inquiry*, Vol. 25, July 1987, Western Economic Association International.

"The Establishment of Central Banking," by Kevin Dowd, reprinted from *The State and the Monetary System*, 1989. Copyright © 1989 by Kevin Dowd.

"The Banking Business: Fundamentals," by Barry N. Siegel, reprinted from *Money, Banking and the Economy: A Monetaristic View*, 1982, Harcourt Brace & Company.

"Lessons of the German Inflation," by Henry Hazlitt, reprinted with permission from *The Inflation Crisis, and How to Resolve It*, 1978, published by The Foundation for Economic Education, Irvington-on-Hudson, New York.

"The Consequences to Society of Changes in the Value of Money," by John Maynard Keynes, reprinted from *A Tract on Monetary Reform*, 1974, Cambridge University Press.

"Money and Interest Rates," by William Poole, reprinted with permission from *Money and the Economy*, 1978, Addison Wesley Longman. Copyright © 1978 by Addison Wesley Longman.

"Inflation, the Misdirection of Labor and Unemployment," by F.A. Hayek, reprinted from *Full Employment at Any Price?*, 1975, Institute of Economic Affairs. Copyright © 1975 by Institute of Economic Affairs.

"A Cash-Balance Interpretation of Depression," by Leland Yeager, reprinted from *The Southern Economic Journal*, Vol. 22, No. 4, April 1956, The Southern Economic Association.

"The Genesis of the Depression," by Lionel Robbins, reprinted from *The Great Depression*, 1971, by permission from Ayer Co. Publishers, Inc., N. Stratford, New Hampshire 03590.

"The Biggest Scam in History," by James Ring Adams, reprinted from *The Big Fix*, 1990, by permission of John Wiley & Sons, Inc.

"The Necessary and the Desirable Range of Discretion to be Allowed to a Monetary Authority," by Jacob Viner, reprinted from *In Search of a Monetary Constitution*, edited by Leland B. Yeager, 1962, by permission of Harvard University Press.

"The Gold Standard: Myths and Realities," by Michael David Bordo, reprinted from *Money in Crisis* by Barry N. Siegel, 1984, by permission of Pacific Institute for Public Policy Research.

"Choice in Currency: A Way to Stop Inflation," by F.A. Hayek, 1976, Institute of Economic Affairs.

"Free Banking and Monetary Reform," by George Selgin, reprinted from *The Theory of Free Banking*, 1988, Rowman & Littlefield and Cato Institute.

Contents

PART I: INSTITUTIONS

1. Why Bother?
   J. Huston McCulloch — 3

2. The Theory of Money
   Carl Menger — 12

3. The Evolution of a Free Banking System: A Reappraisal
   George Selgin and Lawrence White — 23

4. The Establishment of Central Banking
   Kevin Dowd — 42

5. Wildcat Banking, Banking Panics, and Free Banking in the United States
   Gerald P. Dwyer — 68

6. The Evolution of the Bank Regulatory Structure
   F. Ward McCarthy, Jr. — 88

PART II: THEORY

7. The Banking Business: Fundamentals
   Barry N. Siegel — 109

8. Why Does Velocity Matter?
   Daniel L. Thornton — 131

9. Lessons of the German Inflation
   Henry Hazlitt — 139

10. The Consequences to Society of Changes in the Value of Money
    John Maynard Keynes — 151

11. Money and Interest Rates
    William Poole — 178

12. The Natural Rate of Unemployment: Concepts and Issues
    Stuart E. Weiner — 190

13.	Inflation, the Misdirection of Labour and Unemployment F.A. Hayek	201
14.	A Cash-Balance Interpretation of Depression Leland Yeager	212
15.	The Genesis of the Depression Lionel Robbins	221
16.	Are Banking Crises Free-Market Phenomena? George Selgin	239
17.	The Biggest Scam in History James Ring Adams	252

PART III: POLICY

18.	The Necessary and the Desirable Range of Discretion to be Allowed to a Monetary Authority Jacob Viner	267
19.	The Gold Standard: Myths and Realities Michael David Bordo	287
20.	Choice in Currency: A Way to Stop Inflation F.A. Hayek	316
21.	Free Banking and Monetary Reform George Selgin	326
22.	The Lender of Last Resort: Alternative Views and Historical Experience Michael David Bordo	333

Part I: Institutions

1. Why Bother?

J. Huston McCulloch

Money—a generally accepted medium of exchange—is not a costless institution. Substantial resources had to be channelled to the mining industry to support past metallic monetary systems. Even today's fiat money systems involve tremendous resources, including the administrative and research staffs of central banks, to operate. Add to this the substantial costs of periodic episodes of inflation and deflation, and it is easy to see that monetary exchange is expensive. So "Why Bother?" Why not just abandon money altogether and rely on barter instead? A simple answer is that money overcomes the difficulties inherent in barter. In the essay that follows, J. Huston McCulloch explains just what these difficulties are and how monetary exchange avoids them. —G.S., Ed.

****

One of the questions that most troubles people when they consider the role of money in the economy is, "Why bother?" We sell goods and services for money only in order to be able to buy other goods and services. Why not get back to nature by trading goods and services directly? At best, the intervention of money seems like an unnecessary nuisance that only obscures the underlying economic relations. Some claim it is more like a carcinogenic contaminant that poisons society.

1.1 THE POSSIBLE IMPOSSIBILITY OF BARTER

Consider, for example, an economy consisting of a butcher and a baker. The butcher would prefer to have a loaf of bread to a steak that he happens to have on hand, and the baker, who has such a loaf of bread, would rather trade it for a steak. They could just trade steak for bread without using money at all. For this example *barter*—the mutually advantageous direct exchange of goods or services for other goods or services—is adequate to achieve an optional reallocation of the goods in the economy.

If we consider a slightly more complicated situation, however, we discover that a market economy based entirely on voluntary exchange might not be able to function efficiently by barter alone. Suppose there were a third individual—a candlestick maker—who was in possession of a third good: a candle. Suppose now that the butcher would be willing to exchange his steak for some bread, but would rather eat the steak himself than have a candle. The baker is an avid bookworm and would rather read than eat, so she prefers the candle to her loaf of bread. She is a vegetarian, however, and so would sooner eat bread than steak. The candlestick maker prefers the steak to his candle, and his candle to the bread.

In this simple economy no barter is possible. That is, there are no *direct* exchanges that are mutually advantageous to the pair of persons involved. The butcher and the baker can't barter because, if they traded their goods, the baker would be stuck with the steak and therefore worse off. The butcher and the candlestick maker can't barter, because the butcher wouldn't consent. The baker and the candlestick maker can't barter, because then the candlestick maker would be worse off. If the economy were confined to barter, each individual would end up with his or her second-most-favorite good, even though goods are present in the economy to satisfy each person's fondest desire.

With only three people and three goods, we have to think a little in order to work up an example in which barter is impossible. But in a modern industrial economy, with millions of variations of commodities and millions of individuals each specialized in the production of just a few of these commodities, barter is totally unworkable because of the vast number of situations like this that might arise.

In our extremely simple three-person economy, it is obvious how everyone could be made better off by rearranging ownership through a dictatorial decree instead of through voluntary exchange. For instance, suppose the baker seizes power. If she orders the butcher to give the candlestick maker his steak, directs the candlestick maker to give her his candle, and then gives the butcher her bread, everyone will be better off.* It would also be within her power, however, to decree the first two transactions, keep the bread (along with the candle) for herself, and then move in with the candlestick maker, leaving the butcher empty-handed! To protect the powerless, it is desirable to rule out involuntary reallocations. But would it still be possible to make everyone better off?

1.2
INDIRECT EXCHANGE

It would be possible, but only through a process of *indirect exchange*. Suppose that the butcher goes to the baker and proposes an exchange of steak for bread. The baker will turn him down, but might add that she *would* be willing to accept a candle in exchange for her bread. Now the butcher approaches the candlestick maker and asks if he will give him some bread for his steak. The candlestick maker replies that he would if he had some, but that all he has is a candle, which he would be willing to trade for the steak. If the butcher remembers that the baker was willing to take a candle for a loaf of bread, he will go ahead and trade steak for candle. Then he returns to the baker and trades the candle for the bread. They all end up with their most desired commodity, entirely through voluntary exchange. But the first exchange was not barter, because the butcher did not receive a good he planned to use himself. On the contrary, he accepted a good he valued less highly than the good he gave up, simply because he believed it had exchange value somewhere else. The candle in this example serves as a *medium of indirect exchange*. It serves the same monetary function as the silver coin or green piece of paper that the worker accepts for his labor, in the belief that he can trade the coin or paper for the goods he really wants.

In this economy there is no particular reason for the candle to be singled out as the monetary medium. If, instead, the baker had spoken first with the candlestick maker and then with the butcher, the steak could have been the medium of indirect exchange. If the candlestick maker had gone to the butcher and then to the baker, the bread could have been used as money.

---

*In an economy with extensive division of labor, centrally directed redistribution encounters the additional problem that it is no longer obvious how to make everyone as well off as possible without making anyone worse off. This may be too complex a problem to solve centrally.

Notice that whichever good is used as money, its value in exchange must be established before it will be accepted in its monetary role. If the butcher had gone to the candlestick maker directly, without first speaking with the baker, he would not have traded his steak for the candle because he would not have known that the candle could be traded for the bread that he really wanted. Before he would accept the candle he had to have established, some time in the past, the terms on which it could be traded for what he was really after. Its value to him as money rests on its past exchange value (which he assumes carries over into the future), rather than on its future usability.

Notice also that the monetary commodity (the candle, for example) must be held for a period of time by someone like the butcher who wants it solely for its monetary function. This means that there are two sources of demand for the monetary commodity: first, the ordinary demand on the part of people like the baker who want the candle for its actual use value, and, second, the purely monetary demand.

1.3
THE PROBLEM IN DIAGRAMS

The situations we have just described may be a little easier to visualize diagrammatically than verbally. Let A, B, and C represent the three individuals and let a, b, and c represent the goods with which each, respectively, is initially endowed. Individual A prefers b to a and a to c. In economic jargon, he obtains higher *utility* or satisfaction from consuming b than a, and higher utility from consuming a than c. He might prefer c to nothing at all, but still would rather have a or, better yet, good b. We can represent these preferences symbolically as "$b > a > c$." The preferences and initial endowments of all three individuals are represented in Figure 1-1:

Individual	Preferences	Initial endowment
A	$b > a > c$	a
B	$c > b > a$	b
C	$a > c > b$	c

Figure 1-1. An economy in which no barter is possible.

Barter is impossible, since if A and B exchanged goods, B would be worse off. If A and C traded, A would be worse off, and if B and C traded, C would be worse off. Everyone could be made better off by decree, as in Figure 1-2, but dictatorship is liable to lead to abuse of power, as in Figure 1-3.

Individual	Initial endowment	Final endowment
A	a	b
B	b	c
C	c	a

Figure 1-2. One possible reallocation by decree.

Individual	Initial endowment	Final endowment
A	a	—
B	b	b,c
C	c	a

Figure 1-3. Another possible reallocation by decree.

The necessary reallocation can be achieved entirely through voluntary exchange, but only provided one of the goods acts as a medium of indirect exchange. If good c is used, the two transactions shown in Figure 1-4 can take place. As Figure 1-5 demonstrates, good a could serve the monetary function equally well.

Individual	Initial endowment	Intermediate endowment	Final endowment
A	a	c	b
B	b	b	c
C	c	a	a
	first exchange	second exchange	

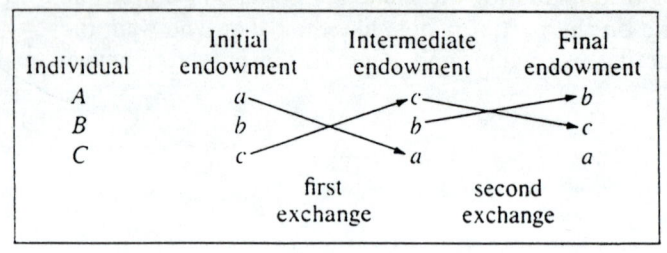

Figure 1-4. Reallocation by indirect exchange; A uses c as money.

Individual	Initial endowment	Intermediate endowment	Final endowment
A	a	b	b
B	b	a	c
C	c	c	a
	first exchange	second exchange	

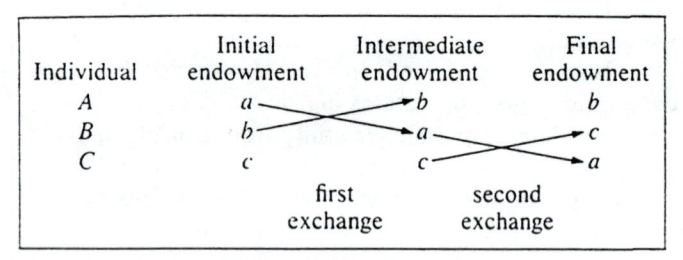

Figure 1-5. Reallocation by indirect exchange; B uses a as money.

1.4 THE EVOLUTION OF A COMMON MONETARY MEDIUM

Of course you shouldn't give up one good for another you value less unless you have reason to believe that someone else will give you something you value more in exchange for it. There are two reasons why a person might acquire a good: He might want to use it himself, or he in turn might think that it has exchange value. If there already is a good that is being used by a significant number of people as a medium of indirect exchange, that good is especially attractive to other people as a medium of indirect exchange. For this reason, the use of any particular commodity as money will be contagious; the right money to use is the money that everyone else uses. There is therefore a tendency for one commodity to be singled out as the *common* medium of indirect exchange, or as *the* money of the community (see Figure 1-6).

Which commodity is singled out is largely an historical accident. Some can be ruled out because they lack certain desirable properties:

Figure 1-6. Commodity money.
By permission of Johnny Hart and Creators Syndicate, Inc.

It helps if a medium of indirect exchange is durable, portable, and divisible. Clams are unsatisfactory because they perish quickly. Sand is no good because enough sand to pay for a day's food would be impossible to carry, assuming it had any value at all. But there is no way to deduce from this list of properties that gold, silver, and genuine Federal Reserve Notes will have a monetary function, while platinum, tin, and first edition Elvis Presley records will not.

The development of money is very similar to the development of language. It is fundamentally arbitrary which grunt or series of noises corresponds to an object such as fire. But once some people have started to use a particular noise to mean fire, other people will be inclined to adopt the same noise, since there is a ready-made circle of people who accept that meaning. Therefore there is a tendency in any society for *one* noise to be singled out as *the* noise for fire. Some noises can be ruled out because they lack certain desirable properties: a word should be pronounceable, concise, and unique. Thus "Fire!" is much handier in an emergency than "Xanhaglushonaipoferoleaghnin!" especially if the latter expression also means "What's for dinner?" and "Good night." But there is no way to deduce from these rules that "fire" will be the noise that is settled upon and not "fuego" or "$\phi\omega\tau\acute{\iota}\alpha$," noises that are recognized in some circles.

1.5
FROM COMMODITY MONEY TO FIAT MONEY

The inconvertible paper money or *fiat money* that we have in the United States today bears little resemblance to commodity money, be it gold, silver, or candles. Such a fiat money, however, must have evolved from an historical commodity-type money. Let us see how this might happen.

The butcher in our example may find it inconvenient to actually carry a candle around with him during the period between the time he sells his steak and the time he buys the bread. The candle may break, melt in the sun's heat, or otherwise deteriorate in appearance as he carries it around. He may instead prefer to ask the candlestick maker to mark the candle "sold" and give him a paper receipt that will entitle him or anyone else presenting it to take actual delivery of the candle. The baker will probably be willing to accept the receipt as readily as the monetary commodity itself, and people who use candles only as money will actually prefer such receipts.

These receipts, backed one-for-one with actual candles, closely resemble the *gold certificates* and *silver certificates* that once were issued by the U.S. government as money. Each of these certificates promised to pay a certain amount of gold or silver, and the gold or silver necessary to redeem each one was actually in the Treasury's vaults. Such money certificates have the advantage that they can at little cost be issued in multiple denominations, in which the monetary commodity itself would be inconveniently bulky, or in fractional denominations, into which it might not be practical to divide the monetary commodity.

In a complex economy, the monetary demand for the monetary commodity will be so great relative to its commodity demand that only a small fraction of the people who acquire money certificates will actually want to redeem them in order to consume the monetary commodity. It follows that in practice, issuers of money certificates will ordinarily find they can get away with keeping only *fractional reserves* of the monetary commodity. The candlestick maker, for example, might be able to get away with paying his workers and wax suppliers with paper notes that promise to pay one candle on demand, and still actually be able to keep that promise while keeping only one candle on hand for every five notes he circulates.

Once money substitutes such as 100% reserve money certificates or fractional reserve notes have for all practical purposes replaced the monetary commodity as the circulating medium, the final step to fiat money can be taken. Recall that the people who accept these notes as money are doing so not because they want to redeem them, but only because they want to trade them for the goods they really want to acquire. They value these notes each time they accept them on the basis of the prior determination of their purchasing power. If the candlestick maker's shop were now to burn down, taking all the candle reserves with it, this recollection of the candle notes' prior purchasing power would be unaltered. People in the economy would have to use something as money, and the right money to use is the money which is historically customary in the society in question, in this case candle notes. People would therefore continue to use the candle notes as money, and the notes would continue to have value, even though they were now entirely irredeemable and unbacked in terms of candles. The fact that those people who really wanted to cash them in for candles would no longer be able to do so means that there would be some reduction in demand for them and some fall in their purchasing power. But since the monetary demand was the bulk of the demand for the candle notes, this fall would be minor and might go entirely unnoticed. Candle notes would become a pure fiat money.

The expression "fiat money" suggests that it springs into existence from the government's fiat or decree, much as the sun comes into existence when, in the Latin version of Genesis, God says *"Fiat lux"* ("Let there be light."). In fact, however, the government has no such divine powers of creation. Although inconvertible fiat money is a practical form of money (with some drawbacks, to be sure), it must have evolved through a long historical process, as described above, from a prior commodity money. This commodity money itself was not arbitrarily established by the government, but was the process of a further historical competition among rival commodities. Government action has profoundly modified this evolution at times, often in unintended ways. But still the government is incapable of endowing fiat money with value out of thin air.

The U.S. dollar is an example of this evolution. At first the dollar was a gold or silver coin. Later some of these were replaced by gold and silver certificates. In 1913 *Federal Reserve Notes* were introduced which did not actually purport to be dollars, but rather were merely promises *to pay* dollars on demand. At first each one-dollar Federal Reserve Note was backed by 40¢ worth of gold plus more than 60¢ worth of obligations payable in the immediate future in gold dollars. Prior to 1933 they were freely convertible into gold, but since 1973 they have been totally inconvertible into anything. Today's dollars simply say

FEDERAL RESERVE NOTE
THE UNITED STATES OF AMERICA
ONE DOLLAR

The Government still has a gold stock that in some sense "backs" the dollar, but that could be entirely sold off without directly affecting the dollar's value. Today's dollar is essentially a pure fiat money, although this is only a recent stage in its evolution.

1.6
SECONDARY
FUNCTIONS OF MONEY

Money ordinarily serves as the economy's customary *unit of account*, as a *standard of deferred payment*, and as a *store of value* in addition to its function as a medium of exchange. Only the medium of exchange function (or medium of indirect exchange, to be precise, since direct exchange doesn't require a medium) is essential, however. The medium of indirect exchange will tend to serve these other functions, but they are not necessary.

Once the economy settles on a common medium of indirect exchange, all goods that are traded will be traded for that medium, money. Therefore goods automatically have their values computed in terms of the monetary good. It would be inconvenient to keep accounts in anything but money, since an extra conversion would be necessary. Therefore prices are ordinarily quoted, and account books are ordinarily kept, in units of the circulating money. If the purchasing power of money is very uncertain, however, this will not necessarily be the case. During the German hyperinflation of 1923, for example, the rapidly depreciating *Reichsmark* continued to function as money. But its value was so uncertain that stores began to price goods in terms of U.S. dollars instead of *Reichsmarks*. The amount to be paid had to be determined by multiplying the dollar-denominated price by the current price of the dollar in the foreign exchange market. Money had ceased to serve as the unit of account.

Provided the future purchasing power of money is relatively predictable, it also makes sense to write loan contracts in terms of monetary units. Insisting on a more exotic form of repayment would greatly reduce the number of people who would be willing to lend you money. But money will not necessarily be the standard of deferred payment. When inflation is unpredictable, it becomes more and more likely that people will prefer to receive deferred payments in terms of real purchasing power, with the exact number of dollars to be determined at repayment time, on the basis of some price index.

Money necessarily serves as a store of value from the instant it is received to the instant it is spent. Sometimes, however, it is used as a store of value over unusually long periods of time. A person might prefer to literally stash away dollar bills rather than lend them out at interest if he doesn't trust banks or corporate bonds. As long as the purchasing power of money is relatively stable, it makes a lot of sense to do this hoarding in terms of money, since it is directly exchangeable for a variety of goods. If the person were to fill his basement with sacks of pre-1964 silver coins instead, as in Figure 1-7, he would first have to convert his dollars into silver.

"Papa doesn't want Tsi Tsu in the bedroom while he's hiding his little nest egg."

Figure 1-7. When money is stable in purchasing power, it is often used directly as a *store of value*. But this is only a *secondary* function of money, since in periods of rapid inflation a nonmonetary commodity (such as gold or silver in today's economy) would be more suitable, in spite of the turnaround costs of converting money into the commodity and back again.
(Drawing by Booth; ©1979 The New Yorker Magazine, Inc.)

Then when he was ready to exchange his hoard for consumables, he would have to convert the silver back into money. If the market for silver had not changed in the meanwhile, he would take a loss, since coin dealers are in business to make a profit over and above their expenses and would only take back the silver at a price somewhat below the one at which they sold. Hoarding money instead of commodities eliminates the take of these middlemen. But again, money's function as a long-range store of value is not essential. In highly inflationary times it would be wiser to hoard nonmonetary commodities, in spite of the loss due to turnaround costs.

In short, the unit of account, standard of deferred payment, and store of value functions of money are only *secondary functions*. The only really indispensable role of money in the economy is its role as medium of indirect exchange.

Problem 1-1.
Using the preferences and initial endowments of Figure 1-1, show the sequence of exchange through which good *b* could serve as a medium of indirect exchange.

Problem 1-2.
Given that A initially owns a, B owns b, and C owns c, find another set of preferences other than those given in Figure 1-1 under which everyone could be made better off, yet for which barter is impossible.

NOTE: Solutions are gathered at the end of the book. For best results, the student should work through each problem to a numerical solution *before* looking at the answers.

REFERENCES*
The theory of the nature of money that we have presented here was originated by Carl Menger, *Principles of Economics* (Glencoe, Illinois: Free Press, 1950; originally published 1871), particularly Chapter 8, and by Ludwig von Mises, *The Theory of Money and Credit* (New Haven, Connecticut: Yale Univ. Press, 1953; originally published 1912).

For the fascinating history of the Hershey Bar standard, read R. A. Radford's article "The Economic Organization of a P.O.W. Camp," *Economic Journal* (November, 1945), pp. 189–201.

Terms to Remember
Barter
Indirect exchange
Medium of indirect exchange
Utility
Fiat money
Gold certificate
Silver certificate
Fractional reserves
Federal Reserve Note
Secondary functions of money
Unit of account
Standard of deferred payment
Store of value

*A few references follow each chapter for the student who wishes to look more deeply into the subject matter. They are certainly not meant to be exhaustive.

2. The Theory of Money
Carl Menger

The idea that "money is a creature of the state" was once commonplace, and is still occasionally encountered. According to it, the institution of monetary exchange was the invention of primitive rulers, and the first coins were likewise the innovation of some ancient government. Carl Menger, founder of the Austrian School of economists, was among the first economists to dispel this misconception. Drawing on both economic theory and anthropological evidence, Menger argued that money was not "invented" by anyone or by any government. It was, rather, a product of "spontaneous evolution"—an unintended outgrowth of numerous individuals' rational pursuit of their self-interest. "On The Theory of Money" is a section from Menger's famous Principles of Economics, *summarizing his theory of how money evolved.*
—G.S., Ed.

****

1. THE NATURE AND ORIGIN OF MONEY [1]

IN THE EARLY stages of trade, when economizing individuals are only slowly awakening to knowledge of the economic gains that can be derived from exploitation of existing exchange opportunities, their attention is, in keeping with the simplicity of all cultural beginnings, directed only to the most obvious of these opportunities. In considering the goods he will acquire in trade, each man takes account only of their use value to himself. Hence the exchange transactions that are actually performed are restricted naturally to situations in which economizing individuals have goods in their possession that have a smaller *use value* to them than goods in the possession of other economizing individuals who value the same goods in reverse fashion. A has a sword that has a smaller use value to him than B's plough, while to B the same plough has a smaller use value than A's sword—at the beginning of human trade, all exchange transactions actually performed are restricted to cases of this sort.

It is not difficult to see that the number of exchanges actually performed must be very narrowly limited under these conditions. How rarely does it happen that a good in the possession of one person has a smaller use value to him than another good owned by another person who values these goods in precisely the opposite way at the same time! And even when this relationship is present, how much rarer still must situations be in which the two persons actually meet each other! A has a fishing net that he would like to exchange for a quantity of hemp. For him to be in a position actually to perform this exchange, it is not only necessary that there be another economizing individual, B, who is willing to give a quantity of hemp corresponding to the wishes of A for the fishing net, but also that the two economizing individuals, with these specific wishes, meet each other. Suppose that Farmer C has a horse that he would like to exchange for a number of agricultural implements and clothes. How unlikely it is that he will find another person who needs his horse and is, at the same time, both willing and in a position to give him all the implements and clothes he desires to have in exchange!

This difficulty would have been insurmountable, and would have seriously impeded progress in the division of labor, and above all in the production of goods for future sale, if there had not been, in the very nature of things, a way out. But there were elements in their situation that everywhere led men inevitably, without the need for a special agreement or even government compulsion, to a state of affairs in which this difficulty was completely overcome.

The direct provision of their requirements is the ultimate purpose of all the economic endeavors of men. The *final end* of their exchange operations is therefore to exchange their commodities for such goods as have use value to them. The endeavor to attain this final end has been equally characteristic of all stages of culture and is entirely correct economically. But economizing individuals would obviously be behaving uneconomically if, in all instances in which this final end cannot be reached *immediately and directly,* they were to forsake approaching it altogether.

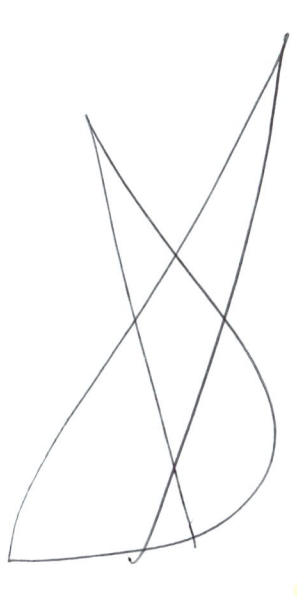

Assume that a smith of the Homeric age has fashioned two suits of copper armor and wants to exchange them for copper, fuel, and food. He goes to market and offers his products for these goods. He would doubtless be very pleased if he were to encounter persons there who wish to purchase his armor and who, at the same time, have for sale all the raw materials and foods that he needs. But it must obviously be considered a particularly happy accident if, among the small number of persons who at any time wish to purchase a good so difficult to sell as his armor, he should find any who are offering precisely the goods that he needs. He would therefore make the marketing of his commodities either totally impossible, or possible only with the expenditure of a great deal of time, if he were to behave so uneconomically as to wish to take in exchange for his commodities only goods that have use value to himself and not also other goods which, although they would have commodity-character to him, nevertheless *have greater marketability than his own commodity.* Possession of these commodities would considerably facilitate his search for persons who have just the goods he needs. In the times of which I am speaking, cattle were, as we shall see below, the most saleable of all commodities. Even if the armorer is already sufficiently provided with cattle for his direct requirements, he would be acting very uneconomically if he did not give his armor for a number of additional cattle. By so doing, he is of course not exchanging his commodities for consumption goods (in the narrow sense in which this term is opposed to "commodities") but only for goods that also have commodity-character to him. But for his less saleable commodities he is obtaining others of greater marketability. Possession of these more saleable goods clearly multiplies his chances of finding persons on the market who will offer to sell him the goods that he needs. If our armorer correctly recognizes his individual interest, therefore, he will be led naturally, without compulsion or any special agreement, to give his armor for a corresponding number of cattle. With the more saleable commodities obtained in this way, he will go to persons at the market who are offering copper, fuel, and food for sale, in order to achieve his *ultimate objective,* the acquisition by trade of the consumption goods that he needs. But now he can proceed to this end much more quickly, more economically, and with a greatly enhanced probability of success.

As *each* economizing individual becomes increasingly more aware of his economic interest, he is led by this *interest, without any agreement, without legislative compulsion, and even without regard to the public interest,* to give his commodities in exchange for other, more saleable, commodities, even if he does not need them for any immediate consumption purpose. With economic progress, therefore, we can everywhere observe the phenomenon of a certain number of goods, especially those that are most easily saleable at a given time and place, becoming, under the powerful influence of *custom,* acceptable to everyone in trade, and thus capable of being given in exchange for any other commodity. These goods were called *"Geld"* [2] by our ancestors, a term derived from *"gelten"* which means to compensate or pay. Hence the term *"Geld"* in our language designates the means of payment as such.[3]

The great importance of *custom* [4] in the origin of money can be seen immediately by considering the process, described above, by which certain goods became money. The exchange of less easily saleable commodities for commodities of greater marketability is in the economic interest of *every* economizing individual. But the actual performance of exchange operations of this kind presupposes a knowledge of their interest on the part of economizing individuals. For they must be willing to accept in exchange for their commodities, because of its greater marketability, a good that is perhaps itself quite useless to them. This knowledge will never be attained by all members of a people at the same time. On the contrary, only a small number of economizing individuals will at first recognize the advantage accruing to them from the acceptance of other, more saleable, commodities in exchange for their own whenever a direct exchange of their commodities for the goods they wish to consume is impossible or highly uncertain. This advantage is *independent of a general acknowledgement of any one commodity as money*. For an exchange of this sort will always, under any circumstances whatsoever, bring an economizing individual considerably nearer to his final end, the acquisition of the goods he wishes to consume. Since there is no better way in which men can become enlightened about their economic interests than by observation of the economic success of those who employ the correct means of achieving their ends, it is evident that nothing favored the rise of money so much as the long-practiced, and economically profitable, acceptance of eminently saleable commodities in exchange for all others by the most discerning and most capable economizing individuals. In this way, custom and practice contributed in no small degree to converting the commodities that were most saleable at a given time into commodities that came to be accepted, not merely by many, but by all economizing individuals in exchange for their own commodities.[5]

Within the boundaries of a state, the legal order usually has an influence on the money-character of commodities which, though small, cannot be denied. The origin of money (as distinct from coin, which is only one variety of money) is, as we have seen, entirely natural and thus displays legislative influence only in the rarest instances. Money is not an invention of the state. It is not the product of a legislative act. Even the sanction of political authority is not necessary for its existence. Certain commodities came to be money quite naturally, as the result of economic relationships that were independent of the power of the state.

But if, in response to the needs of trade, a good receives the sanction of the state as money, the result will be that not only every payment to the state itself but all other payments not explicitly contracted for in other goods can be required or offered, with legally binding effect, only in units of that good. There will be the further, and especially important, result that when payment has originally been contracted for in other goods but cannot, for some reason, be made, the payment substituted can similarly be required or offered, with legally binding effect, only in units of the one particular good. Thus the sanction of the state gives a particular good the attribute of being a universal substitute in exchange, and although the state is not responsible for the existence of the money-character of the good, it is responsible for a significant improvement of its money-character.[6]

2. THE KINDS OF MONEY APPROPRIATE TO PARTICULAR PEOPLES AND TO PARTICULAR HISTORICAL PERIODS

Money is not the product of an agreement on the part of economizing men nor the product of legislative acts. No one invented it. As economizing individuals in social situations became increasingly aware of their economic interest, they everywhere attained the simple knowledge that surrendering less saleable commodities for others of greater saleability brings them substantially closer to the attainment of their specific economic purposes. Thus, with the progressive development of social economy, money came to exist in numerous centers of civilization independently. But precisely because money is a natural product of human economy, the specific forms in which it has appeared were everywhere and at all times the result of specific and changing economic situations. Among the same people at different times, and among different peoples at the same time, different goods have attained the special position in trade described above.

In the earliest periods of economic development, cattle seem to have been the most saleable commodity among most peoples of the ancient world. Domestic animals constituted the chief item of the wealth of every individual among nomads and peoples passing from a nomadic economy to agriculture. Their marketability extended literally to all economizing individuals, and the lack of artificial roads combined with the fact that cattle transported themselves (almost without cost in the primitive stages of civilization!) to make them saleable over a wider geographical area than most other commodities. A number of circumstances, moreover, favored broad quantitative and temporal limits to their marketability. A cow is a commodity of considerable durability. Its cost of maintenance is insignificant where pastures are available in abundance and where the animals are kept under the open sky. And in a culture in which everyone attempts to possess as large herds as possible, cattle are usually not brought to market in excessive quantities at any one time. In the period of which I am speaking, there was no similar juncture of circumstances establishing as broad a range of marketability for any other commodity. If we add to these circumstances the fact that trade in domestic animals was at least as well developed as trade in any other commodity, cattle appear to have been the most saleable of all available commodities and hence the natural money of the peoples of the ancient world.[7]

The trade and commerce of the most cultured people of the ancient world, the *Greeks*, whose stages of development history has revealed to us in fairly distinct outlines, showed no trace of coined money even as late as the time of Homer. Barter still prevailed, and wealth consisted of herds of cattle. Payments were made in cattle. Prices were reckoned in cattle. And cattle were used for the payment of fines. Even Draco imposed fines in cattle, and the practice was not abandoned until Solon converted them, apparently because they had outlived their usefulness, into metallic money at the rate of one drachma for a sheep and five drachmae for a cow. Even more distinctly than with the Greeks, traces of cattle-money can be recognized in the case of the cattle breeding ancestors of the peoples of the *Italian* peninsula. Until very late, cattle and, next to them sheep, formed the means of exchange among the Romans. Their earliest legal penalties were cattle fines (imposed in cattle and sheep) which appear still in the lex Aternia Tarpeia of the year 454 B.C., and were only converted to coined money 24 years later.[8]

Among our own ancestors, the old *Germanic* tribes, at a time when, according to Tacitus, they held silver and earthen vessels in equal esteem, a large herd of cattle was considered identical with riches. Barter stood in the foreground, just as it did among the Greeks of the Homeric age, and cattle again and, in this case, horses (and weapons too!) already served as means of exchange. Cattle constituted their most highly esteemed property and were preferred above all else. Legal fines were paid in cattle and weapons, and only later in metallic money.[9] Otto the Great still imposed fines in terms of cattle.

Among the *Arabs*, the cattle standard existed as late as the time of Mohammed.[10] Among the peoples of eastern Asia Minor, where the writings of Zoroaster, the Zendavesta, were held sacred, other forms of money replaced the cattle standard only quite late, after the neighboring peoples had long gone over to a metallic currency.[11] That cattle were used as currency by the Hebrews,[12] by the peoples of Asia Minor, and by the inhabitants of Mesopotamia, in prehistoric times may be supposed although we cannot find evidence of it. These tribes all entered history at a level of civilization at which they had presumably already gone beyond the cattle standard—if one may be permitted to draw general conclusions, by analogy, from later developments, and from the fact that it appears to be unnatural in a primitive society to make large payments in metal or metallic implements.[13]

But rising civilization, and above all the division of labor and its natural consequence, the gradual formation of cities inhabited by a population devoted primarily to industry, must everywhere have had the result of simultaneously diminishing the marketability of cattle and increasing the marketability of many other commodities, especially the metals then in use. The artisan who began to trade with the farmer was seldom in a position to accept cattle as money; for a city dweller, the temporary possession of cattle necessarily involved, not only discomforts, but also considerable economic sacrifices; and the keeping and feeding of cattle imposed no significant economic sacrifice upon the farmer only as long as he had unlimited pasture and was accustomed to keep his cattle in an open field. With the progress of civilization, therefore, cattle lost to a great extent the broad range of marketability they had previously had with respect to the number of persons to whom, and with respect to the time period within which, they could be sold economically. At the same time, they receded more and more into the background relative to other goods with respect to the spatial and quantitative limits of their marketability. They ceased to be the most saleable of commodities, the *economic* form of money, and finally ceased to be money at all.

In all cultures in which cattle had previously had the character of money, cattle-money was abandoned with the passage from a nomadic existence and simple agriculture to a more complex system in which handicraft was practised, its place being taken by the metals then in use. Among the metals that were at first principally worked by men because of their ease of extraction and malleability were copper, silver, gold, and in some cases also iron. The transition took place quite smoothly when it became necessary, since metallic implements and the raw metal itself had doubtless already been in use everywhere as money in addition to cattle-currency, for the purpose of making small payments.

Copper was the earliest metal from which the farmer's plough, the warrior's weapons, and the artisan's tools were fashioned. Copper, gold, and silver were the earliest materials used for vessels and ornaments of all kinds. At the cultural stage at which peoples passed from cattle-money to an exclusively metallic currency, therefore, copper and perhaps some of its alloys were goods of very general use, and gold and silver, as the most important means of satisfying that most universal passion of primitive men, the desire to stand out in appearance before the other members of the tribe, had become goods of most general desire. As long as they had few uses, the three metals circulated almost exclusively in finished forms. Later, circulating as raw metal, they were less limited as to use and had greater divisibility. Their marketability was neither restricted to a small number of economizing persons nor, because of their great usefulness to all peoples and easy transportability at relatively slight economic sacrifices, confined within narrow spatial limits. Because of their durability they were not restricted in marketability to narrow limits in time. As a result of the general competition for them, they could be more easily marketed at economic prices than any other commodities in comparable quantities (p. 227). Thus we observe an economic situation in the historical period following nomadism and simple agriculture in which these three metals, being the most saleable goods, became the exclusive means of exchange.

This transition did not take place abruptly, nor did it take place in the same way among all peoples. The newer metallic standard may have been in use for a long time along with the older cattle-standard before it replaced the latter completely. The value of an animal, in metallic money, may have served as the basis for the currency unit even after metal had completely displaced cattle as currency in trade. The Dekaboion, Tesseraboion, and Hekatomboion of the Greeks, and the earliest metallic money of the Romans and Gauls were probably of this nature, and the animal picture appearing on the pieces of metal was probably a symbol of this value.[14]

It is, to say the least, uncertain whether copper or brass, as the most important of the metals in use, were the earliest means of exchange, and whether the precious metals acquired the function of money only later. In eastern Asia, in China, and perhaps also in India, the copper standard experienced its most complete development. In central Italy an exclusively copper standard also developed. In the ancient cultures on the Euphrates and Tigris, on the other hand, not even traces of the former existence of an exclusively copper standard are to be found, and in Asia Minor and Egypt, as well as in Greece, Sicily, and lower Italy, its independent development was arrested, wherever it had existed at all, by the vast development of Mediterranean commerce, which could not be carried on adequately with copper alone. But it is certain that all peoples who were led to adopt a copper standard as a result of the material circumstances under which their economy developed, passed on from the less precious metals to the more precious ones, from copper and iron to silver and gold, with the further development of civilization, and especially with the geographical extension of commerce. In all places, moreover, where a silver standard became established, there was a later transition to a gold standard, and if the transition was not always actually completed, the tendency existed nevertheless.

In the narrow commerce of an ancient Sabine city with the surrounding region, and in keeping with the early simplicity of Sabine customs, when the cattle-standard had outlived its usefulness, copper best served the practical purposes of the farmers and of the city dwellers as well. It was the most important metal in use, certainly the commodity whose marketability extended to the largest number of persons, and the quantitative limits of its marketability were wider than those of any other commodity—the most important requisites of money in the primitive stages of civilization. It was, moreover, a good whose easy and inexpensive preservation and storage in small amounts and whose relatively moderate cost of transportation qualified it to a sufficient degree for monetary purposes within narrow geographical limits. But as soon as the area of trade widened, as the rate of commodity turnover quickened, and as the precious metals became more and more the most saleable commodities of a new epoch, copper naturally lost its capacity to serve as money. With the trade of this people extending over the whole world, with the rapid turnover of their commodities, and with the increasing division of labor, each economizing individual felt more and more the need of carrying money on his person. With the progress of civilization, the precious metals became the most saleable commodities and thus the natural money of peoples highly developed economically.

The history of other peoples presents a picture of great differences in their economic development and hence also in their monetary institutions. When Mexico was invaded for the first time by Europeans, it appears already to have reached an unusual level of economic development, according to the reports published by eye-witnesses about the condition of the country at that time. The trade of the ancient Aztecs is of special interest to us for two reasons: (1) it proves to us that the economic thinking that leads men to activity directed to the fullest possible satisfaction of their needs is everywhere responsible for analogous economic phenomena, and (2) ancient Mexico presents us with the picture of a country in the state of transition from a pure barter to a money economy. We thus have the record of a situation in which we can observe the characteristic process by which a number of goods attain greater prominence than the rest and become money.

The reports of the conquistadors and contemporary writers depict Mexico as a country with numerous cities and a well organized and imposing trade in goods. There were daily markets in the cities, and every five days major markets were held which were distributed over the country in such a way that the major market of any one city was not impaired by the competition of that of a neighboring city. There was a special large square in each city for trade in commodities, and in it a particular place was assigned for each commodity, outside of which trade in that commodity was forbidden. The only exceptions to this rule were foodstuffs and objects difficult to transport (timber, tanning materials, stones, etc.). The number of people assembled at the market place of the capital, Mexico, was estimated to have been 20,000 to 25,000 for the daily markets, and between 40,000 and 50,000 on major market days. A great many varieties of commodities were traded.[15]

The interesting question that arises is whether, in the markets of ancient Mexico, which were similar in so many ways to those of Europe, there had also already appeared phenomena analogous in nature and origin to our money.

The actual report of the Spanish invaders is that the trade of Mexico, at the time they first entered the country, had long since ceased to move exclusively within the limits of simple barter, and that some commodities had instead already attained the special status in trade that I discussed more extensively earlier—that is, the status of money. Cocoa beans in small bags containing 8,000 to 24,000 beans, certain small cotton handkerchiefs, golds and in goose quills that were accepted according to size (balances and weighing instruments in general being unknown to the Mexicans), pieces of copper, and finally, thin pieces of tin, appear to have been the commodities that were readily accepted by everyone (as money), even if the persons receiving them did not need them immediately, whenever a direct exchange of immediately usable commodities could not be accomplished.

Eye-witnesses mention the following commodities as being traded on the Mexican markets: live and dead animals, cocoa, all other foods, precious stones, medicinal plants, herbs, gums, resins, earths, prepared medicines, commodities made of the fibers of the century plant, of palm leaves, and of animal hair, articles made of feathers, and of wood and stone, and finally gold, copper, tin, timber, stones, tanning materials, and hides. If we consider not only this list of commodities but also (1) the fact that Mexico, at the time of its discovery by Europeans, was already a developed country with some industry and populous cities, (2) that since the majority of our domestic animals were unknown to them, a cattle-standard was entirely out of the question, (3) that cocoa was the daily beverage, cotton the most common clothing material, and gold, copper, and tin the most widely used metals of the Aztec people, and (4) that the nature of these commodities and the fact of their general use gave them greater marketability than all other commodities, it is not difficult to understand exactly why these goods became the money of the Aztec people. They were the natural, even if little developed, currency of ancient Mexico.

Analogous causes were responsible for the fact that animal skins became money among hunting peoples engaged in external trade. Among hunting tribes there is naturally an oversupply of furs, since providing a family with food by means of hunting leads to so great an accumulation of skins that at most only a competition for especially beautiful or rare kinds of skins can arise among the members of the hunting tribe. But if the tribe enters into trade with foreign peoples, and a market for skins arises in which numerous consumable goods can, at the choice of the hunters, be exchanged for furs, nothing is more natural than that skins will become the most saleable good, and hence that they will come to be preferred and accepted even in exchanges taking place between the hunters themselves. Of course hunter A does not need the skins of hunter B that he accepts in an exchange, but he is aware that he will be able to exchange them easily on the markets for other goods that he does need. He therefore prefers the skins, even though they also have only the character of commodities to him, to other commodities in his possession that are less easily saleable. We can actually observe this relationship among almost all hunting tribes who carry on foreign trade with their skins.[16]

The fact that slaves and chunks of salt became money in the interior of Africa, and that cakes of wax on the upper Amazon, cod in Iceland and Newfoundland, tobacco in Maryland and Virginia, sugar in the British West Indies, and ivory in the vicinity of the Portuguese colonies, took on the functions of money is explained by the fact that these goods were, and in some cases still are, the chief articles exported from these places. Thus they acquire, just as did furs among hunting tribes, a preeminent marketability.

The local money-character of many other goods, on the other hand, can be traced back to their great and general use value locally and their resultant marketability. Examples are the money-character of dates in the oasis of Siwa, of tea-bricks in central Asia and Siberia, of glass beads in Nubia and Sennar, and of ghussub, a kind of millet, in the country of Ahir (Africa). An example in which both factors have been responsible for the money-character of a good is provided by cowrie-shells, which have, at the same time, been both a commonly desired ornament and an export commodity.[17]

Thus money presents itself to us, in its special locally and temporally different forms, not as the result of an agreement, legislative compulsion, or mere chance, but as the natural product of differences in the economic situation of different peoples at the same time, or of the same people in different periods of their history.

1. Theodor Mommsen, *Geschichte des römischen Münzwesens*, Berlin, 1860, pp. v-xx, and 167 ff.; Carnap, "Zur Geschichte der Münzwissenschaft und der Werthzeichen," *Zeitschrift für die gesammte Staatswissenschaft*, XVI (1860), 348-396; Friedrich Kenner, "Die Anfänge des Geldes in Alterthume," *Sitzungsberichte der Kaiserlichen Akademie der Wissenschaften zu Wien: Philologisch-Historische Classe*, XLIII (1863), 382-490; Roscher, *op cit.*, pp. 36-40; Hildebrand, *op. cit.*, p. 5; Scheel, *op. cit.*, pp. 12-29; A. N. Bernardakis, "De l'origine des monnaies et de leurs noms," *Journal des Economistes*, (Third Series), XVIII (1870), 209-245.
2. For obvious reasons, the words "*Geld*" and "*gelten*" in this and the following sentence are left untranslated.—TR.
3. See the first two paragraphs of Appendix I (p. 312) for material originally appearing here as a footnote.—TR.
4. Custom as a factor in the origin of money is stressed by Condillac, *op. cit.*, pp. 286-290 and by G. F. Le Trosne, *De l'intérêt social*, Paris, 1777, pp. 43 f.
5. See Appendix J (p. 315) for material originally appended here as a footnote.—TR.
6. See Stein, *op. cit.*, p. 55; especially also Karl Knies, "Ueber die Geldentwerthung und die mit ihr in Verbindung gebrachten Erscheinungen," *Zeitschrift für die gesammte Staatwissenschaft*, XIV (1858), 266; and Mommsen, *op. cit.*, pp. vii-viii.
7. See the last two paragraphs of Appendix I (p. 313) for material appended here as a footnote in the original.—TR.
8. August Böckh, *Metrologische Untersuchungen über Gewichte, Münzfusse und Masse des Alterthums*, Berlin, 1838, pp. 385 ff., 420 ff.;

Mommsen, *op. cit.*, p. 169; Friedrich O. Hultsch, *Griechische und römische Metrologie*, Berlin, 1862, pp. 124 ff., 188 ff.

9. Wilh. Wackernagel, "Gewerbe, Handel und Schifffahrt der Germanen," *Zeitschrift für deutsches Alterthum*, IX (1853), 548 ff.; Jakob Grimm, *Deutsche Rechtsalterthümer*, 4th edition prepared by A. Heusler and R. Hübner, Leipzig, 1899, II, 123-124; Ad. Soetbeer, "Beiträge zur Geschichte des Geld- und Münzwesens in Deutschland," *Forschungen zur deutschen Geschichte*, I (1862), 215.

10. Aloys Sprenger, *Das Leben und die Lehre des Mohammad*, Berlin, 1861-65, III, 139.

11. Friedrich v. Spiegel, *Commentar über das Avesta*, Wien, 1864-68, I, 94 ff.

12. Moritz A. Levy, *Geschichte der jüdischen Münzen*, Leipzig, 1862, p. 7.

13. Roscher, *op cit.*, note 5 on p. 309.

14. Plutarch, *Lives*, with an English translation by Bernadotte Perrin, London: William Heinemann, 1914, I, 55; Pliny, *The Natural History*, translated by John Bostock and H. T. Riley, London: H. G. Bohn, 1856, IV, 5-6; Heinrich Schreiber, "Die Metallringe der Kelten als Schmuck und Geld," *Taschenbuch für Geschichte und Alterthum*, II, 67-152, 240-247, and III, 401-408.

15. Francesco Saverio Clavigero, *The History of Mexico*, Richmond, 1806, II, 188 ff.

16. A beaver skin is still the unit of exchange value in several regions of the Hudson's Bay Company. Three martens are equal to one beaver, one white fox to two beavers, one black fox or one bear equal to four beavers, and one rifle equal to 15 beavers ("Die Jäger im nördlichen Amerika," *Das Ausland*, XIX, no. 21, [Jan. 21, 1846], 84). The Estonian word *"raha"* (money) has in the related language of the Laplanders the meaning of fur (Philipp Krug, *Zur Münzkunde Russlands*, St. Petersburg, 1805). On fur money in the Russian middle ages, see the report by Nestor (A. L. Schlözer, translator, *Nestor, Russische Annalen*, Goettingen, 1802-1809, III, 90). The old word, *"kung"* (money) really means marten. As late as 1610 a Russian war chest containing 5450 rubles in silver and 7000 rubles worth of fur was taken. (See Nikolai Karamzin, *Geschichte des russischen Reichs*, Riga, 1820-1833, XI, 183). See also Roscher, *op. cit.*, p. 309, and Heinrich Storch, *Handbuch der National-Wirthschaftlehre*, ed. by K. H. Rau, Hamburg, 1820, III, 25-26.

17. Roscher, *op. cit.*, note 13 on pp. 313-314.

3. The Evolution of a Free Banking System
George Selgin and Lawrence White

Menger's theory refers only to the evolution of a pure commodity money, e.g., gold or silver coin. Modern monetary systems, however, can also make use of various forms of bank money—redeemable bank notes and checkable deposits—which are an economical substitute for commodity money. In "The Evolution of a Free Banking System" Selgin and White extend Menger's theory of "spontaneous evolution" to account for the emergence of banks, bank money, and related institutions such as clearinghouses. Because their goal is to understand the workings of a completely unregulated or "free" banking system, Selgin and White abstract from all government regulation: their hypothetical banking system is one that develops in a world of pure laissez-faire. —G.S., Ed.

****

INTRODUCTION

In recent years monetary theorists have produced a substantial literature on the properties of a completely unregulated monetary system.[1] Their assumptions concerning the institutional features of such a system have ranged from the proliferation of numerous competing private fiat currencies at one extreme to the complete disappearance of money at the other. While these assumptions have generated clear-cut and provocative conclusions, their plausibility or realism in light of historical experience is open to serious doubt. These doubts may unfortunately suggest that any discussion of an unregulated monetary system (or free banking system) must be tenuous and highly speculative. This study shows, to the contrary, that important institutional features of a free banking system, in particular the nature of payment media, can be realistically grounded by constructing a logical explanation of its evolution.

The method of logical evolutionary explanation has previously been applied to monetary institutions by John Hicks (1967) and Carl Menger (1892), among others. The present study integrates and extends work along their lines. The method is employed here in the belief that it has been unduly neglected in recent work, not that it is the only valid method for theoretically explaining institutional arrangements. The more standard method of building explicit transactions costs or informational imperfections or asymmetries into an optimization model has unquestionably been useful in the task of explaining why banks exist as intermediaries (Anthony Santomero [1984, 577–80] surveys this literature).

Our investigation derives arrangements that would have arisen had state intervention never occurred. The results should therefore help to identify the degree to which features of current monetary and banking institutions are rooted in market forces and the degree to which they have grown out of regulatory intervention. Such information gives important clues about how future deregulation would modify institutions. We show that sophisticated monetary arrangements emerge in the absence of regulation. No strong claims are advanced here about the welfare properties of these arrangements.[2] We aim to establish the most credible path for unrestricted monetary evolution, but certainly not the only possible path. Economists who find other institutional outcomes more plausible for an unregulated system will, we hope, similarly try to explain why and how those outcomes would emerge.

The evolution of a free banking system, following the emergence of standardized commodity money, proceeds through three stages. These are, first, the development of basic money-transfer services which substitute for the physical transportation of specie; second, the emergence of easily assignable and negotiable bank demand liabilities (inside money); and third, the development of arrangements for the routine exchange ("clearing") of inside monies among rival banks. The historical time separating these stages is not crucial. The path of development, rather than being one of steady progress as pictured here, may in practice involve false starts or creative leaps. What is essential is that, by an invisible-hand process, each stage is the logical outgrowth of the circumstances that preceded it. In other words, each successive step in the process of evolution originates in individuals' discovery of new ways to promote their self-interest, with the outcome an arrangement at which no individual consciously aims.

COMMODITY MONEY

Because the use of money logically and historically precedes the emergence of banking firms, we begin with an account of the origin of money. Our account follows that of Menger (1892), who furnished an invisible-hand explanation, consistent with historical and anthropological evidence, of how money originated as a product of undesigned or spontaneous evolution.[3] Menger's theory shows that no state intervention is necessary in order to establish a basic medium of exchange or unit of account. It also provides a useful prototype for our explanations of how subsequent banking institutions evolve in spontaneous fashion.

In premonetary society, traders relying upon barter initially offer goods in exchange only for other goods directly entering their consumption or household production plans. The number of bargains struck this way is small, owing to the well-known problem of finding what William Stanley Jevons termed a "double coincidence of wants." Before long some frustrated barterer realizes that he can increase his chances for success by adopting a two-stage procedure. He can trade his wares for some good, regardless of its direct usefulness to him, which will more easily find a taker among those selling what he ultimately wants. It follows that the earliest media of exchange are simply goods perceived to be in relatively widespread demand. The widening of demand for these things owing to their use as media of exchange reinforces their superior salability. Other traders eventually recognize the gains achieved by those using indirect exchange, and emulate them, even though they may be unaware of the reason for the advantages of using a medium of exchange. This emulation further enhances the acceptance of the most widely accepted media, elevating one or two goods above all others in salability. The snowballing of salability results in the spontaneous appearance of generally accepted media of exchange. Eventually traders throughout an economy converge on using a single commodity as a generally accepted medium of exchange, i.e., as money.

Historical evidence on primitive monies indicates that cattle were often the most frequently exchanged commodity, and that a standardized "cow" was the earliest unit of account. Cattle were a poor general medium of exchange, however, because of their relative nontransportability and nonuniformity. Not until the discovery of metals and of methods for working them did the use of money replace barter widely.[4] According to Jacques Melitz (1974, 95), common attributions of moneyness to primitive media, especially nonmetallic "moneys" (with the exception of cowries in China), warrant skepticism because many of these media (e.g., the Yap stones of Melanesia) do not meet any reasonably strict definition of money.

The emergence of coinage can also be explained as a spontaneous development, an unplanned result of merchants' attempts to minimize the necessity for assessing and weighing amounts of commodity money received in exchange. Merchants may at first mark irregular metallic nuggets or pieces after having assessed their quality. A merchant recognizing his own or another's mark can then avoid the trouble and cost of reassessment. Marking gives way to stamping or punching, which eventually leads to specialists making coins in their modern form. Techniques for milling coin edges and covering the entire surface with type provide safeguards against clipping and sweating and so allow coinage to serve as a guarantee of weight as well as of quality. Arthur R. Burns (1927a, 297–304; 1927b, 59) has illustrated this process with evidence from ancient Lydia, where coins of electrum (a naturally occurring silver-gold alloy) came into early use.

Absent state interference, coinage is a private industry encompassing various competing brands. Under competition coins are valued according to bullion content plus a premium equal to the marginal cost of mintage. The demand for readily exchangeable coins promotes the emergence of standard weights and fineness. Nonstandard coins must circulate at a discount because of the extra computational burden they impose, so that their production is unprofitable. States seem to have monopolized coinage early in history, but not by outcompeting private mints. Rather, the evidence suggests that state coinage monopolies were regularly established by legal compulsion and for reasons of propaganda and monopoly profit. State-minted coins functioned both as a symbol of rule and as a source of profits from shaving, clipping, and seigniorage. For these reasons coinage became a state function throughout the world by the end of the seventh century (Burns 1927a, 308; 1927b, 78).

BANKING FIRMS

The counting and transporting of coin entail considerable inconvenience. Traders, particularly those frequently making large or distant exchanges, will naturally seek lower-cost means of transferring ownership of money. One likely locus for development of such means is the market where local coins are exchanged for foreign coins. Standard coins may differ interlocally even in the absence of local state interventions because of geographic diseconomies in reputation building for mints. A coin-exchange market then naturally arises with interlocal trade. A trader who uses a money changer must initially count and carry in local coin each time he wants to acquire foreign coin, or vice versa. He can reduce his costs by establishing a standing account balance, to build up at his convenience and draw upon as desired. The money changer's inventories equip him to provide such accounts, which constitute demand deposits, and even to allow overdrafts. These deposits may originally be nontransferable. But it will soon be apparent, where one customer withdraws coins in order to pay a recipient who redeposits them with the same exchange banker, that the transfer is more easily made at the banker's place of business, or more easily yet by persuading the banker to make the transfer on his books without any handling of coins. Thus trading individuals come to keep money balances with agencies which can make payments by ledger-account transfers.

Money-transfer services of this sort, provided by money changers and bill brokers in twelfth-century Genoa and at medieval trade fairs in Champagne, mark the earliest recorded forms of banking.[5] In time all the major European trading centers had what Raymond de Roover (1974, 184) calls "transfer banks." De Roover comments that "deposit banking grew out of [money-changing] activity, because the money changers developed a system of local payments by book transfer." In our view, however, the taking of deposits on at least a small scale logically *precedes* the development of book-transfer methods of payment.

Money-transfer services may also develop in connection with deposits made for safekeeping rather than for money changing. The well-known story of the origins of goldsmith banking in seventeenth-century England illustrates this development. Wealthy persons may temporarily lodge commodity money with scriveners, goldsmiths, mintmasters, and other reputable vault-owners for safekeeping. Coin and bullion thus lodged must be physically withdrawn and transferred for its owner to use it as a means of payment. Exchanges in which the recipient redeposits the coins or bullion in the same vault (like redeposits with a money changer or bill broker) can obviously be accomplished more easily by making the transfer at the vault, or better yet by simply notifying the vault's custodian to make the transfer on his books. In England, scriveners were the earliest pioneers in the banking trade; in Stuart times they were almost entirely displaced by goldsmith bankers. English goldsmiths evidently became transfer bankers when they "began to keep a 'running cash' for the convenience of merchants and country gentlemen" (de Roover 1974, 83–84). The confiscation by Charles I of gold deposited for safekeeping at the royal mint ended that institution's participation in the process of banking development. Private mints, had they been permitted, would have been logical sites for early banking activities.

Transfer banking is not connected with intermediation between borrowers and lenders when the banker acts strictly as a warehouseman, giving deposit receipts which are regular warehouse dockets. The strict warehouse banker is a bailee rather than a debtor to his depositors and can make loans only out of his personal wealth. Two conditions make it possible, however, to take advantage of the interest income available from lending out depositors' balances, even while satisfying depositors' desire to have their funds withdrawable on demand: (1) money is fungible, which allows a depositor to be repaid in coin and bullion not identical to that he brought in, and (2) the law of large numbers with random withdrawals and deposits makes a fractional reserve sufficient to meet actual withdrawal demands with high probability even though any single account may be removed without notice. (Interestingly, these conditions may also be met in the warehousing of standard-quality grain, so that fractional-reserve "banking" can likewise develop there, as Jeffrey C. Williams [1984] has shown.) The lending of depositors' balances is an innovation that taps a vast new source of loanable funds and alters fundamentally the relationship of the banker to his depositor customers.

Historically in England, according to R. D. Richards (1965, 223), "the bailee . . . developed into the debtor of the depositor; and the depositor became an investor who loaned his money . . . for a consideration." Money "warehouse receipts" became merely ready promissory notes. W. R. Bisschop (1910, 50n) reports that English warehouse bankers had become intermediaries by the time of Charles II (1660–85): "Any deposit made in any other shape than ornament was looked upon by them as a free loan." Competition for deposits prompted the payment of interest on deposits, and the attractiveness of interest on safe and accessible deposits in turn apparently made the practice of depositing widespread among all ranks of people (Powell 1966, 56–57).

TRANSFERABLE INSTRUMENTS

Under these circumstances the effective money supply obviously becomes greater than the existing stock of specie alone. The most important banking procedures and devices, however, have yet to develop. Many purchases are still made with actual coin. Bank depositors, in order to satisfy changing needs for money at hand, make frequent withdrawals from and deposits into their bank balances. These actions may in the aggregate largely cancel out through the law of large numbers. But they require the banks to hold greater precautionary commodity money reserves, and consequently to maintain a larger spread between deposit and loan rates of interest, than is necessary when payments practices become more sophisticated. Greater sophistication comes with the emergence of negotiable bank instruments, able to pass easily in exchange from one person to another, which replace coin and nonnegotiable deposit receipts in transactions balances. The use of coin is also superseded by the development of more efficient means for the bank-mediated transfer of deposits.

Assignability and negotiability may develop through several steps. Initially the assignment of deposited money (whether "warehoused" or entrusted to the banker for lending at interest) by the depositor to another party may require the presence of all three parties to the exchange or their attorneys. Money "warehouse receipts" (or promissory notes) and running deposit balances cannot be assigned by the owner's endorsement without the banker acting as witness. An important innovation is the development of bank-issued promissory notes transferable by endorsement. Assignable notes in turn give way to fully negotiable bank notes assigned to no one in particular but instead payable to the bearer on demand. A parallel development is the nonnegotiable check enabling the depositor to transfer balances to a specific party, in turn giving way to the negotiable check which can be repeatedly endorsed or made out "to cash."[6] Thus the modern forms of inside money—redeemable bearer bank notes and checkable deposits—are established. Once this stage is reached it is not difficult for bankers to conceive what Hartley Withers (1920, 24) has called "the epoch-making notion"—in our view it is only an incremental step—of giving inside money not only to depositors of metal but also to borrowers of money. The use of inside money enhances both customer and bank profits, so that only the possible reluctance of courts to enforce obligations represented by assigned or bearer paper stands in the way of its rapid development.

In England bearer notes were first recognized during the reign of Charles II, about the time when warehouse banking was giving way to fractional-reserve transfer banking. At first the courts gave their grudging approval to the growing practice of repeated endorsement of promissory notes. Then after some controversy, fully negotiable notes were recognized by Act of Parliament. In France, Holland, and Italy during the sixteenth century merchants' checks "drawn in blank" circulated within limited circles and may have cleared the way for the appearance of bank notes (Usher 1943, 189; Richards 1965, 46, 225).

REGULAR NOTE-EXCHANGE

Further economies in the use of commodity money require more complete circulation of inside money in place of commodity money, and more complete development of bank note and check clearing facilities to reduce the need for commodity money reserves. It is relatively straightforward to show that bankers and other agents pursuing their self-interest are indeed led to improve the acceptability of inside money and the efficiency of banking operations.

At this stage, although bank notes are less cumbersome than coin, and checkable deposits are both convenient for certain transactions and interest paying, some coin still remains in circulation. Consumers trust a local bank's notes more than a distant bank's notes because they are more aware of the local notes' likelihood of being honored and more familiar with their appearance (hence less prone to accepting forgeries). It follows that the cost to a bank of building a reputation for its issues—particularly regarding note convertibility—is higher in places further from the place of issue and redemption. The establishment of a network of bank branches for redemption is limited by transportation and communication costs. In the early stages of banking development the par circulation of every bank's notes and checks is therefore geographically relatively limited.[7] People who generally hold the inside money of a local bank but who do business in distant towns must either take the trouble to redeem some of their holdings for gold and incur the inconvenience of transporting coin, or suffer a loss in value on their notes by carrying them to a locale where they are accepted only at a discount, if at all. (The alternative practice of keeping on hand notes from each locality they deal with is likely to be prohibitively costly in terms of foregone interest.) In general, a brand of inside money will initially be used only for transactions in the vicinity of the issuer, and coin will continue to be held alongside notes of like denomination. The use of commodity money in circulation requires banks to hold commodity reserves greater than those required by the transfer of inside money, because the withdrawal of commodity money for spending generates more volatile reserve outflows than the spending of notes or deposits.

In this situation, profit opportunities arise which prompt actions leading to more general acceptance of particular inside monies. The discounting of notes outside the neighborhood of the issuing bank's office creates an arbitrage opportunity when the par value of notes (i.e., their face redemption value in commodity money) exceeds the price at which they can be purchased for commodity money or local issues in a distant town plus (secularly falling) transaction and transportation costs. As interlocal trade grows, "note brokers" with specialized knowledge of distant banks can make a business, just as retail foreign-currency brokers do today, of buying discounted nonlocal notes and transporting them to their par circulation areas or reselling them to travelers bound for those areas. Competition eventually reduces note discounts to the level of transaction and transportation costs plus a factor for redemption risk. By accepting the notes of unfamiliar banks at minimal commission rates, brokers unintentionally increase the general acceptability of notes, and promote their use in place of commodity money.

To this point we have implicitly assumed that banks refuse to accept one another's notes. This is not unreasonable; banks have as many reasons as other individuals do to refuse notes unfamiliar to them or difficult to redeem. They have in addition a further incentive for refusing to accept notes from rival banks, which is that by doing so they help to limit the acceptability of these notes, thereby enhancing the demand for their own issues. To cite just one historical illustration of this, the Bank of Scotland and the Royal Bank of Scotland—the first two banks of issue located in Edinburgh—refused to accept the notes of "provincial" banks of issue for a number of years (see Checkland [1975, 126]).

Nevertheless note brokerage presents opportunities for profit to bankers. Banks can out-compete other brokers because, unlike other brokers, they can issue their own notes (or deposit balances) to purchase "foreign" notes and need not hold costly till money. Each bank has an additional incentive to accept rival notes: larger interest earnings. If the notes acquired are redeemed sooner than the notes issued, interest-earning assets can be purchased and held in the interim. This profit from "float" can be continually renewed. In other words, a bank can maintain a permanently larger circulation of its own notes by continually replacing other notes with its own, and correspondingly can hold more earning assets than it otherwise could. If other banks are simultaneously replacing Bank *A*'s notes with their own, there may be no absolute increase in *A*'s circulation compared to the situation in which no bank accepts rival notes. But there will be an increase compared to Bank *A* not accepting, given whatever policies rivals are following, so that the incentive remains. (We argue below that in fact an indirect consequence of *other* banks' par acceptance of Bank *A* notes will be an absolute increase in *A*-note-holding in place of specie-holding.) Where transaction and transportation costs and risks are low enough, competition for circulation will narrow the brokerage fee to zero, that is, will lead the banks to general acceptance of one another's notes at par. The development of par acceptance by this route does not require that the banks explicitly and mutually agree to such a policy.

An alternative scenario, which assumes strategic behavior by the banks, leads to the same result. A bank may aggressively purchase foreign notes in the markets, and then suddenly return large quantities to their issuers for redemption in commodity money, hoping to force an unprepared issuer to suspend payments. The aggressor hopes to gain market share by damaging a rival's reputation or even forcing it into liquidation. These tactics, historically known as "note-picking" and "note-duelling," initially provoke the other issuers to respond in kind. Collecting and redeeming the first bank's notes not only returns the damage, but helps replenish the other banks' reserves. Purchasing its rivals' notes at par allows a bank to collect them in greater quantities, and may therefore be adopted. (Arbitrage-redemption of notes paid out precludes paying a price above par.) In the long run, nonaggression among banks should emerge, being less costly for all sides. Note-picking and note-duelling are costly and ineffectual ways to promote circulation when others do likewise. Banks thus find it profitable to take rivals' notes only as these are brought to them for deposit or exchange, and to return the collected notes to their issuers promptly in exchange for commodity money reserves. This result is contrary to Eugene Fama's (1983, 19) suggestion that note-duelling will persist indefinitely. It is an example of the "tit for tat" strategy, as discussed by Robert Axelrod (1984), proving dominant in a repeated-game setting.[8] Again, no explicitly negotiated pact is necessary. It only takes a single bank acting without cooperation from other banks to nudge the rest toward par acceptance (zero brokerage fees) as a defensive measure to maintain their reserves and circulation.

In New England at the beginning of the nineteenth century the Boston banks gave the nudge that put the whole region—with its multitude of "country" banks of issue far removed from the city—on a par-acceptance basis (Trivoli 1979). In Scotland the Royal Bank, when it opened for business in 1727, immediately began accepting at par the notes of the Bank of Scotland, at that time its only rival, and instigated a short-lived note duel. One response by the Bank of Scotland, later widely adopted, is notable: the bank inserted a clause into its notes giving it the option (which it did not normally exercise) of delaying redemption for six months, in which event it would pay a bonus amounting to 5 percent per annum (Checkland 1975, 60, 67–68). In both places, established banks, even after they had begun accepting each other's notes at par, sometimes refused to take the notes of new entrants. They soon changed their policies because the new banks that accepted and redeemed their notes were draining their reserves, while the established banks could not offset this without engaging in the same practice.

Banks that accept other banks' notes at par improve the market for their own notes and, unintentionally, for the notes that they accept. This makes a third scenario possible: If two banks both understand these circulation gains, they may explicitly enter a mutual par-acceptance arrangement. Others will emulate them, leading to general par acceptance. This explanation, previously offered by White (1984a, 19–21), assumes slightly more knowledge on the part of banks than the first two scenarios. Historical evidence of such explicit arrangements in Scotland is provided by Munn (1975).

Statistics from Boston dramatically illustrate the mutual circulation gains from acceptance arrangements. From 1824 to 1833 the note circulation of the Boston banks increased 57 percent, but the Boston circulation of country banks increased 148 percent, despite the Boston banks' intent to drive the country banks out of business (Lake 1947, 186; Trivoli 1979, 10–12). There is room for all banks to gain because the spread of par acceptance makes inside money more attractive to hold relative to commodity money. Since notes from one town are now accepted in a distant town at par, there is no longer good reason to lug around commodity money. As par note acceptance developed in Scotland, Canada, and New England—places where note issue was least restricted—during the nineteenth century, gold virtually disappeared from circulation. (Small amounts of gold coin were still used in these places at least in part because of restrictions upon the issue of "token" coin and of small-denomination notes. In an entirely free system, such restrictions would not exist.) In England and the rest of the United States, where banking (and note issue in particular) were less free, gold remained in circulation.

Even the complete displacement of commodity money in circulation by inside money does not, however, exhaust the possibilities for economizing on commodity money. Much of the specie formerly used in circulation to settle exchanges outside the banks may still be needed to settle clearings among them. Banks can substantially reduce their prudentially required holdings of commodity money by making regular note exchanges which allow them to offset their mutual obligations. Only net clearings rather than gross clearings are then settled in commodity money. The probability of any given-sized reserve loss in a given period is accordingly reduced (by the law of large numbers) and each bank can prudently reduce its ratio of reserves to demand liabilities.

The gains to be had from rationalization of note exchange are illustrated by the provincial Scottish banks before 1771, which practiced par acceptance without regular exchange. Note duelling among these banks was not uncommon (Leslie 1950, 8–9; Munn 1981, 23–24), and to guard against redemption raids they had to keep substantial reserves. Munn's figures (1981, 141) show that their reserves during this period were typically above 10 percent of total liabilities. This contrasts with reserve ratios of around 2 percent that were typical after note clearings became routine. The advantages of regular note exchange are great enough to have secured its eventual adoption in every historical instance of relatively free plural note issue.

CLEARINGHOUSES

The most readily made arrangements for note exchange are bilateral. In a system of more than two issuers, however, multilateral note exchange provides even greater economies. Reserve-holding economies result from the offsetting of claims that would otherwise be settled in specie. Multilateral clearing also allows savings in time and transportation costs by allowing all debts to be settled in one place and during one meeting rather than in numerous scattered meetings.

The institutional embodiment of multilateral note and deposit exchange, the clearinghouse, may evolve gradually from simpler note-exchange arrangements. For example, the note-exchange agents of banks *A* and *B* may accidentally meet each other at the counter of bank *C*. The greater the number of banks exchanging bilaterally, the less likely it is that such an encounter could be avoided. It would be natural for these two agents to recognize the savings in simple time and shoe-leather costs from settling their own exchange then and there, and from agreeing to do it again next time out, and then regularly. From a set of there bilateral settlements around one table it is not a large step toward the computation and settlement of combined net clearing balances. Once the advantages of this arrangement become clear to management, particularly the reserve-holding economies which may not have concerned the note porters, the institution will spread. Fourth, fifth, and subsequent banks may join later meetings. Or similar regular few-sided exchanges may be formed among other groups of banks, either independently or by one of the first three banks, whose meetings are later combined with the meetings of the original group. Eventually all the banks within an economy will be connected through one or a small number of clearinghouses.

The histories of the best-known early clearinghouses, in London, Edinburgh, and New York, all conform to this general pattern. J. S. Gibbons (1858, 292) reports that in New York the impetus for change from numerous bilateral exchanges to combined multilateral exchange came from note porters who "crossed and re-crossed each other's footsteps constantly." Among the London check porters, as related by Bisschop (1910, 160), "occasional encounters developed into daily meetings at a certain fixed place. At length the bankers themselves resolved to organize these meetings on a regular basis in a room specially reserved for this purpose."

The settlement of interbank obligations is initially made by physical transfer of commodity money at the conclusion of clearing sessions. Banks will soon find it economical to settle instead by means of transferable reserve accounts kept on the books of the clearinghouse, echoing the original development of transfer banking. These accounts may be deposits or equity shares denominated in currency units. As a transfer bank, the clearinghouse need not hold 100 percent reserves, and can safely pay its members a return (net of operating costs) by holding safe earning assets. This development reduces a member bank's cost of holding reserves, but does not eliminate it because alternative assets yield a higher return. Unless regulated directly by the clearinghouse, a bank's reserve ratio is determined by precautionary liquidity considerations depending mainly on the volume and volatility of net clearings and the clearinghouse penalty for reserve deficiency (see Ernst Baltensperger [1980, 4–9] and Santomero [1984, 584–86]).

Once established, a clearinghouse may serve several purposes beyond the economical exchange and settlement of interbank obligations. It can become, in the words of James G. Cannon (1908, 97), "a medium for united action among the banks in ways that did not exist even in the imagination of those who were instrumental in its inception." One task the clearinghouse may take on is to serve as a credit information bureau for its members. By pooling their records, banks can learn whether loan applicants have had bad debts in the past or are overextended to other banks at present, and can then take appropriate precautions (Cannon 1910, 135). Through the clearinghouse banks can also share information concerning bounced checks, forgeries, and the like.

The clearinghouse may also police the soundness of each member bank in order to assure the other member banks that notes and deposits are safe to accept for clearing. As part of this function, banks may be required to furnish financial statements and may have their books audited by clearinghouse examiners. The Chicago clearinghouse insisted on statements as early as 1867, and in 1876 gained the right to carry out comprehensive examinations whenever desired, to determine any member's financial condition (James 1938, 372–73, 499). Regular examinations began in 1906 (Cannon 1910, 138–39). Other clearinghouses, such as the Suffolk Bank and the Edinburgh clearinghouse, took their bearings mainly from the trends of members' clearing balances and traditional canons of sound banking practice. Those two clearinghouses enjoyed such high repute as certifying agencies that to be taken off their lists of members in good standing meant a serious loss in reputation and hence business for an offending bank (Trivoli 1979, 20; Graham 1911, 59).

It is possible that a clearinghouse may attempt to organize collusive agreements on interest rates, exchange rates, and fee schedules for its members. However, rates inconsistent with the results of competition would tend to break down under unregulated conditions, for the standard reason that secretly underbidding a cartel has concentrated benefits and largely external costs. A clear example of this comes from Scottish experience (Checkland 1975, 391–427). The Edinburgh banks set up a committee in 1828 to set borrowing and lending rates. The Glasgow banks joined a new version of the committee in 1836, at which time it represented the preponderance of Scottish banks in number and in total assets. Though not a clearinghouse association itself, the committee had much the same membership as the Edinburgh clearinghouse. In spite of repeated formal agreements, the committee could not hold members to its recommended interest rates. Not until after entry to the industry was closed in 1844 did the agreements become at all effective.

Perhaps the most interesting of all the roles a clearinghouse may perform is to assist its members in times of crisis (see Cannon [1910, 24]). If a bank or group of banks is temporarily unable to pay its clearing balances, or if it experiences a run on its commodity money reserves, the clearinghouse can serve as a medium through which more liquid banks lend to less liquid ones. It provides the framework for an intermittent, short-term credit market similar to the continuous federal funds market from which reserve-deficient American banks presently borrow. Another possible emergency function of clearinghouses is note issue. This function is called for when member banks are artificially restricted from issuing, as for example U.S. banks were by the bond-collateral requirements of the National Banking Acts, so that the banks are not able independently to fulfill all of their depositors' requests for hand-to-hand means of payment. Currency shortages occurred frequently in the United States during the second half of the nineteenth century, and clearinghouses helped to fill the void caused by deficient note issues of the National Banks.[9]

THE MATURE FREE-BANKING SYSTEM

We are now in a position to describe a mature free banking system, using historical evidence to illuminate its likely structural and operational characteristics. Evidence on industry structure from Scotland, Canada, Sweden, and elsewhere indicates that unregulated development does not produce natural monopoly, but rather an industry consisting of numerous competing banking firms, most having widespread branches, all of which are joined through one or more clearinghouses. In Scotland there were nineteen banks of issue in 1844, the final year of free entry. The largest four banks supplied 46.7 percent of the note circulation. In addition to their head offices the banks had 363 branch offices, 43.5 percent of which were owned by the largest (measured again by note issue) four banks.[10]

The banks in the mature system issue inside money in the shape of paper notes and demand deposit accounts (checkable either by paper or electronic means) that circulate routinely at par. Banks may also issue redeemable token coins, more durable but lighter and cheaper, to take the place of full-bodied coins as small change. Each bank's notes and tokens bear distinct brand-name identification marks and are issued in the denominations the public is most willing to hold. Because of the computational costs that would be involved in each transfer, interest is not likely to accrue on commonly used denominations of bank notes or tokens, contrary to the hypothesis of Neil Wallace (1983) that all currency would bear interest under laissez-faire.[11] Checkable accounts, however, provide a competitive yield reflecting rates available on interest-earning assets issued outside the banking system.

Checkable bank accounts are most familiarly structured as demand deposits, i.e., liabilities having a predetermined payoff payable on demand. An important reason for this structure is that historically a debt contract has been easier for the depositor to monitor and enforce than an equity contract which ties the account's payoff to the performance of a costly-to-observe asset portfolio. The predetermined payoff feature, however, raises the possibility of insolvency and consequently of a run on the bank if depositors fear that the last in line will receive less than a full payoff. One method of forestalling runs that may prevail in an unregulated banking system is the advertised holding of a large equity cushion, either on the bank's books or off them in the form of extended liability for bank shareholders. If this method were inadequate to assure depositors, banks might provide an alternative solution by linking checkability to equity or mutual-fund-type accounts with postdetermined rather than predetermined payoffs. The obstacles to such accounts (asset-monitoring and enforcement costs) have been eroded over the centuries by the emergence of easy-to-observe assets, namely publicly traded securities. Insolvency is ruled out for a balance sheet without debt liabilities, and the incentive to redeem ahead of other account holders is eliminated. An institution that linked checkability to equity accounts would operate like a contemporary money-market mutual fund, except that it would be directly tied into the clearing system (rather than having to clear via a deposit bank). Its optimal reserve holdings would be determined in the same way as those of a standard bank.

The assets of unregulated banks would presumably include short-term commercial paper, bonds of corporations and government agencies, and loans on various types of collateral. Without particular information on the assets available in the economy, the structure of asset portfolios cannot be characterized in detail, except to say that the banks presumably strive to maximize the present value of their interest earnings, net of operating and liquidity costs, discounted at risk-adjusted rates. The declining probability of larger liquidity needs, and the trade-off at the margin between liquidity and interest yield, suggest a spectrum of assets ranging from perfectly liquid reserves, to highly liquid interest-earning investments (these constitute a "secondary reserve"), to less liquid higher-earning assets. Thus far, because the focus has been on monetary arrangements, the only bank liabilities discussed have been notes and checking accounts. Unregulated banks would almost certainly diversify on the liability side by offering a variety of time deposits and also traveler's checks. Some banks would probably become involved in such related lines of business as the production of bullion and token fractional coins, issue of credit cards, and management of mutual funds. Such banks would fulfill the contemporary ideal of the "financial supermarket," with the additional feature of issuing bank notes.

Commodity money seldom if ever appears in circulation in the mature system, virtually all of it (outside numismatic collections) having been offered to the banks in exchange for inside money. Some commodity money will continue to be held by clearinghouses so long as it is the ultimate settlement asset among them. At the limit, if inter-clearinghouse settlements were made entirely with other assets (perhaps claims on a super-clearinghouse which itself holds negligible commodity money), and if the public were completely weaned from holding commodity money, the active demand for the old-fashioned money commodity would be wholly nonmonetary. The flow supply formerly sent to the mints would be devoted to industrial and other uses. Markets for those uses would determine the relative price of the commodity. The purchasing power of monetary instruments would continue to be fixed by the holder's contractual right (even if never exercised) to redeem them for physically specified quantities of the money commodity. The problem of meeting any significant redemption request (e.g., a "run" on a bank) could be contractually handled, as it was historically during note-duelling episodes, by invoking an "option clause" that allows the bank a specified period of time to gather the necessary commodity money while compensating the redeeming party for the delay. The clause need not (and historically did not) impair the par circulation of bank liabilities.

This picture of an unregulated banking system differs significantly in its institutional features from the visions presented in some of the recent literature on competitive payments systems. The system described here has assets fitting standard definitions of money. Banks and clearinghouses hold (except in the limit), and are contractually obligated to provide at request, high-powered reserve money (commodity money or deposits at the clearinghouse), and they issue debt liabilities (inside money) with which payments are generally made. These features contrast with the situation envisioned by Black (1970) and Fama (1980), in which "banks" hold no reserve assets and the payments mechanism operates by transferring equities or mutual fund shares unlinked to any money.

Bank reserves do not disappear in the evolution of a free banking system, as analyzed here, because the existence of bank liabilities that are promises to pay presupposes some more fundamental means of payment that is the thing promised. Individuals may forgo actual redemption of promises, preferring to hold them instead of commodity money, so long as they believe that they will receive high-powered money if they ask for it. Banks, on the other hand, have a competitive incentive to redeem one another's liabilities regularly. So long as net clearing balances have a positive probability of being nonzero, reserves will continue to be held. In a system without reserve money it is not clear what would be used to settle clearing balances. In a commodity-money system, the scarcity of the money commodity and the costliness of holding reserves serve to pin down the price level and to limit the quantity of inside money. In money-less systems it is not always clear what forces limit the expansion of payment media nor what pins down the price level. Nor are these things clear, at the other extreme, in a model of multiple competing fiat monies.[12]

Our analysis indicates that commodity-based money would persist in the absence of intervention, for the reason that the supreme salability of the particular money good is self-reinforcing. This result contradicts recent views (see Black [1970], Fama [1980], Greenfield and Yeager [1983], Yeager [1985]) that associate complete deregulation with the replacement of monetary exchange by a sophisticated form of barter. (To be sure, Greenfield and Yeager recognize that their system would be unlikely to emerge without deliberate action by government, particularly given a government-dominated monetary system as the starting point.) In an economy with commodity-based money, prices are stated in terms of a unit of the money commodity, so the question of using an abstract unit of account does not arise as it does in a sophisticated barter setting.[13] Even if actual commodity money were to disappear from reserves and circulation, the media of exchange would not be "divorced" from the commodity unit of account; they would be linked by redeemability contracts. We can see no force severing this link. Contrary to Woolsey (1985), the renunciation of commodity redemption obligations is not compelled by economization of reserves. Thus we find no basis for the spontaneous emergence of a multicommodity monetary standard or of any pure fiat monetary standards, such as contemplated in works by Hall (1982), Woolsey (1984), Klein (1974), and Hayek (1978). In short, unregulated banking would be much less radically unconventional, and much more akin to existing financial institutions than recent literature on the topic suggests.

One important contemporary financial institution is nonetheless missing from our account, namely the central bank. We find no market forces leading to the spontaneous emergence of a central bank, in contrast to the view of Charles Goodhart. (For this discussion a central bank is closely enough defined, following Goodhart [1985, 3–8], as an agency with two related powers: monetary policy, and external regulation of the banking system.) Goodhart (1985, 76) argues that the development of a central bank is "natural" because "the natural process of centralization of interbank deposits with leading commercial banks tends toward the development of a banks' club" which then needs an independent arbiter. But even on his own account the forces that historically promoted centralized interbank deposits were *not* "natural" in any laissez-faire sense. They stemmed crucially from legal restrictions, particularly the awarding of a monopoly of note issue or the suppression of branch banking. Where no legislation inhibits the growth of branched banking firms with direct access to investment markets in the economy's financial center, and able to issue their own notes, it is not at all apparent that profit seeking compels any significant interbank depositing of reserves. Walter Bagehot (1873, 66–68) argued persuasively that "the natural system—that which would have sprung up if Government had let banking alone—is that of many banks of equal or not altogether unequal size" and that in such a system no bank "gets so much before the others that the others voluntarily place their reserves in its keeping." None of the relevant historical cases (Scotland, Canada, Sweden) shows any significant tendency toward interbank deposits.

We have seen that reserves do tend to centralize, on the other hand, in the clearinghouses. And clearinghouses, as Gorton (1985a, 277, 283; 1985b, 274) has recently emphasized, may take on functions that are today associated with national central banks: holding reserves for clearing purposes, establishing and policing safety and soundness standards for member banks, and managing panics should they arise. But these functional similarities should not be taken to indicate that clearinghouses have (or would have) freely evolved into central banks. The similarities instead reflect the preemption of clearinghouse functions by legally privileged banks or, particularly in the founding of the Federal Reserve System (Gorton 1985a, 277; Timberlake 1984), the deliberate nationalization of clearinghouse functions. Central banks have emerged from legislation contravening, not complementing, spontaneous market developments.[14]

Notes

The authors are indebted to the Institute for Human Studies for the opportunity to work together on this article, and to Chris Fauvelas, David Glasner, Israel Kirzner, Hu McCulloch, Mario Rizzo, Kurt Schuler, Richard J. Sweeney, and anonymous referees for useful comments. The Scaife Foundation provided support for White's research.

1. See for example Black (1970), Klein (1974), Hayek (1978), Fama (1980), Greenfield and Yeager (1983), Wallace (1983), White (1984b), O'Driscoll (1985), and Yeager (1985).
2. We have each made normative evaluations of free banking elsewhere: Selgin (1988, chaps. 8–10); White (1984a, chap. 5; 1984b).
3. See also Menger (1981, 260–62). The same view appears in Carlisle (1901, 5) and Ridgeway (1892, 47). A more recent version of Menger's theory is Jones (1976). For a secondary account of Menger's theory, see O'Driscoll (1986).
4. See Menger (1981, 263–66); Ridgeway (1892, 6–11); and Burns (1927a, 286–88). On some alleged nonmetallic monies of primitive peoples, see Quiggen (1963).
5. See Usher (1943), de Roover (1974, chaps. 4, 5), and Lopez (1979).
6. On the historical development of bank notes and checks in Europe, see Usher (1943, 7–8, 23).
7. See White (1984a, 84–85) for nineteenth-century views on geographic diseconomies in note circulation.
8. An example of the explicit adoption of "tit for tat" by an exhausted note-duelling bank is given by Munn (1981, 24).
9. See Cannon (1908), Andrew (1908), Smith (1936), Timberlake (1984),

and Gorton (1985a).
10. These figures are based on data in White (1984a, 37). A recent econometric study of economics of scale in banking is Benston, Hanweck, and Humphrey (1982).
11. See White (1984a, 8–9; 1987).
12. Taub (1985) has shown that a dynamic inconsistency facing issuers in Klein's (1974) model will lead them to hyperinflate.
13. This point is emphasized by White (1984c). For additional criticism of the Black-Fama-Yeager literature, see O'Driscoll (1985), Hoover (1985), and McCallum (1984).
14. On the appearance of central banks in several nations, see Smith (1936); on Canada in particular see Bordo and Redish (1985).

References

Andrew, A. Piatt. 1908. "Substitutes for Cash in the Panic of 1907." *Quarterly Journal of Economics* (August): 497–596.

Axelrod, Robert. 1984. *The Evolution of Cooperation*. New York: Basic Books.

Bagehot, Walter. 1873. *Lombard Street: A Description of the Money Market*. London: Henry S. King.

Baltensperger, Ernst. 1980. "Alternative Approaches to the Theory of the Banking Firm." *Journal of Monetary Economics* 6 (January): 1–37.

Benston, George, J., Gerald A. Hanweck, and David B. Humphrey. 1982. "Scale Economies in Banking: A Restructuring and Reassessment." *Journal of Money, Credit, and Banking* (November): 435–54.

Black, Fischer. 1970. "Banking and Interest Rates in a World Without Money: The Effects of Uncontrolled Banking." *Journal of Bank Research* 1 (Autumn): 9–20.

Bisschop, W. R. 1910. *The Rise of the London Money Market, 1640–1826*. London: P. S. King & Son.

Bordo, Michael, and Angela Redish. 1985. "Why Did the Bank of Canada Emerge in 1935?" Manuscript.

Burns, A. R. 1927a. "Early Stages in the Development of Money and Coins." In *London Essays in Economics in Honour of Edwin Cannan*, edited by T. E. Gregory and Hugh Dalton. London: George Routledge & Sons.

———. 1927b. *Money and Monetary Policy in Early Times*. New York: Alfred E. Knopf.

Cannon, James G. 1908. "Clearing Houses and the Currency." In *The Currency Problem and the Present Financial Situation*, edited by E.R.A Seligman. New York: Columbia University Press.

———. 1910. *Clearing Houses*. Washington, D. C.: Government Printing Office.

Carlisle, William. 1901. *The Evolution of Modern Money*. London: Macmillan.

Checkland, S. G. 1975. *Scottish Banking: A History, 1695–1973*. Glasgow: Collins.

de Roover, Raymond. 1974. *Business, Banking, and Economic Thought in Late Medieval and Early Modern Europe*, edited by Julius Kirshner. Chicago: University of Chicago Press.

Fama, Eugene F. 1980. "Banking in the Theory of Finance." *Journal of Monetary Economics* 6 (January) 39–57.

———. 1983. "Financial Intermediation and Price Level Control." *Journal of Monetary Economics* (July): 7–28.

Gibbons, J. S. 1858. *The Banks of New York: Their Dealers, the Clearing House, and the Panic of 1857*. New York: D. Appleton Co.

Goodhart, Charles. 1985. *The Evolution of Central Banks: A Natural Develop-

ment? London: Suntory-Toyota International Centre for Economics and Related Disciplines/London School of Economics and Political Science.

Gorton, Gary. 1985a. "Clearinghouses and the Origin of Central Banking in the United States." *Journal of Economic History* 42 (June): 277–83.

―――. 1985b. "Banking Theory and Free Banking History: A Review Essay." *Journal of Monetary Economics* 16 (September): 267–76.

Graham, William. 1911. *The One Pound Note in the History of Banking in Great Britain*, 2d ed. Edinburgh: James Thin.

Greenfield, Robert L., and Leland B. Yeager. 1983. "A Laissez-Faire Approach to Monetary Stability." *Journal of Money, Credit, and Banking* 15 (August): 302–15.

Hall, Robert E. 1982. "Explorations in the Gold Standard and Related Policies for Stabilizing the Dollar." In *Inflation: Causes and Effects*. edited by Robert E. Hall. Chicago: Chicago University Press for the National Bureau of Economic Research.

Hayek, F. A. 1978. *The Denationalisation of Money*, 2d ed. London: Institute of Economic Affairs.

Hicks, John. 1967. "The Two Triads, Lecture I." In *Critical Essays in Monetary Theory*. Oxford: Clarendon Press.

Hoover, Kevin D. 1985. "Causality and Invariance in the Money Supply Process." Doctoral dissertation, Oxford University.

James, F. Cyril. 1938. *The Growth of Chicago Banks*. New York: Harper & Brothers.

Jones, Robert. 1976. "The Origin and Development of Media of Exchange." *Journal of Political Economy* 84 (November): 757–75.

Klein, Benjamin. 1974. "The Competitive Supply of Money." *Journal of Money, Credit, and Banking* 6 (November): 423–53.

Lake, Wilfrid S. 1947. "The End of the Suffolk System." *Journal of Economic History* (November): 183–207.

Leslie, J. O. 1950. *The Note Exchange and Clearing House Systems*. Edinburgh: William Blackwood.

Lopez, Robert S. 1979. "The Dawn of Medieval Banking." In *The Dawn of Modern Banking*. New Haven: Yale University Press.

McCallum, Bennett T. 1984. "Bank Deregulation, Accounting Systems of Exchange, and the Unit of Account: A Critical Review." Carnegie-Rochester Conference Series on Public Policy (Autumn): 3–45.

Melitz, Jacques. 1974. *Primitive and Modern Money*. Reading, Mass.: Addison-Wesley.

Menger, Carl. 1892. "On the Origin of Money," translated by Caroline A. Foley. *Economic Journal* 92 (June): 239–55.

―――. 1981. *Principles of Economics* [1871]. New York: New York University Press.

Munn, Charles. 1975. "The Origins of the Scottish Note Exchange." *Three Banks Review* 107: 45–60.

―――. 1981. *The Scottish Provincial Banking Companies, 1747–1864*. Edinburgh: John Donald.

O'Driscoll, Gerald P., Jr. 1985. "Money in a Deregulated Financial System." Federal Reserve Bank of Dallas *Economic Review* (May): 1–12.

―――. 1986. "Money: Menger's Evolutionary Theory." *History of Political Economy* 18 (Winter): 601–16.

Powell, Ellis T. 1966. *The Evolution of the Money Market, 1385–1915*. New York: Augustus M. Kelley.

Quiggen, A. Hingston. 1963. *A Survey of Primitive Money: The Beginning of Currency*. London: Methuen.

Richards, R. D. 1965. *The Early History of Banking in England*. New York: Augustus M. Kelley.

Ridgeway, William. 1892. *The Origin of Metallic Currency and Weight Standards*. Cambridge: Cambridge University Press.

Santomero, Anthony M. 1984. "Modeling the Banking Firm: A Survey." *Journal of Money, Credit, and Banking* (November): 576–602.

Selgin, George A. 1988. *The Theory of Free Banking.* Totowa, N. J.: Rowman and Littlefield.

Smith, Vera C. 1936. *The Rationale of Central Banking.* London: P. S. King & Son.

Taub, Bart. 1985. "Private Fiat Money with Many Suppliers." *Journal of Monetary Economics* 16 (September): 195–208.

Timberlake, Richard H. 1984. "The Central Banking Role of Clearing-House Associations." *Journal of Money, Credit, and Banking* 16 (February): 1–15.

Trivoli, George. 1979. *The Suffolk Bank: A Study of a Free-Enterprise Clearing System.* Leesburg, Va.: Adam Smith Institute.

Usher, Abbott Payson. 1943. *The Early History of Deposit Banking in Mediterranean Europe.* Cambridge: Cambridge University Press.

Wallace, Neil. 1983. "A Legal Restrictions Theory of the Demand for "Money" and the Role of Monetary Policy." *Federal Reserve Bank of Minneapolis Quarterly Review* (Winter): 1–7.

White, Lawrence H. 1984a. *Free Banking in Britain: Theory, Experience, and Debate, 1800–1845.* Cambridge: Cambridge University Press.

———. 1984b. "Free Banking as an Alternative Monetary System." In *Money in Crisis: The Federal Reserve, the Economy, and Monetary Reform,* edited by Barry N. Siegel. Cambridge, Mass.: Ballinger Publishing.

———. 1984c. "Competitive Payments Systems and the Unit of Account." *American Economic Review* (September): 699–712.

———. 1987. "Accounting for Non-interest-bearing Currency: A Critique of the Legal Restrictions Theory of Money." *Journal of Money, Credit, and Banking* 19 (November): 448–56.

Williams, Jeffrey C. 1984. "Fractional Reserve Banking in Grain." *Journal of Money, Credit, and Banking* (November): 488–96.

Withers, Hartley. 1920. *The Meaning of Money.* London: John Murray.

Woolsey, W. William. 1984. "The Multiple Standard and the Means of Exchange." Manuscript, Talledega College, Al.

———. 1985. "Competitive Payments Systems: Comment." Manuscript, Talledega College.

Yeager, Leland B. 1985. "Deregulation and Monetary Reform." *American Economic Review* (May): 103–7.

4. The Establishment of Central Banking
Kevin Dowd

Unlike commodity money, fractional reserve banking, and clearinghouses, central banks have not been products of "spontaneous order." Instead, they have been established deliberately, through legislation. Here author Kevin Dowd reviews the origins of two of the most influential central banks: the Bank of England and the Federal Reserve System. --G.S., Ed.

* * *

A central bank is not a natural product of banking development. It is imposed from outside or comes into being as the result of Government favours.

(Vera Smith 1936)[1]

5.1 Introduction

We turn now to the historical experience of state intervention into the monetary system. This chapter deals with the establishment of central banking, while the next deals with its historical record. We shall see how British and American monetary history confirms many of the conclusions we reached earlier about the benefits of *laisser-faire* banking and the potential damage that can be done by state intervention. For accounts of other countries' experience, the following references might prove to be useful: for Canada, see Bordo and Redish (1988), Chisholm (1979, 1983), Schuler (1985, 1988a,b) and Shortt (undated); for China, see Selgin (1987); for France, see Nataf (1987) and E. White (1988); for Sweden, see Jonung (1985) and Sandberg (1978); and for Switzerland, see Weber (1988). The experience of these countries appears to be broadly consistent with the conclusions that we draw from British and American monetary history.

We begin with the establishment of central banking in Britain.

5.2 The Early History of the Bank of England[2]

A recurrent theme in English history is the government's perpetual shortage of money. The monarchs could always levy taxes, of course, but only with their subjects' consent, and they were often forced to make concessions to obtain it. Over time the need for taxes grew, but so did the accumulated concessions and the potential for conflict between sovereign and Parliament. The Tudor monarchs were generally skilful enough to avoid major confrontations with Parliament, but the needs of the state continued to grow, and when the relatively inept Stuarts succeeded to the throne a major confrontation was almost inevitable. It came with the Civil War (1642–50).

The war failed to solve the underlying problem. After the Restoration Charles II soon found himself in financial straits and decided to borrow the money he needed from the London goldsmiths, rather than ask Parliament for it. He could not repay and repudiated the debts in 1672. This action caused much distress and badly damaged the Government's credit for years to come. Some twenty years later William III needed money to wage war against France but was faced with high interest rates reflecting the Government's poor credit. He was therefore very receptive when a Scottish financier, William Paterson, suggested a scheme in which he and a group of other financiers would advance the Government a loan in return for the right to set up a bank to issue loans and print banknotes. The bank was to be known as the Governor and Company of the Bank of England, and it was set up in 1694.

The early history of the Bank can be summarised as a series of purchases of privileges by the Bank from the Government. Originally, the Bank made a loan to the Government of £1,200,000 in return for the right to issue notes to the same amount. These amounts were extended in 1697, when it was also stipulated that the Bank should enjoy a monopoly of chartered banking in England and the privilege of limited liability for its shareholders. These were the beginnings of the Bank's monopoly powers. In 1709 these were extended further when a law was passed to limit competition to companies with less than 6 partners with unlimited liability. The capital of any other bank was therefore limited to what could be provided by up to 6 partners, and in an industry where there were economies of scale this meant that English banks were severely under-capitalised. The effects of this were very detrimental:

> The hunger for credit persisted . . . and reliable aggregations of capital from among more than six moderately wealthy persons were impossible. The consequence was that petty shopkeepers and tradesmen set up everywhere as bankers to supply the demand for credit . . . (But) With every threat of a Stuart rising or a foreign invasion the more timid people rushed to the banks to exchange their notes for gold. Only the wealthy banks could stand such runs, and the petty shopkeeping banks failed on all such occasions in scores, dragging down with them their clients . . . (Meulen 1934, pp 95–6)

It was widely believed at the time that the instability of English banks was due, not to their under-capitalisation, but to their freedom to set their own terms of redemption and issue small notes. This led to demands for legislative action, and Parliament responded by prohibiting option clauses throughout the UK in 1765, by prohibiting notes of less than £1 in England and Wales in 1775, and then by extending this ban to notes of less than £5 in 1777. The suppression of option clauses forced banks to redeem on demand and made them vulnerable to runs on their liquidity, while the suppression of small notes meant that the majority of trades now had to conduct business using the more expensive medium of coins. This ban also hindered the growth of small banks since new banks relied, to a large extent, on the issue of small notes to gain acceptance.

The sale of privileges to the Bank continued throughout the eighteenth century. As Smith (1936, p. 11) put it:

> The result of the accumulation of an array of privileges was to give the Bank of England a position of prestige and influence in the financial world such as to cause small private banks to experience

difficulties in continuing to compete in the same line of business, and in London the majority of private note issues had been abandoned by about 1780. A further effect was that the smaller banks began to adopt the practice of keeping balances with the Bank of England, which was thus already beginning to acquire the characteristics of a Central Bank.

The process of the Government raiding the Bank's larder eventually culminated in the suspension of the convertibility of the Bank's notes. When the French revolutionary wars broke out, the Government repeatedly applied to the Bank for more loans. The Bank felt obliged to comply, although it did so under protest, but the strain on its reserves proved too much, and in the end the Government had to authorise the Bank to suspend specie payments. In effect, the Government had first made the Bank insolvent, and then legalised its insolvency.

After the suspension, Bank of England notes went to a discount against gold, and specie disappeared from everyday circulation. To all intents and purposes the Bank's notes were legal tender, although they were not made so officially until 1812. The use of the Bank's notes was encouraged further by the authorisation to issue small notes, which was motivated by a desire to economise on specie. Increasingly, the other banks came to look upon Bank notes as backing for their own issues, and they continued to do so even after convertibility had been restored and Bank of England notes again ceased to be legal tender. The nation's stock of gold was therefore concentrated more and more in the vaults of the Bank of England, and this, together with the Bank's unique note-issuing privileges, meant that the Bank came to be looked upon as the ultimate — and indeed, only — source of help in liquidity panics. This was gradually to force the Bank to accept a role as lender of last resort and custodian of the nation's monetary system.

We now leave England for a while and turn to Scotland.

5.3 The Development of Free Banking in Scotland[3]

The development of banking in Scotland took a very different course from that of banking in England. The first Scottish bank was the Bank of Scotland, which received its charter from the Scottish Parliament in 1695. This charter gave it the rights to limited liability and a monopoly of the note issue in Scotland until 1716. Despite its title, the Bank of Scotland was not a state bank, and its charter prohibited it from lending to the Government. Shortly after its foundation, the Act of Union of 1707 merged the Scottish and English Parliaments, and the new Westminster Parliament was distinctly unsympathetic to the Bank because of its suspected Jacobite leanings. It therefore ignored the Bank's pleas not to charter a rival bank — the Royal Bank of Scotland — in 1727.

Warfare between the banks broke out on the same day the second bank opened. Each side tried to drive the other out of business by collecting its notes and presenting them for summary redemption. It became apparent, however, that though these 'note duels' could inflict considerable damage, neither bank was going to put the other out of business. The banks gradually realised this and a more peaceful note exchange began to develop which eventually led to a formal note-exchange agreement in 1751. The competition continued on other fronts, nonetheless, and it led to some major banking innovations. In 1728 the Royal Bank instituted the cash credit account, a form of overdraft which individuals could use, provided they presented evidence of sound character and two or more co-signatories who accepted liability for the loan. This allowed individuals to borrow money without the need for extensive collateral of their own. Meanwhile, in the same year the Bank of Scotland (the 'Old Bank') began offering interest on its deposits, and the following year it introduced a cash credit account of its own. It followed these innovations, in 1730, with the introduction of the option clause to protect itself from sudden demands for redemption.

The next move in the banks' rivalry was the establishment of the Glasgow Ship Bank in 1749 by the Old Bank, to win business away from the Royal Bank. The latter responded by setting up the Glasgow Arms Bank the next year. The two Glasgow banks then turned against the Edinburgh banks by issuing their own notes, and a new bank war followed. The bank war proved inconclusive, so an attempt was made to set up a cartel and agree on a market share-out. That attempt proved to be unsuccessful, and so the banks settled down to an uneasy coexistence. In the meantime, a new chartered bank came on the scene with the British Linen Company, which obtained its charter in 1746. Originally set up to promote the linen trade, it started banking and eventually dropped the linen trade altogether. New banks continued to enter the field in the late 1750s and early 1760s and they began to offer notes for smaller amounts (less than £1) which helped to alleviate the inconveniences caused by the lack of an adequate coinage. The banks also adopted the Old Bank's practice of inserting option clauses into their bank note contracts to protect their liquidity. Both small notes and option clauses were controversial, though, and they were suppressed by Act of Parliament in 1765[4]. After this, Scottish free banking was never entirely 'free'.

The innovations continued. In 1771 all the major Scottish banks finally agreed to accept each other's notes at par and to exchange them at a regular clearing. This helped to promote the demand for each bank's notes, but it also contributed significantly to the stability of the banking system by providing a rapid and effective check against any bank that over-issued its notes. The 1770s also saw the establishment of the first successful branch banks, and branch banking rapidly spread.

The stability of the Scottish system was demonstrated by the episode of the Ayr bank failure. The management of this bank engaged on a reckless expansion of its loan business and soon found itself in serious difficulties. It managed to remain solvent only by borrowing from bankers in London, but its steadily mounting debts forced it into bankruptcy in 1772 just 3 years after it opened. The public suffered no losses from the failure, and all the creditors were eventually paid off in full. Any inconvenience the public might have suffered was reduced by the policy of the Old Bank and the Royal Bank to accept the notes of the Ayr Bank at par; they did this to attract more deposits and to put more of their own notes into circulation. The collapse of the Ayr Bank inflicted serious losses on the bank's proprietors (who were liable for all its debts) and on some smaller banks that had circulated its bills, but the major banks and the public suffered little or nothing. Such were the effects of the most serious bank collapse during the free banking period.

The Scottish banking system was as able to weather external shocks as internal ones. Two of the most significant were in 1797 and 1825–6. The first was when the Bank of England suspended convertibility — this caused a brief panic in Edinburgh, and the major Scottish banks temporarily suspended as well. The panic subsided, however, and the Scottish banks soon resumed their normal redemption policies and maintained them for the rest of the Restriction period. This indicates, incidentally, how competition forced the banks to maintain convertibility. The second shock was the crisis of 1825–6, 'a panic so tremendous that its results are well remembered after nearly fifty years' as Bagehot (1873, p. 138) later described it. This panic shook the English banking system to its foundations, and virtually every bank in the country had to apply to the Bank of England for assistance. The strength of the Scottish banking system is perhaps illustrated by the fact that not a single Scottish bank felt the need to apply to the Bank of England, despite the close links between the English and Scottish financial systems.

Scottish bank notes were widely accepted, not just in Scotland but in much of northern England as well. The esteem in which Scottish notes were held is well illustrated by a memorial sent by the representatives of the border areas of Northumberland and Westmoreland to Parliament, when it was proposed to prohibit the Scottish £1 note in 1826. The memorial outlined the reasons for the strength of the Scottish banks and continued:

> The natural consequence has been that Scotch notes have formed the greater part of our circulating medium, a circumstance in which we have reason to rejoice, since, in the course of the last 50 years, with the solitary exception of the Falkirk bank, we have never sustained the slightest loss from one acceptance of Scotch paper; while, in the same period, the failures of banks in the north of England have been unfortunately numerous, and have occasioned the most ruinous losses to many who were little able to sustain them.[5]

Another indication of the relative losses suffered by the public in Scotland and England is given by White (1984b, p. 41) who reports an estimate of the losses from all Scottish bank failures, up to 1841, of only £32,000. Against this, losses the previous year in London alone were said to have been twice that amount.

The fifty years or so after the Ayr Bank episode saw the further development and consolidation of the Scottish banking system. The smaller note-issuing banks gradually disappeared, and branch-banking continued to spread. The smaller banks that remained tended to be specialist firms which kept accounts with the larger banks and did not issue notes. This indicated that there were substantial but limited economies of scale in the note-issuing business, and there was certainly no tendency for any one bank of issue to drive the others out. In other words, while there were economies of scale there was no evidence of natural monopoly in the note-issuing business or any other aspect of banking.

The system of free banking in Scotland appears to have promoted the country's economic development in various ways: by making credit available to promote industry and commerce; by encouraging habits of thrift and industry among the population; by encouraging the use of bank liabilities as media of exchange to reduce transactions costs; and by providing the people with a stable monetary system which protected them against disturbances. An indication of how much the banking system might have contributed to Scotland's economic development is given by Cameron (1967, pp. 94–5). He points out that per-capita income in Scotland in 1750 was probably only half that in England, and yet it nearly equalled England's income by 1845. Scotland's much more rapid economic progress over this period was attained despite a number of obvious disadvantages — its greater political instability, inferior infrastructure and greater distance from export markets — and Cameron concludes that the only advantages it could have had, relative to England, would have been its superior educational and banking systems. It therefore seems reasonable to suppose that Scotland's better economic progress was due in some considerable part to its superior banking system.

5.4 British Controversies Over Central Banking[6]

While the roots of the free banking idea can be traced to Adam Smith (1776)[7] and Jeremy Bentham (1788)[8], it was not until the 1820s that it began to acquire anything like a significant following. The immediate antecedents to free banking can be found in the agitation in the early 1820s for the 6-partner rule against joint-stock banking in England to be abolished. This agitation appeared to start with James Mill's *Elements of Political Economy*, in 1821, and a pamphlet by Thomas Joplin in 1822. They argued that the joint-stock organisation was more suited to banking than a partnership, and cited the example of Scotland as evidence. Their claims seemed to be borne out by the disastrous crisis of 1825–6 which shook the English financial system to its foundations:

> The crash of 1825–26 brought down a number of England's most reputable country banks and London banking houses as well as scores of smaller banks. A single month in 1825 saw 73 banks stop payment, only 10 of which eventually resumed business. One member of Parliament took note that 700 or 800 country banks — virtually the entire industry — had asked the Bank of England for assistance during the general panic. The Bank of England itself, in the words of Bagehot 'was within an ace of stopping payment' due to depleted specie reserves. (White 1984b, p. 47)

This crisis led the Prime Minister, Lord Liverpool, to declare:

> The present system is one of the fullest liberty as to what is rotten and bad, but one of the most complete restriction as to all that is

good. By it a cobbler or cheesemonger, without any proof of his ability to meet them, may issue his notes, unrestricted by any check whatever; while, on the other hand, more than six persons, however respectable, are not permitted to become partners in a bank with whose notes the whole business of the country might be transacted.[9]

The result was the Act of 1826 which allowed joint-stock banks of issue in England — provided only that they were more than 65 miles from London. Thus the Bank's monopoly position was perhaps weakened in one respect,[10] but confirmed in another.

About the same time, proposals began to be put forward to abolish the Bank of England's privileges altogether and establish free banking in England. One such proposal came from Sir Henry Parnell, who put forward the idea in a meeting of the pro-free-trade Political Economy Club in 1826. He argued that the issue of bank notes should be entirely free, and was severely critical of the 1826 Act which left untouched the greater evil to be remedied in the Bank of England. He was much impressed by the evidence brought by Scottish bankers to the Commons Committee of 1826, and repeatedly stressed the role of the note-clearing system in limiting over-issue among competitive banks. Because of this, he wrote:

> no such thing as an excess of paper or as a depreciation of paper can take place for want of a sufficiently early and active demand for gold. If in England the power of converting paper into gold has not prevented an excess of paper, because the demand does not occur until long after the excess has taken place, this is to be attributed to the system of English banking.[11]

These claims provoked a number of critical responses, all of which disputed the claim that the clearing system would discipline over-issue. J. R. McCulloch (1831), for example, argued that a bank which expanded its note issues under competitive conditions of issue would be able to force the other banks to expand along with it, but the free bankers were quick to counter that this argument ignored the reserve losses which the expanding bank would face in the course of its expansion. G. W. Norman (1837), however, argued that the clearing system would not work because competition would force the banks to expand together. The premise of Norman's argument is dubious, as we discussed in Chapter 2, but in any case the reserve losses of the system as a whole would still exert the necessary discipline. The most famous argument, however, and one to which the free bankers never gave a clear response, was the argument put forward by the Irish economist Mountiford Longfield about the clearing system not disciplining over-issue because a bank which expanded its loans would also expand the payments it had falling due to it. We discussed this argument in Chapter 2, where we noted its invalidity because it is not sufficient to expand loans in order to increase the note circulation, and because the argument fails to allow for the time lag between the loan expansion and their repayment. We now return to the main storyline.

The calls for free banking from Parnell and others acquired additional force because the Bank's charter was due to expire in 1833. This put the Bank's defenders under considerable pressure, and it was doubtful whether Parliament would allow the Bank's privileges to be extended. As early as 1826 Lord Liverpool and Frederick John Robinson wrote in a letter to the Bank's directors: 'With respect to the extension of the term of their exclusive privileges . . . it is obvious . . . that Parliament will never agree to it. Such privileges are out of fashion, and what expectation can the Bank under present circumstances entertain that theirs will be renewed?'[12]

The threat was sufficiently strong that at least one of the Bank's proprietors in 1832 advised his colleagues to agree to give up the note-issuing monopoly in return for some form of compensation.[13] That same year, the Leader of the Commons, Lord Althorp, moved for an investigation in view of the coming expiry of the Bank's charter. The issue to be determined was the conditions under which individuals should be allowed to issue money. A Secret Committee was set up to deliberate the issue, but the Chancellor made a deal with the Bank to extend the charter and pushed the Committee to a quick decision to recommend renewal. The vast majority of witnesses were London bankers and brokers who recommended the renewal of the charter but were hardly in a position to offend the Bank, while many witnesses who would have opposed renewal were not even called.[14] On the Committee, Parnell alone voted against renewal and afterwards complained that the proceedings were *ex parte* and one-sided'.[15] When the issue came back before the House, Lord Althorp then made his position clear: 'My opinion is, that if you contrive an adequate check upon the conduct of a single bank, it will be more advantageous that such single bank should manage the circulation of the country, than that it should be left to the competition of different and rival establishments.'[16] In the event, a majority of MPs agreed with him, and it was decided to renew the Bank's charter until 1844.

In retrospect, this was probably the best chance the free bankers had to abolish the Bank of England's monopoly. The decision to renew the Bank's charter was greeted with many protests, and proposals for free banking continued to come from various quarters, both inside and outside Parliament, but as time went on the focus of public debate appeared to shift from the issue of whether there should be a central bank to the question of what rules it should follow. It was ironic that this increasing antipathy to free trade in banking came at about the same time as the idea of general free trade was gaining ground:

> There was an increasing feeling that the note issue should be concentrated in a single agency, either the Bank of England or a newly created National Bank . . . Spokesmen for the country banks tried to make the most of the idea that there was a conflict between the principles of free trade and a monopoly of the note issue. They had little success, and at the same time that free trade sentiment was gaining ground in the field of trade and business there was a growing acceptance of the idea that note issue was not a business activity, but a function of government. The idea was expressed in many ways, and by many people, but the summary statement of Thomas Spring Rice, Chancellor of the Exchequer, in the debate on the Bank of Ireland bill in 1839, gave what appears to have been the preponderance of public opinion: 'I deny the applicability of the general principle of the freedom of trade to the question of making money'. (Fetter 1965, pp. 173–4)[17]

Whether or not this view represented the preponderance of public opinion in 1839, it certainly did later.

In the late 1830s the Bank came under renewed criticism for its alleged responsibility for the monetary disturbances of the period. A defence in 1837 of the Bank by one of its directors, John Horsley Palmer, laid the blame with the country banks' allegedly reckless credit policies. This pamphlet itself provoked a lot of criticism, and in the subsequent controversies three different schools of thought could be discerned: the free bankers argued that the problem could be cured by convertibility and competition, and that no fundamental solution could be found while the monopoly of the Bank remained. As one of their leaders, Samuel Bailey, said in 1837, under a monopoly, 'the necessity will exist of having recourse to arbitrary assumptions and empirical expedients', but under free banking, 'the currency will be capable of adapting itself by those insensible contractions and expansions which no human sagacity can ever effect, to the perpetually varying wants of the community'.[18] The second view blamed the monetary disturbances on the Bank of England and especially on the country banks, and recommended legislation to ensure that the note issue was properly regulated. This position was to crystalise into the currency school.[19] Their position is well summarised in the words of S. J. Loyd, one of their leading proponents: 'With respect to a paper currency ... *a steady and equable regulation of its amount by fixed law* is the end to be sought'.[20] The third point of view put some of the blame on the Bank, but argued that it should simply hold a larger specie reserve. This point of view was put forward by Thomas Tooke and later evolved into the banking school. The currency and banking schools disagreed over the precise remedy to the problem, but they had a common and deep-rooted hostility to the free bankers, and the free bankers, in turn, were hostile to both schools as defenders of the Bank's privileges.

As the Bank's charter came up for renewal in 1844 the controversy tended to focus on the currency school's recommendations to regulate the Bank of England and the banking school's opposition to them. The currency school had a powerful ally in the Prime Minister, Sir Robert Peel, and in 1844 Peel was able to get their proposals enacted. Under this Act, the Bank of England was to be split into completely separate Issue and Banking Departments, and the former was to maintain a 100 per cent marginal reserve requirement beyond a fixed authorised note issue. All the Bank's other business was to be done by the Banking Department. Entry to the note-issue business was closed, and the note issues of banks in England and Wales were to be frozen. If any bank of issue failed or gave up its right of note issue, the fiduciary issue of the Bank was allowed to rise by two-thirds of the lapsed issue. The ban against banks of issue having offices within 65 miles of London also remained in force. It is significant that the main provisions of the Act were suggested to the Government by the Bank, whose management apparently saw the implementation of the Currency School proposals as a way of safeguarding their monopoly and giving them an 'automatic rule' they could apply which would shield them from public criticism. A second Act the next year froze the authorised note issues of the Scottish banks as well, and obliged them to maintain 100 per cent marginal reserve ratios against further issues. These Acts effectively centralised the note issue throughout the whole of the United Kingdom. Free banking in Scotland had been sacrificed to satisfy Peel's desire to unify the UK monetary system.

The reaction to these Acts from those who had advocated free banking was limited. In large part this was because the Acts bought off many of the interested parties. Much of the agitation for free banking had come from bankers, and the Acts effectively made note issuing a cartel by banning new entrants and freezing market shares. The suppression of competition was thus a windfall gain to existing note issuers, and this went a long way to silencing any other criticisms they might have made of the Act. More spirited reactions came from other quarters. James Wilson, the first editor of *The Economist*, condemned the Acts as entrenching the cause of the evil — the monopoly position of the Bank of England — and complained:

> We have never been able to discover any good ground for the objections which appear to exist in the minds of a large portion of even the most uncompromising free traders, against the application of the same principles to banking, and especially to the issue of notes payable on demand. Nor have we ever been able to elicit any satisfactory reasons for their objections; which the more we have considered the more we are satisfied are based on groundless fears and misapprehensions. (Wilson 1847, p. 281)

Further proposals for free banking continued after the setbacks of 1844 and 1845, but it slowly became apparent that the two Acts were there to stay despite the subsequent monetary crises that seemed to bear out their critics. Fewer people were willing to countenance radical proposals for monetary reform, and such proposals therefore seemed increasingly irrelevant. Writers like Herbert Spencer in the 1850s continued to advocate free banking, and Walter Bagehot in the 1870s accepted it in principle,[21] but regarded himself as too much of a realist to think it had any chance of being adopted, and after their generation no-one of any prominence supported free banking, even in principle. The old controversies about free banking were gradually forgotten, and it came to be accepted, more or less without question, that free banking must be unsound.

This completes our discussion of the establishment of central banking in England. We now turn to the history of banking in the United States.

5.5 The Early History of Banking in the USA[22]

While English banking was dominated from an early stage by the Bank of England, and Scotland enjoyed relatively free banking until Peel abolished it, the United States of America experienced a wide variety of monetary experiments that ranged between more regulated versions of free banking and less complete versions of what can only very roughly be described as 'central banking'. If Scotland enjoyed *freedom*, and the English system was *centralised*, the US system was one of 'decentralisation without freedom' as Smith (1936, p. 36) rather aptly described it, and the USA opted for fully fledged central banking only at the comparatively late date of 1913.

The first major monetary experiment in the USA was the founding of the Bank of North America to help finance the War of Independence. After the war was over, however, there was considerable agitation to abolish the Bank. It was argued that the Confederation Congress had no authority to grant bank charters, and that the authority to do so lay with the states because they had had that authority as colonies before independence, and had not granted it to Congress or relinquished it by joining the federation. The agitation eventually had the desired effect and the Bank's charter was repealed.

It was not long, though, before attempts were made to replace the Bank. The leading inspiration was Alexander Hamilton, who submitted a proposal for a new national bank — the (first) Bank of the United States — in 1790. Hamilton had considerable influence on the American banking system, not only on this occasion but later on as well because much later, legislation was based on his original ideas. The proponents of the Bank argued that a national bank would serve a number of purposes: it would help spread banking, and thereby facilitate the conversion of 'dead' gold and silver into productive capital; it would be able to provide the federal government with funds in an emergency; it would assist the federal government in the collection of taxes; and, by setting up branches, it would help to unify the all-too-fragmentary American banking system. Another argument for chartering the Bank was that the federal government would get a free share in it, worth around $2 million. The Act was passed and the Bank came into operation in 1791. The Bank was to be the depository of all federal balances and had the right to open branches in any state it chose. It proceeded to alienate other banks and was steadfastly opposed by the states' rights lobby. Its opponents were sufficiently strong that when the Bank's charter came up for renewal in 1811 they were able to prevent it and let the charter lapse.

In the meantime, many banks were set up under the separate legal systems of different states. The states' legal frameworks varied considerably, but they typically involved applying for a charter from the local legislature. The charter would give the shareholders some form of limited liability (usually fixed at twice the value of the capital subscribed) and placed restrictions on the ratio of note issues to capital. Banks were frequently obliged to make special loans to the states that chartered them, and these loans often weakened their liquidity and undermined their capital values, and thereby made them more prone to fail. The state charter system also had other adverse consequences. The fact that charters only permitted banks to have offices in the state (and sometimes only the county) where they were chartered prevented a branch-banking system from developing, and this caused two major problems:

- It increased banks' vulnerability by restricting their opportunity to diversify their portfolios;
- It raised the costs of redeeming notes. This hindered the development of an effective note-clearing system and created problems of note depreciation and over-issue. Banks of issue were smaller and more numerous, and their notes often found their way to other counties or states where they sold at discounts reflecting the high costs of redeeming them and the unfamiliarity of the banks that issued them. The high cost of redemption in turn reduced the frequency of redemption and relaxed one of the constraints against over-issue;

Had a branch-banking system been allowed to develop (as it was in Scotland and Canada) the banks would have been less vulnerable because they would have held more diversified portfolios, and they could have exploited economies of scale in the note-issue business in order to reduce the number of different notes, and to reduce the costs and increase the frequency of redemption. This, in turn, would have reduced over-issues and helped to 'equalise the exchanges' between different banknotes. As we shall see, these problems caused by a unitary banking system are a persistent theme in US monetary history.[23]

In 1812 war broke out again with Britain. At first, the US government tried to cover its revenue needs by issuing loans, but it resorted to the issue of interest-bearing Treasury notes when these measures proved insufficient. A large number of banks bought these and used them to expand their own issues. This expansion of paper led to a shortage of specie, and most banks were forced to suspend convertibility. The result was monetary chaos. Different banks depreciated their currencies to different degrees, and it became impossible to maintain any kind of reliable medium of account. One consequence of this was to throw the government's finances into complete confusion:

> The Treasury . . . received duties in the bank notes of the port at which the goods were entered. Consequently there was a further advantage to import commodities at the port of entry where the currency was most depreciated. Hence Philadelphia and Baltimore enjoyed a period of great apparent prosperity, for, in July, 1815, New York paper was at 14% discount, and Baltimore paper at 16%, compared with Boston paper or silver . . .
> The government suffered the greatest loss and embarrassment from the derangement of the currency. Boston was the money market of the country, and there were heavy disbursements there, which must all be made at specie par; but there was no revenue there, all being obtained further south in depreciated notes. If any one had any payments to make at Boston to the Treasury, he bought notes of the suspended banks to the southward with which to do it. (Sumner 1986, p. 66)

Gresham's Law ensured that specie and the notes of specie-paying banks were effectively replaced by depreciated paper.

The combination of the deranged currency and the government's fiscal needs led to new calls for a national bank. A bill to establish such a bank was passed by Congress, but vetoed by President Madison early in 1815. The pressure for it intensified, however, and an Act the next year provided for the establishment of the Second Bank of the United States. This Bank was very similar to its predecessor: the government took a large (subsidised) stake in its capital; it had a 20-year charter and the monopoly of the government's deposits; and it had the right to set up branches anywhere in the Union it pleased. It was expected to provide a 'uniform currency' — i.e. to equalise the exchange rates of different banknotes across the country — and to act as the government's fiscal agent. To provide a uniform currency, it sought not only to provide a note issue of its own, but also to get other banks to peg their notes to it. In order to persuade them to do this, the Bank promised to provide them with support in the event of an emergency. This was the first time that an American national bank had explicitly accepted the role of lender of last resort.

In 1817 there was a temporary resumption of specie convertibility. It was temporary because the Bank, instead of attempting to reduce the state banks' issues, proceeded to encourage them further using its own notes as a basis. In over-extending itself, the Bank fed a further round of inflation and brought itself to the brink of bankruptcy in 1818. Its only possible response was to curtail its lending, which brought on a financial crisis. This produced widespread bankruptcies and a new suspension of convertibility in 1819.

After this inauspicious start, the Bank was gradually able to recover and its performance improved considerably. Convertibility was restored in 1821, and there were relatively few monetary disturbances throughout the 1820s. The Bank's reputation improved, and it began to look as if it would be accepted as an essential feature of the American monetary system. In the late 1820s, however, the Democrats went on the attack again and accused the Bank of violating its charter and meddling in politics.[24] When Andrew Jackson declared war on the Bank, all the old objections about its constitutionality and states' rights took new life again. The Bank, he declared, was 'unauthorized by the Constitution, subversive of the rights of the states, and dangerous to the liberties of the people'.[25] Jackson's election as President made it clear that the Bank was in serious trouble, and in 1833 he ordered the government's deposits to be removed from it. Not long afterwards he vetoed the bill to renew the Bank's charter, and the charter lapsed in 1836.

After this, the federal government abstained from any major attempts to legislate banking for nearly thirty years and left the field wide open to the states. There followed a fascinating period characterised by a wide variety of monetary experiments. This period is generally known — somewhat inaccurately, as we shall see — as the free banking period. We shall deal with this in the next section.

5.6 The Free Banking Period

The federal withdrawal gave the states free rein to pass whatever banking legislation they wished and a number of states then proceeded to enact free banking laws. The first states were Michigan, in 1837, and New York and Georgia in 1838. Others followed suit afterwards. While they varied from state to state, 'free banking laws' had the following general features:[26]

- Anyone could set up a free bank who could raise the capital to do so, subject to a minimum capital requirement which varied from state to state.
- Free banks had to secure their note issues with deposits of certain specified types of bonds that were to be deposited with the state auditor. The types of bonds eligible varied, but they were usually state and sometimes federal bonds.
- The notes of free banks had to be redeemable on demand, and a bank was to be liquidated and its assets sold off to pay its creditors if it refused to honour a single note. The noteholders usually had first preference on the assets of a liquidated bank.
- The shareholders of free banks were generally allowed some form of limited liability. The usual limit was twice the value of their capital subscription.

The first provision made entry to the banking industry free, subject only to a minimum size restriction, but the second and third provisions were potentially destabilising — the second because it forced the banks to buy state bonds and thereby made them vulnerable to fluctuations in their prices, and the third because it implied a prohibition of option clauses with which banks might have been able to protect their liquidity.

The experiences of different states varied dramatically. The free-banking experiments were successful in New York, Ohio and Louisiana, for example, but in others the result was less satisfactory. According to one modern account, 'Banks of very dubious soundness would be set up in remote and inaccessible places "where only the wildcats throve". Bank notes would then be printed, transported to nearby population centers, and circulated at par. Since the issuing bank was difficult and often dangerous to find, redemption of bank notes was in this manner minimized' (Luckett 1980, p. 23). An alleged instance of this 'wildcat banking' was in Michigan, after its first attempt at free banking. There, the bank commissioners complained that, 'gold and silver flew around the country with the celerity of magic; its sound was heard in the depths of the forest, yet like the wind one knew not whence it came or whither it was going . . .'.[27] Dramatic accounts like these left a strong but misleading impression on popular memories of the free banking period. A more accurate view — and a more valuable one, I would suggest, because it is contemporary — was presented by the state auditor of Indiana in his report of 1856:

> The experiment of free banking in Indiana, disastrous as it has been in some particulars, has demonstrated most conclusively the safety and wisdom of the system. The original bill was crude and imperfect, admitting of such construction as held out to irresponsible men

> inducement and facilities for embarking largely in the business of banking, without the ability to sustain themselves in a period of revulsion.
>
> That revulsion came . . . and yet the loss to which the noteholder was necessarily subjected, in many cases did not exceed 5%, and in no case exceeded 20% of the amount in his hands.[28]

Two questions then arise: (i) How successful was free banking generally?, and, (ii) Why were some experiments with free banking apparently more successful than others?

A tentative answer to the first question is suggested by the recent work of Rockoff (1974), Rolnick and Weber (1983, 1984, 1985, 1986) and Economopoulos (1988). This suggests that traditional accounts of the free banking period have tended to over-emphasise wildcatting and exaggerate the losses that noteholders suffered. Rolnick and Weber also find no evidence of contagion effects which would lead a run on one bank to spread to another, and they conclude that the main source of the free bank failures was external shocks. (We shall return to these shocks later.) This suggests a reasonably good general track record.

This leaves the question of why some free banking experiments seemed to be more successful than others. The different outcomes can be explained by several factors. One factor is the differences which existed both in the legal frameworks under which banks operated, and in the standards of law enforcement. For instance, in some cases the state auditor was satisfied if banks had the prescribed assets in the right places when he made his periodic — and predictable — visits, and he seldom made much effort to check that those assets were there the rest of the time. This gave wildcatters the opportunity to render the inspections ineffective by passing the same assets around from one bank to another as the auditor made his round.[29] Another, perhaps more important, difference in the legal framework was that some states intervened to suspend convertibility. This was the case with Michigan's first free banking experiment, for instance. This led to wildcat banking because the suspension of convertibility removed the main check against over-issue, and so a monetary explosion was to be expected. (See also Chapter 4, note 15. It is also worth noting that even after this disaster Michigan tried again at free banking, about 20 years later, and this time the experiment was successful.)

The second reason — and possibly the most important one — for the variance in the success of free banking is to be found in the combination of the bond deposit provision and the state of different states' finances. In their papers, Rolnick and Weber have argued that the main cause of the free bank failures was the capital losses inflicted on them by falls in the values of the bonds in their portfolios. These are the shocks that we referred to earlier. Their reasoning is that when falls in bond prices make a bank's net worth sufficiently negative, then it will choose to fail because, by doing so, it can pass on part of the capital loss to the noteholders. They also present empirical evidence that gives their 'falling asset price' theory a considerable amount of empirical support.[30]

The Rolnick-Weber analysis explains the free bank failures in terms of falling asset prices, but it is an incomplete explanation because it does not explain *why* the failed banks suffered the capital losses they did. I suggest that some indication of the reason for the capital losses can be gleaned from the history of state finances at the time. If one looks at bond prices for the period one cannot help being struck by their very wide discrepancies (see Homer 1963, Martin 1856, or some of the data given by Rolnick and Weber). For example, US and Massachussetts bonds tended to trade at or above par most of the time, and they show relatively little price variability, while Illinois and Indiana bonds traded below par most of the time and showed far greater price variability. In the course of 1842, for example, the prices of both bonds fell by over 70 per cent and even after that the gap between the highest and lowest price in any given year was about 20–30 per cent of the price of the bond. These bonds were obviously very risky and their holders must frequently have suffered large capital losses.

The history of the period strongly suggests that these discrepancies between different state bond prices can be traced to differences in states' public finances. In virtually every case, the large falls in bond prices were associated with speculation — which sometimes proved to be correct — that the states in question were about to default on their debts. Indiana, for example, had defaulted on its debt during 1841 and there were fears that it might do so again. This evidence therefore seems to point to the conclusion that the cause of the falling bond prices that put most of the failed free banks out of business was the instability of some states' finances.[31]

This explanation seems to be confirmed by Rockoff (1974, p. 163) who reports 6 cases of wildcat banking out of 18 cases of free banking, and that 3 of these (Wisconsin, Illinois and New Jersey) 'can be traced to the linking of the supply of currency to the debt of another state', while another (ie, Minnesota) was 'clearly due to efforts by the state to force its bonds to a higher price than they were currently bringing in the market'. The last two were Indiana and Michigan after its first free banking law was passed in 1837, and we have discussed these already.

Free banking spread relatively slowly after the initial spurt of free banking laws, and some states preferred entirely different monetary regimes. Some set up a monopoly bank of issue (such as Ohio in 1845), while others, like Arkansas, preferred to prohibit banking altogether. Their residents then turned to out-of-state notes instead. State authorities tried to discourage this but they could not prevent it. Their attempts raised the costs of redeeming notes and thereby weakened the market forces that would have maintained their value and quality. The result was that these states generally ended up with worse currencies than the free banking states, and their governments had no control of the currency either.[32] The success of free banking encouraged other states to adopt it, and there was a pronounced drift towards it in the 1850s. Illinois,[33] Ohio and Massachussetts[34] adopted free banking in 1851, and Indiana and Wisconsin followed them shortly afterwards, while Michigan adopted free banking (again) in 1857, Iowa and Minnesota in 1858 and Pennsylvania in 1860. By the eve of the Civil War, over half the states in the Union had adopted it.

This period witnessed several other interesting monetary experiments besides the free banking laws. One of these was the spread of the Suffolk system which helped to check over-issue and 'equalise the exchanges' by ensuring a speedy redemption of notes.[35] As we have already seen, a major weakness of the US banking system was that it was highly fragmented and this fragmentation raised redemption costs with the consequences we have already discussed. Some banks tried to exploit the possibilities this raised by placing themselves at a distance from large centres of population and putting out large note circulations which were costly to redeem. City banks found themselves at a relative disadvantage because their notes were easier to redeem and they were often frustrated to find that out-of-town banks were able to secure most of the note issue in the cities, and yet still remain liquid. To counter this, the Boston banks tried a number of methods to collect the notes of out-of-town banks and return them for redemption. The most successful of these was the Suffolk system, named after the Suffolk Bank of Boston which initiated it. The idea behind it was that the banks which joined it would have their notes redeemed at par by the Suffolk and contribute to a fund which would be used to pay the expenses of redeeming all other notes they received (principally out-of-town notes).

The adoption of the system ensured that country banks notes were rapidly redeemed and their note issues curtailed. It also had the effect of equalising the exchanges between different notes, both because the Suffolk promised to accept members' notes at par, and because the rapid note return ensured that note issues did not get far out of line. The strength of the system was that non-members had an incentive to join or else to set up rival systems. This was because their notes would be sent for redemption anyway, and the scheme reduced the costs to each bank of redeeming other banks' notes. As a result, the Suffolk system spread quite rapidly to cover most of New England, and was copied elsewhere. The Suffolk system, like the Scottish note-clearing system, demonstrates that many functions often associated with central banking — like the existence of a centralised note exchange to ensure rapid redemption and to equalise the exchanges — do not require central banks to operate them, and arise spontaneously under competitive conditions.

A less successful experiment of the period was the safety-fund system. This was a system adopted in several states in which banks were made to pay into an insurance fund designed to protect noteholders in the event that a bank went bankrupt. Unlike clearing systems, such as the Suffolk scheme, safety fund schemes did not arise from the free market but were imposed on the banks by legislation. They are interesting to modern economists because they are very similar to contemporary deposit insurance schemes and, indeed, can be regarded as forerunners to them.

The most ambitious safety fund, which was set up in 1829, was in New York.[36] Each year banks paid in their subscriptions and there were no claims at all on the fund for the first few years. The system contained the seeds of its own destruction, however, because it involved an implicit subsidy to take risks and because nothing was done to ensure that the insurance premia were actuarially sound. As a result, the fund was in fact accumulating an actuarial deficit while it still seemed to be in surplus, and all that was required to break the fund was a major crisis. This occurred in the early 1840s, when 11 safety fund banks went bankrupt, and the fund could not meet its liabilities. The fund was effectively bankrupted, and while the remaining banks were made to put more capital into it, it never properly recovered and was wound up some years later. Other safety funds elsewhere met similar fates.

This concludes our discussion of the free banking period. As we have seen, the different monetary experiments of this period produced some significant successes but also some costly failures. It is probably fair to say that the successes were due in large part to the freedom the banks enjoyed to respond to the demands of the market-place. The evidence also appears to be consistent with the view that the failures were due either to inappropriate regulations (as with the free bank failures) or to other misguided interventions (as with the safety funds). In effect, there was a process of competition between the monetary systems of different states, and there was a tendency to abandon experiments which failed, and to copy those that worked (like the Suffolk system and New York-style free banking), and this produced a substantial improvement in the quality of American banking as time went on. But then the Civil War came and the federal government once more started to legislate on banking.

5.7 The National Banking System[37]

The start of the Civil War had an immediate impact on the banking system since the southern banks repudiated their debts to northern banks when they seceded from the Union. The northern banks managed to shoulder the loss, but they soon came under renewed pressure again, this time from the federal government. The Secretary of the Treasury was finding it difficult to raise sufficient money by borrowing from the public, so he drew up a plan to borrow $50 million in specie from the banks. At the same time he started to issue US notes which the banks were obliged to redeem in specie. The resulting pressure on the banks' reserves forced them to suspend convertibility at the end of 1861. After this, there followed three issues of irredeemable legal tender of $150 million each and these produced a substantial inflation.

The federal government then decided to raise more money from the banks by adopting the bond deposit principle at the federal level. This was the origin of the National Banking System which was established by the National Banking Acts of 1863 and 1864.[38] Under the new system, any group of five or more could form a note-issuing bank, provided that their capital was not less than $50,000, and provided that their note issues were secured by deposits of United States bonds.[39] (This raised the demand for US bonds, and therefore increased their price.) The Treasury would have first lien on the assets of a failed bank, and shareholders would be subject to double liability. The Treasury would protect noteholders by redeeming the notes of any failed bank, thus maintaining the free circulation of notes, even after the bank that issued them had gone out of business. The national banks also had to maintain a minimum ratio of 25 per cent between their holdings of legal tender reserves and the sum of their notes and deposits, and these reserves included US Government bonds and 'greenbacks' as well as specie. (This also increased the demand for federal liabilities.) Finally, the national banks had to pay a tax of 1 per cent on their notes, and of 0.5 per cent on their deposits and their capital not invested in US bonds. The Act also made allowance for state banks to enter the scheme and become national banks, but as they did not enter sufficiently quickly, another Act of 1865 put a 10 per cent annual tax on their note issues, and this effectively killed off the state banks of issue.

The National Banking System was neither a fully-fledged central banking system nor free banking, though it had some resemblances to each one. It had a number of serious defects:

(1) It explicitly discouraged a branch-banking system by requiring that a bank could only carry on business at the place named on its certificate of association. The USA thus continued to be saddled with the defects of a unitary banking system.

(2) The restrictions it placed on the note issue seriously stunted the development of the banking system because the US economy was still at a stage where the issue of notes was an important source of profits for a bank, and so restrictions on their issue erected a significant entry barrier (see Sylla 1972). These restrictions would therefore have forced the public to use alternative media of exchange — coin, illegal currencies (see Timberlake 1981) and, in more sophisticated circles, cheques — and it would have deprived them of banks that would otherwise have been established. This in turn would have hindered the contribution that the banking system could have made to the country's economic development, and as Sylla (1972) pointed out, this would have been particularly important in the more backward areas where banks would have had difficulty even getting started. These problems were compounded even further in the early days of the National Banking System because of an arbitrary limit of $300 million which was placed on the note supply. Notes were to be allocated across regions on the basis of population and economic activity, but in practice the banks of the New England, Middle Atlantic and East North Central regions got very disproportional shares, and the rest of the country had to make do with what was left. The $300 million limit was raised by $54 million in 1870, and then abolished altogether in 1875. Shortly thereafter, however, the price of US bonds rose to well above par and it was seldom worthwhile to issue notes anyway.[40]

(3) The bond deposit provision tied the note supply to price of federal debt. The note supply was then forced to contract as

the federal government ran surpluses during the post-bellum years and bought back much of its debt, and in the process raised its price. As Cagan (1963, pp. 22–3) put it, the profitability of note issuing:

> depended crucially on the prices of the US bonds eligible to serve as collateral. When from 1864 to 1880 these bonds sold at or just above par, the issuance of notes returned a handsome profit. I have calculated the rate of return on the capital tied up in issuing the notes . . . to be 31% per year in 1879 and 21% in 1880. Shortly thereafter, however, the Treasury began to run a budget surplus . . . As a result, large premiums appeared, which sharply reduced the profitability of issuing notes. . . . In January, 1882 . . . the return to issuing notes fell to . . . 9% per year. Banks earned almost as much on other assets. In subsequent years the return on notes fell even below the average return on other assets. Consequently, new issues ceased, and many banks retired part of their outstanding notes. The total quantity outstanding declined from around $300 million at the beginning of the 1880s to $126 million at the end of that decade. Their circulation expanded again in the 1890s when the high premiums on US bonds fell sharply.

(4) The restrictions on the note supply often prevented it responding appropriately to changes in the demand for notes. This was the problem of the 'inelasticity' of the note supply which attracted increasing attention as time went on. This problem was particularly acute in the autumn when there was a seasonal rise in the demand for notes, but the banks were able to respond only to the extent that they could continue to satisfy their bond deposit and reserve ratio requirements. This led to very considerable interest rate fluctuations and made the US banking system peculiarly liable to panics:

> A series of acute financial crises occurred in fairly quick succession — 1873, 1884, 1890, 1893, 1907. Crises occurred on most of these occasions in London as well, but they were nothing like as stringent. Money rates in New York rose to fantastic heights as compared with London, and there was one other even more marked dissimilarity. In America there took place in three out of the five cases (1873, 1893 and 1907) widespread suspensions of cash payments, either partial or complete, with currency at a premium over claims on bank accounts. (Smith 1936, p. 133)

It is important to stress that these suspensions occurred not because the banks had no specie — they generally did — but principally because they were not allowed to issue additional notes. In the terminology we introduced in Chapter 3, these were deposit runs rather than note runs.

The problem of liquidity shortages in a crisis gave rise to the institution of clearing houses to deal with it. These originated in an agreement among the New York banks during the 1857 crisis to expand their loans together so that no bank would lose reserves to the others. In later crises, the banks agreed to *clearing-house loan certificates* — interest-bearing notes which the banks used to settle accounts with each other. Apart from ensuring that banks did not lose reserves to each other during a crisis, they also contributed to the system's overall liquidity at a time when liquidity was most needed, and clearing houses had very strong incentives to support their member-banks.[41] As time went on, the institution of clearing houses spread, and other types of certificate were invented. The value of clearing-house loan certificates and similar instruments ran into hundreds of millions, and their usefulness was widely recognised. They were also technically illegal, but the government wisely decided not to prosecute their issuers. A contemporary writer summarised the situation in the following way:

> Most of this currency was illegal, but no one thought of prosecuting or interfering with its issuers . . . In plain language, it was an inconvertible paper money issued without the sanction of law, . . . yet necessitated by conditions for which our banking laws did not provide . . . when banks were being run upon and legal money had disappeared in hoards, in default of any legal means of relief, it worked effectively and doubtless prevented multitudes of bankruptcies which otherwise would have occurred. (Andrew 1908, pp. 515–6)

It is an unfortunate state of affairs when the government feels it cannot implement the law because of the damage it would cause.[42]

These repeated crises gave rise to much controversy and numerous plans for reform. A growing school of thought maintained that the solution to the problems of the US monetary system was to establish a central bank on the European model, and the controversy over whether the USA should establish a central bank intensified after the crisis of 1907. Congress responded to that crisis by passing the Aldrich–Vreeland Act to authorise the issue of 'emergency currency' as a stopgap measure, and to establish a National Monetary Commission to report on banking reform. The Commission was particularly impressed by the way in which European central banks were able to handle liquidity crises by centralising reserves and acting as lenders of last resort. It tended to assume that the greater stability of the European financial systems was due to their having central banks, rather than to other defects of the American banking system, and it did not take arguments for free banking particularly seriously. The Commission therefore recommended the establishment of an American central bank — a Federal Reserve System of 12 regional Federal Reserve Banks which would be owned by banks which were members of the System.[43] The Federal Reserve System would be run by a Federal Reserve Board and would be responsible for issuing notes, keeping the reserves of member-banks and setting interest rate policy. Congress accepted these recommendations and the Federal Reserve Act was passed in 1913. The Federal Reserve started operations the next year.

5.8 Some Conclusions

This completes our account of the establishment of central banking in Britain and the USA. As we have seen, the monetary experiences of these two countries are very different, but they both show similar basic themes:

- Central banking did not arise 'spontaneously' as a result of market failures, but as a consequence of specific state interventions and the problems those interventions created.
- State intervention was generally motivated by the desire to raise revenue or to correct for problems caused by earlier intervention. It was not motivated by market failures *per se*.
- The effect of intervention was to destabilise the banking system and occasionally to debase the value of the currency.
- Free banking (or something close to it) was tried successfully in both nations and suppressed for fundamentally political reasons.

We shall now proceed to the next chapter and consider the historical record of central banking.

Notes

1. Quoted from Smith (1936, p. 148).
2. This section draws heavily on White (1984b), Meulen (1934) and Smith (1936), and to a lesser extent on MacLeod (1896), Andréades (1909) and Clapham (1945).
3. This section and the next are distilled from Cameron (1967), Checkland (1975), Kerr (1918), Meulen (1934), Munn (1981), Smith (1936) and White (1984b). The Scottish free banking experience has provoked a great deal of recent controversy. To avoid too long a digression on this controversy in the main text, we defer our discussion to an appendix of this chapter.
4. Option clauses have received a bad press since the controversy of the 1760s. I have argued in Chapter 2 and elsewhere (Dowd 1988d and Chappell and Dowd 1988) that this judgment might be premature and that option clauses are potentially very useful.
5. Quoted in Meulen (1934, p. 139).
6. The standard references to the UK monetary debates are Smith (1936), Viner (1937), Mints (1945), Fetter (1965) and, more recently, White (1984b). The reader should also refer to Rothbard's review (1988) of White. According to Rothbard, White 'conflates two very distinct schools of free bankers: (1) those who wanted free banking in order to promote monetary inflation and cheap credit, and (2) those who, on the contrary, wanted free banking in order to arrive at hard, near-100% specie money' (p. 234). He argues that only two of White's heroes, Robert Mushet and Sir Henry Parnell, were clearly hard-money men, and he presents evidence to suggest that a number of the remainder — Sir John Sinclair, Poullett Scrope, James Gilbart, James Wilson, and possibly even Samuel Bailey — were unsound on the 'real bills' issue. Rothbard is quite right to suggest that some of these make uncomfortable allies for modern free bankers. However, his claim that White himself is fundamentally unsound — 'a variant of a banking-school inflationist' (p. 239) — is uncalled for. White's statement of the fallacy of the 'real bills' doctrine(s) (pp. 120–2) is clear evidence of the soundness of his position.

While on the subject of White's account of the controversies, Munn also comments on White's rather uncritical treatment of certain writers (p. 341). Dr Munn also points out that, 'White virtually ignores the writing of Scottish bankers. Hugh Watt, Scotland's most experienced banker, gets very little attention and Alexander Blair, the most senior banker, is ignored altogether. Neither of these men would have found themselves in complete sympathy with White's views . . .' (loc. cit.).

7. In Book 2, Chapter 2 of the *Wealth of Nations*, Smith gave a qualified support to free banking. He suggested that banks should be compelled to redeem their notes on demand, and that notes for less than a certain sum should be prohibited, but that banks should otherwise be left free.
8. Bentham's main concern in his *Defence of Usury* (1788) was to attack the usury laws, but in the process he also came out against other restrictions on banks. However, he did not develop these comments into a detailed argument for free banking.
9. Quoted in Meulen (1934, p. 113).
10. In fact, it is questionable whether the Act involved much liberalisation of the Bank's monopoly. As Joplin appears to have been the first to realise, the earlier Acts implicitly defined banking as involving the issue of notes and this definition had to be construed strictly since the Acts were penal statutes. This meant that the six-partner rule did not apply to banks that refrained from issuing notes. This was never tested in the courts, however, and all the 1826 Act did, in this respect, was to clarify the matter.
11. Quoted in Smith (1936, p. 63).
12. Quoted in White (1984b, p. 61).
13. White (1984b, pp. 65–7).
14. See the *Digest* of evidence presented before the Bank Charter Committee of 1832.
15. See White (1984b, p. 66) and Halevy (1961, pp. 86–7). The quote is from White.
16. Quoted in White (1984b, p. 67).
17. This of course raises the question of why people who are fundamentally sympathetic to *laisser faire* in most trades should have rejected *laisser faire* in banking. Perhaps part of the mystery is resolved by Rothbard (1988, pp. 234–7) who presents evidence that a number of contemporary UK writers supported the currency principle in order to achieve an outcome they interpreted as fundamentally *laisser faire*. He states:

    the fervent desire of Richard Cobden, along with other Manchesterians and most other currency school writers, was to remove government or bank manipulation of money altogether and to leave its workings solely to the free-market forces of gold or silver. Whether or not Cobden's proposed solution of a state-run bank was the proper one, no one can deny the fervor of his *laisser-faire* views or his desire to apply them to the difficult and complex case of money and banking. (p. 237)

18. Quoted in White (1984b, p. 132).
19. I take the currency school position to be the advocacy of a monopoly note issue for the Bank of England with a legislated 100 per cent marginal reserve requirement. I take the banking school position to be the defence of the legislative status quo, albeit with a recommendation that the Bank should hold greater reserves. Given these definitions, both schools were fundamentally opposed to free banking. Note, however, that Rothbard (1988) implicitly defines the currency and banking schools quite differently, and it is this that leads him to talk of currency school writers who were sympathetic to free banking (see n. 17).
20. Quoted in Smith (1936, p. 69).
21. For more on Bagehot's views on free banking, see Chapter 2, note 23.
22. This account of early US banking history relies primarily on Sumner (1896), Smith (1936) and Hammond (1957).

23. An interesting question is why branching restrictions were able to persist so long. The answer, presumably, is that they persisted because the small banks lobbied to keep them.
24. For a good discussion of political movements in the Jacksonian period see Blau (1947).
25. Quoted in Dunne, p. 2.
26. For the first condition see Rolnick and Weber (1984), p. 270; for second and fourth see Rolnick and Weber (1984), table one; and for the third see Rolnick and Weber (1984), p. 271.
27. Quoted in Rockoff (1974, p. 146).
28. Quoted in Rockoff (1974, p. 151).
29. Smith (1936, pp. 45-6). A curious and relatively neglected feature of US banking history is the importance of fraud as a cause of bank failure. This appears to be a persistent theme:

> Fraud has always been a major problem for banks because they deal in very large quantities of the most easily fenced of all commodities — money. In the United States over the period 1865-1931, fraud and violations of the law were cited by the Comptroller of the Currency as the cause most responsible for failures of national banks. Frauds also are responsible for the most costly losses to depositors and the insurance agencies. . . . The ratio of the number of citations for fraud to the total number of identified causes of failures ranges from 63% over the years 1914-1920 to 18% over the decade 1921-1929. For the period 1934-1958, the Federal Deposit Insurance Corporation reports that for 'approximately one-fourth of the banks, defalcation or losses attributable to financial irregularities by officers and employees appear to have been the primary cause of failure' . . . During 1959-1971, fraud and irregularities were responsible for 66% of the failures. (Benston et al 1986, pp. 2-3)

30. For example, Rolnick and Weber (1984, p. 288) find that 79 per cent of the failures they consider occurred during the relatively short periods (i.e. 7 years out of 22) when bond prices were falling.
31. A possible objection to this needs to be considered. King (1983, p. 147) disputes the argument that the bond deposit provision caused these failures and argues that, 'there are natural means for any bank to undo any pure portfolio restriction. Banks should simply have as owners or creditors individuals who would otherwise hold amounts of government debt.' This 'irrelevance theorem' is an important result, but it does not strictly apply here because of the shareholders' limited liability. Suppose that a portfolio restriction is imposed on a bank and it arranges a swap with someone who would otherwise have held the assets it is required to hold. Now suppose that there is a sufficiently large fall in the value of those assets. Had there been no restriction, the person who held the assets would have had to take the capital loss. With the restriction and the swap, however, bank shareholders would be able to take advantage of their limited liability by declaring the bank bankrupt in order to pass the capital loss onto the bank's creditors. In the former case the bank would have continued in business, in the latter it would not. This justifies the claim in the text that the portfolio restriction and the capital loss can produce a different outcome in the presence of limits to the shareholders' liability.
32. Sumner (1896, pp. 415-6).
33. For more on Illinois' free banking experience, see Economopoulos (1988).
34. The case of Massachussetts is rather interesting. Although the 'free banking' law was passed in 1851, no free banks were set up under it until 1859. The reason appears to be that the banks would have had to back their note issues with the bonds of New England states or municipalities, and for most of the 1850s the prices of these were apparently well above par on account of their scarcity (see Rockoff 1974, p. 149). Free banks in Massachussetts were therefore 'priced out' of the market. In a sense, their problem was

the opposite of that of free banks elsewhere — bond prices were too high, not too low.
35. For more on the Suffolk system, see Trivoli (1979).
36. This account of the New York Safety Fund is based on Smith (1936, p. 43) and King (1983).
37. Our discussion of the National Banking System is based on Sumner (1896), Smith (1936) and Timberlake (1984).
38. The passing of these Acts owed a great deal to the emergency atmosphere created by the Civil War rather than to any clearly established defects of the existing system. As Cagan (1963, p. 16) states, Secretary Chase:

> proposed a new, uniform currency backed by US bonds to replace state notes, appealing to the difficulties of Treasury finance complicated by the war as well as to the permanent advantages such a reform of the currency system would bring. When he first made the proposal, Congress would not even take it up for debate. But by 1863, when hopes for an early Union victory had dimmed and the mounting expenditures cast doubt on the Treasury's ability to finance such a large military effort, the proposal took on the character of a war measure. The opposition weakened, and the bill passed by a narrow majority.
>
> Had the southern representatives and senators been attending the Congress in Washington, their concern for states' rights would almost certainly have prevented the passage of the bill. The National Banking System can therefore be said to be a direct consequence of the Civil War.

39. In addition, the 1865 Act prohibited note issues in excess of 90 per cent of a bank's paid-in capital. It also imposed a 25 per cent specie or greenback reserve requirement against note issues, though this latter restriction was abolished in 1874 (see Cagan 1963, pp. 18–9).
40. Another potentially dangerous feature of the National Banking System was that it made bank notes effectively indistinguishable since, in the last resort, the Treasury committed itself to redeem them at par. Had there been no other externally imposed restrictions on the note issue, banks would have had no incentive to restrict their issues, and a monetary explosion might have occurred of the kind discussed in note 15 of the last chapter. I should like to thank Catherine England for bringing this to my attention.
41. The reserve-centre banks also supported out-of-town banks during crises: 'Critics charged that New York banks protected themselves in times of crisis and shortchanged their correspondents. The opposite was, in fact, true, and central reserve-city banks' loans rose in these periods, providing assistance to the interior banks. Interest rates on these loans did rise, but that was what any sound institution, commercial or central bank, would do.' (Eugene White (1983, pp. 73–4))
42. Cannon (1901, pp. 103–4) had somewhat earlier arrived at a similar conclusion about the usefulness of clearing-house loan certificates. As he put it, when discussing the 1893 crisis:

> The only avenue of relief provided by the laws was the issue of additional national bank-notes, but . . . it was apparent that the national banks were bound hand and foot by indiscreet legislation, and were therefore unequal to the task of extending the relief so much needed, and which, under more favorable laws, might easily have been supplied. . . . The remedy that was applied affords one of the finest examples the country has ever seen of the ability of the people when left to themselves to devise impromptu measures for their own relief. The most potent factors in staying the force of the panic were the clearing-house loan certificates issued by the clearing-house associations throughout the country.

43. For good discussions of the political and legislative background to the Act, see Dunne (undated), Dewald (1972) and West (1977). Note that while Dewald tends to see the measures adopted as more or less inevitable, Dunne sees them more as a combination of legislative accidents.

5. Wildcat Banking, Banking Panics, and Free Banking in the United States

by Gerald P. Dwyer

Prior to the Civil War, note-issuing banks were chartered by State governments. It was once widely assumed that many, if not most, of these banks were fly-by-night or "wildcat" firms, set up by unscrupulous entrepreneurs who profited by saddling their clients with worthless currency. New research, however, casts a much more favorable light on the pre–Civil War currency system, suggesting that State-chartered banks of issue may not have been so bad after all. –G.S., Ed.

****

From 1837 to 1865, banks in the United States issued currency with no oversight of any kind by the federal government. Many of these banks were part of "free banking" systems in which there was no discretionary approval of entry into banking.[1] A note received in a transaction might indicate that it was issued by, say, the Atlanta Bank. This banknote was used for payments in transactions and was redeemable on demand at the Atlanta Bank for a specified quantity of specie, gold or silver. These notes were used in transactions just as checks are today. In important respects, though, they were quite different from today's checks. Notes were passed from one person to another and yet another before being returned to the bank. They were the bank's obligations, not bank customers' obligations. Because there was no central bank and no government insurance, the ultimate guarantee of a banknote's value was the value of the bank's assets.

Free banking in the United States sometimes has been equated with "wildcat banking," a name that suggests that opening a bank has much in common with drilling for oil. Drilling for oil is not an obvious analogy for a sound banking system. Use of the word *wildcat* to mean "reckless" or "financially unsound" apparently arose in Michigan in the 1830s, when bankers supposedly established free banks in inaccessible locations "where the wildcats roamed."[2] In the free banking period such locations benefited banks because they hampered noteholders' attempts to redeem notes, and banks with fewer notes redeemed could hold less specie and generate higher net revenue for their owners.

More generally, when banks issue notes, a major issue for banking laws and holders of banknotes is enforcement of banks' contracts to redeem the notes. If a bank issues notes in good faith that they can be redeemed as promised, the issue is simply contract enforcement. If a bank issues notes

The author is a visiting scholar in the financial section of the Atlanta Fed's research department and a professor in the Department of Economics at Clemson University. He thanks Robert Bliss, R. Alton Gilbert, R.W. Hafer, George G. Kaufman, Will Roberds, Hugh Rockoff, Arthur Rolnick, George Selgin, Larry Wall, and Eugene N. White for helpful comments.

with no prospect that they can be redeemed, the issue becomes prevention of fraud, or what is "essentially counterfeiting." Milton Friedman (1960, 6) suggests,

> It so happens that the contracts in question are peculiarly difficult to enforce and fraud peculiarly difficult to prevent. The very performance of its central function requires money to be generally acceptable and to pass from hand to hand. As a result, individuals may be led to enter into contracts with persons far removed in space and acquaintance, and a long period may elapse between the issue of a promise and the demand for its fulfillment. In fraud as in other activities, opportunities for profit are not likely to go unexploited.

Free banks did not always redeem their notes as promised, and there are fabulous stories of fraudulent activities, stories that appear frequently in histories of free banking and general histories of banking. For example, in an examination report for Jackson County Bank in Michigan in 1938, the state bank commissioners report that they found the account books had accountholders' names written in pencil and their balances written in pen. In addition, they examined the bank's specie.

> Beneath the counter of the bank, nine boxes were pointed out by the teller, as containing one thousand dollars each. The teller selected one of the boxes and opened it; this was examined and appeared to be a full box of American half dollars. One of the commissioners then selected a box, which he opened, and found the same to contain a superficies only of silver, while the remaining portion consisted of lead and ten penny nails. The commissioner then proceeded to open the remaining seven boxes; they presented the same contents precisely, with a single exception, in which the substratum was window glass broken into small pieces. (U.S. Congress 1839-40, 1109)

Whether or not this story is typical of Michigan's free banks, free banking in that state in the 1830s was a failure, with noteholders suffering heavy losses. In fact, in his influential history of banking, Bray Hammond concludes that people in states where banking was prohibited "were better off than the people of Michigan, Wisconsin, Indiana, and Illinois," who had free banking (Hammond 1957, 626).

Was free banking in the United States so bad that people would have been better off with no banks at all? One way of approaching this question is to ask, Did noteholders suffer substantial losses from holding free banks' notes? If those losses were substantial, were they generally associated with difficulties in enforcing the contract between noteholders and banks, fraud, or both? This issue is not of only historical interest because, as discussed in Box 1, free banks' notes have similarities to some forms of electronic money. Recent research makes it possible to provide more informed answers to these questions than was possible even as recently as 1980.[3]

The Spread of Free Banking

After the Second Bank of the United States' federal charter expired in 1836, the various states provided the legal framework for banking, and there was no banking system operating under federal government law. Prior to free banking, limited-liability organizations were permitted to issue notes if the legislature granted a charter for that specific purpose. Free banking opened up note issuance to limited-liability organizations without discretionary approval by a legislature, as in earlier years, or by a banking regulator, as in later years (Gerald C. Fischer 1968, 177-84). Free banking ended in 1865 when the federal government imposed a tax on state banknotes.

Chart 1 shows a map of the United States in 1860 and the years that the states adopted free banking. Three states adopted free banking in the 1830s: Michigan, Georgia, and New York. The rest that adopted free banking did so in 1849 and later years.

Overview of Free Banking

The free banking systems in the various states had many things in common.[4] The defining characteristic of free banking is that if the requirements of a given state's free banking law are met, any person or group of persons is permitted to open a bank.

Opening a Bank. Prior to opening a bank, subscriptions for a minimum amount of capital funds were required. When subscribing for stock, a person commonly paid in some of the funds and promised to provide additional funds up to the amount subscribed. The law generally required that a minimum amount of funds be paid in before the bank could begin operation. Some states also limited the maximum amount of capital in any one bank. An abbreviated balance sheet for a free bank, shown in Table 1, is helpful for understanding free banks' note issuance. The capital funds appear on the balance sheet as equity capital, a liability. The balance sheet also includes an asset, loans to stockholders, to illustrate the offset for capital subscribed but not paid in.[5] In addition to being liable for their subscribed capital, the bank's stockholders often were subject to double liability: when the bank closed, each stockholder could also be required to pay an additional amount equal to the stockholder's subscribed capital.

Issuing Currency. Banks were permitted to issue banknotes that circulated from hand to hand much as Federal Reserve notes do today. In order to issue notes, banks were required to make a security deposit with the state banking authority. The state banking authority then signed the notes and provided them to the bank.

Box 1
Free Banks' Notes and Electronic Money

Will electronic money resemble the banknotes circulated in the U.S. free banking period?[1] Walter Wriston (1995, 1996; Bass 1996), a former Chairman of Citicorp, and others have suggested that money used for transactions on the Internet may resemble nineteenth-century banknotes more than it will today's money.

Actually, only a subset of what often is called electronic money is "money" in the economic sense, and most of that subset is more similar to money orders or cashier's checks than banknotes. The confusion between money and other means of payment arises even in the economics literature, so confusion in the popular literature is not surprising. Friedman and Schwartz (1970, chaps. 2 and 3) provide an accessible discussion of the definition and measures of money. For example, even though a credit card can be used to make purchases, neither a credit card nor its unused balance is money. When someone uses a credit card to buy a dinner, the purchaser is promising to pay later with money.

Some electronic payment schemes, such as one run by a company called First Virtual, make no pretense at introducing electronic money. First Virtual holds buyers' credit card numbers on a computer inaccessible from the Internet and verifies the authenticity of a purchase. In effect, First Virtual adds an intermediary to transactions. Several other payment schemes focus on preserving anonymity for the buyer but do not introduce the equivalent of currency that can be received and spent repeatedly without involving the money issuer or another third party.

The electronic payment schemes closest to electronic currency are the use of "electronic wallets" and "money modules." These schemes, which require hardware not now widely available in the United States, make it possible to transfer balances from one person's wallet or module to another without another party to the transaction.

Compared with paper currency, checks, and credit cards, such electronic currency would have some advantages for buyers and sellers who want to conduct transactions on the Internet. One advantage is that electronic currency can preserve the anonymity of a transaction in the same way that paper currency does. Probably more important to most people, electronic currency could be used for simple transactions on the Internet between people who do not have enough transactions or the reputation to acquire a merchant credit card account. It also is possible that electronic money could be simpler for international transactions than money denominated in local currency, partly because it is relatively expensive to convert from one currency to another in small amounts.

As of this writing, an institution located in the United States attempting to issue private money would confront substantial legal issues and taxes that might make such an issue impractical. The costs of domestic and international communication on the Internet, however, are effectively the same. Hence, despite impediments in the United States, developing private money offshore in a less restrictive jurisdiction could create a viable alternative even for transactions between U.S. residents.

There may be similarities between electronic money and free banks' notes. Electronic money is likely to consist of uninsured liabilities of private individuals or companies. If so, perhaps the most immediate lessons from free banking are that (1) consumers are not sheep waiting to be sheared (2) attention must be paid to the importance of the assets into which the electronic money is convertible and to the issuer's reputation for making the conversion as promised.

Note

1. Levy (1994) and Flohr (1996) provide accessible introductions to electronic money. Schneier (1996, 139-47), the standard nontechnical source of information on cryptography, provides some details about how one form of electronic money can be securely implemented and references to discussions of other forms of electronic money.

The free banking laws specified acceptable assets that could be deposited. They generally allowed deposits only of selected state bonds, known as state stocks at the time, and U.S. government bonds, both of which traded on the New York Stock Exchange. The marketability of these bonds simplified valuing the notes, which contributed to their widespread use. As Eugene N. White (1995) indicates, it also contributed to eliminating earlier legal restrictions on low-denomination banknotes. As long as the security's value was at least as high as the security deposit required for the outstanding notes, the bank received the interest on the bonds. As Table 1 shows, the bonds deposited were an asset of the bank and the notes were a liability. States required that bonds be valued at the lesser of par value (face value) or market value, and some states permitted banks to issue notes only up to a fraction, for example 90 percent, of the bonds' par or market value.

If the security deposit's value fell below the notes' value, banks were required to add bonds to the security deposit or to decrease their notes outstanding. These changes in bonds or notes were necessary until the security's value was at least as high as the notes' value. If the bank failed to make up the deficiency in its security deposit within a limited time, the bank was closed, and the bank's security deposit was used to pay noteholders on a pro rata basis. The bank's bonds were sold, and noteholders received the lesser of the proceeds or the notes' par value. Any excess of the bonds' value above the value of outstanding notes was returned to the bank's owners. If the proceeds from selling the security deposit were less than the notes' par value, the noteholders could file suit against the bank and its stockholders for the deficiency up to the limits of the bank's and stockholders' liability. This procedure was used for winding up the security deposit if the bank closed for any other reason as well.

Par Conversion on Demand of Banknotes Required. Banks were required by law to convert their notes into specie at the notes' face value on demand. As shown on the balance sheet in Table 1, banks held some specie in order to honor this legal requirement.[6] The free banks were fractional-reserve institutions: they held specie that was a fraction of their outstanding notes.

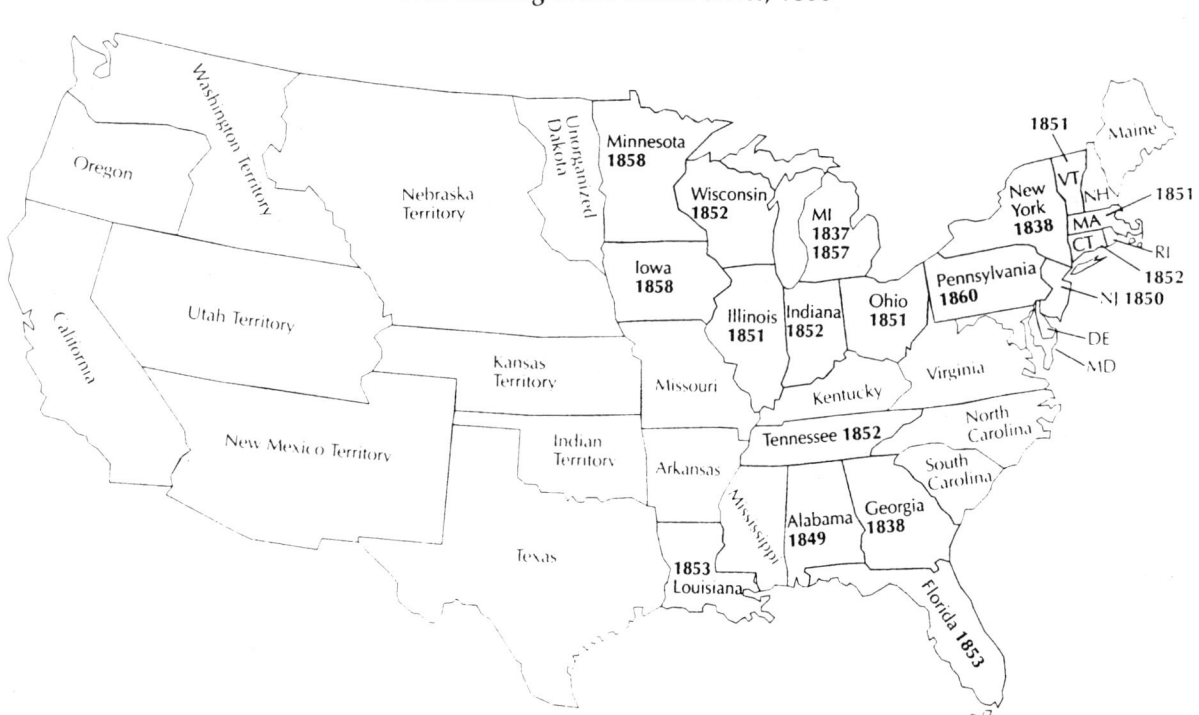

Chart 1
Free Banking in the United States, 1860

The eighteen states shaded had adopted free banking by 1860. Only Michigan, Georgia, and New York did so in the 1830s, with the rest starting in 1849 or later.
Sources: Rockoff (1975, 3) and Thorndale and Dollarhide (1987, 8).

Banks were penalized for failing to convert notes into specie at par value on demand. If a bank failed to redeem its notes at par on demand, a noteholder could formally protest to the banking authority. The bank had a grace period within which it could redeem the protested notes. Otherwise, the banking authority closed the bank and wound up the bank's security deposit. Even if the bank redeemed the notes during the grace period, some states required the bank to make an additional payment to the protesting noteholder for the time and trouble of protesting the notes.

Bank Runs Possible. The requirement that banks convert notes into specie at par on demand created the possibility of a bank run. Because banks held fractional reserves of specie, they could not instantaneously honor all noteholders' requests for specie. Banks could honor such requests only over time as they reduced their outstanding loans or exchanged assets for specie. Hence, noteholders' demand for converting notes into specie could create a liquidity problem for a bank. If noteholders thought it likely that a bank would not be able to continue to convert its notes into specie at par, they had an incentive to exchange the bank's notes for specie. The noteholders then could hold the specie or banknotes issued by another bank and wait to see whether the bank kept its notes convertible into specie.

A more widespread event possible with required convertibility of notes at par is a run on a banking system or, more traditionally and colorfully, a banking panic. For banknotes, a banking panic is a decrease in the demand for banks' notes associated with an increase in noteholders' estimated probability that banks will temporarily or permanently fail to redeem the notes at par value. While "panic" is the traditional name for such an event, people did not generally, if ever, panic in the sense of having "unreasoning fear." Rather, people had good reason to be apprehensive about whether the banks could continue redeeming their notes at par. In a banking panic, unlike a run on an individual bank, noteholders did not simply exchange their specie for notes issued by other banks. Instead, they held the specie or exchanged it for notes issued by banks not in the banking system.

Locations of Banks. Free banks were permitted to have an office at only one location. This restriction did not prevent individuals from owning or operating more than one bank if they so wished, however. Scattered records indicate that some people owned shares in several banks in one or more states, but there is no systematic evidence on how common such ownership was.

Some states required that banks locate their offices in an area with a minimum number of people. For example, Illinois in 1857 adopted a law requiring that banks be located in cities, towns, or villages with at least 200 people, and Wisconsin in 1858 adopted a similar restriction. Apparently, these laws were adopted to prevent banks from locating in out-of-the-way places, thereby hampering redemption of their notes.

Information about Banks' Activities. Free banking laws required that information be made available to the public about the banks' activities. The laws required that banks submit periodic reports, at least annually and sometimes quarterly, and the state banking authority publish the reports in selected newspapers. The state banking authority also had the power to examine the banks and determine the veracity of their reports.

Table 1
Abbreviated Balance Sheet for a Free Bank

Assets		Liabilities	
Bonds deposited with state banking authority	$50,000	Notes	$50,000
Loans to stockholders	15,000	Equity capital	50,000
Specie	5,000		
Loans	30,000		
Total	$100,000		$100,000

In addition to this required information, various trade publications known as banknote reporters specialized in reporting the values of banks' notes.[7] Under typical circumstances, notes could be exchanged for specie at the issuing bank itself at zero discount: one dollar of notes could be exchanged for one dollar of specie. A bank's notes might well be used in transactions at locations far from the bank, though, and rather than trading at par value the notes would trade at discounts from par at such locations. For example, discount rates for Indiana banks' notes were quoted in New York City. If the discount rate was 1.5 percent for a bank's notes, a person in New York City with $100 in Indiana notes could exchange them for $98.50 of specie. A person holding banknotes in New York City or elsewhere could, if it was the more advantageous course, send the banknotes back to the Indiana bank for redemption at their face value in specie.

Usually, the discount reflected the transportation cost and interest forgone due to the time required to return the notes (Charles W. Calomiris and Larry Schweikart 1991; Gary Gorton 1996). As Gorton (1996) shows, new banks had higher discounts on average because new banks had not yet established a reputation for reliably redeeming their notes. In addition, notes issued by banks that were ceasing operations traded at discounts that reflected the interest forgone due to waiting for redemption and the amount that noteholders expected to receive (Gerald P. Dwyer Jr. and Iftekhar Hasan 1996). Notes issued by banks that were likely to fail traded at discounts greater than usual even before closing. These excess discounts reflected the probability of failure, the payment that noteholders expected to receive, and the interest forgone while waiting for the payment.

Early Experience with Free Banking

Of the early adopters of free banking, Michigan and New York provide an informative contrast. Michigan's experience commonly is regarded as a fantastic failure of free banking and New York's as a solid success.[8]

A Fiasco—Michigan in 1837 and 1838. In 1837, shortly after it became a state, Michigan adopted the first free banking law in the United States.[9] This law was based on a proposed bill in New York and generally was similar to the typical free banking environment outlined above.

There were important differences, though, between Michigan's law and later ones. In free banking systems in the United States, the security deposit was the minimal guarantee of the notes' value. Michigan's free banking law provided that this security deposit consist "either of bonds and mortgages upon real estate within this state or in bonds executed by resident freeholders of the state" (Michigan 1837a, "An Act to organize and regulate banking associations," Section 11). Possible problems with bonds and mortgages on real estate, though, include inflated appraisals and depreciated real estate values when selling large amounts of real estate in security deposits. In Michigan, as bank commissioner Alpheus Felch (1880, 120) indicates, real estate values were far below appraised values when the free banks were closing en masse. The subterfuges possible with personal bonds, which are guarantees by individuals, are obvious.[10]

As events unfolded, Michigan's problems were compounded by a nationwide suspension of specie payments shortly after the state adopted free banking. This suspension of payments occurred for reasons unrelated to free banking in Michigan (Richard H. Timberlake 1993), but it affected free banking in the state. In a suspension of specie payments, banks did not redeem their notes, and under Michigan law, such a suspension by any bank implied that the bank must be closed. In 1838, Michigan amended its law to permit banks to suspend specie payments and after the number of banks quickly doubled further amended its law to prohibit new banks from suspending payments.[11] This suspension was especially problematic for the new Michigan banking system, which did not have an established reputation for reliably redeeming its notes. In addition, it probably did not help that Michigan was a frontier state at the time. Before the advent of the telegraph, let alone modern communications, acquiring information was a slower and more expensive process than today, which would compound the lack of information about the new banks and banking system.

The increase in the number of banks in Michigan was large, and their openings were followed quickly by their demises.[12] In January 1837 there were nine banks in Michigan. By December 1837 there were eighteen banks, and two months later, forty. By September 1839, only nine remained (U.S. Congress, 1840-41, 1449). These numbers are only estimates because it was hard for Michigan's bank commissioners to be sure how many banks ever opened (U.S. Congress, 1839-40, 1107, 1128). In a preamble to recommending repeal of the free banking law, the bank commissioners waxed eloquent, claiming,

> The singular spectacle was presented, of the officers of the State seeking for banks in situations the most inaccessible and remote from trade, and finding at every step an increase of labor by the discovery of new and unknown organizations. Before they could be arrested, the mischief was done; large issues were in circulation, and no adequate remedy for the evil. (U.S. Congress 1839-40, 1129)[13]

Commissioners' reports on some banks are readily available along with many accompanying depositions (U.S. Congress 1839-40). In at least a few cases, according to depositions by available bank officials, the banks were started without any intent of ever redeeming notes. In fact, notes were put into circulation without meeting legal requirements such as having the signature of a bank commissioner on the notes or providing the security deposit for the notes. Such activities were illegal under the law, and the simplest interpretation is that the banknotes were fraudulent if not counterfeit.[14]

It is easy to see how issuing notes and absconding with the proceeds could increase the wealth of a bank's organizers. For the cost of printing up notes, the issuer could use the notes to buy other assets and then skip town with those assets. The balance sheet in Table 2 illustrates the strategy. None of the bank's capital is paid in. The bank's capital is exactly offset by a loan to the owners. The notes are created and issued by making a loan to the owners. If the owners provide personal bonds to start the bank or an inflated appraisal on real property, and if they dispose of the notes and avoid their legal liability after the bank closes, they gain by the full amount of the notes' value.

As long as the person initially receiving the notes does not realize that the notes soon will be worthless—otherwise they will not take them—creating the banknotes increases the owners' wealth. Such a situation cannot be expected to persist, however. Receivers of such notes soon will notice their rapid decrease in value and will accept the notes at a discount if they may have a positive value or will not accept them at all if they certainly will be worthless. Free banking's rapid demise in Michigan itself suggests the promptness of such responses.

Estimates of noteholders' losses from these extraordinary developments are rough at best. In January 1839 the bank commissioners estimated that free banks were authorized to issue more than $4 million of notes and that "at a low estimate, near a million dollars of the notes of insolvent banks are due and unavailable in the hands of individuals" (U.S. Congress 1839-40, 1128-29).[15] It is not clear how many notes were issued. The commissioners indicate that "about forty banks" began operation. Their discussions of individual banks indicate that they thought that about seventeen banks had sufficiently large security deposits to cover their notes.[16] Discussing unredeemed notes, an 1839 Attorney General's report suggests that about $2 million was outstanding toward the end of 1839, and free banks redeemed these notes at about 39 cents on the dollar (Hugh Rockoff 1985). This redemption rate suggests that noteholders' losses were about 60 percent of the par value of these notes, or on the order of $1 million to $1.2 million. Noteholders' actual losses in these banks were reduced by any discount on the notes from their face value when issued.

Even though the estimate is rough, an approximate estimate of noteholders' total losses is $1.2 million. If the free banks had issued $4 million in notes at par value, noteholders lost about 30 percent of the par value of all free banks' notes. The 60 percent loss rate based on $2 million of notes is an overestimate, and the 30 percent loss rate based on $4 million of notes probably is an underestimate. In either case, noteholders' losses on banknotes are substantial.

A Success—New York. The events in Michigan are spectacular, but besides not lasting very long themselves, they also did not persist in the sense that they did not reappear in other states. In 1838, while Michigan was suffering through its debacle, New York passed the free banking law that its legislature had been debating for several years. New York's free banking system is widely regarded as notably successful.

Table 2
Abbreviated Balance Sheet for a Michigan Wildcat Bank

Assets		Liabilities	
Loans to stockholders	$100,000	Notes	$50,000
		Equity capital	50,000
Total	$100,000		$100,000

New York required that banks' security deposits consist of New York state government bonds or bonds and mortgages on real estate. Available evidence suggests that the bonds and mortgages on real estate were less of a problem than in Michigan.

Chart 2 shows losses suffered by noteholders in New York free banks for the years available, 1842 to 1863.[17] The annual loss rates on New York notes were relatively high in the 1840s—4 percent in 1842, 0.2 percent in 1844, and 0.4 percent in 1848—and then never again as high as 0.1 percent. Noteholders' loss rates of less than 0.1 percent in later years are not obviously more than their losses from inadvertently destroying or misplacing notes.

Losses on total notes give a picture of the typical noteholders' losses, but they do not show the losses suffered by those who held notes issued by the banks that failed—banks that ceased operation and paid noteholders less than the par value of their notes. Chart 3 shows the losses per dollar of notes in failed

Chart 2
Loss Rate on Total Notes in New York Free Banks, 1842-63[a]

Percent of Notes Outstanding

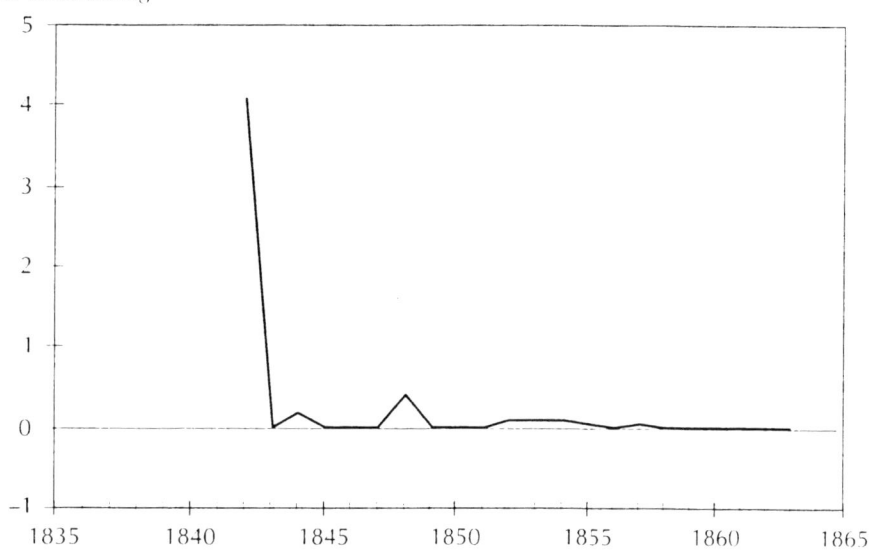

While Michigan's free banking efforts seemed to fail dismally, New York's free banking system is widely regarded as successful.

[a] The only dates for which information is available.

Source: King (1983).

Chart 3
Loss Rate on Notes in Failed New York Free Banks, 1840-63[a]

Percent of Notes Outstanding

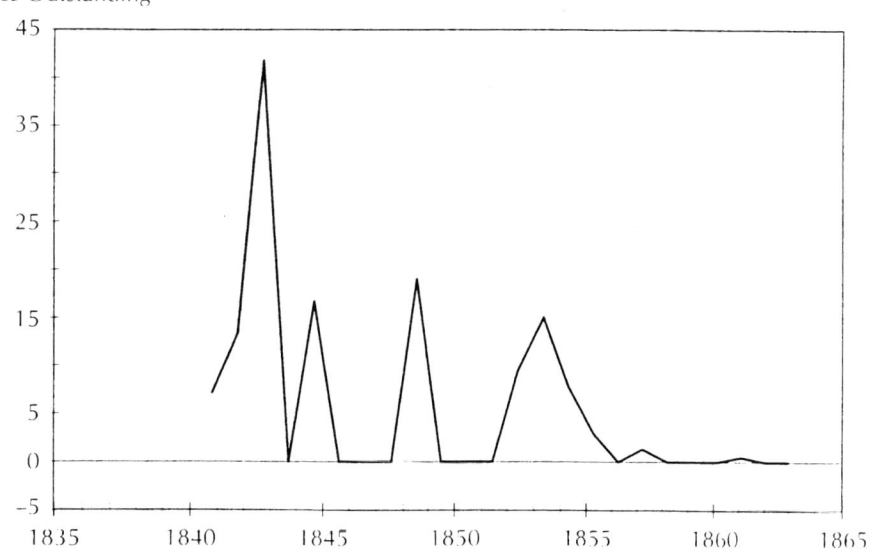

Losses on total notes (Chart 2) give a picture of the typical noteholders' losses, but they do not show the losses suffered by those who held notes issued by banks that failed, ceasing operation and paying noteholders less than the note's par value.

[a] These data include 1840 and 1841 whereas the aggregate losses shown in Chart 2 do not because data on total notes are not available for those years.

Source: King (1983).

New York free banks from 1840 to 1863.[18] For a few years, noteholders' loss rates on these banks' notes are relatively high. Nonetheless, loss rates on failed banks' notes show the same pattern of declining losses over time as do noteholders' loss rates on all notes. The highest loss rate is 42 percent in 1842, within the range of estimated loss rates for Michigan a few years earlier. In the 1840s, the annual average loss rate is 9.8 percent; in the 1850s, it is 3.7 percent; and in the four years of the 1860s, it is 0.1 percent. Although the loss rate borne by those who held failed banks' notes sometimes is substantial, even this loss rate decreases over time.

It is easy to overstate the significance of these losses. This pattern of zero losses by some and sometimes nontrivial losses by others means that in turn misfortune was borne by some and not by others. During this period, banknote reporters made it relatively low cost to be informed about the value of banks' notes. While the more informed had an incentive to shift these losses to the less informed, in the absence of evidence, it is hard to say more.[19] Even the annual average loss rate on notes in the small proportion of banks that failed in the 1850s is only 3.7 percent. The overall loss rate for that decade is less than 0.1 percent.

Free Banking in Selected States

As Chart 1 indicates, most states that adopted free banking did so in the 1850s, after New York had about fifteen years' experience with the banking system. Besides experiences of the early adopters of free banking, it is informative to examine what happened in selected states that adopted free banking later and apparently had substantial problems.[20] Extreme examples can be the best teachers, but it is important to realize that they are not representative examples. Indiana, Illinois, and Wisconsin had particularly bad experiences with their free banking systems, as indicated by Hammond's conclusion cited earlier that people in these states would have been better off with no banks at all than with free banking.

Bank Entry and Failures. Table 3 summarizes free banks' entry and exit in these three states from the inception of free banking to 1863. In the table, a bank is listed as ceasing operation if it closed and the bank's security deposit was sufficient to redeem all of the bank's notes at their face value. A bank is listed as failing if it closed and the bank's security deposit was not sufficient to redeem all of the bank's notes at their face value.[21] A noticeable aspect of Table 3 is the large amount of entry and exit. Much of this activity simply reflects people starting banks and later closing them because it was optimal to do so. There is no obvious reason to be more concerned about it than to be concerned about grocery stores beginning and ceasing operation.[22]

While the timing differs between the states, the failures in each state are clustered in specific time periods. In Indiana, 68 banks started in the first three years of free banking in the state, and only 38 existed at the end of that period. Eighty-seven percent of the banks in Illinois closed at the start of the Civil War, and most of them failed. Out of 108 banks at the start of 1861 in Wisconsin, 36 failed and 15 ceased operation in the

Was free banking in the United States so bad that people would have been better off with no banks at all?

next two years. As mentioned above, these states are not typical. They are chosen for discussion precisely because they have notorious episodes in which many banks closed.

Wildcat Banking. Were the occasional large numbers of banks that failed wildcat banks with reckless or financially unsound operations?[23] By themselves, high failure rates do not mean that banks are operating recklessly. Conversely, banks that remain open for a long period may well be operating recklessly.

Duration before Failure. Although eventual failure rates are unreliable measures of banks' ex ante riskiness, Arthur J. Rolnick and Warren E. Weber (1984) use the duration of a bank's existence as a measure of whether a bank is a wildcat bank. They define a bank as a wildcat bank if it failed within a year after beginning operation. This definition is relatively straightforward, and it is possible to determine whether any particular bank failed shortly after opening. In addition, it focuses on one aspect of wildcat banking: starting a bank and absconding with one-time gains from starting it. Using this definition, Rolnick and Weber (1984) and

Table 3
Free Banks Entering and Exiting in Indiana, Illinois, and Wisconsin, 1853-63

Period	Entry	Ceased Operation	Failed	Closed[a]	Number of Banks
Indiana					
− Dec 53	30				30
Dec 53 − Jul 54	19		1	2	46
Jul 54 − Jan 56	19	7	10	10	38
Jan 56 − Jul 56	2	4		3	33
Jul 56 − Jul 57	5	7	2	3	26
Jul 57 − Jan 58		7			19
Jan 58 − Jan 59	1	4			16
Jan 59 − Jan 60	1				17
Jan 60 − Jan 61	2		1		18
Jan 61 − Jan 62					18
Jan 62 − Jan 63		1			17
Illinois					
− Apr 53	23				23
Apr 53 − Apr 54	8	2			29
Apr 54 − Jan 56	15	9			35
Jan 56 − Nov 56	16	3	2		46
Nov 56 − Jan 58	4	5	2		43
Jan 58 − Oct 58	5	1			47
Oct 58 − Jan 60	29	1			75
Jan 60 − Oct 60	20				95
Oct 60 − Apr 62	5	3	80		17
Apr 62 − Jan 63	8				25
Wisconsin					
− Jan 53	2				2
Jan 53 − Jan 54	8				10
Jan 54 − Jan 55	14	1			23
Jan 55 − Jan 56	10	3			30
Jan 56 − Jan 57	17	2			45
Jan 57 − Jan 58	26	3			68
Jan 58 − Jan 59	34	3			99
Jan 59 − Jan 60	16	8			107
Jan 60 − Jan 61	7	5	1		108
Jan 61 − Jan 62	2	12	35		63
Jan 62 − Jul 62		3	1		59

[a] Unknown whether bank ceased operation or failed. In addition, there are six Indiana banks for which dates of operation are not available. Three of these ceased operation and one failed, and it is unknown whether the other two ceased operation or failed.

Sources: Rolnick and Weber (1982); Economopolous, unpublished data.

Andrew Economopolous (1988, 1990) clearly have shown that wildcat banking was unimportant if not irrelevant in Indiana, Wisconsin, and Illinois.

Rockoff (1975) suggested, for reasons outlined in Box 2, that wildcatting might be due to bonds in the security deposit being valued at par rather than market value. Subsequent research into state laws and regulators' operations in states, though, has found bonds being valued at the lesser of par or market value in every case except New York from 1838 to 1840 (Rolnick and Weber 1984; Economopolous 1988). Legislators in New York and other states learned from New York's problems in its earliest years and did not repeat the mistake.

Bank Owners Highly Leveraged in Their Ownership. Rolnick and Weber's measure of wildcat banking is not informative about whether a bank was operating in a highly leveraged and possibly reckless manner. The president of a competitor of free banks suggested that anyone with relatively little funds could organize a free bank (Hugh McCulloch 1888, 125-26). If a bank's organizer has some funds, borrows more, and uses the funds to buy state bonds, then the organizer can use the state bonds as security for notes. In exchange for the deposited bonds, the state banking authority sends notes to the organizer, and the organizer uses the notes to buy more bonds. This process continues until the organizer uses the notes to pay off the original loan. A possible end result of this process is the balance sheet in Table 4. Nothing in the balance sheet suggests a bank with reckless operations. The bank's ratio of notes to capital is one, and the bank has sufficient bonds deposited to pay off noteholders and a substantial loan portfolio. The loans just happen to be loans to the bank's owners.

Why would anyone organize such a bank? As long as it is solvent, the bank receives the interest on the bonds held by the state banking authority. In the example in Table 4, starting with, say, $5,000, the bank's owner is receiving interest on $50,000 in bonds. The bank's owner is highly leveraged in this transaction, but it is not apparent on the bank's balance sheet.[24] There are three aspects of this operation that are particularly pertinent. First, the bonds held by the state banking authority are available to pay noteholders.

Second, if the loans are collectible, noteholders are covered even against relatively large losses on the state bonds. The owner is liable for the loan to the bank, and, generally speaking, the owner also is liable for

Box 2
Valuation of Bonds Deposited as Security

The valuation of bonds as security for banknotes had important effects on how free banking worked. As Rockoff (1975) points out, if the bond security was valued at more than its market value, individuals had an incentive to buy bonds, issue notes, and abscond with the proceeds. For example, if someone could buy $80,000 worth of bonds at current market prices and the bonds were valued as security at their face value of, say, $100,000, and the notes could be passed for more than $80,000, say $90,000, there is a one-time gain of $10,000 in starting the bank. If the owner could avoid being sued for noteholders' losses, for example by leaving the court's jurisdiction, this difference between the amount received for the notes and the market value of the bonds created an incentive to start a bank and let it fail quickly.

After a few years of free banking's operation, legislators were aware of this incentive. Initially, from 1838 to 1840, bond security in New York was valued at its par value, which can be and was greater than some bonds' market value. In 1840, New York amended its law to require that the bond security be valued at the lesser of par or market value, a requirement followed by other states.

While addressing one problem, this provision of free banking laws was associated with another problem. Because bonds were valued at the lesser of par or market value, everything else the same, banks found it in their interest not to buy bonds trading at prices much above their par value. Bonds purchased at prices above par value could be used to support notes only equal to the bonds' par value. A smaller issue of notes decreased the bank's loans and its income. If banks are attempting to maximize expected income, other things the same, they prefer not to buy bonds trading well above their par value. Banks' risk aversion can, of course, cause banks to buy bonds trading well above par if such bonds are less risky than bonds trading closer to par value. In effect, banks face a trade-off between their risk and their return, which is absent if bonds are valued at market price, no matter what their par value. This provision may explain why Illinois and Wisconsin banks held large amounts of southern bonds, which had unfortunate consequences when prices of those bonds fell at the start of the Civil War.

the amount of equity capital again should it fail. In the example in Table 4, the owner is liable for an additional $95,000 over and above the $5,000 of personal funds invested in the bank. If the bank's owner has substantial additional assets that are difficult to move beyond the jurisdiction of the state's courts, the owner can be forced to make these payments with the result that the noteholders are unlikely to suffer losses.

Third, this banking operation has substantial value to the bank's owners *as long as the bank continues to operate* because the owner continues to receive interest on the state bonds. The owner has no incentive to

Table 4
Abbreviated Balance Sheet for a Free Bank, With the Owner Highly Leveraged in Its Organization

Assets		Liabilities	
Bonds deposited with state banking authority	$50,000	Notes	$50,000
Loans to stockholders	45,000	Equity capital	50,000
Specie	5,000		
Total	$100,000		$100,000

abscond with funds because the bank's positive present value is due solely to continuing to receive the interest on the bonds, not because of any one-time gain from starting the bank.

Nonetheless, there is a sense in which the bank is a risky venture for noteholders: the ultimate funds available to noteholders are the security deposit and the owner's assets, not the security deposit and a more diversified loan portfolio. Unfortunately, little direct can be said about the value of loan diversification to noteholders without detailed data on banks' loan portfolios and bank owners' assets.

Remote Location. A quite different but simple way of thinking about wildcatting is in terms of the word's apparent origin: remote locations that hamper note redemption. Such locations can be associated with reckless operations because outside knowledge about such banks' operations might be quite limited. Did free banks locate in remote and inaccessible places?

Chart 4 shows maps of Indiana, Illinois, and Wisconsin in 1860, indicating the population and the number of banks in each county. There is no obvious pattern to the location of Indiana banks, other than perhaps some tendency for them to be along the Ohio River on the southern boundary and along state borders generally. Each county with three banks has a major town: from north to south, Indianapolis, Evansville, and Terre Haute. Banks in Wisconsin generally are located in the more populous and more accessible downstate counties. Banks in Illinois generally are located in the southern part of the state near the Ohio River, across the Mississippi River from St. Louis and in Bloomington. A striking aspect of the map for Illinois is the almost complete absence of free banks in the most populous county, Cook County. There were many private banks in Cook County, and these banks made loans there. Illinois free banks themselves made fewer loans than other banks because a usury law applied to free banks but not other lenders, including private banks (F. Cyril James 1938, 233). Free banks could circumvent the usury law by lending their notes to affiliated private banks that made loans at higher interest rates. Hence, while Illinois banks located in accessible locations, they apparently found it expedient to issue notes from offices in less populous locations than Chicago.

Episodic Factors External to the Banking Systems. If wildcat banking is not the explanation of why so many banks closed, what is? In the case of Indiana, a change in a law in Ohio was the initiating factor in the Indiana free banks' problems. Indiana banknotes circulated in other states, and evidence suggests that a relatively large amount of Indiana banknotes was used in transactions in Ohio, partly because of relatively high taxes on banks in Ohio (Hasan and Dwyer 1994, 275–78). Indiana's free banks encountered difficulties when Ohio passed a law in May 1854 that made it illegal as of October 1, 1854, for anyone in Ohio to use small banknotes issued by banks in other states. This decrease in the demand for Indiana banknotes resulted in the return of the notes for redemption and decreases in the prices of Indiana bonds, which were about two-thirds of the banks' security deposits.

Chart 5 shows prices of Indiana bonds with a 5 percent coupon for this period. For comparison, Chart 5 also shows the prices of U.S. government bonds and other state government bonds with data available for at least half of the period. As the chart shows, Indiana bond prices were above 96 percent of par through the middle of August 1854, after which they fell about 10 percent for two months. The trough in bond prices is in December 1854. This decrease is after the change in

Ohio's law and coincides with the organized expulsion of notes from Ohio. In the absence of any other developments concerning Indiana's debt, the timing suggests that the decrease in the demand for Indiana banknotes and consequently Indiana bonds was a result of the Ohio law.[25]

In 1861, however, the decrease in bond prices occurred before the Illinois and Wisconsin free banks' difficulties and is an important factor in those difficulties.[26] Chart 6 shows prices of bonds that were 10 percent or more of the aggregate portfolio of banks in either state in 1861; it also shows U.S. bond prices for comparison.[27] All of these bonds have 6 percent coupon rates.[28] The prices of southern and border state bonds fell before the Civil War and then fell dramatically the same week that Confederates fired on Fort Sumter and Lincoln responded by ordering a blockade and calling up troops.[29] The low prices occurred in June 1861, and bond prices increased thereafter to the end of 1862. While bond sales by banks may have affected the bond prices' movements, the Civil War itself is the initiating factor that resulted in many banks failing in Illinois and Wisconsin.

Banking Panics. Even though the initiating factors are different in 1854 in Indiana and in 1861 in Illinois and Wisconsin, subsequent events are strikingly similar. In each of these instances, there was a banking panic that affected banks in the banking system.

In all three states, discount rates on notes in banknote reporters indicate that the market value of all banks' notes fell quite substantially. Table 5 shows discount rates for banknotes in each of these states during these episodes. In Indiana at the end of 1853, the discount rates on banknotes were 1.5 percent. By December 1854, almost 90 percent of the Indiana free banks had discount rates of 25 percent or more. A typical New York City holder of an Indiana bank's notes lost almost 25 percent of the notes' value. This loss reflected a change from a situation with expected redemption on demand at face value to a nonzero probability of the bank closing, with delayed redemption of the notes and the possibility of receiving less

Table 5
Discount Rates on Notes and Changes in Notes Outstanding in Indiana in 1854, Illinois in 1861, and Wisconsin in 1861

	Indiana	Illinois	Wisconsin
		Discount Rates	
Date	12/53	6/60	6/60
Discount rate	1.50	2.25	2.75
Percent of banks with this discount rate and higher	100	97.5	97.1
Date	12/54	6/61	6/61
Discount rate	25	60	20
Percent of banks with this discount rate and higher	89	100	100
		Percentage Change in Banknotes Outstanding	
Period	10/54 to 1/56	1/60 to 1/62	1/60 to 1/62
Percentage change	−44.7	−84.2	−59.8

Sources: Discount rates in 1853 and 1854 are from *Thompson's Bank Note and Commercial Reporter*, December 15, 1853, and December 1, 1854. Discount rates in 1860 and 1861 are from *Hodge's Journal of Finance and Bank Reporter*, June 9, 1860, and June 22, 1861. The data on Indiana, Illinois, and Wisconsin banknotes are from U.S. Congress (1863-64, Table 2, 216-17).

Chart 4
Population and Number of Free Banks by County in Wisconsin, Illinois, and Indiana, 1860

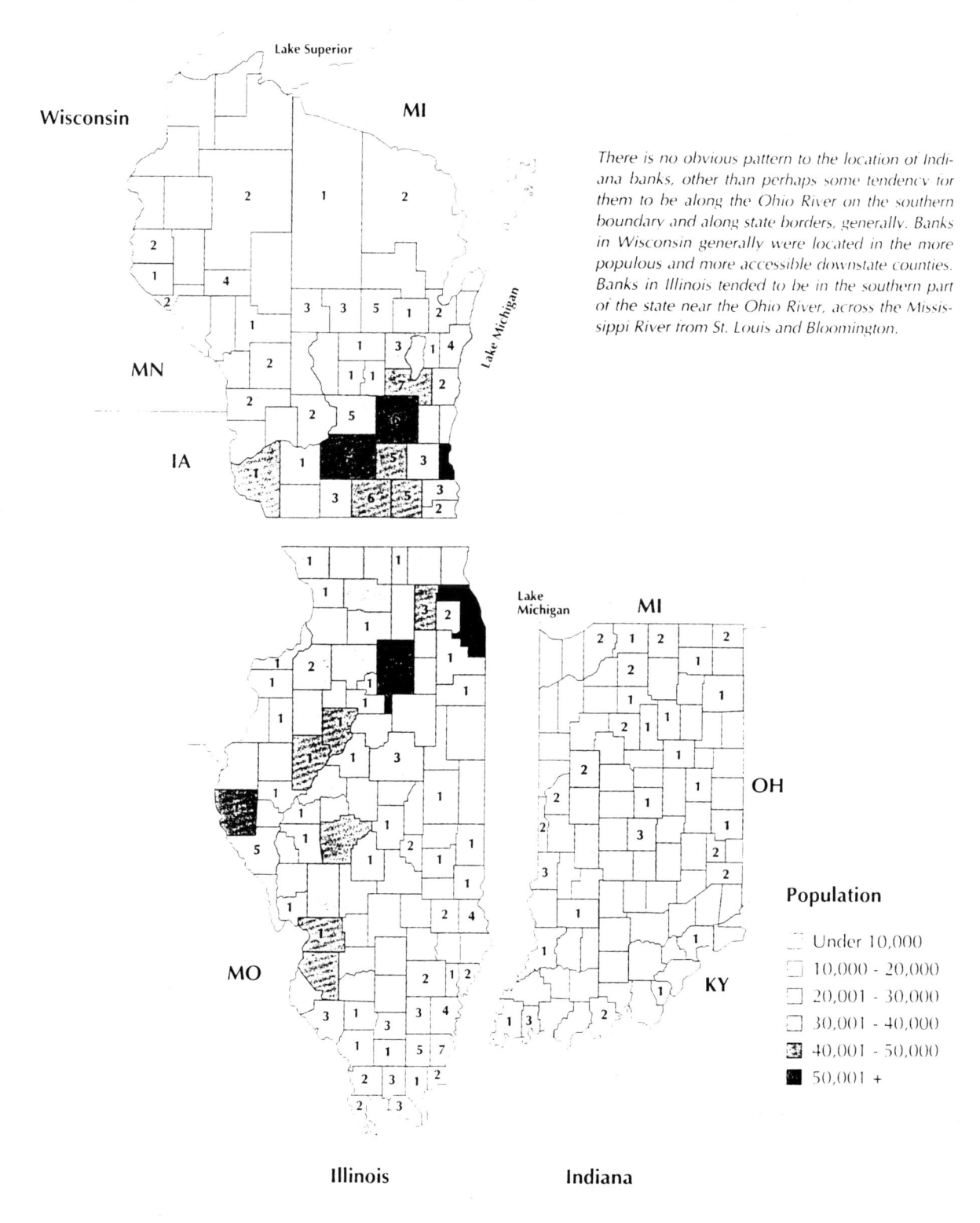

There is no obvious pattern to the location of Indiana banks, other than perhaps some tendency for them to be along the Ohio River on the southern boundary and along state borders, generally. Banks in Wisconsin generally were located in the more populous and more accessible downstate counties. Banks in Illinois tended to be in the southern part of the state near the Ohio River, across the Mississippi River from St. Louis and Bloomington.

Population
- Under 10,000
- 10,000 - 20,000
- 20,001 - 30,000
- 30,001 - 40,000
- 40,001 - 50,000
- 50,001 +

Source: Thorndale and Dollarhide (1987, 381 [Wisconsin], 105 [Illinois], and 112 [Indiana]).

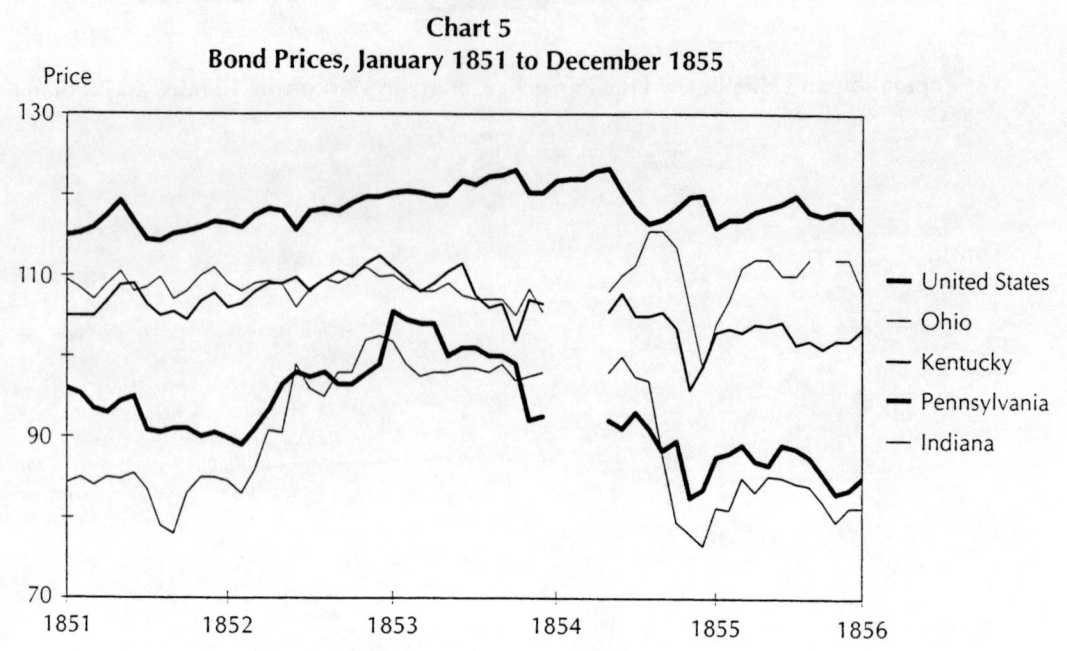

**Chart 5
Bond Prices, January 1851 to December 1855**

Indiana's free banks encountered difficulties when Ohio passed a law in May 1854 that made it illegal as of October 1, 1854, for anyone in Ohio to use small banknotes issued by banks in other states. This decrease in demand for Indiana banknotes resulted in the return of the notes for redemption and decreases in the prices of Indiana Bonds.

Note: Gaps in state data indicate that data were unavailable.

Source: See data appendix (available on request).

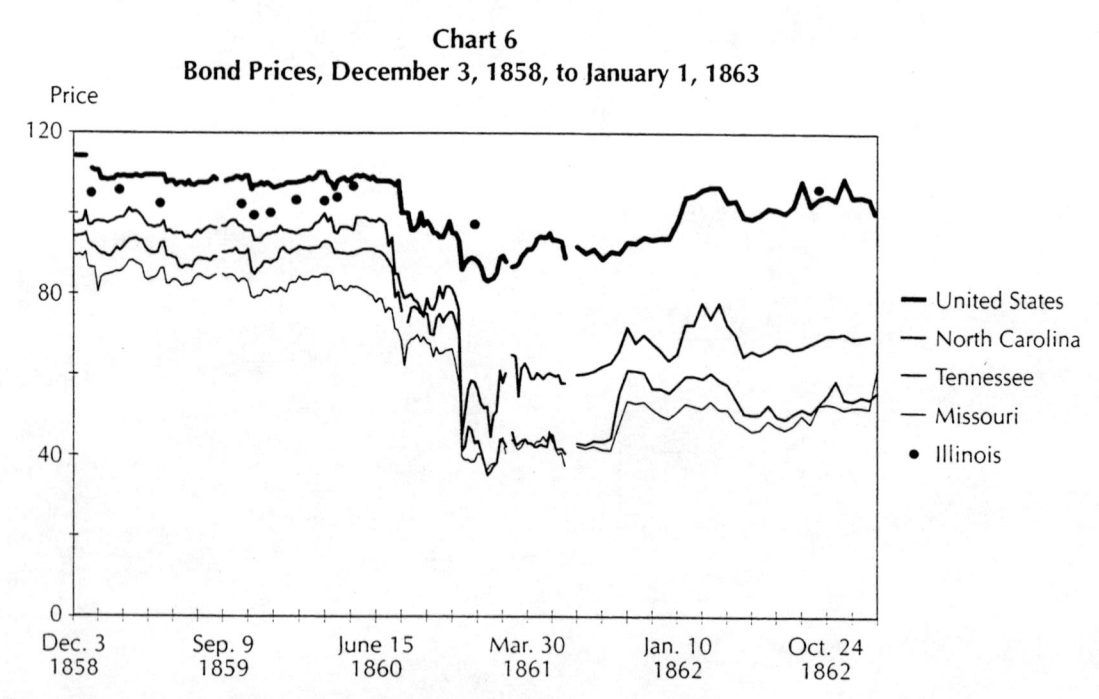

**Chart 6
Bond Prices, December 3, 1858, to January 1, 1863**

The prices of southern and border state bonds fell before the Civil War and then fell dramatically the same week that the Confederates fired on Fort Sumter.

Note: Only fragmentary data on Illinois bond prices are available.

Source: See data appendix (available on request).

than the notes' face value. In Illinois and Wisconsin in 1861, quite different initiating developments—the onset of the Civil War—had similar effects.

These discount rates are greater than noteholders' losses. While loss rates are not known for all Indiana banks that ceased operations in 1854 and 1855, noteholders' average loss rate even on notes issued by a typical bank known to have failed is 12 percent, and the maximum known loss rate on notes issued by an Indiana bank that failed in 1854 and 1855 is 20 percent. This average loss rate in failed banks is far less than the discount rates of at least 25 percent on almost all banks' notes and also is small in comparison with losses in the 1830s in Michigan and losses in 1842 in New York.[30] Holders of notes from a typical bank in Wisconsin suffered losses of about 7.2 percent, and holders of Illinois notes suffered larger losses, about 22.2 percent.

These developments in all three states also are followed by substantial contractions in the amount of notes outstanding. From October 1854 to January 1856, Indiana banknotes outstanding fell by about 45 percent. From January 1860 to January 1862, Wisconsin banknotes outstanding fell by about 60 percent and Illinois banknotes fell by an even larger 84 percent.

In response to these developments, bankers attempted to coordinate their responses and reassure noteholders that some banks were solvent. In Indiana in 1854 and in Wisconsin in 1861, the free banks suspended payments.[31] A detailed comparison of Illinois and Wisconsin indicates that the suspension of payments had substantial effects (Dwyer and Hasan 1996). The suspension of payments explains much of the difference between 87 percent of Illinois banks closing and 47 percent of Wisconsin banks closing. In addition to decreasing the number of banks that ceased operations, the joint suspension decreased noteholders' losses by about 20 percentage points. Besides being similar in the 1854 and 1861 episodes, bankers' coordinated responses, including the suspensions of payments, are similar to bankers' responses to runs on the banking system in the National Banking period.[32]

Conclusion

Free banking in the United States was not the disaster portrayed by some, but it also was not problem-free. The early years of free banking were troubled. Holders of Michigan notes lost 30 to 60 percent of the notes' value. In 1842 holders of New York notes lost 4 percent of the notes' value and holders of failed banks' notes lost 42 percent. With the exception of episodic events that generated atypical losses, free banking's performance improved over time. This improvement is associated with, and possibly due to, adjustments in the laws in response to problems that arose. In the 1850s, a substantial number of states adopted free banking laws.

Free banking in Indiana, Illinois, and Wisconsin are alleged later instances of reckless banking. There is no evidence that free banks in these states generally were characterized by continuing fraud to transfer wealth from passive noteholders to shrewd bankers. There also is little evidence supporting a generalization that these free banks were imprudent, let alone financially reckless. The episodic difficulties faced by free banks were not self-induced implosions. In these instances, banks' losses occurred sporadically when developments outside the banking systems decreased the demand for the banks' notes or decreased the value of the banks' assets. These episodic difficulties resulted in banking panics, and bankers, legislators, and bank regulators dealt with the panics in ways that anticipated developments in the subsequent National Banking period.

Free banking disappeared when it was taxed out of existence by the federal government in 1865. This action was not due to apparent dissatisfaction voiced by citizens of free banking states. In fact, the national banking law adopted during the Civil War included many provisions similar to the free banking laws. Nonetheless, it is an open question whether some feasible banking system other than free banking would have improved people's well-being in free banking states.

Notes

1. "Free banking" is the name used for these banking laws at the time, and this usage of the term is clear in context. This period was not one of laissez-faire banking, in which the only laws applied to banks are those applying to similar firms whether or not they are financial institutions. Free banking laws in the United States included many detailed provisions of the laws that applied to banking and not other businesses, some of which had unfortunate effects.

    It is ironic that the banks in the United States most similar to laissez-faire banks, private banks, have received little study. It is difficult to know even how many private banks there are at any time, let alone anything about them. Because private banks are not incorporated, do not have limited liability, and are subject only to general laws, there is very little documentary evidence, and none of it is readily available. Individuals or partnerships in the United States long have been unable to issue notes, but private banks face the same issues in the deposit and loan business as do today's commercial banks.

2. According to the *New Shorter Oxford English Dictionary*, the use of the word *wildcat* for a reckless or unsound operation arose in the early 1800s. The usual basis of the name, as in Hammond (1957, 600-601), for example, is the explanation in the text. Dillistin (1949, 60-63) argues for a different, strained interpretation.

3. Rockoff (1975) was the first economist in many years to examine U.S. free banking. L. White (1984) explored free banking in Britain, including its intellectual history, and Rolnick and Weber (1983; 1984; 1985; 1988) wrote an influential series of papers investigating U.S. free banking. In recent years, there has been a torrent of research on free banking all over the world. Dowd (1992) includes nine papers on some of these free banking episodes. Selgin and White (1994) survey much of the research on free banking. This research into free banking is part of an examination of basic issues concerning monetary and banking systems analyzed in recent years by Hayek (1978), Friedman and Schwartz (1986), Goodhart (1988), and others. Other studies include a classic analysis by Smith ([1936] 1990) and more recent analyses by Bordo and Schwartz (1995), Goodhart (1994), Roberds (1995), Schwartz (1993), and Selgin (1993; 1994).

4. This summary is based on Dewey (1910), Hammond (1957), Rolnick and Weber (1984), Hasan and Dwyer (1994), and Dwyer and Hasan (1996).

5. Loans to stockholders generally are not so obvious on available free banks' balance sheets.

6. Although they legally could demand it, noteholders did not necessarily require specie in exchange for the banknotes. They often accepted notes issued by other banks.

7. Dillistin (1949) provides detailed information on the reporters, and Gorton (1996) provides an economic analysis of the discount rates.

8. Georgia is the remaining state that adopted free banking in the 1830s. Georgia never had more than two free banks, however; hence, the history of free banking in Georgia is not particularly informative and is not examined in this paper. Schweikart (1987) and Scott (1989) provide overviews of banking in Georgia before the Civil War.

9. There are no histories of banking in Michigan that include this period. The available information is limited because fire destroyed the Michigan bank commissioners' records (Rolnick and Weber 1983, 1089). Felch's (1880) recollections of this period, during which he was a legislator and a bank commissioner, provide an informative but prejudiced overview. The reports by the bank commissioners printed in the House Executive Documents (U.S. Congress 1837-38, 1839-40) also are informative. Shade (1972) examines the relationship between banks and politics in the Old Northwest: Ohio, Indiana, Illinois, Michigan, and Wisconsin.

10. These problems apparently became clear quickly. The original banking bill including personal bonds in the security deposit was approved March 15, 1837, but was amended to include only bonds and real estate mortgages on December 30, 1837 (Michigan 1838, "An Act to amend an act entitled 'An Act to organize and regulate banking associations' and for other purposes," Section 6).

11. The laws are "An Act suspending, for a limited time certain provisions of law, and for other purposes," approved June 22, 1837 (Michigan 1837b), and "An Act to amend an act entitled 'An act suspending for a limited time certain provisions of law, and for other purposes'," approved December 28, 1837 (Michigan 1838).

12. Shade (1972, 36-37) indicates that the Michigan legislature granted nine new charters in 1836 in addition to the existing charters and passed the free banking law after receiving eighteen requests for new charters in its 1837 session.

13. Given today's banking laws or, for that matter, later free banking laws, it is natural to suppose that banks were required to inform the bank commissioners before opening. This was not the case, though. Free banks in Michigan were required to file applications with the treasurer and clerk of the county in which they intended to open their office, not with the bank commissioners (Michigan 1837a, "An Act to organize and regulate banking associations," Section 1).

14. Dillistin (1949, chap. 2) is the best single source on counterfeiting of free banks' notes.

15. At least one of the commissioners, Alpheus Felch, was not favorably disposed to free banking. He was one of four legislators out of thirty-nine to vote against the original free banking law (Felch 1880, 115; Shade 1972, 37). He also was one of the Supreme Court justices who ruled in litigation in 1844 that the free banking law was unconstitutional (Rockoff 1985, 886). This $1 million estimate seems to be the estimate that Felch (1880) relies on, contrary to Rockoff's supposition (1985, 887).

16. These evaluations range from tentative ones of "hope no loss" to definite ones of "no possible loss."

17. These losses are the difference between the par value of the notes and the dollar amount received from the banking

regulator and do not allow for the forgone interest in the meantime or later recoveries from the banks or their stockholders.

18. These data include 1840 and 1841, whereas the aggregate losses do not, because reliable data on total notes are not available for 1840 and 1841 (King 1983, 147).

19. In Wisconsin in 1861, banks decided not to accept ten banks' notes at par and announced it only after some businesses had paid workers in those banks' notes (Krueger 1933, 82-85). The result was a riot.

20. At the start of the Civil War, Tennessee free banks had problems similar to those in Illinois and Wisconsin, but the surviving data do not include noteholders' losses (Pierce and Horning 1991).

21. Noteholders may have been paid the face value of their notes even if the bank's security deposit was insufficient to redeem the notes at face value. The available information from the states' archives is on note redemption by the security deposit, which does not include information on payments from other sources. Even if a noteholder was paid face value, the payment was delayed and the present value would have been less than the face value. There is insufficient information available to reliably calculate such present values. Not having such present values, though, is a second-order problem compared with not having information on all payments to noteholders.

22. Increased entry, though, can be associated with increased competition, which is desirable. On the basis of raw numbers, Ng (1988) suggests that free banking did not increase bank entry. Using an economic model, though, Economopolous and O'Neill (1995) provide evidence that free banking did increase entry. Bodenhorn (1990) presents evidence that free banking was also associated with more changes in banks' market ranks. Kahn's (1985) computations indicate that free banks had a shorter life expectancy than chartered banks, which is not obviously undesirable anyway. These computations are vitiated, though, by an assumption that the probability of closing is the same every year, an assumption grossly at variance with the data.

23. Rockoff (1975, 4-5) defines a wildcat bank as a free bank that cannot continuously redeem its notes. He later (1991,

96-103) elaborates on his views of wildcat banking and distinguishes them from Rolnick and Weber's views.

24. Interestingly, Bodenhorn and Haupert (1995) provide evidence that free banks issued too few notes to maximize their net revenue.

25. The relative price of Indiana bonds rose in 1852 at least partly due to a change in the way interest was paid. Before 1853, one-fifth of the interest on the bonds was paid in bonds on which interest would not be paid until 1853. Indiana began paying all of the promised interest in 1853.

26. Details are provided in Rolnick and Weber (1984), Economopolous (1988), Hasan and Dwyer (1994), Dwyer and Hasan (1996), and the earlier work referenced in these papers.

27. Movements of northern states' bond prices generally are similar to movements of U.S. bond prices.

28. Only fragmentary data on Illinois bonds prices are available in *Bankers' Magazine*, the source of the bond prices. There is no evidence of changes in bond prices specific to Illinois in Chart 6, although nontrivial transitory changes could be concealed by the paucity of observations. There is no evidence, though, of events other than the bank failures that might have affected prices of Illinois bonds.

29. It is less surprising that Missouri bonds fell as much as southern bonds when one recalls that Missouri was under martial law with a provisional state government for the duration of the war (Brownlee 1958). Ratchford (1941, 124-25) indicates that Missouri paid no interest on its bonds from the outbreak of the Civil War until the ratification of a Reconstruction-era constitution in 1866.

30. The loss rates for Michigan and New York are weighted-average loss rates for all banks, and the loss rates for Indiana, Illinois, and Wisconsin are simple average loss rates across banks.

31. As in Michigan in 1838, the state legislatures suspended the provision of the free banking laws that would have revoked banks' charters because they failed to redeem their notes.

32. Dwyer and Gilbert (1989) and Calomiris and Gorton (1991) summarize these later episodes. Sprague (1910) and Friedman and Schwartz (1963) provide detailed information and analysis.

References

Bass, Thomas A. "The Future of Money." Interview with Walter Wriston. *Wired* 4 (October 1996): 140-43, 200-05.

Bodenhorn, Howard. "Entry, Rivalry, and Free Banking in Antebellum America." *Review of Economics and Statistics* 72 (November 1990): 682-86.

Bodenhorn, Howard, and Michael Haupert. "Was There a Note Issue Conundrum in the Free Banking Era?" *Journal of Money, Credit, and Banking* 27 (August 1995): 702-12.

Bordo, Michael D., and Anna J. Schwartz. "The Performance and Stability of Banking Systems under 'Self-Regulation': Theory and Evidence." *Cato Journal* 14 (Winter 1995): 453-79.

Brownlee, Richard S. *Gray Ghosts of the Confederacy: Guerrilla Warfare in the West, 1861-1865.* Baton Rouge, La.: Louisiana State University Press, 1958.

Calomiris, Charles W., and Gary Gorton. "The Origins of Banking Panics: Models, Facts, and Bank Regulation." In *Financial Markets and Financial Crises*, National Bureau of Economic Research Project Report, edited by R. Glenn Hubbard, 109-73. Chicago and London: University of Chicago Press, 1991.

Calomiris, Charles W., and Larry Schweikart. "The Panic of 1857: Origins, Transmission, and Containment." *Journal of Economic History* 51 (December 1991): 807-34.

Dewey, Davis R. *State Banking before the Civil War*. National Monetary Commission. Washington: Government Printing Office, 1910.

Dillistin, William H. *Bank Note Reporters and Counterfeit Detectors*. New York: American Numismatic Society, 1949.

Dowd, Kevin. *The Experience of Free Banking*. London: Routledge, 1992.

Dwyer, Gerald P., Jr., and R. Alton Gilbert. "Bank Runs and Private Remedies." Federal Reserve Bank of St. Louis *Review* 71 (May/June 1989): 43-61.

Dwyer, Gerald P., Jr., and Iftekhar Hasan. "Suspension of Payments, Bank Failures, and the Nonbank Public's Losses." Federal Reserve Bank of Atlanta Working Paper 96-3, May 1996.

Economopolous, Andrew. "Illinois Free Banking Experience." *Journal of Money, Credit, and Banking* 20 (May 1988): 249-64.

———. "Free Bank Failures in New York and Wisconsin: A Portfolio Analysis." *Explorations in Economic History* 27 (1990): 421-41.

Economopolous, Andrew, and Heather O'Neill. "Bank Entry during the Antebellum Period." *Journal of Money, Credit, and Banking* 27 (November 1995): 1071-85.

Felch, Alpheus. "Early Banks and Banking in Michigan." *Pioneer Collections: Report of the Pioneer Society of the State of Michigan* 2 (1880): 111-24.

Fischer, Gerald C. *American Banking Structure*. New York: Columbia University Press, 1968.

Flohr, Udo. "Electric Money." *Byte* 21 (June 1996): 74-84.

Friedman, Milton. *A Program for Monetary Stability*. New York: Fordham University Press, 1960.

Friedman, Milton, and Anna J. Schwartz. *A Monetary History of the United States, 1867-1960*. Princeton, N.J.: Princeton University Press, 1963.

———. *Monetary Statistics of the United States*. New York: National Bureau of Economic Research, 1970.

———. "Has the Government Any Role in Money?" *Journal of Monetary Economics* 17 (January 1986): 37-62.

Goodhart, Charles. *The Evolution of Central Banks*. Cambridge, Mass.: MIT Press, 1988.

———. "The Free Banking Challenge to Central Banks." *Critical Review* 8 (Summer 1994): 411-25.

Gorton, Gary. "Reputation Formation in Early Bank Notes." *Journal of Political Economy* 104 (April 1996): 346-97.

Hammond, Bray. *Banks and Politics in America from the Revolution to the Civil War*. Princeton, N.J.: Princeton University Press, 1957.

Hasan, Iftekhar, and Gerald P. Dwyer Jr. "Bank Runs in the Free Banking Period." *Journal of Money, Credit, and Banking* 26 (May 1994): 271-88.

Hayek, F.A. *The Denationalization of Money—The Argument Refined*. 2d ed. London: Institute of Economic Affairs, 1978.

Hodge's Journal of Finance and Bank Reporter, June 9, 1860, and June 22, 1861.

James, F. Cyril. *The Growth of Chicago Banks*. New York: Harper and Brothers Publishers, 1938.

Kahn, James A. "Another Look at Free Banking in the United States." *American Economic Review* 75 (September 1985): 881-85.

King, Robert G. "On the Economics of Private Money." *Journal of Monetary Economics* 12 (July 1983): 127-58.

Krueger, Leonard Bayliss. *History of Commercial Banking in Wisconsin*. University of Wisconsin Studies in the Social Sciences and History, no. 18. Madison: University of Wisconsin, 1933.

Levy, Steven. "E-Money (That's What I Want)." *Wired* 2 (December 1994): 174-79, 213-19.

McCulloch, Hugh. *Men and Measures of Half a Century*. New York: Charles Scribners Sons, 1888.

Michigan. *Acts of the Legislature of the State of Michigan Passed at the Annual Session of 1837*. Detroit, Mich.: John S. Bagg, 1837a.

———. *Acts of the Legislature of the State of Michigan Passed at the Special Session of 1837*. Detroit, Mich.: John S. Bagg, 1837b.

———. *Acts of the Legislature of the State of Michigan Passed at the Adjourned Session of 1837 and the Regular Session of 1838*. Detroit, Mich.: John S. Bagg, 1838.

Ng, Kenneth. "Free Banking Laws and Barriers to Entry in Banking, 1838-1860." *Journal of Economic History* 48 (December 1988): 877-89.

Pierce, Sarah B., and Bruce C. Horning. "The Free Banking Era in Tennessee." Vanderbilt University. Unpublished paper, 1991.

Ratchford, B.U. *American State Debts*. Durham, N.C.: Duke University Press, 1941.

Roberds, William. "Financial Crises and the Payments System: Lessons from the National Banking Era." Federal Reserve Bank of Atlanta *Economic Review* 80 (September/October 1995): 15-31.

Rockoff, Hugh. *The Free Banking Era: A Reexamination*. New York: Arno Press, 1975.

———. "New Evidence on Free Banking in the United States." *American Economic Review* 75 (September 1985): 886-89.

———. "Lessons from the American Experience with Free Banking." In *Unregulated Banking: Chaos or Order?*, edited by Forrest H. Capie and Geoffrey E. Wood, 73-109. New York: St. Martin's Press, 1991.

Rolnick, Arthur J., and Warren E. Weber. "The Free Banking Era: New Evidence on Laissez-Faire Banking." Federal Reserve Bank of Minneapolis Research Department Staff Report 80, 1982.

———. "New Evidence on the Free Banking Era." *American Economic Review* 73 (December 1983): 1080-91.

———. "The Causes of Free Bank Failures." *Journal of Monetary Economics* 14 (October 1984): 269-91.

———. "Banking Instability and Regulation in the U.S. Free Banking Era." Federal Reserve Bank of Minneapolis *Quarterly Review* 9 (Summer 1985): 2-9.

———. "Explaining the Demand for Free Bank Notes." *Journal of Monetary Economics* 21 (January 1988): 47-71.

Schneier, Bruce. *Applied Cryptography*. 2d ed. New York: John Wiley and Sons, Inc., 1996.

Schwartz, Anna J. "Are Central Banks Necessary?" *Critical Review* 7 (Spring-Summer 1993): 355-70.

Schweikart, Larry. *Banking in the American South from the Age of Jackson to Reconstruction*. Baton Rouge, La.: Louisiana State University Press, 1987.

Scott, Carole E. "Antebellum Banking in Georgia and South Carolina." In *Essays in Economic and Business History*, edited by Edwin J. Perkins. Selected Papers from the Economic and Business History Historical Society, vol. 8. Los Angeles: Department of History, University of Southern California, 1989.

Selgin, George. "The Rationalization of Central Banks." *Critical Review* 7 (Spring-Summer 1993): 335-54.

———. "Are Banking Crises Free-Market Phenomena?" *Critical Review* 8 (Fall 1994): 591-608.

Selgin, George, and Lawrence H. White. "How Would the Invisible Hand Handle Money?" *Journal of Economic Literature* 32 (December 1994): 1718-49.

Shade, William Gerald. *Banks or No Banks: The Money Issue in Western Politics, 1832-1865*. Detroit, Mich.: Wayne State University Press, 1972.

Smith, Vera C. *The Rationale of Central Banking*. 1936. Reprint. Indianapolis: Liberty Press, 1990.

Sprague, O.M.W. *History of Crises under the National Banking System*. U.S. National Monetary Commission. Washington: Government Printing Office, 1910.

Thompson's Bank Note and Commercial Reporter, December 15, 1853, and December 1, 1854.

Thorndale, William, and William Dollarhide. *Map Guide to the U.S. Federal Censuses, 1790-1920*. Baltimore, Md.: Genealogical Publishing Co., Inc., 1987.

Timberlake, Richard H. *Monetary Policy in the United States: An Intellectual and Institutional History*. Chicago: University of Chicago Press, 1993.

U.S. Congress. House. Executive Document 79. 25th Cong., 2d sess., 1837-38.

———. Executive Document 172. 26th Cong., 1st sess., 1839-40.

———. Executive Document 111. 26th Cong., 2d sess., 1840-41.

———. Executive Document 20. 38th Cong., 1st sess., 1863-64.

White, Eugene N. "Free Banking, Denominational Restrictions, and Liability Insurance." In *Money and Banking: The American Experience*, 99-117. The George Edward Durell Foundation. Fairfax, Va.: George Mason University Press, 1995.

White, Lawrence H. *Free Banking in Britain: Theory, Experience, and Debate: 1800-1845*. Cambridge: Cambridge University Press, 1984.

Wriston, Walter. "Money: Back to the Future." *Wall Street Journal*, November 24, 1995, A8.

———. "Money—Back to the Future?" Lecture given at Claremont-McKenna College, November 20, 1996.

6. The Evolution of the Bank Regulatory Structure: A Reappraisal

F. Ward McCarthy, Jr.

It is common for people, including economists, to assume that government regulations are motivated by considerations of public welfare only, and that regulatory changes contribute to steady improvements in economic institutions. Whatever the validity of this view applied to industry in general, there is much reason for doubting its validity with regard to the banking industry. As F. Ward McCarthy Jr. makes clear in the following essay, government regulations of banking in the U.S. has often been motivated by considerations of public finance rather than public welfare. The result has been a series of banking arrangements more well-suited for generating revenue for the government than for encouraging economic stability and growth. —G.S., Ed.

****

INTRODUCTION

The banking industry is regulated by an elaborate institutional structure that exercises extensive authority over virtually every aspect of banking activity. The sheer size and complexity of the system is overwhelming and has been a source of confusion in the administration of the supervision and regulation of banks. For this very reason, the Task Group on Regulation of Financial Services, chaired by Vice President George Bush, has studied the federal regulatory structure in order to reorganize and improve it. The agency reorganization proposed by the Task Group, however, merely rearranges authority under the existing agency structure and does not reduce the number of bank regulators.

A first step toward resolution of the reorganization dilemma is to gain a better understanding of the origin and development of the institutions that comprise the current regulatory framework. Students of bank regulation offer two familiar explanations for government control of banking. Public regulation of banking is typically rationalized on the idealistic grounds that it enhances economic stability by fostering honest and sound practices. An alternative view disputes the existence of the correspondence between regulation and the public interest and regards public regulation as a means of protecting the banking industry from competition. While each of these perspectives contributes to our understanding of government regulation of banking, neither provides an adequate explanation of the genesis and development of the institutional structure of the regulatory framework. In order to understand this evolution, it is necessary to recognize that government regulation of the banking industry has enhanced the revenue generating capabilities of government authorities. The institutional structure of bank regulation has served as an instrument of public finance.

This article traces the major developments in the evolution of the bank regulatory structure in this country in order to gain some insight into the process that generated the current regulatory framework. Two major themes are developed: (1) government intervention in banking was motivated by considerations of public finance and (2) there has been a pronounced reluctance of government agents to divest themselves of regulatory authority once they have gained it.

The article begins with an examination of the colonial period when government control of banking was initiated and the principle of government intervention was established. Section II explains the postcolonial development of charter regulation under state legislative control and notes the attempt to establish federal regulatory authority through the central bank functions of the First and Second Banks of the United States. Section III discusses the erosion of state legislative control of bank entry and the implementation of free banking over the second quarter of the century. The reestablishment of dual federal and state regulatory control under the National Bank Act, and the extension of federal regulatory authority through the creation of the Federal Reserve System are examined in sections IV and V, respectively. Section VI presents a brief review of the reform measures of the 1930s that established the Federal Deposit Insurance Corporation and extended the authority of the Federal Reserve System. Concluding remarks are offered in section VII.

I.
THE ORIGINS OF GOVERNMENT REGULATION OF BANKING

The prevailing public policy regarding banking during the colonial period[1] was to substitute government control for market competition. Colonial governments promoted government financial interests and obstructed the development of private banking organizations. Due to this government intervention, public enterprises dominated the colonial banking era and private banks seldom survived.

The precedent for government control of banking in the colonies was established in 1690 when the Commonwealth of Massachusetts became the first American government to circulate an inconvertible paper currency. The notes were issued in anticipation of taxes to replenish a treasury that had been depleted by an unsuccessful military expedition. Over the next several years the colony accommodated treasury deficits by expanding note issues, delaying or extending redemption periods and replacing redeemed issues with more tax anticipation notes. This inflationary finance contributed to a general depreciation of paper currencies, a disappearance of precious metals from circulation, and a decreased public willingness to pay taxes. Nonetheless, these first issues of paper currency established the pattern for early monetary and banking developments. By 1712 six other colonies had followed the example of Massachusetts and were utilizing public banks as an expeditious method of public finance.[2]

Colonial governments guarded the right to circulate paper currency as a privileged monopoly and, in so doing, impeded private banking institutions.[3] If the purpose of this policy can be deduced from its effects, then the motivation clearly was to enhance the ability of colonial governments to raise revenue. In the absence of market discipline, colonial governments were free to exploit their self-imposed monopoly power and to reap the financial benefits of regulation by circulating a variety of currencies through their banks.[4]

Even when regulatory action was rationalized as being in the public interest, the government often was a beneficiary of the intervention. For example, in 1714 the Commonwealth of Massachusetts rejected a private proposal for a land-collateralized private note issue as contrary to the public interest.[5] The Massachusetts General Court's objection to the proposal centered on two issues: (1) the inadequacy of real estate as security for note issue, and (2) the inequity of granting the privileges and profit opportunities of note issue to private individuals. The colony promptly revealed its true intentions, however, when it agreed to accommodate the private demands for currency by issuing its own treasury bills backed by real estate. Although this note issue was intended to diminish support for the private bank, it actually did the reverse. For this application of a double standard "increased the zeal and raised a strong resentment"[6] in those who supported the development of private banks.

Eventually the conflict between private and public bank interests was decided by crown authorities who had ultimate jurisdiction over such matters because the colonies were part of the realm of England and subject to English law. British authorities were initially sympathetic to private banks and countermanded colonial government policies that conflicted with English law. In 1735, the Lords of Trade[7] in London overruled Massachusetts legislation that explicitly prohibited the circulation of notes by a private partnership. The Lords recognized that private credit issues were permissible under common law as long as the notes were not made legal tender. This ruling effectively removed the major constraint on private banking.

The view that the business of banking could be conducted independently of government influence prevailed, however, for only a short period. In 1741, Parliament extended the principal provisions of the so-called "Bubble Act" of 1720 to the colonies.[8] The purpose of the original act was to strengthen the British government's control over unincorporated joint-stock companies.

The occasion for the extension of this legislation to the colonies was the establishment of a private land bank in Massachusetts, a revival of the abortive 1714 proposal. Opposing the new land bank were those who distrusted private ownership of the bank and feared that it would lead to an increase in the volume of bills of credit circulating in the colony.[9] Chief among the opponents was the governor of the colony who published a proclamation warning that the land bank notes were fraudulent and harmful to trade. Since the governor and his supporters lacked the legal authority to restrain the land bank, they petitioned Parliament to do so. In passing the extension to the Bubble Act, Parliament referred explicitly to the land bank as one of the offenders which was to be suppressed. In so doing, Parliament reversed the earlier position taken by Whitehall in upholding the legality of private banks and paper money issues in the colonies, and firmly established the requirement of government sanction as a major principle of bank

II.
CHARTER REGULATION

The experience of the colonial era influenced both the post-colonial regulatory framework and the commercial banking industry that developed within this framework. To avoid repetition of the colonial experience with inflationary paper currency issues, the Constitution prohibited the individual states from issuing paper money. This restriction prevented the reappearance of public banks and created the potential for private enterprise banking.

This potential, however, was not realized because the individual state governments had the incentive to utilize banking as an instrument of public finance just as the colonial governments had done. State governments were able to circumvent restrictions on direct monetary authority by chartering banks as corporations with the power to issue debt obligations.[10] Government control of banking was perpetuated because state-chartered banks could legally circulate the paper currency that the states themselves could not. As a result, commercial banking in America began with incorporation and the specific governmental sanction of charter regulation.

Under charter regulation, which characterized the first fifty years of commercial banking, the establishment of a new bank required a charter that was granted only by a special legislative act.[11] This enabled the legislatures to control the number of banks in operation and set the range of the permissible and obligatory activities for banking institutions. Charter regulation, then, presented state governments with a potential source of revenue because a charter conferred a valuable corporate privilege on terms specified by the state. States were able to exact favorable financial arrangements in the form of bonuses and low-interest loans in exchange for granting banks the opportunity to earn monopoly profits.

In order to enhance the stature of government-sanctioned banks, charters were often couched in language designed to encourage public acceptance of chartered institutions. Of far greater significance to the value of a charter, however, was the conviction that a charter also conferred a monopoly privilege. The earliest chartered banks were understood to be monopolies even when monopoly power was not explicitly granted. Of course, this interpretation of charter rights was encouraged by those possessing charters, but also was reinforced by a commonly held misconception regarding competition. New institutions, chartered or unchartered, were thought to represent an inherent threat to the stability of all banking interests. In short, competition was viewed as an evil. This misconception prevailed for several years even after experience proved it to be indefensible.

For example, there were no provisions in the original charter of the Bank of North America granting exclusive rights to banking in Pennsylvania.[12] Nonetheless, the bank maintained its monopoly for ten years after its establishment in 1781 because of fears that banking could not survive under a competitive framework. The fear of competition stemmed from the erroneous assumption that the specie requirements of an additional bank would prevent the possibility of profitable bank operations.

> A new bank produces no new deposits of specie. There is not a dollar more money added to the circulation. A new bank divides the deposits of specie and of course diminishes the advantages of credit. For it is manifest that two banks with small capitals will do less than one bank with both capitals. Besides the ordinary banking risks, each institution is in danger from the others.[13]

Even after events demonstrated that bank entry and competition did not have the feared effects, opposition to competitive banking remained among both those who wished to maintain monopoly power and those who wished to restrain it. Established banking institutions continued to resist new entry in order to maintain their monopoly privileges and profits. These monopoly privileges, in turn, induced a popular resentment of banks, the privileged status of which was seen as smacking of aristocracy, as constituting a threat to the existence of individual freedom, and as being in need of restraint. In short, contemporary popular opinion equated corporate power with monopoly power. For this reason, an increase in the number of bank charters was interpreted as an "expansion of privilege rather than a division of it,"[14] and a restriction on the number of corporations was viewed as the effective method of limiting monopoly power. Ironically, the opponents of banking formed a coalition with established banking interests in pursuit of the common goal of restricting bank entry.

Although the states succeeded in limiting the number of banks by controlling entry, charters were not indispensable in the early years of charter regulation. In fact, some banks operated for years without receiving legislative sanction. This practice, however, was curtailed around 1800 with the appearance of so-called "restraining acts." These laws attempted to restrict banking to chartered banks and made it illegal for anyone unauthorized by law to become a member or a proprietor of any banking institution. As a consequence of the restraining laws, the common law right to borrow was distinguished from the right to borrow by issuing obligations intended to circulate as money; the business of banking was legally reserved to corporations chartered by the state.[15] This legal restraint on entry permitted the state legislatures to solidify their control of banking and protected the monopoly power of chartered institutions from encroachment by private non-sanctioned interests.

Once the restraints on unincorporated banking were in effect, the competition for new bank charters intensified. As the demand for banking services grew with economic expansion, more entrepreneurs attempted to enter the banking industry. State legislators, who controlled the rights to a valuable franchise, were solicited both by existing charter-holders who lobbied to protect their privileges and by would-be bankers who lobbied for new charters. Thus, in the early part of the 19th century, banking was an integral part of the political system.

Since they were bargaining from a position of strength, state legislatures were able to insist on a variety of favorable financial arrangements in exchange for the profit opportunities conferred by charters. The allure of profits was also strong enough to motivate aspiring charter holders to provide a variety of pecuniary inducements to individual legislators. Charges of corruption were widespread and were proven in some cases.[16] Although monopoly banking privileges were diluted as state-chartered banks grew more numerous, the benefits of any resulting competition were severely limited. Indeed, many chartered banks were handicapped from the start because they were forced to fulfill unsound commitments as the price of obtaining a charter.

The federal government did not have the constitutional authority to regulate banks by statute, but exerted a strong regulatory influence through the First (1791-1811) and Second (1816-1836) Banks of the United States which were chartered by Congress.[17] The First Bank of the United States was established to serve as a fiscal agent for the Treasury, to furnish credit to the federal government, and to issue a uniform national paper currency. Although it was federally chartered, it was mostly privately owned and was intended to compete with other private commercial banks. The First Bank was not established as a central bank. That is, it was not intended to serve as a central depository, clearinghouse and lender of last resort for a banking system. Indeed, there was no integrated banking system as such. For when the First Bank was chartered in 1791, each of the four banks in existence comprised an isolated banking system of its own and did not need any of the functions provided by a central bank. Furthermore, while Congress's right to charter any bank was hotly disputed, its right to charter a central bank was not even considered a possibility under contemporary interpretations of the Constitution. A central bank was a genus that had not been clearly differentiated from other banks by 1791.

Much to the chagrin of the state governments, however, the First Bank emerged as a central bank and the general regulator of money and state chartered banking institutions.[18] Because of its size, fiscal agency functions, large reserve holdings and interstate branches, the First Bank was able to constrain the activities of the state banks by presenting the notes of state banks for redemption in specie. In so doing, the First Bank imposed restraints on the note issues of state banks and, consequently, the public finance potential of state chartering authority. This role was later adopted and expanded by the Second Bank of the United States which attempted to assert itself in central bank activities.[19] Even though central bank authority was not prescribed by statute, the bank "performed these functions deliberately and avowedly—with a consciousness of quasigovernmental responsibility and of the need to subordinate profit and private interest to that responsibility."[20]

Early attempts by the states to check the authority of the Second Bank by taxation were curtailed by the Supreme Court in the McCulloch v. Maryland case of 1819. The Court was petitioned to rule in a suit brought against the Second Bank by the state of Maryland for failure to pay a tax that the state imposed on all banks not chartered by the Maryland legislature. Similar taxes had been imposed or were being considered by a number of other states opposed to the Second Bank. The case was of immediate importance because the taxes were a threat to the existence of the Bank, but the more important issue was the extent and strength of federal powers. In upholding the Second Bank as a legitimate exercise of the implied "necessary and proper" powers delegated to the federal government by the Constitution, the Court ruled the Maryland tax to be an unconstitutional "power to destroy" federal government authority:

> If the states may tax one instrument employed by the [federal] government in the execution of its powers, they may tax any and every other . . . means employed by the [federal] government, to an excess that would defeat all the ends of [federal] government.

This Supreme Court ruling helped to extend the life of the Second Bank until its charter expired in 1836. However, partly because it was generally believed that the Bank had extended its powers without license at the expense of state governments, bills for renewal of the Bank's charter were first vetoed by President Jackson and then delayed indefinitely. This effectively curtailed federal central banking activities until the organization of the Federal Reserve System in 1913, and returned the control of bank regulation to the individual states.

III.

THE FREE BANKING ERA

Public dissatisfaction with both the corruption and instability of the banking system under charter regulation led to the development of several experimental regulatory systems.[21] Two of the most important of these systems were free banking and the safety fund system, both of which apparently had their American origin in New York state.

In 1825, a New York legislative committee report recommended reform of the chartering system. The reform was intended to eliminate the parceling of monopoly banking privileges so that "whatever advantages are to be derived from banking operations all citizens would be free to enjoy alike."[22] The following year, a similar committee report decried the charter system as "odious to the free spirit of our civil institutions" and detrimental to sound banking because the "[c]onfidence, induced by the supposed sanctity of a charter, enables the unworthy and dishonest managers of [a bank's] concerns to flood the country with a circulation"[23] that would not exist otherwise. This committee recommended the removal of legislative control of entry and an increase in competition to improve public welfare and the performance of the banking system. Within a year plans for a banking system with easier entry and increased competition were proposed. However, the state legislature was able to resist, at least temporarily, the political pressure to divest itself of its chartering authority.

Instead, the state satiated public demands for reform when it enacted the Safety Fund Act which introduced the idea of guaranteeing creditors against loss due to bank failure. Under the safety fund system, the state maintained its ability to utilize the banking system as an instrument of public finance because the legislature maintained control over the issue and terms of bank charters. In addition, each bank was required to contribute a portion of its capital to a fund which was to be used to liquidate the liabilities, capital stock excluded, of failed banks participating in the system. The contributions to this fund were controversial for two reasons. First, bankers objected to being subjected to the additional costs of safety fund membership because they already contributed to the state legislature in return for the grant of a charter. Second, critics of the system noted that the flat rate contribution to the fund meant that low risk banks subsidized bankers with high risk preferences. The uniform contribution did not reflect the relative riskiness of the individual contributors as would a fee that varied directly with risk. In addition, by eliminating the risk assumed by the public, the uniform contribution also reduced public incentive to monitor and discipline individual bank behavior. This aspect of the plan was soundly criticized by opponents who anticipated the recent problems associated with the flat rate premium of FDIC deposit insurance[24] by some one hundred and fifty years.

> The gravest objection to the system, is the creation of the *Bank fund*, by the half per cent annual contribution of the banks. This is represented by the "Union Committee," as being one of those defects "endangering the soundness of the currency," and also "unjust," inasmuch as it renders banks responsible for others, over which they have no control; as offering a "premium in favor of misconduct, at the expense of those which are wisely and cautiously managed; . . ."[25]

In addition to introducing an insurance principle to bank regulation, the Safety Fund Act did initiate the transfer of the authority of direct state control of banking from special legislative statute to delegated authority. The law provided for three bank commissioners. One was appointed by the state governor and the other two were appointed by the banks. These commissioners were empowered to examine the condition of banks and apply for injunctions against those which were judged to violate safety fund law provisions. The supervisory powers furnished in this legislation formed the basis of current bank supervision.

In 1838 New York removed the requirement of specific legislative sanction for bank entry when it passed free banking legislation.[26] In permitting banking to be open to an indefinite and unlimited number of banks, this free banking act was both revolutionary and controversial. It departed from the legal convention of granting incorporation through special enactment and delegated the powers to charter an unlimited number of corporations to an administrative authority.[27] In the spirit of laissez faire, it restored the common law right to engage in the business of banking and disassociated banking from the status of privileged monopoly that had characterized banking from early colonial times.

Free banking, however, did not completely eliminate either legal restrictions on entry or portfolio restrictions designed to aid states in raising revenue. Under free banking, prospective bankers were entitled to a charter only if they met minimum legal capital requirements. Banks chartered under free banking laws were entitled to issue their own notes but were required to deposit designated state government bonds as security for all notes issued. This security requirement helped to supply a market for government bonds and compensated the states for the loss of the financial assistance that was routinely required from banks under state charter regulation. In addition to these restrictions, free banks were required to redeem all circulating notes on demand in specie, and were entitled to earn interest on the securities as long as they remained solvent. If a free bank failed to redeem its notes, the state closed the bank and reimbursed the noteholders with the proceeds of a sale of the bank's assets.

The success of free banking as a reform movement is a point of considerable debate. The traditional appraisal of free banking, which is used as support for government regulation, is that it was dismal. The system has been judged harshly because of its heterogeneous currency and because it witnessed many bank failures, failures which caused note holders to suffer losses which were substantial in some cases. To critics of free banking, the period is characterized by the behavior of the so-called wildcat banks which gained infamy due to their purported success in exploiting the potential for fraud in the free banking system. The Governor of Indiana expressed his concern with wildcat banks in an 1853 address:

> The speculator comes to Indianapolis with a bundle of bank notes in one hand and the stock in the other; in twenty-four hours he is on the way to some distant point of the Union to circulate what he denominates a legal currency authorized by the Legislature of Indiana. He has nominally located his bank in some remote part of the State, difficult of access, where he knows no banking facilities are required, and intends that his notes shall go into the hands of persons who will have no means of demanding their redemption.[28]

However, episodic evidence of the exploits of wildcat banks leaves a stronger impression of the difficulties associated with free banking than a more complete view of the experience would justify. Evidence of satisfactory performance can be found in the statements of contemporaries who were intimately connected to the banking of the era. For example, the state auditor of Indiana appraised the results of free banking much more favorably than one might have expected in light of the governor's speech three years earlier.

> The experiment of free banking in Indiana, disastrous as it has been in some particulars, has demonstrated most conclusively the safety and wisdom of the system. The original bill was crude and imperfect, admitting of such construction as held out to irresponsible men inducement and facilities for embarking largely in the business of banking, without the ability to sustain themselves in a period of revulsion. That revulsion came . . . and yet the loss to which the bill-holder was necessarily subjected, in many cases, did not exceed five per cent, and in no case exceeded twenty per cent of the amount in his hands.[29]

Recent study of the free banking era provides more conclusive evidence that the experience under free banking varied considerably and that the kind of misconduct conventionally attributed to wildcat banking was atypical.[30] Many banks were profitable and, of the banks that did fail, many redeemed their notes at par. Many of the difficulties of the period occurred in the first few years of free banking and seem to have been associated with the organizational difficulties of instituting the system. For example, the free banking system in New York was a disaster initially, but after some of its defects were corrected it became the model for other free banking states. Moreover, the regulations imposed on free banks may themselves have been a source of instability. For example, the requirement that government bonds be deposited as security for bank notes increased bank exposure to term structure risk and forced the retirement of bank notes as bond prices fell. Recent evidence suggests that regulated free bank portfolios were more important determinants of bank failure than misconduct or mismanagement.

Despite its alleged failures, the free banking movement gained widespread acceptance. By 1860, more than half of the thirty-two states, including some of the most populous, possessed some form of free banking. Moreover, in 1863, some of the features of free banking were initiated on a national level with the passage of the National Bank Act and the establishment of the National Banking System.

IV.
THE NATIONAL BANKING SYSTEM

The idea for a national system of banks evolved over a long period of time. In the McCulloch v. Maryland case of 1819, the Supreme Court established the constitutional foundations of a national banking system. A decentralized system was advocated as early as 1834 by banking reformers who were opposed to the financial power of a central bank and favored "abolishing all monopoly, and for substituting in the place of a National Bank a National System of Banking."[31] Long before the National Bank Act, it was recognized that a system of national banks could be organized to provide the national currency desired by some bank reformers. Moreover, it was also understood that the circulation of a national currency backed by federal government securities could help to create a market for government bonds and satisfy the funding needs of the federal government even in the absence of a central bank like the Bank of the United States. For example, Millard Fillmore, the Comptroller of the Currency in New York, who advocated the extension of free banking throughout the country, noted that should

> Congress authorize such notes as were secured by stocks of the United States, to be received for public dues to the National treasury, this would give such notes a universal credit, co-extensive with the United States, and leave nothing further to be desired in the shape of a national paper currency. This would avoid all objection to a national bank, by obviating all necessity for one for the purpose of furnishing a national currency. The National Government might be made amply secure.[32]

However, neither a national currency nor a national banking system was feasible given the prevailing political climate and the acceleration of the free banking movement during the antebellum period. It was only because the Civil War put great financial pressure on the federal government to exploit the revenue generating potential of a national currency that a national banking system was established.

The first federally sponsored proposal for a system of national banks appeared in the Annual Report of the Secretary of the Treasury in 1861. In this Report, Secretary Chase outlined a plan for a national system based on the principles of New York's free banking law. He advocated a free banking framework "because it has the advantage of recommendation from experience. It is not an untried theory. In the State of New York and in . . . other States it has been subjected . . . to the test of experiment, and has been found practicable and useful."[33] Of course, Chase's plan differed from the New York plan or any state free banking system because it substituted federal control of a national currency backed by United States securities for the heterogeneous banknote issues of the individual banks.

As was the case with previous instances of government intervention, a national banking system was rationalized as being in the public interest. For example, Chase hailed the proposed national currency as potentially "the safest currency which this country has ever enjoyed."[34] As was the case with previous instances of government intervention, however, the government also was intended to be a beneficiary of the control scheme. Chase argued that national banks would provide the "further advantage of a large demand for government securities . . . [and] increased facilities for obtaining the loans required by the war."[35] Indeed, Chase clearly viewed the banking system as a potential source of financial assistance for the beleaguered United States Treasury. In the absence of a central bank, a national currency backed by federal government securities was the most convenient means of tapping this source:

> To enable the government to obtain the necessary means for prosecuting the war to a successful issue, without unnecessary cost, is a problem which must engage the most careful attention of the legislature.
> The Secretary has given to this problem the best consideration in his power, and now begs leave to submit to Congress the result of his reflections.
> The circulation of the banks of the United States constitutes a loan without interest from the people to the banks, costing them nothing except the expense of issue and redemption and the interest on the specie kept on hand for the latter purpose; and it deserves consideration whether sound policy does not require that the advantages of this loan be transferred, in part at least, from the banks, representing only the interests of the stockholders, to the government, representing the aggregate interests of the whole people.[36]

There was considerable opposition to a national system. The first two attempts to enact legislation authorizing a national currency and a national banking system were defeated in spite of recommendations of the Secretary of the Treasury and the President. In 1863, however, Congress established the National Banking System by enacting the National Currency Act, now known as the National Bank Act.[37] The original bill passed the Senate by only two votes and, given the antifederal persuasion of the southern states, the bill would not have been enacted had the South been represented in Congress.

The act marked the beginning of the dual banking system, the division of regulatory authority between state and federal governments. The law provided the federal government with the authority to charter and supervise national banks and to regulate the national currency by establishing the Office of the Comptroller of the Currency within the Treasury Department. Since the national banking system was modeled after free banking, a group of five or more persons was permitted to form a national bank by satisfying the minimum statutory capital requirement and filing articles of association with the Comptroller. Each national bank also was required to deposit United States bonds with the Comptroller and in exchange received national bank notes equal to 90 percent of the lesser of the par or market value of the deposited bonds. The act also imposed a number of restrictions on bank activity that were rationalized as enhancing bank soundness and financial stability including: (1) a requirement to maintain reserves against both deposit and note liabilities,[38] (2) restrictions on the scope of operations primarily to accepting deposits and making short-term, self-liquidating loans to business,[39] and (3) a requirement to provide periodic reports of condition to the Comptroller.

Two factors hindered the growth of the National Banking System initially. First, most bankers preferred to continue to conduct business under state charters which typically had fewer restrictions and offered more attractive profit opportunities than national charters. In addition, the Comptroller exercised arbitrary discretion in granting charters, discretion that discouraged entry. In considering charter applications the Comptroller made subjective appraisals both of the economic potential of the community and the extent of potential competition and also required the endorsement of a prominent citizen or, sometimes, even a member of Congress.[40] This policy was neither consistent with the Congressional design for an expanding national banking system nor was it specifically granted by an allegedly free-bank statute.

Strong measures, however, were soon taken to coerce greater participation in the national banking system. In 1865 Congress imposed a ten percent tax on any bank paying out state bank notes after July 1, 1866. In his speech proposing the bill[41] on February 27, 1865, Senator John Sherman left no room for doubt that the tax was intended to eliminate state banking by prohibiting profitable issue of state bank notes:

> A still more important feature of this bill is the section to compel the withdrawal of State bank notes . . . national banks were intended to supersede the State banks. Both cannot exist together . . . the power of taxation cannot be more widely exercised . . .[42]

Resistance to the national banking legislation remained strong. A Maine bank challenged the tax and the constitutionality was tested in the Veazie Bank v. Fenno[43] case which was considered by the Supreme Court in 1869. The bank contended that the tax was a direct tax that had not been apportioned among the states as required by the Constitution. Furthermore, it argued that the tax exceeded Congressional authority because it impaired a franchise granted by the state. The Court, however, absolved Congress of any wrongdoing, confirmed the validity of the tax and disposed of any lingering notion of states' rights regarding currency issues. The reasons for the decision, which virtually assured the expansion of the national system first proposed by former Secretary of the Treasury Chase, were summarized in the statement of the by-then Chief Justice of the Supreme Court Chase:

> . . . the judicial cannot prescribe to the legislative departments of the Government limitations upon the exercise of its acknowledged powers. The power to tax may be exercised oppressively . . . [and not] be pronounced contrary to the Constitution [by the Judiciary] . . . [Furthermore] [i]t cannot be doubted that under the Constitution [Congress is given] the power to provide a circulation of coin . . . [and] bills of credit. . . . Having thus, in the exercise of undisputed Constitutional powers, undertaken to provide a currency for the whole country, it cannot be questioned that Congress may, constitutionally, secure the benefit of it to the people by appropriate legislation.[44]

In rejecting the majority opinion, the dissenting justices argued that the decision had no historical or legal precedent. State banking organizations had been accepted members of the financial community since the early years of the nation and their constitutionality had been upheld by the Supreme Court twenty-two years earlier in the Briscoe v. Bank of Kentucky case. In the view of the dissenting justices, the tax was "an unprecedented amputation of state authority."[45]

Through its power to tax, Congress persuaded a large number of state banks and new entrants to apply for a national charter. Ambitions, however, for a banking system comprised solely of nationally chartered banks were never realized because the tax on state bank notes did not effectively restrain state banks. By the time the tax on state bank notes was imposed, deposits were supplanting currency as the primary medium of exchange, and commercial banking was emerging as a profitable deposit banking business immune to the Congressional tax on state bank notes. As the innovation of deposit banking spread, state banking underwent a resurgence. The less restrictive state charters again were potentially more profitable than national charters, just as they had been before the tax on state bank notes. With much more limited corporate powers, national banks were never able to attain the supremacy envisioned by the creators of the National Bank Act.

V.
THE REFORM MOVEMENT AND THE ADVENT OF THE FEDERAL RESERVE SYSTEM

The period between 1875 and 1913 was marked by a series of attempts to remedy perceived inadequacies in the banking system. The retirement of bond-backed national bank notes and greater utilization of private clearinghouse arrangements were central to the reform movement. Congress was slow to respond to this reform agitation that endorsed a decrease in federal regulatory authority, but eventually responded by enacting legislation roughly based on clearinghouse principles. In so doing, however, Congress expanded and solidified the federal government's control over the banking industry and enhanced the revenue-generating capabilities of the federal regulatory framework with the formation of the Federal Reserve System in 1913.

The primary motivation for reform was the vulnerability of the financial system to liquidity crises and panics. Contemporary observers focused on two essential causes of this instability: (1) the pyramiding of reserves and (2) the alleged inelasticity of the money supply.[46]

Pyramiding occurred because banks operated on a fractional reserve system that permitted them to hold part of their required reserves as deposits with other banks. So-called country banks maintained reserve deposits at designated reserve city banks, and the latter held deposits at central reserve city banks. Reserve city and central reserve city banks held only a fractional reserve against the reserve deposits they held for other banks and thus were able to use some of the reserve deposits of depositing banks to meet their own required reserves. As a consequence, the actual cash reserve was a smaller fraction of aggregate deposits than the numerical reserve ratios stipulated by statute for individual institutions. Moreover, reserves tended to be highly concentrated in the large money center banks that had a significant correspondent business. While a fractional reserve banking system is vulnerable to bank runs in the absence of a lender of last resort, this pyramiding of reserves sometimes exacerbated the problem. Any systematic drain on the reserves of a sizable group of banks caused a liquidity problem for the large city correspondents as the banks experiencing the drain would have to draw down their reserve deposits at the city banks. A sustained large drain could cause problems of crisis proportions. This reserve system obviously affected the deposit-to-currency convertibility and, consequently, the total amount of money available.

The alleged inelasticity of national bank notes was viewed as a separate defect of the system. This was so because the size of the note issue was determined by the level of government debt and, therefore, was fairly rigidly fixed within short periods of time.[47] National bank notes did not satisfy the popular notion of an elastic currency because they did not vary with cyclical and seasonal fluctuations in business activity. For this reason, reformers considered a currency based on national bank notes to be a serious flaw in the financial system.

In order to remedy these perceived defects, reformers recommended both a move away from a bond-secured currency and the development of a market mechanism to serve a lender of last resort function. Two of the most important reform measures based on these ideas were the "Baltimore Plan" of the 1894 American Bankers Association convention and Theodore Gilman's "Graded Banking System."[48] The Baltimore Plan focused on currency reform as the remedy to financial instability and proposed revisions of the National Bank Act including amendments (1) to repeal the requirement that federal government bonds be deposited as security for bank notes, (2) to provide for a new national currency backed by bank assets, and (3) to provide for the relief of liquidity crises with the circulation of an emergency currency issued under heavy taxation in order to encourage retirement after the emergency.

Like the Baltimore Plan, the "Graded Banking System" stressed the ability of banks to generate reserves to meet short-term increases in the demand for currency as the key to the stability of the banking system. This proposal called for the organization of clearinghouse associations to perform the lender of last resort function. Clearinghouses developed in this country in order to facilitate interbank transactions, and eventually operated in all of the reserve cities of the national bank system and in other financial centers. Clearinghouses, though privately owned by the member banks they served, nevertheless functioned like a central bank in at least two ways: first, by requiring member banks to hold a cash reserve against deposit liabilities, and second, by creating new reserves for member institutions in emergencies. Also, the clearinghouses innovated new arrangements to help their members cope with panics. For example, clearinghouses attempted to alleviate the problem of reserve drain, without the costly procedure of maintaining 100 percent reserves, by utilizing emergency currencies to stretch the reserve base of member banks in order to relieve liquidity crises.[49] These clearinghouse innovations have been recognized as the market's response to the need for central bank functions and "the specifically American solution to a problem with which central banks in other great commercial nations were faced."[50]

The principles embodied in clearinghouse arrangements and currency reform represented a potentially effective means of rectifying the unstable characteristics of the banking system and, for this reason, were central to a number of reform proposals considered by Congress. Such proposals, however, were opposed in some quarters because they diluted the federal government's control over the banking system, threatened the financial power that the bond-backed currency provided to the federal government, and sanctioned private competition in the issue of currency.[51] Congress was reluctant to adopt any reform that diluted federal regulatory authority.

In fact, no substantial reform legislation emerged from Congress for several years. After the financial panic of 1907, a panic marked by a widespread run on banks and an inability of those institutions to convert deposits into cash upon demand, the Aldrich-Vreeland Act was enacted in an attempt to establish a mechanism to relieve liquidity crises and to prevent bank failures in a way similar to that practiced by clearinghouses. The Aldrich-Vreeland Act was the first legislation to provide for a currency backed by short-term assets and "also marked the first tendency for legislation to [encourage] . . . centralization and cooperation among banks."[52] The act, however, did not bring about any major reduction in federal control of banking. First, it was only a temporary measure. Second, it established the Secretary of the Treasury as the regulator of the emergency currency of the National Currency Associations. More significantly for basic reform, however, it did establish the National Monetary Commission to study the currency and banking situation and report its findings to Congress.

After the National Monetary Commission completed its deliberations on domestic and foreign banking practices, it submitted a summary of the perceived defects of the banking system and remedies for these defects. The Commission's reform proposal, known as the Aldrich Plan, called for the establishment of a National Reserve Association to be comprised of a central executive office and fifteen branches, each of which was to be divided into local associations. The organizational structure of the National Reserve Association was modeled after the clearinghouse system and it was intended to function as a clearinghouse. Senator Aldrich was quite explicit on this matter:

> The organization proposed is not a bank, but a cooperative union of all the banks of the country for definite purposes and with very limited and clearly defined functions. It is, in effect, an extension, an evolution of the clearing-house plan modified to meet the needs and requirements of an entire people.[53]

Membership in the National Reserve Association was to be voluntary and the entire paid-in capital stock was to be owned by the members. National banks were to be able to join without any qualifications, while state banks and trust companies needed only to conform to specified reserve and capital requirements to become members. Under the Aldrich Plan, the government had little control over banking because the Commission adhered to the principle that practitioners were the best qualified to manage clearinghouse operations. The Commission also sought to remove the incentive for members to manipulate the organization for profit by placing a ceiling on the dividends that the stockholders could receive. The National Reserve Association was intended to be responsive to the public interest and insulated from conflict of interest.

The great central banking potential that clearinghouse operations offered was never realized because federal authorities would not relinquish regulatory authority. The control of the National Reserve Association became the focal point of the contemporary dialogue on reform. The Aldrich proposal was criticized for promoting monopolistic tendencies because the procedure for selecting directors gave greater influence to banks with a larger number of shares in the National Reserve Association. Critics also noted the virtual absence of government control over the Reserve Associations. The sharpest critics dismissed the National Reserve Association as a poorly disguised scheme for a central bank.[54]

Congress, however, was not content to remedy these perceived defects. It was simply opposed to the privately controlled structure of the National Reserve Association and determined to replace it with a government-controlled institution, although there was disagreement concerning the degree of centralization of that authority. Ultimately, Congress established the Federal Reserve System. That System was intended to serve the same clearinghouse functions as the National Reserve Association and consequently, had an organization that was quite similar to that of the National Reserve Association except, of course, that the Federal Reserve was under closer control of the federal government.[55] The capstone of the system, the Federal Reserve Board, was located in Washington and, with the exception of its *ex officio* members (the Secretary of the Treasury and the Comptroller), all of its members were Presidential appointees.[56]

While proponents of the Federal Reserve Act criticized the Aldrich Plan for proposing a central bank, they declined to recognize the central bank features of the Federal Reserve System.[57] The central authority was depicted as a benign coordinating agency that would function as a public utility or perhaps even a "supreme court of American finance." The assumption underlying this view obviously was diametrically opposed to the laissez faire principle that the National Monetary Commission adopted when it recommended the Aldrich Plan. The proponents of the Federal Reserve Act also declined to recognize the potential for political conflict embodied in the central organization and occasionally invoked a "people-control-it-through-the-government"[58] doctrine to dismiss this notion. Federal government control of the Federal Reserve was considered to be a strong feature because it placed "great power in the hands of the people."[59] Carter Glass was one of the more eloquent adherents to this principle.

> No financial interest can prevent or control [the Board]. It is an altruistic institution, a part of the Government itself, representing the American people, with powers such as no man would dare misuse . . . strictly a board of control . . . doing justice to the banks, but fairly and courageously representing the interests of the people . . . the task of political control [of the Board] is the expression of a groundless conjecture.[60]

The major point of departure for adversaries of the proposed Federal Reserve System was the central organization which made the system a central bank. The "public control doctrine" simply was not acceptable to those who embraced the practical view that "control through a Government bureau, by political appointees, is not synonymous with control by the people and for the people."[61] This view also had its spokesman in Congress.

> This bill creates a "central bank." This plan is much more centralized, autocratic, and tyrannical than the Aldrich plan. It is true that we are to have 12 regional banks; but these are but the agents of the grand central board, which absolutely controls them. The power is not with them; they are not in any material matter given the right of independent action; they must obey orders from Washington.[62]

The Federal Reserve Act did not repeal the National Bank Act or abolish the Office of the Comptroller of the Currency, but rather superimposed a second regulatory system on the existing National Banking System and created a second regulatory agency. In so doing, federal authorities strengthened their control over national banks by requiring the latter to become members in the Federal Reserve System, even though bankers had little representation in the System's central decision-making process. Also, by vesting new regulatory authority in this second regulatory agency, Congress created a new avenue to bring state-chartered banks under the scope of federal control, preempted profitable operations of private clearinghouses and permitted the federal government to maintain exclusive control over the issue of paper currency.

In enacting the Federal Reserve Act, Congress

diluted the authority of the Comptroller and camouflaged the link between the Treasury and bank regulation. There was a conscious decision not to sever this link completely, however. Indeed Congress declined to abolish the Office of the Comptroller of the Currency or to put it under the control of the Federal Reserve System despite sentiment to extinguish "remnants of an undemocratic, antiquated and dangerous"[63] system.

In addition, Congress established the Federal Reserve to function as an instrument of public finance. Because the Fed was granted the authority to purchase and rediscount assets in exchange for its own non-interest-bearing liabilities, Fed operations were potentially quite profitable. Section 7 of the Federal Reserve Act required that "all net earnings [of the Federal Reserve Banks] shall be paid to the United States as a franchise tax." While the Act provided for the retirement of national bank notes, it attempted to ensure the continuation of a strong market for government bonds by authorizing every Federal Reserve bank to "buy . . . bonds and notes of the United States . . . with a maturity . . . not exceeding six months, issued in anticipation of the collection of taxes." Section 4 also authorized the issue of Federal Reserve bank notes "under the same conditions and provisions of law as relate to the issue of circulating notes of national banks secured by bonds of the United States bearing the circulating privilege, except that the issue of such notes shall not be limited to the capital stock" of each Federal Reserve Bank. Finally, Congress spelled out the relationship of the new Federal Reserve System to the U. S. Treasury Department as follows:

> Nothing in this Act contained shall be construed as taking away any powers heretofore vested by law in the Secretary of the Treasury which relate to the supervision, management, and control of the Treasury Department and bureaus under such department, and wherever any power vested by this Act in the Federal Reserve Board or the Federal Reserve Agent appears to conflict with the powers of the Secretary of the Treasury, such powers shall be exercised subject to the supervision and control of the Secretary of the Treasury.[64]

Almost from the start, the Comptroller of the Currency and the Fed were in conflict. The controversy revolved around bank supervisory and examination functions and the authority of the Fed to have access to the information gathered by the Comptroller in examination reports.[65] The Fed believed that access to information on bank financial conditions was necessary to the proper discharge of its responsibilities. The Comptroller, however, was reluctant to share confidential information with the Fed, and for a period of time only sent abstracts of examination reports to the Fed. The Comptroller's position seemed to be based on the notion that access to confidential financial information on the banking system was not vital to the successful operation of the new central bank. This attitude was reflected in a report written by a committee that was commissioned by the Comptroller to study the jurisdictional issue:

> In requesting access to the complete reports of examination, the Federal Reserve banks appear to be operating upon the assumption that the credit extended by them is an extra hazardous risk and of an abnormal character justifying them in demanding information not exacted by other banking institutions and in no way relating to the solvency of the bank. This point of view is not warranted by past banking experience and if the extending of accommodations is to be restrictive and surrounded with burdensome exactions, the success of the system is in jeopardy.[66]

In any event, the Comptroller declined to cooperate with the Fed or explain what purpose this confidential information served to the Treasury Department.

The friction between the two federal agencies eventually put the Comptroller's office in jeopardy. By 1921, Congress had introduced a number of bills to abolish the Comptroller's Office and resolutions to investigate the agency's behavior. Opponents of the Comptroller argued that it would be more democratic if the autocratic powers exercised by the Comptroller were vested in a board.[67] It was argued that the Federal Reserve Act had made the Comptroller redundant and that its continued existence would constitute an unnecessary source of "costly delays, duplication of work, inefficiency and unbearable irritation."[68] These accusations, predictably, were denied by the Comptroller. Nothing of significance came of any of these bills or resolutions, in part because the relations between the two agencies did improve after 1923. Without the embarrassment of open hostilities between the two federal agencies, Congressional incentive to rectify the overlapping authority disappeared.

VI.

THE EXTENSION OF THE FEDERAL BANK REGULATORY STRUCTURE

The advent of the reformed and dually executed

federal regulatory framework coincided with fundamental changes in the financial environment in the United States. The outbreak of European hostilities in 1914 presented unusual demands for funds and stimulated activity in the financial services industries. After the United States entered the war, the integration of commercial and investment banking activities was encouraged by the federal government which enlisted broad commercial bank support in underwriting and distributing Liberty Bonds to help finance the government's enormous demand for funds. Participation in this distribution provided many commercial banks with the expertise necessary for expanded securities operations and helped to educate a general public that became more willing to invest funds in the capital markets during the ensuing era of prosperity.

Consequently, even after the war, commercial bank involvement in all aspects of the securities markets continued to increase. The general prosperity enabled many nonfinancial corporations to reduce indebtedness to banks or to utilize the accommodative securities markets as a substitute for bank loans to finance business.[69] Commercial borrowing at banks declined, threatening the profitability of traditional loan activities and leaving the banking industry with surplus funds. Many banks relied on the longer term capital markets to offset the reduction in loan revenue. Since state banks were not constrained by federal regulations, they directly accelerated their activity in the investment banking business; national banks were forced to rely more on trust company or securities affiliates. By the mid 1920s, investment banking and security services had become so popular with the public that many banks found it necessary to provide investment services in order to remain competitive.

Both branch banking and securities activities of national banks were the focus of reform proposals prior to the depression. While the national banking system was growing relative to state-chartered banking in terms of numbers,[70] the proportion of total deposits attributable to national banks was declining due to the attrition of many of the larger national banks. These defections reflected an effort to gain access to the most favorable regulatory framework. For example, many national banks were able to increase their branching capabilities[71] by converting to state charters or merging with a state bank and retaining state-charter status. National banks seeking more direct participation in the securities business had the same incentives to operate under state regulation. As a consequence, the Comptroller was especially concerned that national bank powers be broadened in order to curtail national bank defections.[72] The so-called McFadden Act, which was passed in 1927, included provisions intended to equalize competition between national and state banks. The law reduced inequities in branching regulations and granted explicit authority to national banks to buy and sell marketable securities.

Shortly thereafter, commercial bank involvement in securities activities accelerated as commercial banks became aggressive innovators in the investment banking industry. By the end of the 1920s, "commercial banks and their security affiliates occupied a position in the field of long-term financing equal to that of private investment bankers, both from the standpoint of investment banking machinery and from the standpoint of the volume of securities underwritten and distributed by the two groups of institutions."[73]

Following the stock market crash of 1929 and the subsequent collapse of the banking system, however, concern for more rigid control over banking activities, especially investment practices, resurfaced. In 1930, Congressional committees studied the causes of the 1929 collapse, which many believed to be the root cause of the economic and financial distress. Bank investment practices, especially the extent to which bank credit had been funneled into the stock market, became the focus of investigation and criticism. Indeed, to many who witnessed the developments of the late 1920s, the sequence of events seemed to provide formidable evidence of commercial bank culpability:

> No sooner had the McFadden Act taken effect, then the great bull market had gotten underway! During the period from 1928 through 1930, commercial banks had substantially increased their share of the new bond issues and had begun to make inroads in the equities market.[74]

In addition, the Congressional investigations exposed instances of conflict of interest, speculative abuse and personal enrichment by officials at some of the larger commercial banks. These revelations helped to reinforce a general impression of bank culpability and put the banking community on the defensive. Although the scope and pervasiveness of these abuses are still subject to debate, the dramatic nature of the Congressional hearings had a strong influence on public sentiment, and thereby contributed to both the lack of public confidence in the banking system and to the popular belief that stronger

Land Security." The preamble recited that the decline in trade necessitated a greater circulation of a medium of exchange.

[6] Hutchinson, **History of Massachusetts from 1628 to 1774,** as quoted in White [55], p. 390.

[7] In 1696, Parliament created the Board of the Lords of Trade and Plantations to oversee the colonies, make them more useful to England and suppress industries detrimental to England's interests.

[8] The act is entitled "For restraining and preventing several unwarrantable schemes and undertakings in His Majesty's colonies and plantations in America." The act states that all clauses of the Bubble Act "did do and shall extend to and are and shall be in force and carried into execution" in America.

[9] The colony of Massachusetts was an aggressive note issuer and, with the exception of 1732 and 1739, issued bills every year between 1702 and 1741 inclusive. There was also a large inflow from Rhode Island, often referred to as the most reprobate of the colonies for its lack of monetary restraint.

[10] The constitutionality of state banks was upheld in Briscoe v. Bank of Kentucky, 36 U.S.(11 Pet.) 257 (1837). The Supreme Court ruled that state banks could issue notes, even when stock in the state bank was held by the state.

[11] With the two notable exceptions of the First and Second Banks of the United States, each of which was chartered by Congress, charter regulation was essentially a system under the control of the individual states. However, Congress also sanctioned the Bank of Pennsylvania in 1780 which was established to furnish supplies for the Continental armies and ceased operations in 1784. In 1781, Congress approved a charter for the Bank of North America although there was doubt concerning Congressional legal authority to grant a corporate charter since the power to incorporate was universally accepted as an implied and exclusive right of the individual state legislatures. Consequently, the bank also obtained charters from the states of Delaware, Massachusetts, New York and Pennsylvania.

[12] For an excellent discussion of this controversy see Anna J. Schwartz, "The Beginning of Competitive Banking in Philadelphia, 1782-1809" [38], pp. 417-432.

[13] From "On Banks" an article written anonymously in the *Gazette of the United States,* March 10, 1792, as quoted in Schwartz [38].

[14] Bray Hammond, **Banks and Politics in America** [19], p. 67.

[15] These restraining acts also gave birth to the unregulated financial sector because they did not prohibit other incorporated and unincorporated businesses outside the field of banking, such as canal companies and water companies, from going into debt by issuing notes. These notes often were accepted as money.

[16] One historian described the chartering process in New York:

> The evidence . . . afforded a most disgusting picture of the members of the legislature . . . and indeed of the degradation of human nature itself. The attempt to corrupt, and in fact, corruption itself, was not confined to any one party. It extended to individuals of all parties.

Jabez Hammond, **History of Political Parties in New York.** Albany, 1843, I, p. 337 as quoted in Hammond, "Free Banks and Corporations: The New York Free Banking Act of 1838" [18], p. 190.

[17] There are no clauses in the Constitution pertaining to banking, per se. The monetary clauses of the Constitution are:

> Article 1, section 8 which gives Congress the power
>
> "To regulate Commerce with foreign Nations, and among the several States, and with the Indian Tribes; To establish an uniform Rule of Naturalization, and uniform Laws on the subject of Bankruptcies throughout the United States; To coin Money, regulate the Value thereof, and of foreign Coin, and fix the Standard of Weights and Measures. . . ."
>
> Article 1, section 10 which restrains state activities to the extent that
>
> "No State shall enter into any Treaty, Alliance, or Confederation; grant Letters of Marque and Reprisal; coin Money; emit Bills of Credit; make any Thing but gold and silver Coin a Tender in Payment of Debts; pass any Bill of Attainder, ex post facto Law, or Law impairing the Obligation of Contracts, or grant any Title of Nobility."
>
> Article 1, section 8, clause 18 which concluded the specific grants of power by granting Congress the power
>
> "To make all Loans which shall be necessary and proper for carrying into Execution the foregoing Process, and all other processes vested by this Constitution in the Government of the United States or any Department or Officer thereof."

[18] Richard H. Timberlake, Jr. **The Origins of Central Banking in the United States** [43], p. 10.

[19] The Second Bank of the United States did not always impose restraint on state bank note issues. Initially the bank's policy was expansive in order to appease state banks and encourage them to redeem their notes in specie. The Second Bank agreed to exchange its own notes for a large sum of state bank notes, to hold these state bank notes in its vault and to accommodate state currency needs during financial crises. It was not until the latter part of the decade that the Second Bank began to redeem state bank notes on a large scale. See Murray N. Rothbard, **The Panic of 1819: Reactions and Policies** [37].

[20] Hammond, **Banks and Politics** [17], p. 324. See also Timberlake, **The Origins of Central Banking** [43], chaps. 3 and 4, for a discussion of the role of the Second Bank of the United States.

[21] Prohibition was not uncommon. Arkansas, California, Iowa, Oregon and Texas all prohibited banking for various periods.

[22] New York State Senate Journal, 1825, as quoted in Robert E Chadduck, **The Safety Fund Banking System in New York 1829-1866** [4], p. 371.

[23] Report of the committee on banks and insurance companies on petitions. Albany, 1826. As quoted in Chadduck [4], p. 372.

[24] For a discussion of the current controversy see Eugenie D. Short and Gerald P. O'Driscoll, Jr., "Deregulation and Deposit Insurance" [39], pp. 11-23.

[25] An anonymous pamphleteer, as quoted in Fritz Redlich, **The Molding of American Banking, Men and Ideas** [31], vol. 1, p. 93.

[26] Michigan passed the first free bank act in 1837.

[27] As early as 1811 small manufacturing firms were permitted to incorporate without special legislative sanction. Toward the latter part of the period of charter regulation, legislation was passed to charter a specified number of banks, but there were no laws permitting general incorporation of banks until free banking.

[28] As quoted in Knox [23], p. 318.

[29] As quoted in Hugh Rockoff, **The Free Banking Era: A Re-Examination** [34], p. 22.

[30] The remainder of this section is based on the following: Rockoff [34]; Arthur J. Rolnick and Warren E. Webber, "New Evidence on the Free Banking Era [35], and "The Causes of Free Bank Failures; A Detailed Examination" [36].

[31] "Essays on the Currency on Which is Proposed the Enactment by Congress of a General Bank Law" Boston, 1834, quoted in Leonard C. Helderman, **National and State Banks** [20].

[32] Buffalo Historical Society Publications, X, pp. 282-283, quoted in Helderman [20].

[33] **Report of the Secretary of the Treasury on the State of the Finances for the Year Ending June 30, 1861** [32], p. 19.

[34] Ibid., p. 19.

[35] Ibid.

[36] Ibid., p. 17.

[37] The original national banking law was approved on February 25, 1863 and was entitled "An act to provide a national currency, secured by a pledge of United States stocks, and to provide for the circulation and redemption thereof." This law was repealed and a revised version was enacted July 3, 1864. On June 10, 1874 Congress declared that the act "shall hereafter be known as the National Bank Act."

[38] For an excellent discussion of the rationales and functions of reserve requirements, see Marvin Goodfriend and Monica Hargraves, "A Historical Assessment of the Rationales and Functions of Reserve Requirements" [16].

[39] This concept of the proper functions of banking, widespread in the 19th century, is frequently referred to as the "banking principle" and was derived from the "real bills" doctrine. The "banking principle" and other 19th century banking theories are discussed in Loyd W. Mints, **A History of Banking Theory** [25].

[40] Ross M. Robertson, **The Comptroller and Bank Supervision** [33], pp. 57-69.

[41] An act to amend an act entitled "An act to provide internal revenue to support the Government, to pay interest on the public debt, and for other purposes," approved June 13, 1864.

[42] As quoted in Walter Wyatt, "Constitutionality of Legislation Providing for a Unified Commercial Banking System" [57], p. 244.

[43] 75 U.S.(8 Wall) 533.

[44] Wyatt [57], pp. 245-246.

[45] Gerald T. Dunne, **Monetary Decisions of the Supreme Court** [8], p. 50.

[46] Friedman and Schwartz note that this view of inelasticity was due partly to a failure to recognize fully the significance of deposits as money, and partly "[to] a particular manifestation of the ubiquitous 'real bills' doctrine." Milton Friedman and Anna Jacobson Schwartz, **A Monetary History of the United States 1867-1960** [13], p. 169.

[47] In order to increase its note circulation, a national bank required time to (1) purchase the government bonds that serve as security, (2) transfer the bonds to the United States Treasurer, (3) notify the Comptroller to forward the notes and (4) transport the notes.

[48] Theodore Gilman, **A Graded Banking System** [14].

[49] R. H. Timberlake, Jr., "The Central Banking Role of Clearing-House Associations" [42], p. 4.

[50] Redlich [31], part II, p. 158.

[51] The utility of clearinghouse issues was recognized by many of its harshest critics. The major criticism of clearinghouse operations is that they were illegal because the federal government exercised an exclusive authority to issue money. For a discussion of this point, see Timberlake, "The Central Banking Role of Clearing-House Associations" [42], pp. 14-24.

[52] Robert Craig West, **Banking Reform and the Federal Reserve 1863-1923** [52], p. 51.

[53] As quoted in West, **Banking Reform** [52], p. 73.

[54] See Timberlake, **Origins of Central Banking** [43], p. 192. It was very important that any reform measure avoid the appearances of a central bank. A central bank was offensive to both those who feared large bank domination of the financial system and those who feared political control. In the words of a contemporary:

> No, there is no way possible to keep a central bank free from Wall St., without [it.] it couldn't be a success, again you can't keep it out of the hands of Monopolists and politics, . . .

M. Lauretson, president of the First State Bank of Tyler, Minnesota as quoted in Eugene N. White, **The Regulation and Reform of the American Banking System, 1900-1929** [54], p. 93.

[55] The striking similarity between the Aldrich Plan and the Federal Reserve Act is documented in Paul M. Warburg, **The Federal Reserve System, Its Origins and Growth** [48], pp. 178-406.

[56] The idea of the Board has been attributed to political expediency. (For details, see West [52], chaps. 5 and 6.) President Wilson is often credited with this suggestion. However, the idea probably originated with Professor J. Laurence Laughlin who recommended a central board in his reform proposal called "Plan D." See J. Laurence Laughlin, **The Federal Reserve Act: Its Origins and Problems** [24].

[57] Carter Glass denied that the Fed was a central bank after it had been in operation for almost a decade.

> "What are these regional banks?
> There is no mystery about them . . . they are banks of banks. They do not loan, can not loan, a dollar to any individual in the United States . . . but only to stockholding banks . . .
> At the head of these 12 regional banks we put a supervisory board. It is not a central bank."

Carter Glass. "Truth About the Federal Reserve System." Speech in the Senate of the United States, January 16-17, 1922 [15], p. 8.

[58] Timberlake, **Origins of Central Banking** [43], p. 194.

[59] H. H. Seldomridge, 60th Congress, 1st session, as quoted in Timberlake, **Origins of Central Banking** [43], p. 194.

[60] Carter Glass, as quoted in Timberlake, **Origins of Central Banking** [43], pp. 193-194.

[61] Frank Mondell, 60th Congress, 1st session, as quoted in Timberlake, **Origins of Central Banking** [43], p. 195.

[62] Horace M. Towner, 63rd Congress, 2nd session, as quoted in West, **Banking Reform** [52], p. 119.

[63] Paul M. Warburg, "Political Pressure and the Future of the Federal Reserve System" [49], p. 72.

[64] Federal Reserve Act, section 10. The legislative history of this passage gives little insight into its intent

because it was not debated in Congress. The provision appeared during the Senate discussion of the bill on one of the several new prints of the bill intended to incorporate minor changes. No one directly claimed authorship, although the Senate Committee chairman implied that it was suggested by the Treasury. Regardless of its intent, it contributed to the jurisdictional friction between the two federal agencies. For a discussion of this passage in the law, see A. D. Welton, "The Reserve Act in Its Implicit Meaning" [51], p. 57.

[65] Robertson [33], p. 107.

[66] Quoted in Robertson [33], p. 108.

[67] Congressional Record, 65 Congress, 3rd session, 1919.

[68] Warburg, "Political Pressure" [49], p. 72.

[69] Lauchlin B. Currie, "The Decline of the Commercial Loan" [5], and William N. Peach, **The Security Affiliates of National Banks** [27], chaps. 2 and 4.

[70] Raymond P. Kent, "Dual Banking Between the Two World Wars" in **Banking and Monetary Studies** [22], p. 45.

[71] The National Bank Act did not forbid branching by national banks. However, the Comptroller interpreted the law to preclude branching. See Robertson [33], pp. 57-69.

[72] See for example the **Annual Report**, Comptroller of the Currency, 1924.

[73] Peach [27], p. 20.

[74] Edwin J. Perkins, "The Divorcement of Commercial and Investment Banking: A History" [29], p. 500.

[75] See, for example: Friedman and Schwartz [13], chaps. 7 and 8 and Clark Warburton, **Depression, Inflation and Monetary Policy: Selected Papers, 1945-1953** [50], chaps. 14 and 15.

[76] After the panic of 1907, Kansas, Mississippi, Nebraska, North and South Dakota, Oklahoma, Texas and Washington passed laws establishing bank deposit guarantee systems.

[77] Susan Estabrook Kennedy, **The Banking Crises of 1933** [21], p. 216.

[78] See Goodfriend and Hargraves [16] on this point, especially pp. 13-16.

1. Burns, Helen M. *The American Banking Community and New Deal Banking Reforms 1933-1935.* Westport, Conn.: Greenwood Press, 1974.

2. Cagan, Phillip. "The First Fifty Years of the National Banking System—An Historical Appraisal." In *Banking and Monetary Studies.* Edited by Deane Carson. Homewood, Ill.: Richard D. Irwin, 1963.

3. Carosso, Vincent P. *Investment Banking in America: A History.* Cambridge: Harvard University Press, 1970.

4. Chadduck, Robert E. *The Safety Fund Banking System in New York 1829-1866.* Prepared for the National Monetary Commission, 1910; reprint ed., New York: Johnson Reprint Corporation, 1972.

5. Currie, Lauchlin B. "The Decline of the Commercial Loan." *Quarterly Journal of Economics* 45 (August 1931).

6. Davis, Joseph Stancliffe. *Essays in the Earlier History of American Corporations.* Cambridge: Harvard University Press, 1917; reprint ed., New York: Russell and Russell, 1965.

7. Dewey, Davis R. *Financial History of the United States.* New York: Augustus M. Kelley, 1968.

8. Dunne, Gerald T. *Monetary Decisions of the Supreme Court.* New Brunswick, N. J.: Rutgers University Press, 1960.

9. Eliason, A. D. *The Rise of Commercial Banking Institutions in the United States.* New York: Burt Franklin, 1970.

10. *Federal Reserve Act as Amended Through 1976.* Washington: Board of Governors of the Federal Reserve System, 1976.

11. "Federal Reserve Act of 1913." In *First Annual Report of the Federal Reserve Board 1914*, pp. 25-44. Washington: Board of Governors of the Federal Reserve System, 1915.

12. Federal Reserve Committee on Branch, Group, and Chain Banking. "The Dual Banking System in the United States." Prepared for the Federal Reserve System. Washington: Federal Reserve Board, n.d.

13. Friedman, Milton, and Schwartz, Anna Jacobson. *A Monetary History of the United States 1867-1960.* Princeton: Princeton University Press, 1963.

14. Gilman, Theodore. *A Graded Banking System.* Boston and New York: Houghton Mifflin, 1898.

15. Glass, Carter. "Truth About the Federal Reserve System." Speech in the Senate of the United States, January 16-17, 1922.

16. Goodfriend, Marvin, and Hargraves, Monica. "A Historical Assessment of the Rationales and Functions of Reserve Requirements." *Economic Review,* Federal Reserve Bank of Richmond (March/April 1983).

17. Hammond, Bray. *Banks and Politics in America.* Princeton: Princeton University Press, 1957.

18. ———. "Free Banks and Corporations: The New York Free Banking Act of 1838." *Journal of Political Economy* 44 (April 1936).

19. Hedges, Joseph Edward. *Commercial Banking and the Stock Market Before 1863.* Baltimore: Johns Hopkins Press, 1938.

20. Helderman, Leonard C. *National and State Banks,* n.d.

21. Kennedy, Susan Estabrook. *The Banking Crisis of 1933.* Lexington, Ky.: University Press of Kentucky, 1973.

22. Kent, Raymond P. "Dual Banking Between the Two World Wars." In *Banking and Monetary Studies.* Edited by Deane Carson. Homewood, Ill.: Richard D. Irwin, 1963.

23. Knox, John Jay. *A History of Banking in the United States.* New York: Bradford Rhodes and Company, 1900.

24. Laughlin, J. Laurence. *The Federal Reserve Act: Its Origins and Problems.* New York: The Macmillan Company, 1933.

25. Mints, Loyd W. *A History of Banking Theory.*

Chicago: University of Chicago Press, 1975.

26. *Original Acts Pertaining to National Banks in Chronological Order*, vol. 1. Washington: U. S. Comptroller of the Currency, n.d. (Processed.)

27. Peach, William N. *The Security Affiliates of National Banks*. Baltimore: Johns Hopkins Press, 1940.

28. Peltzman, Sam. "Toward a More General Theory of Economic Regulation." *Journal of Law and Economics* 19 (August 1976).

29. Perkins, Edwin J. "The Divorcement of Commercial and Investment Banking: A History." *The Banking Law Journal* 68 (June 1971).

30. Posner, Richard A. "Theories of Economic Regulation." *Bell Journal of Economics* 5 (Autumn 1974).

31. Redlich, Fritz. *The Molding of American Banking, Men and Ideas*. 2 vols. New York: Johnson Reprint Co., 1968.

32. *Report of the Secretary of the Treasury on the State of the Finances for the Year Ending June 30, 1861*. Washington: Government Printing Office, 1861.

33. Robertson, Ross M. *The Comptroller and Bank Supervision*. Washington: U. S. Comptroller of the Currency, 1968.

34. Rockoff, Hugh. *The Free Banking Era: A Re-Examination*. New York: Arno Press, 1975.

35. Rolnick, Arthur J., and Webber, Warren E. "New Evidence on the Free Banking Era." *American Economic Review*, 73 (December 1983).

36. ———. "The Causes of Free Bank Failures: A Detailed Examination." Federal Reserve Bank of Minneapolis, July 1983. (Mimeographed.)

37. Rothbard, Murray N. *The Panic of 1819: Reactions and Policies*. New York and London: Columbia University Press, 1962.

38. Schwartz, Anna J. "The Beginning of Competitive Banking in Philadelphia, 1782-1809." *The Journal of Political Economy* 55 (October 1947).

39. Short, Eugenie D., and O'Driscoll, Gerald P. Jr. "Deregulation and Deposit Insurance." *Economic Review*, Federal Reserve Bank of Dallas (September 1983).

40. Sprague, O. M. W. *History of Crises Under the National Banking System*. Prepared for the National Monetary Commission, 1910; reprint ed., New York: Augustus M. Kelley, 1968.

41. Stigler, George J. *The Citizen and the State: Essays on Regulation*. Chicago: University of Chicago Press, 1975.

42. Timberlake, Richard H., Jr. "The Central Banking Role of Clearing-House Associations," n.d. (Mimeographed.)

43. ———. *The Origins of Central Banking in the United States*. Cambridge: Harvard University Press, 1978.

44. U. S. Comptroller of the Currency. *Annual Report, December 1, 1924*. Washington: Government Printing Office, 1924.

45. U. S. Congress. House. *Amendments to Federal Reserve Act*. H.R. Report 1026 to Accompany S. 5236, 65th Cong., 3rd sess., 1919.

46. ———. *Changes in the Banking and Currency System of the United States*. H.R. Report 69 to Accompany H.R. 7837, 63rd Cong., 1st sess., 1913.

47. U. S. National Monetary Commission. "Report of the National Monetary Commission," "Suggested Plan for Monetary Legislation," and "Suggested Plan for Monetary Legislation—Revised Edition." In *Publications of the National Monetary Commission*, vol. I. Washington: U. S. Government Printing Office, 1912.

48. Warburg, Paul M. *The Federal Reserve System, Its Origins and Growth*, vol. 1. New York: The Macmillan Company, 1930.

49. ———. "Political Pressure and the Future of the Federal Reserve System." In *The Federal Reserve System—Its Purposes and Work*. The American Academy of Political and Social Science Annals 99 (January 1922).

50. Warburton, Clark. *Depression, Inflation and Monetary Policy: Selected Papers, 1945-1953*. Baltimore: Johns Hopkins Press, 1966.

51. Welton, A. D. "The Reserve Act in Its Implicit Meaning." In *The Federal Reserve System—Its Purposes and Work*. The American Academy of Political and Social Science Annals 99 (January 1922).

52. West, Robert Craig. *Banking Reform and the Federal Reserve 1863-1923*. Ithaca: Cornell University Press, 1977.

53. ———. "Bank Regulation in the United States from the Colonial Period to the Present." Federal Reserve Bank of Kansas City, n.d. (Mimeographed.)

54. White, Eugene N. *The Regulation and Reform of the American Banking System, 1900-1929*. Princeton: Princeton University Press, 1983.

55. White, Horace. *Money and Banking*. Boston: Ginn and Company, 1935.

56. Willis, Henry Parker. *The Federal Reserve System*. New York: The Ronald Press Company, 1923.

57. Wyatt, Walter. "Constitutionality of Legislation Providing for a Unified Commercial Banking System for the United States." *Nineteenth Annual Report of the Federal Reserve Board, 1932*. Washington: Government Printing Office, 1933.

The views expressed in this article are those of the author and do not necessarily reflect the opinions of the Federal Reserve Bank of Richmond or the Board of Governors of the Federal Reserve System.

Part II: THEORY

7. The Banking Business: Fundamentals
Barry N. Siegel

What role do commercial banks play in the economy? What is the connection between bank lending and the "creation" of bank money? Perhaps the easiest way to answer these questions is to imagine the steps involved in setting up a new commercial bank. —G.S., Ed.

****

A commercial bank is a firm (usually a corporation chartered by a state or the federal government) whose business it is to receive demand deposits and pay customers' checks drawn upon them, to receive time deposits and pay interest upon them, to make loans to business and consumer borrowers, to invest in government and privately issued securities, to collect checks for customers' credit transactions, to certify depositors' checks, and to issue cashiers' checks.

Many commercial banks do more. Some issue credit cards, manage payrolls for business customers, pay bills for household customers, underwrite security issues, operate trust departments for investments of wealthy individuals, buy and sell foreign currencies, and so forth. In short, many banks are so-called "department stores of finance."

Most of these activities are not peculiar to commercial banking. Other financial institutions also engage in them. But commercial banks are peculiar in the degree to which they specialize in the acceptance and creation of demand deposits. No other financial institution has such a large proportion of its deposits subject to withdrawal or transfer immediately upon receipt of an order by a customer. That being so, commercial bank deposits serve as media of exchange to a far greater extent than do the deposit liabilities of any other financial intermediary.

The demand deposit function of commercial banks has long made them a special object of control and regulation by the monetary authorities. Banks must keep reserves as dictated by the authorities and submit to a variety of regulations designed to make them sound financial institutions. Few other industries are so thoroughly regulated.

The monetary nature of demand deposits makes commercial banks a favorite object of study by monetary economists. These economists believe that interactions between the supply and demand for money are a major source of variations in prices, production, and employment in modern industrial economies. For that reason, they must study the business of commercial banking. The information gleaned helps them understand the forces that underlie fluctuations in the economy at large.

4.1
Commercial banks as firms

The term "commercial banks" arises from the ideas of nineteenth century theorists. These theorists believed that banks should confine their leading to short-term loans for commercial purposes, such as loans to farmers to harvest their crops and inventory loans to merchants and manufacturers.

They believed loans of this sort to be self-liquidating because the goods pledged as collateral[1] against them would, upon sale in the near future, make money available to repay the loans. This doctrine, variously identified as the *commercial loan theory* or the *real bills doctrine*, was popular in both the United States and in Great Britain.

The doctrine made sense in at least one respect: Because demand deposits are a major source of funds to the individual bank, and because these deposits are subject to immediate loss on written order of a customer who wishes to withdraw money or to write a check payable to someone not a depositor in the bank, the individual bank must maintain a *liquid position*. A bank has a liquid position if it has at its disposal cash, or ready access to cash, sufficient to meet unexpected demands by depositors. If a bank makes long-term loans, it freezes its assets in a form that reduces its liquid position. Short-term loans, properly staggered, usually assure a bank that each day or week a number of loans will be repaid, making funds available in the event demand depositors should impose an extraordinary drain upon its resources.

Banks no longer adhere rigorously to the commercial loan theory. They now lend to consumers, make long-term loans, and offer business loans unsecured by inventories or other forms of collateral. Even so, the concept embodied in the term "commercial banks" reminds us of the special problems faced by an institution having a principal liability subject to payment on demand. These problems explain a good deal of the behavior of commercial bankers.

4.1.1
Balance sheets

A step-by-step description of the setting up and operation of a bank is the best way to describe its peculiarities as a business institution. For this purpose, we must first discuss an essential tool of the monetary economist's trade—the balance sheet.

The financial position of an economic unit is described by the money values of its assets, liabilities, and net worth. Assets are the things the unit owns. Liabilities are its debts. The net worth of the unit is calculated by subtracting its liabilities from its assets. Because liabilities represent outside claims on assets, net worth stands for the unit's residual claims on its assets. If it were to liquidate assets and pay off its debtors, it would be left with cash equal to its net worth.

These considerations allow us to put a unit's assets, liabilities, and net worth into an algebraic identity:

$$\text{assets } (A) = \text{liabilities } (L) + \text{net worth } (NW)$$

This identity is also described by a balance sheet, such as the one given here for a hypothetical family:

Jones Family Financial Position
(Dec. 31, 1978)

A		L + NW	
Cash	$ 1,000	Mortgage	$ 40,000
Stocks and bonds	10,000	Other debts	2,000
House	50,000	Net worth	41,000
Furniture	15,000		
Car	5,000		
Clothing, etc.	2,000		
Total	$ 83,000	Total	$ 83,000

Several properties of the balance sheet are worth emphasizing:

1. All items are recorded as of a given date.
2. Total assets must always equal the sum of liabilities and net worth. This property arises from the description of net worth as the economic unit's residual claims on its assets.
3. Use of one asset to purchase another changes the _composition of assets_, but leaves the _total value_ of assets and _net worth unchanged_. Thus, the net worth and total assets of the Jones family would be unchanged if it used $500 of its cash to buy a dining room table.
4. Assets purchased on credit increase assets and liabilities equally, leaving net worth unchanged.
5. Use of an asset to pay off debt reduces assets and liabilities equally, leaving net worth unchanged.
6. An increase in net worth can occur in four ways: (a) saving, (b) endowment, (c) capital gains, and (d) stealing. Saving occurs when an economic unit decides to use a portion of its income to purchase an asset or to reduce its debts. An endowment is a gift from some other unit. A capital gain is an increase in the market value of the assets held by the unit. An example would be an increase in the market value of the Jones family home. Stealing speaks for itself.
7. A decrease in net worth can also occur in four ways: (a) consumption, (b) gifts, (c) capital losses, and (d) theft losses. Consumption represents the deterioration or depletion of assets. Unless an economic unit replaces consumption with fresh saving, its net worth will decline. Decreases in net worth by way of gifts of assets to outside units, by way of reductions in market value of assets, or by way of losses through theft are self-explanatory.

An important implication of these principles is that no single item on a balance sheet can change without alteration of another. Using the balance sheet to record changes in the economic status of a unit requires a _double entry accounting system_. Changes in any asset category must be accompanied by an opposite change in another asset category or an equal change in liabilities or in net worth. The same is true of changes in terms on the right side of the balance sheet. This property of balance sheet accounting helps to make it an important tool for analyzing the effects of the actions of banks and of the monetary authorities.

4.1.2
Setting up a bank

To go into the banking business, it is necessary to form a corporation, to obtain sufficient capital, and to acquire a charter.

Banks need capital to purchase buildings, equipment, and supplies and to invest in earning assets. They also need capital as a cushion to pay off their creditors should the need arise. A bank acquires capital by selling shares and by accumulating a surplus in excess of those shares—first, by charging share holders a premium for their purchases of capital stock and, second, by retaining profits not distributed to share holders in the form of dividends. In an accounting sense, the capital recorded on a bank's balance sheet is its net worth.

Banks obtain charters from state banking supervisors or from the Comptroller of the Currency, an official of the U.S. Treasury with the responsibility of administering national banks under the National Banking Act of 1863. A bank can apply for a charter under either kind of authority, but it cannot get a charter from both. At the end of 1979, there were about 4,600 national banks and more than 10,000 state banks chartered by 50 different state banking departments.

A bank cannot acquire a charter without satisfying minimum capital requirements laid down by the chartering authorities. The requirements differ between the authorities, but in general they depend upon the size of the community in which the bank wishes to operate. In all cases, the authorities require capital to be fully paid in cash before permitting a bank to open its doors for business.

Now, let us trace through the opening of a new bank and watch its progress as it develops its operations. After obtaining a charter and selling $5 million worth of stock, the bank's balance sheet would look like this:

A		$L+NW$	
Cash	$5,000,000	Capital stock and surplus	$5,000,000

One of the bank's decisions may be to join the Federal Reserve System. If it has a federal charter, it must belong to the System. If it has a state charter, it has a choice. If our bank joins, it becomes a *member bank* of the System. Before passage of the 1980 Monetary Control Act, only member banks had to satisfy the reserve requirements and other regulations of the System. Privileges of membership included the ability to borrow from the local Federal Reserve bank and use of the System's check clearing and wire facilities. Now, all banks are subject to reserve requirement regulations of the Fed and have privileges similar to those of members.

The initial steps in opening a bank include the purchase of a building, equipment, and supplies; investing a portion of its cash in earning assets; and, in preparation for conducting its deposit business, placing a portion of its cash on reserve at the regional Federal Reserve bank. Each of these acts affects the bank's balance sheet on the asset side.

To show the changes prior to displaying the revised balance sheet we employ what is known in the trade as a T-account. The T-account is a record of the financial transactions of a bank. Information recorded on the T-account is posted on the balance sheet in order to show how the transactions have transformed the composition of the bank's assets, liabilities, and net worth.

Suppose the bank puts $1 million into a building and supplies. The T-account would record this act as follows:

A		$L+NW$
Cash	−$1,000,000	
Buildings and supplies	+$1,000,000	

Next, record a $3 million investment in government bonds and a shift of $800 thousand of cash to the bank's deposit at the Fed:

A		L+NW
Cash	−$3,800,000	
Deposit at Fed	+$ 800,000	
Government bonds	+$3,000,000	

Notice that all of the changes are recorded on the asset side of the balance sheet. The net worth of the bank is as yet untouched—its ownership position remains intact. Even so, the new balance sheet has a decidedly different look. It now shows the bank as a going concern, ready for business, and already earning interest for its stock holders:

A		L+NW	
Cash	$ 200,000	Capital	$5,000,000
Deposit at Fed	800,000		
Government bonds	3,000,000		
Buildings and supplies	1,000,000		
	$5,000,000		

4.1.3
Deposit and clearing operations

The next step is to attract demand deposits. Demand deposits expand a bank's power to lend or to invest in securities. Except for interest-bearing NOW accounts issued to individuals and nonprofit organizations, the law currently prohibits payment of interest on demand deposits. Thus, dollars a bank attracts and holds in the form of demand deposits contribute much to its profits. Although the contribution is diminished somewhat by the requirement, legal as well as self-imposed, to hold a fraction of deposits as reserves—vault cash (currency and coin in the vault or till) or deposits in the Fed—the lure of profits leads banks to desire large numbers of demand deposit customers.

Suppose our bank attracts $10 million of demand deposits. Most, if not all, such deposits would be in the form of checks the new customers have written on deposits in banks they are deserting. The initial entries in our bank's books would be:

A		L+NW	
Cash items in the process of collection	+$10,000,000	Demand deposits	+$10,000,000

Note, our bank does not yet have the additional cash. It must first *collect* the funds from the other banks. It usually does so by forwarding the checks drawn upon them to the local Federal Reserve bank. The Fed then adds $10 million to our bank's deposits and subtracts $10 million from the deposits of the other banks. The transactions look like this:

Our Bank

A		L + NW
Cash items in the process of collection	−$10,000,000	
Deposits at Fed	+$10,000,000	

Other Banks

A		L + NW	
Deposits at Fed	−$10,000,000	Demand deposits	−$10,000,000

Federal Reserve Bank

A	L + NW	
	Deposits of our bank	+$10,000,000
	Deposits of other banks	−$10,000,000

The check clearing system provided by the Fed is a major convenience. Before the advent of the Federal Reserve System, banks leaned heavily upon clearing house systems of their own. Even today there are a number of such clearing houses located in various cities. Banks daily receive checks drawn upon other banks, and the other banks receive checks drawn upon them. By establishing and working through clearing houses, banks avoid the need to present checks directly to the individual banks upon which they have been drawn. Instead, they send the checks to their clearing houses and receive credit for their total value.

For each bank, the clearing house figures out the balance of payments. When checks drawn against a bank exceed in value the checks it receives, the clearing house requests payment from the bank. When checks a bank receives and presents to the clearing house exceed the value of the ones drawn against it, it gets paid by the clearing house. At the end of each day, after all the smoke has cleared, each bank will have either increased or decreased its position with the clearing house; as a result, it will have either gained or lost cash assets. Taking all banks together, the *net* payments into and out of the clearing house must total zero, because the sums received by banks having positive clearings must match the sums paid out by banks having negative clearings.

The Federal Reserve System is the major clearing house for member banks. Nonmember banks occasionally keep deposits in the Fed for clearing purposes, but they mainly work through larger *correspondent banks*.[2] Correspondent banks are usually members of the Federal Reserve System. State banking laws frequently permit state chartered banks to count deposits in other banks as part of their required reserves. These deposits, in turn, are sought by correspondent banks because they increase their lending power. In return, the correspondent banks use their connections with the Fed to collect and disburse moneys for the nonmember banks.

The Federal Reserve System's clearing facilities are especially useful for banks collecting and disbursing funds to and from different parts of the country. There are 12 Federal Reserve districts, each with its own Federal Reserve bank. There is also an Inter-District Settlement Fund. After receiving checks drawn on banks in other districts, a bank sends them to its own district Federal Reserve bank, receiving in return a credit to its Federal Reserve deposit. The district Federal Reserve bank then sends the check through the Inter-District Settlement Fund for clearing. When a district Federal Reserve bank receives more checks than it sends, its balance at the Fund increases. When clearings go against it, its balance declines.

4.1.4
Bank reserves and reserve requirements

After accepting the $10 million of demand deposits and placing the new cash in its account at the Fed, our bank's balance sheet looks like this:

A		L + NW	
Reserves*	$11,000,000	Demand deposits	$10,000,000
Government bonds	3,000,000	Capital	5,000,000
Buildings and supplies	1,000,000		
	$15,000,000		$15,000,000

*Reserves are cash assets—vault cash plus deposits at the Fed.

Note that "vault cash and deposits at the Fed" have been replaced with the more generic term, "reserves." Banks keep reserves for several purposes. The first is to pay out currency and coin to demand deposit customers who wish to cash checks. If vault cash runs out, banks simply ask the Fed for more, in which case their deposits with the Fed are reduced by an equal amount. The second use of reserves is to make payments to other banks that have received checks drawn upon them by their depositors. Reserves in the form of deposits at the Fed are best for this purpose.

Finally, banks *must* keep some reserves to satisfy requirements laid down by the Federal Reserve System. Required reserves for national banks were first instituted by the National Bank Act of 1863. The concept was carried over to the Federal Reserve Act of 1913, which applied reserve requirements to all member banks, including state member banks as well as national banks. The Banking Act of 1935 gave the Federal Reserve Board power to vary the reserve requirements over a substantial range. Before the 1980 Monetary Control Act, the law permitted the Fed to establish reserve requirements within the following limits for individual banks:

Between 3 and 10 percent of savings and time deposits.

Between 7 and 14 percent of net demand deposits of banks with deposits up to $400 million.

Between 10 and 22 percent of net demand deposits[3] of so-called reserve city banks—banks having $400 million or more in deposits. (Reserve city banks used to be defined as banks located in cities having reserve banks or branches.)

The 1980 Monetary Control Act has changed all this. It set an initial reserve requirement of 3 percent against transaction deposits (demand deposits, NOW accounts, ATS accounts, etc.) of $25 million or less in all depository institutions (banks and thrift institutions, members and nonmembers of the Fed). For transactions accounts exceeding $25 million, it set an initial reserve requirement of 12 percent, but authorized the Federal Reserve Board to change it within a range of 8 to 14 percent. As of December 31, 1981, the Board was required to raise the $25 million break-point for transactions balances of individual banks by 80 percent of the percentage increase in total transactions balances of all depository institutions.

The 1980 law also spoke to reserve requirements on *nonpersonal* time deposits. Each depository institution is required to maintain between 0 and 9 percent reserves against such deposits, as determined by the Fed.

The law provided for an eight-year phase-in of reserve requirements for nonmember depository institutions. It also permitted nonmember banks to hold deposits in correspondent banks that are members of the Fed, provided that the correspondents pass through the reserves to the Fed. Nonbank depository institutions may keep reserves at correspondent institutions holding deposits at the Federal Home Loan Bank Board (S & Ls) or the National Credit Union Central Liquid Facility (credit unions), provided, again, that the reserves are passed through to the Fed. As under the old law, vault cash is an acceptable form of reserves.[4]

An interesting implication of the law is that it cuts across reserve requirements in nonmember state banks. These requirements, which differ from state to state, were put in place in order to assure depositors of the liquidity of the institutions they do business with. Accordingly, state imposed required reserves need not take the form of cash. Instead, many states permit reserves to be held in the form of deposits at correspondent banks (not necessarily passed through to the Fed) and short-term securities, such as U.S. Treasury bills.

Required reserves for banks and thrifts do not increase their liquidity. They are there for a different purpose—monetary control. The Fed attempts to limit the total reserves available to the banking system. The reserve requirements of banks limit the total volume of deposits they can have with their available reserves. Thus, using its powers to manipulate both available reserves and reserve requirements, the Fed influences the size of the deposit portion of the money supply.

4.1.5
Bank lending and deposit creation

When a bank's total reserves exceed its required reserves, it has *excess reserves*. Assume that the Fed's reserve requirement policies lead our hypothetical bank to have a 15 percent average reserve requirement against its demand deposits. This requirement, plus its $10 million of demand deposits, implies a required reserve total of $1.5 million. The bank's total reserves are $11 million; its excess reserves are, therefore, $9.5 million.

This large sum of money is available for a variety of uses. The bank could keep it idle, but that would not be very smart. To be sure, the bank loses some of its reserves every day from cash withdrawals and from checks drawn on its deposits and placed with other banks. But it also gains reserves from cash deposits and from checks drawn on other banks that have come into the possession of its deposit customers. On most days, the bank will lose a little and gain a little. If its average cash holdings are large in relation to its probable net deposit losses, its excess reserves are too large. The bank should, therefore, exchange its surplus reserves for income producing loans and securities. In that way, it can increase its profits.

If our bank lends $9 million of its $9.5 million in excess reserves, its T-account will show the transactions as follows:

A		$L + NW$	
Loans	+$9,000,000	Demand deposits	+$9,000,000

Pay close attention to the way the bank makes its loans. It does not, as would you or I, lend money by reducing its cash assets. *Instead, it simply creates $9 million in new demand deposits.* It does so by crediting the deposit accounts of the borrowers with the new money. In exchange, it receives promissory notes totaling $9 million. In effect, the new deposits it creates are backed by its loan customers' promises to pay. Economists refer to this process as one that *monetizes debt*.

Individual bankers frequently deny that their loan operations monetize debt. From their point of view, they are simply lending money they have received from depositors, or money they have borrowed. They believe they are simply lending the excess reserves generated by such transactions.

But, from the point of view of the whole banking system, every dollar of excess reserves creates an opportunity for banks to expand the total deposits of the system. And any expansion in total deposits represents an increase in the money supply as it is defined by economists and the monetary authorities.

Thus, the $9 million of loan-backed new deposits credited to the deposit accounts of our bank's borrowers is available for their spending. The $10 million of deposits already in the bank is similarly available for spending, since nothing has happened to reduce their amount. The logic is inescapable: By making loans equal to $9 million, our bank has increased the deposit portion of the money supply by an equal amount.

Unless and until the bank reduces its loans, the money supply will continue to be $9 million larger than before.

When borrowers spend the new deposits, the checks drawn on them frequently fall into the hands of other banks. The other banks present the checks to their clearing houses or to the Federal Reserve banks for clearing. If our bank loses $9 million in reserves in this manner, its T-account and that of other banks will read as follows:

Our Bank

A		L+NW	
Reserves	−$9,000,000	Demand deposits	−$9,000,000

Other Banks

A		L+NW	
Reserves	+$9,000,000	Demand deposits	+$9,000,000

Notice, the $9 million of new deposits did not disappear when they were spent. Instead, they appeared at other banks. This confirms the conclusion that banks increase the deposit portion of the money supply when they use excess reserves to increase loans.

At times, bank loans may also increase the currency portion of the money supply. Recall that the money supply is defined as currency and deposits *owned by the nonbank public*. Bank reserves, including vault cash, are not part of the money supply. But, if borrowers decide to take payment on their loans in cash rather than in deposits, the bank's reserves are automatically transformed into money, as the term is officially defined.

As an example of this transformation, assume that our bank lends $500 thousand to a group of borrowers who demand cash, not deposits, in return for the promissory notes they give to the bank. The bank's T-account, and that of the nonbank public (of which the borrowers are a part), would record the transactions as follows:

Our Bank

A		L+NW
Reserves	−$500,000	
Loans	+$500,000	

Nonbank Public

A		L+NW	
Currency	+$500,000	Bank debt	+$500,000

After making its loans, losing the deposits it created to other banks, and losing currency to the nonbank public, our bank's balance sheet looks like this:

	A		L+NW
Reserves	$1,500,000	Demand deposits	$10,000,000
Loans	9,500,000	Capital	5,000,000
Government bonds	3,000,000		
Buildings and supplies	1,000,000		
	$15,000,000		$15,000,000

The bank has just enough reserves to meet the 15 percent reserve requirement laid down by the Fed. This is no accident. Had it lent out more than the original $9.5 million in excess reserves, it would have run the risk of losing more than $9.5 million to other banks and to customers demanding cash. In that event, its reserves would have fallen below $1.5 million, which would have been insufficient to meet the 15 percent reserve requirement against its original $10 million of deposits. Such a failure would have forced it to reduce loans or to borrow in order to restore its reserves to the required level. Otherwise, it would have faced a fine by the Fed.

A bank attempts to protect itself against reserve deficiencies by confining its lending and investing to an amount equal to or less than its excess reserves. Its deposits come to it in two forms. The first are *primary deposits*, which come into being when customers place currency or checks written on other banks into their deposit accounts. The second are *derivative deposits*, which are the demand deposits the bank itself creates in its loan and securities investment activities. Primary deposits are relatively stable, because regular demand deposit customers are continually adding to, as well as drawing down, their deposits. The reserves needed to meet requirements against primary deposits are, therefore, relatively predictable, and the excess reserves they generate can be lent out with little fear.

Derivative deposits are another matter. Borrowers rarely wish to keep them idle. Instead, they generally use them immediately to make payments to their suppliers or creditors. In that event, the bank is likely to lose all or most of these deposits (including the excess reserves upon which they are based) to other banks. When the bank lends more than its excess reserves, it runs the risk of creating a reserve deficiency. In that event, it will be penalized by the Fed, be forced to reduce its loans and investments, or be forced to borrow.

When a bank follows the rule of lending an amount equal to or less than its excess reserves, it can be fairly sure that its reserve losses will not dip deeply into its required reserves. That is because most of the deposits on its books at any moment are likely to be primary deposits. Derivative deposits created by recent loans will have mostly been checked away. So the rule of confining lending to excess reserves is the bank's major device for minimizing costs and embarrassments arising out of reserve deficiencies.

4.2
Time and savings deposits; borrowing and bank capital

The basic nature of the banking business is described by the material in the previous sections of this chapter. We now examine the business in more detail by looking at other sources of funds and the nature of bank assets. In this section, we shall study time and savings deposits, different sources of bank borrowing, and the structure of capital accounts. Section 4.3 deals with bank investments and bank loans. In studying both of these sections, keep in mind the total structure of bank assets and liabilities as illustrated in the following balance sheet, which is a condensed version of the composite balance of the U.S. commercial banking system.

U.S. Commercial Banks—Assets and Liabilities
June 30, 1978
(Billions of Dollars)

A		$L + NW$	
Currency and coin	12.0	Demand deposits	374.7
Reserves with Fed	29.6	Time deposits	365.0
Deposits in other banks	56.0	Savings deposits	226.0
Cash items in process of collection	69.3	Federal funds purchased and securites sold under repurchase agreements	93.2
Securities held	262.3	Other liabilities	54.8
Federal funds sold and securities bought under resale agreements	48.6	Bankers' acceptances outstanding	17.1
Other loans (net)	650.2	Capital	83.7
Other assets	86.5		
Total	1,214.5	Total	1,214.5

Source: Federal Reserve Bulletin, Vol. 65, No. 2, February 1979, A 18. Figures here are summaries of much greater detail in original; hence, they contain small rounding errors.

4.2.1
Bank time and savings deposits

Although demand deposits are a major source of bank funds, time and savings deposits are even more so. On June 30, 1978, for example, time and savings deposits in commercial banks in the U.S. were $591 billion as compared to $375 billion of demand deposits.

Savings and time deposits, as noted in Chapter 2, come in various forms. Savings, or passbook accounts mostly belong to individuals, although a change in regulations in 1975 authorized commercial banks to make them available to business firms in amounts up to $150 thousand per customer per bank. Deposits and withdrawals of savings in this form can be made at any time, although banks may technically require 30 days notice prior to withdrawal. The automatic transfer of savings to checking account service (ATS), authorized by the Fed in 1978, substantially improved the liquidity of savings deposits—in effect, converting them into interest-bearing demand deposits.

Consumer-type time certificates of deposit have specified denominations and fixed terms to maturity at fixed interest rates. Most mature within four years, though regulations now permit banks to issue consumer time certificates with much longer maturities. Savings and loan associations issue similar certificates of deposit. All are subject to stiff interest penalties if redeemed before maturity.

Large certificates of deposit—frequently called CDs—have minimum denominations of $25 thousand, but are usually issued in denominations of $1 million. Although these deposits have fixed terms to maturity, ranging from 1 to 18 months, most of the large CDs issued are negotiable—they can be sold to third parties. There is a very lively CD market, and large firms or wealthy individuals invest heavily in them when they have temporary surplus funds. Small investors have indirect access to CDs when they purchase shares in money market funds, which use pooled funds of small savers to purchase CDs and other large denomination short-term securities. A bank fixes its CD interest rate at the time it sells certificates to initial depositors. However, because the prices of CDs in the secondary market vary, the effective yield to secondary investors may differ from the yield original holders get when they hold them to maturity.

Payment of interest to holders of savings and time deposits makes them less profitable for banks than demand deposits. Even so, there are compensations. Reserve requirements against savings and time deposits are much less than the requirements against demand deposits. In addition, they turn over far less frequently, and to a large degree the turnover is predictable. That is because time certificates of deposit are dated, and customers cannot convert them to cash before redemption dates without incurring interest penalties. Passbook savings accounts are held by household and business customers because they do not plan to use the funds immediately, so it is to their advantage to hold the funds in an interest-earning form.

Payment of daily interest on passbook savings and the advent of ATS accounts have eroded some of the advantages to banks of savings deposits, but the prospect of putting such funds to profitable uses continues to make them attractive.

In 1933, Congress gave the Federal Reserve System power to set interest-rate ceilings on savings and time deposits. The Fed exercises this power under *Regulation Q*. In 1966, Congress extended the regulation to thrift institutions.

In recent years, Regulation Q has become an important instrument of monetary policy. In addition, it has become highly controversial, because it interferes with banks' freedom to manipulate deposit rates in order to attract and maintain savings deposits.[3] In times of rising interest rates on Treasury bills and other short-term market interest rates, people have tended to pull their money out of time and savings deposits in order to reinvest them in other securities. This process is frequently identified by economists with the awkward word, *disintermediation*.

To counter disintermediation, the Federal Reserve in 1978 authorized banks to issue six-month floating rate *money market certificates*. These certificates, which are issued in minimum denominations of $10,000, carry ceiling rates tied to the average interest paid by the U.S. Treasury at its weekly auction of six-month Treasury bills. Regulatory authorities also permit thrift institutions to issue such certificates.

Experience with money market certificates indicates that they are a mixed blessing to banks and other depository institutions. As might be expected, they were an instant hit with households. Their total mounted rapidly as interest rates rose in 1978 and the years that followed. Instead of buying Treasury bills and other short-term securities, savers bought the certificates. From zero in 1978, the amount outstanding in banks rose to over $90 billion by the end of 1979. Even more were issued by thrift institutions.

So disintermediation became less of a problem. Nonetheless, the high interest rates that emerged in those years created a severe earnings problem for banks and thrift institutions. Many loans on their books, particularly mortgage loans, had been made at lower interest rates. The escalating interest costs of money market certificates made many of these loans unprofitable. The inability of banks and thrifts to turn over the loans at higher interest rates severely reduced the overall profitability of their operations.

The T-account treatment of savings and time deposits is straightforward: Assuming the reserve requirement against such deposits averages 5 percent, a $1 million inflow of time deposits increases the excess reserves of a bank by $950 thousand. If the bank lends these reserves, and the derivative demand deposits thus created are checked away, we can show the results of the new time and savings inflow as follows:

A		L + NW	
Reserves	+$ 50,000	Time and savings deposits	+$1,000,000
Loans	+$950,000		

4.2.2
The discount window, federal funds, and other borrowed money

Although deposits are the main source of loanable funds for banks, they also borrow funds. A minor, but very important, source of borrowed funds is the Federal Reserve System. Banks with reserve deficiencies must somehow remove them in order to satisfy their local Federal Reserve banks. To aid banks in such embarrasing situations, every Federal Reserve bank maintains a "discount window"—a loan facility administered by a vice-president of the bank. Banks can use this facility to borrow on a short-term basis, during which time the Fed expects them to get their affairs in order.

The interest rate the Fed charges banks that borrow is called the *discount rate*. The discount rate is not a penalty rate, because it is usually lower than the interest rates banks get from their own loans and security investments. Even so, the Fed discourages continuous borrowing by member banks. If a bank overuses the discount window, it may get a warning letter from its local Federal Reserve bank, or even a refusal of a loan.

Banks also borrow in the *federal funds market*. The term "federal funds" has two meanings. The first refers to interbank lending of funds banks have on deposit with the Federal Reserve System. For many years, banks with reserve deficiencies have borrowed reserves owned by banks with excess reserves. That helps them to avoid trips to the Fed's discount window. Federal funds loans are typically made on an overnight basis in denominations of at least $1 million at an interest rate set in the federal funds market. Federal funds acquired by a bank are free of reserve requirements, so the total sum borrowed is available for use. Federal funds loans are effected by an order to the Fed from the lending bank to transfer immediately part of its reserve balance to the borrowing bank.

Many large banks almost continuously make loans and investments beyond their excess reserves and use steady borrowing of federal funds to make up resulting reserve deficiencies. These borrowings are made easy by the existence of a large number of banks that possess federal funds and that are in contact with brokers who act as intermediaries. Information on the price and availability of federal funds comes through telephone contact, and banks use the Fed's wire system to transfer reserves between lenders and borrowers in different districts.

Federal funds are immediately available funds that come to a bank without a reserve requirement. For that reason, the term has in recent years come to be applied to all such funds, even those not resulting from loan transfers of reserves between banks.

In addition to borrowing from other commercial banks, Federal Reserve regulations permit banks to borrow immediately available reserve free funds from federal agencies, savings and loan associations, mutual savings banks, domestic agencies and branches of foreign banks, and, to a limited extent, government security dealers.

Market terminology has recognized these regulations, and a federal funds loan has now taken on a second meaning—an overnight (and sometimes longer) loan, not just between two commercial banks, but also between two institutions from which banks may borrow free of required reserves. For example, a bank may borrow federal funds from a savings and loan association, and the latter may borrow federal funds from a security dealer. More important, a bank may also lend immediately available reserve funds to its correspondent bank. Traditionally, correspondent balances earned no interest, but now many small banks accumulate large balances with their correspondents and lend them the funds not needed for check clearing or other purposes. In such cases, banks do not use the Federal Reserve wire service to transfer reserve balances. Instead, bookkeeping entries by the lending and borrowing banks reflect the fact that a noninterest-bearing correspondent demand balance has been converted into a federal funds loan.

Another class of transactions generating immediately available funds for a commercial bank is the *repurchase agreement* (RP), sometimes referred to as a "repo" or "buy back." We discussed RPs in Section 2.1.3. An RP occurs when a bank sells a depositor, perhaps a nonfinancial corporation, a security it promises to repurchase the next day. The funds released by such a transaction are free of reserve requirements; hence they are very close to federal funds loans in the senses defined above.

None of the methods of borrowing discussed to this point requires a bank to hold reserves against the liability created by the loan. Even so, the methods vary in terms of their effects upon a bank's balance sheet. For example, a bank borrowing directly from its local Federal Reserve bank receives a credit to its reserve account equal to the size of the loan. Its liabilities and cash assets go up by an equal amount, and because no new deposits are created by the transaction, none of the new reserves contributes to an increase in required reserves—all are available to support the bank's loans and security investments.

A federal funds loan between banks transfers excess reserves from the lending to the borrowing bank. Like funds borrowed from the Fed, excess reserves borrowed from another bank are fully available for loans and investments. But a transfer of excess reserves between banks does not increase the total reserves of the banking system, as does a loan from the Fed to the bank. Instead, the existing reserves in the banking system are put to more intensive use. Thus, both types of loans lead to the same thing—an enlargement of the volume of bank credit and bank deposits of the whole banking system.

Funds borrowed by a bank from a nonbank financial intermediary, such as a savings and loan association, do not generate an equal amount of excess reserves. Suppose, for example, that an S&L has $1 million on deposit with a bank and that, because it does not plan to use the deposit until the next day, it makes a $1 million overnight loan to the bank. The transaction would look like this (assuming a 15 percent reserve requirement):

Bank

A		$L + NW$	
Required reserves	$-\$150,000$	S&L demand deposit	$-\$1,000,000$
Excess reserves	$+\$150,000$	Loan from S&L	$+\$1,000,000$

The transaction releases the reserves *required* against the S&L bank deposit, but it does not release an amount equal to the loan, as in the case of a federal funds loan between two banks.

Because a repurchase agreement is essentially an overnight loan between a depositor and a bank, the balance-sheet interpretation is similar to the one given the S&L loan—an RP also releases required reserves in an amount equal to a fraction of the reduction in demand deposits.

Two other sources of short-term funds for banks are Eurodollars (first discussed in Section 2.1.3) and holding companies.

Eurodollars are dollar-denominated deposits in foreign banks or in overseas subsidiaries of U.S. banks. These deposits obligate overseas banks to pay dollars to holders. When interest rates in Europe exceed rates in the United States, holders of deposits in U.S. domestic banks frequently switch their money abroad. As a result, the foreign banks acquire ownership of deposits in the domestic banks.

When domestic banks are short of reserves, they frequently borrow deposits from their overseas subsidiaries or from foreign-owned Eurodollar banks. Such loans cancel overseas bank deposits in the domestic banks and free required reserves for domestic bank loans.

In 1969, the Fed began to apply reserve requirements to bank borrowings from Eurodollar banks. Although these requirements were smaller than the ones levied against the demand deposits released by the loans, the regulation had the effect of reducing the volume of such borrowings.

Most large banks are owned by holding companies. Before the late 1960s holding companies were used by banks to bring a number of separately chartered banks within their own and other states into a single organization. In 1956 Congress passed the Bank Holding Company Act in order to curb the growth of bank holding companies—the motive was to prevent monopolization of the banking business through the device of holding companies.

But banks could still put themselves under *one-bank holding companies*. These companies engage in a variety of nonbank activities in addition to owning a single bank. In the inflationary environment of the late 1960s, the Fed was using Regulation Q to hold down time deposit interest rates in order to make it difficult for banks to sell CDs. A number of banks organized themselves under one-bank holding companies in order to open up another source of borrowed money. Holding companies are able to borrow money in the commercial paper market. By relending money borrowed in this fashion to their bank subsidiaries, holding companies help them to acquire reserve free funds not subject to Regulation Q. The Fed gave this end run the same treatment it gave bank borrowings in the Eurodollar market. In 1970 it required banks to hold reserves against funds channeled to them out of funds raised in the commercial paper market by their holding companies.

4.2.3
Bankers' acceptances

Another important liability item appearing on the balance sheets of a typical bank is the *banker's acceptance*. Acceptances are one of the oldest financial instruments connected with the banking business. They are jointly created by banks and their business customers, particularly when the latter are engaged in international transactions. A firm without immediate funds to pay for goods it wants to buy draws up an order for a commercial bank to pay. If the firm has good local credit standing, it may convince its bank to guarantee or "accept" the order to pay, in which case it becomes a banker's acceptance. With the bank substituting its own credit standing for that of its customer, the foreign seller of the goods is happy to receive payment in this form. The bank's guarantee allows it to sell the acceptance in the money market and to get its money immediately.

A bank rarely loses money on acceptances; moreover, they are a good source of income because they enable the bank to extract a fee for the service from its business customers. Also, in making its commitment the bank is not directly involving its own funds, which remain free for other loans. In periods of tight money, when funds are particularly difficult to acquire, banks are especially pleased to increase their acceptance business.

4.2.4
Capital accounts

Before we leave the right-hand side of the balance sheet, we should say a word about banks' capital accounts. The accounts consist of stock (par value), surplus, undivided profits, and special reserve accounts. Capital stock is created when a bank issues new stock. When the sales proceeds exceed the par value of the stock, surplus is created. Surplus also changes when the bank's directors vote to transfer funds into the account from undistributed profits instead of retaining them for subsequent distribution to stockholders in the form of dividends. The directors also transfer undistributed profits into a special reserve account to cover losses on bad loans and investments. This act does not involve a special transfer or segregation of funds, but is primarily a device to remove a portion of undivided profits from stockholders' claims to profits.

It is important to note that banks do not actually tuck away cash to match their capital accounts. Capital accounts are simply a measure of the bank's net worth or the claims of its owners to the assets the bank holds in all forms. If the bank wishes to pay off its stockholders, or to increase its dividends, it can draw upon any of its assets. That is, it can acquire the necessary funds by reducing cash, by selling securities, or by reducing loans.

Although all banks acquire their initial funds from capital stock, subsequent increases in loanable funds come mainly from expansion of deposits. Over the last 20 years, bank capital has averaged only about 7 percent of total sources of funds for the U.S. banking system.

4.3
Bank assets

The asset side of a bank's balance sheet also says much about the nature of its business. Generally speaking, assets break down into three major categories—cash, loans, and investments. Cash assets consist of vault cash, reserves with the Fed, balances with other banks, and cash items in the process of collection. Since we have already discussed these items, we shall not give them further attention here, except to say that cash is not the only thing a bank can use to make quick adjustments to a sudden onset of reserve losses. Sales of short-term securities, federal funds loans, and access to the Fed's discount window perform a similar function.

4.3.1
Investments

Bank investments consist of holdings of marketable notes and bonds, mostly U.S. government securities issued by the Treasury or by other U.S. government agencies, and obligations issued by state and local governments. In 1978, for example, U.S. banks held $138 billion of U.S. government Treasury and agency issues and $117 billion of state and local obligations. All other security holdings amounted to a mere $6 billion.

Why do banks invest so much in U.S. government securities? First, U.S. government securities are safe; unlike private securities, there is no default risk attached to them—the money creation and tax powers of the federal government guarantee payment of interest and repayment of principal. Second, there is a wide market for government securities, and banks in need of quick infusions of funds can get them from low-cost quick sales to any of a number of government bond dealers who, in turn, have access to a broad set of potential buyers. Third, banks must have collateral in the form of U.S. government bonds to hold against loans from the Fed and against government deposits, as required by law and regulations. Last, but not least, banks earn interest on their holdings of U.S. government securities.

Interest earnings, together with superior liquidity and safety, make U.S. government bonds a favorite vehicle for bank investments. Even so, banks that are not careful can still lose money on such investments. They must balance their portfolios between long- and short-term bonds. As discussed in Chapter 3, long-term bonds tend to fluctuate more in price in response to interest rate changes than do short-term bonds. A bank that overloads its portfolio with long-term bonds risks selling them at a loss during periods of financial tightness. It is precisely in such periods that interest rates shoot up and depositors start to withdraw their money in large sums.

Banks can, to some extent, avoid losses on long-term bonds by borrowing in the federal funds market, by issuing more CDs, or by borrowing from the Fed. Because these devices may, in some circumstances, be too expensive, it is good strategy for a bank to buy short-term Treasury securities. Although these securities frequently carry lower interest rates than do long-term bonds, their prices do not fluctuate much in response to changes in interest rates, which reduces the risk of capital losses on their sale.

To stay reasonably liquid, therefore, banks frequently hold short-term bonds in their investment portfolios. This practice is so common that bankers regard short-term investments as *secondary reserves*. The Fed does not recognize such reserves; but, from the point of view of the individual bank, price stability and a ready market make short-term U.S. government securities almost as good as the reserves the Fed does recognize.

Bank investments in state and local bonds are a major source of bank income. These investments are unusually attractive because interest income earned from them is exempt from federal taxes.

The tax incentive is powerful. Corporate income taxes go up to 46 percent of net income. A 6 percent state and local bond has a yield equivalent to an 11.1 percent taxable security for a bank in the 46 percent tax bracket.[6]

Despite their profitability, state and local securities do pose a problem for banks. The market for such securities is far more limited than is the market for U.S. government bonds. Moreover, the risk is often much higher. State and local governments frequently twist local bankers' arms to force them to buy local bond issues, particularly when national markets are not being receptive to their issues. A case in point is New York City, which in 1975 was on the verge of defaulting on its bonds. Several of the large banks in the city were for a time unable to collect on their holdings of the city's securities, and they were unable to sell them to anyone else. Although New York's financial problems continue, a solution of sorts has been worked out with a promise by the federal government to guarantee a portion of New York's debt. Even so, this case provides dramatic evidence that investments in state and local securities can be far more risky than many other types of investments.

Bank investments in nongovernment securities are minimal. Bank regulatory agencies do not favor such investments. In fact, the law does not permit banks to buy common stock as investments. Only their trust departments, which manage portfolios of nonbank customers, are permitted to buy common stock. Such investments do not appear on banks' balance sheets.

4.3.2
Bank loans

Over one half of all bank assets consist of loans to business and household customers. Loans are distinguishable from bond investments in two main ways. First, most loans are not negotiable instruments. As a result, they are less liquid than security investments, in the sense that they cannot be sold for cash in an active market.

A second distinction is that a loan is initiated by the borrower. A bank cannot drag a customer off the street and force him to borrow money. In contrast, a bank's security holdings are the result of its own initiatives. When it wants to buy a bond, it simply places an order through an appropriate broker or dealer. The importance of this distinction is that banks need not wait for borrowers to request loans in order to eliminate their excess reserves; they can always invest in short- or long-term bonds.

Commercial and industrial customers borrow from banks for a variety of reasons. Short-term loans provide them with funds to meet payrolls, to stock up on inventories in anticipation of heavy sales, to overcome a temporary shortage of cash needed to repay loans, and so forth. Firms that are good customers of a particular bank frequently acquire *lines of credit*—predetermined amounts the bank is willing to lend them on demand, without going through the formal loan application process. A credit line appears on a bank's balance sheet only when the line is used.

Most short-term loans mature within a year; long-term loans, which firms may use to finance plant and equipment, have durations of 1 to 10 years.

Almost 30 percent of bank loans are mortgage loans, mainly for residential construction. These loans are typically long-lived, running from 10 to 30 years, though the high variability of interest rates in recent years have reduced their maturity to 5–10 years in many cases. In the past, residential mortgage loans were risky, even when secured by property. The Federal Housing Administration now has programs to underwrite and insure a large volume of real estate loans of many types. The programs have virtually removed default risk for lenders. In addition, the secondary market in mortgages, developed in conjunction with Fannie Mae and other federal credit agencies, has increased significantly the liquidity of mortgage loans.

Loans to consumers are the third most important loan category. Although some of these loans are of the single payment type, most are installment loans that borrowers repay over a period of time in small chunks. On June 30, 1978, loans to individuals by all commercial banks were $154 billion, while installment loans were $214 billion. Banks make installment loans for a variety of purposes—auto purchases, home repair and modernization, credit card plans, mobile home purchases, furniture and appliance purchases, and so forth.

Banks today are a major source of consumer credit. Before World War II, they supplied very little credit to consumers, preferring instead to concentrate upon business lending. But, since that war they have found consumer lending to be a very profitable and stable source of business, and they have developed a variety of techniques to handle it—the credit card is one obvious example.

Other important parts of the loan business include federal funds loans to other bankers, loans to finance companies, loans to security brokers and dealers, loans to individuals for the purpose of purchasing or carrying securities, and loans to other depository institutions.

Security loans to individuals are to some extent regulated by the Federal Reserve System. These loans are designed to cover the difference between the purchase price of the securities and the money actually paid for them by the buyers. Security loans, therefore, permit the buyers to speculate with borrowed money. Because such speculation can lead to instability in the stock market, Congress in 1935 authorized the Fed to regulate the maximum credit margin—credit as percentage of the value of a stock at the time of the extension of credit—for stocks purchased by traders and private individuals.

SUMMARY

This chapter provides an overview of the business of banking. Banks have evolved from simple depository institutions into complex organizations with many functions. Their distinctive feature is the checking (demand) deposit function. No other financial institution has such a large proportion of its liabilities subject to sudden call on demand.

Demand deposits in a bank originate with primary deposits of customers and as derivatives of bank lending and investing. Derivative deposits are created when banks make loans and buy securities in order to reduce excess reserves to a minimum. In so doing, banks exchange non-earning assets for earning assets and raise their profits.

The amount of demand deposits banks can have outstanding is legally limited by reserve requirements imposed by the Federal Reserve System authorities. The Fed requires member banks to hold reserves in the form of vault cash or Federal Reserve bank deposits. State banks may satisfy most of their reserve requirements with security holdings or with deposits in other banks that, under the 1980 Monetary Control Act, must pass through required reserves to the Fed.

Other sources of bank funds include time and savings deposits, federal funds loans and repurchase agreements, loans from the Federal Reserve banks, Eurodollars, bank holding companies, and equity capital. Time and savings deposits are less volatile than demand deposits; but, when interest rates are changing rapidly, large inflows or outflows of time and savings deposits occur. Most borrowed money is also short term in nature, and banks that use a lot of it must constantly seek to renew their loans, particularly in the federal funds market. The Federal Reserve banks frown upon continuous borrowing by banks.

Bank assets consist mainly of loans and investments. Investments are mostly in U.S. government and state and local government securities. Aside from earning income, securities frequently act as secondary reserves for a bank. Banks lend money to a wide range of business and household customers. In this respect, they differ from other financial intermediaries, which specialize more in one or another form of lending, such as housing or consumer loans. Even so, banks are a mainstay of the business community, which depends heavily upon short-term bank loans to finance inventories, payrolls, and other expenses.

[1] Collateral is *specific* property a borrower pledges as security for repayment of a loan.

[2] Correspondent banks hold deposits from other banks, providing check collections and other services in exchange. The 1980 Monetary Control Act extends Federal Reserve System clearing privileges to nonmember banks, for a price. Depending on relative costs, nonmember banks may choose to remain with correspondents, or work through the Fed.

[3] Net demand deposits of a bank are its gross deposits minus cash items in the process of collection and demand balances due from other domestic banks. For a review of reserve requirements history, see "Member Bank Reserve Requirements—Heritage From History," *Federal Reserve Bank of Chicago Business Conditions*, June 1972, pp. 2–18.

[4] The details of the law are given in Charles R. McNeill and Denis M. Rechter, "The Depository Institutions Deregulation and Monetary Control Act of 1980," *Federal Reserve Bulletin*, Vol. 66, No. 6, June 1980, pp. 444–453.

[5] The 1980 Monetary Control Act requires elimination of Regulation Q over a six-year period. See Section 7.4.

[6] Let r be the yield on a taxable bond and r' be the yield on a tax-free state and local bond. If the tax rate is t, then the after-tax yield on a taxable bond equals the yield on the tax free bond when $r(1-t) = r'$. To compete with a 6 percent tax-free bond, a taxable bond must therefore yield 11.1 percent to a bank in the 46 percent tax bracket: $r = 6/.54 = 11.1$.

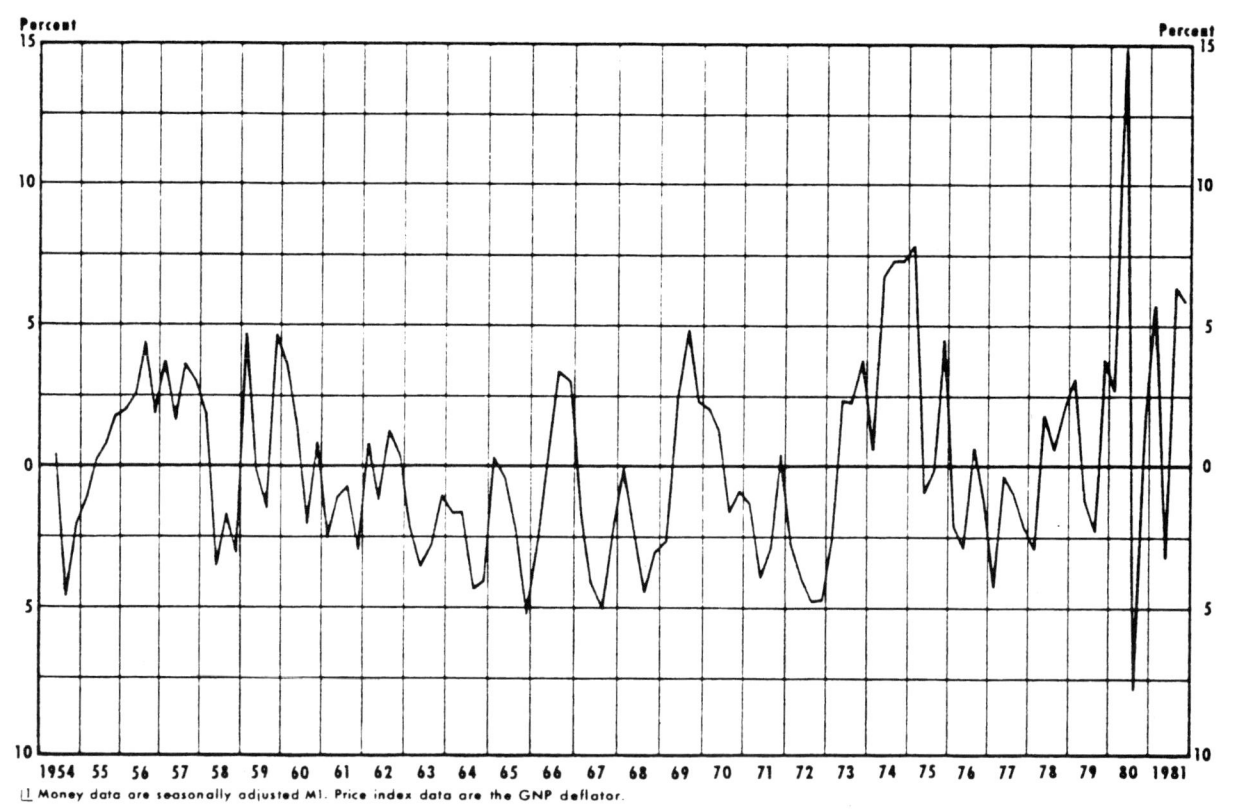

Chart 1
Rate of Price Change minus Rate of Money Growth [1]

[1] Money data are seasonally adjusted M1. Price index data are the GNP deflator.

Figure 1
Level shift in velocity at t_0 with no change in growth rate

Decrease in the growth rate of velocity at t_0

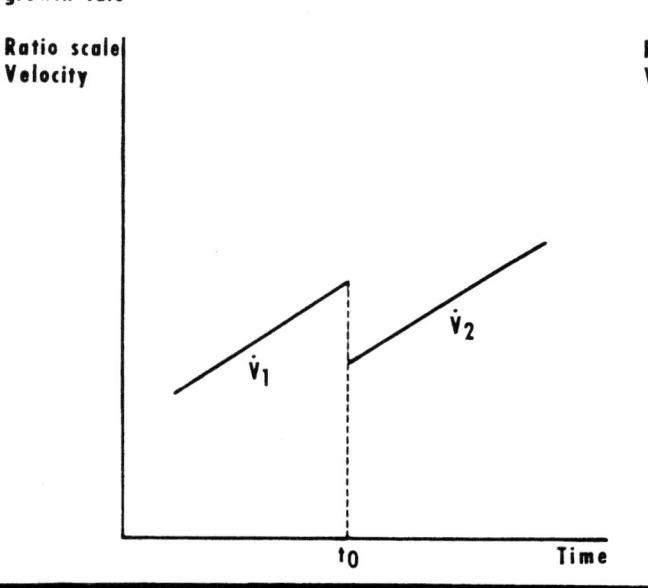

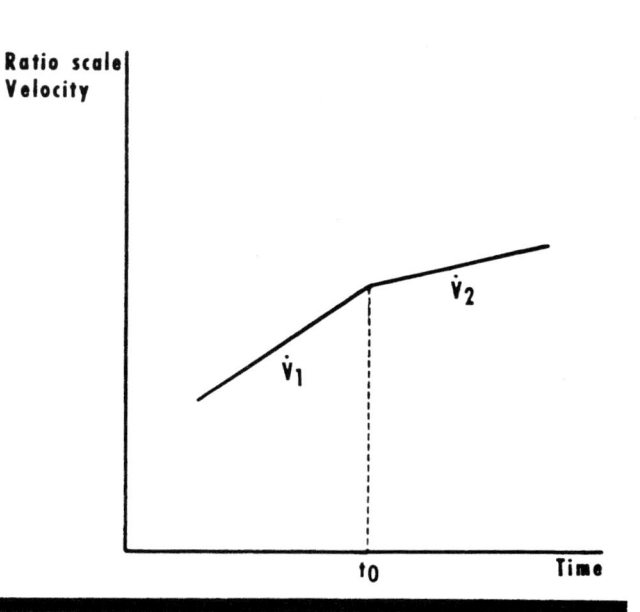

otherwise. Such instability need not result inevitably from policy responses to temporary changes in velocity; nevertheless, the danger is there. Thus, if policymakers suspect that the velocity change they observe is temporary, they may choose to ignore it.[11]

Level Vs. Growth Rate Shifts

Policymakers also must distinguish between changes in the levels of velocity and changes in its growth rate; the policy response will be different in the two cases. To illustrate this, consider the cases depicted in figure 1.[12] In both, $\dot{V}_1$ and $\dot{V}_2$ represent the growth rate of velocity before and after the hypothetical change at time t_0.

In the case of a permanent decline in the *level* of velocity that leaves the growth rates unaffected ($\dot{V}_1 = \dot{V}_2$), a policy response that accelerated the growth of money temporarily until the higher desired level is obtained and then returned money growth to its previous rate would produce an unvarying rate of growth in GNP. In the second case ($\dot{V}_2 < \dot{V}_1$), a compensatory and permanent increase in the growth rate of money at time t_0 is necessary to maintain the growth rate of GNP.

If policymakers failed to respond to the velocity changes depicted in figure 1, the consequences would be different in the two cases. In the first (level-shift) case, there would be a *temporary* reduction in the rate of change of prices or real output, or both. In the long run, however, velocity would return to its former growth rate and, hence, so would the growth of nominal output. In the second case, the growth rate of prices would be lowered *permanently*; in addition, the growth rate of real output may be lowered temporarily if the monetary authority failed to adjust the growth rate of money in response to a permanent decline in velocity growth.

THE VARIABILITY OF VELOCITY

The timing of the policy response to the velocity change, of course, is very important. Unfortunately, it is difficult to determine whether there has been a significant change in velocity, let alone to foresee such a change. Furthermore, it is difficult to differentiate between level and growth rate shifts, and to differentiate between temporary and permanent changes.

In order to see why this might be the case, consider the historical movements in the growth rate of M1 velocity presented in chart 2. This chart shows the quarter-to-quarter growth rate of M1 velocity, a horizontal line showing the average growth rate of M1 velocity for the period II/1954–IV/1981, and dashed lines representing plus or minus two standard deviations of the quarter-to-quarter growth rate of velocity from its mean over this period.[13]

It is obvious that the quarter-to-quarter growth rate of velocity is highly variable. Nevertheless, it falls outside the range of plus or minus two standard deviations in four of the 111 quarters from II/1954–IV/1981. More recently, there have been three occasions during the last six quarters when the growth rate of velocity has fallen outside of this range. A priori, it is difficult to determine whether these apparent shifts are simply temporary movements in the growth rate associated with a permanent change in the level of velocity, a permanent change in the growth rate, or a temporary change in the growth rate associated with a temporary change in the level. Indeed, it is difficult to know whether these changes represent a significant change in velocity. It could be that other factors that affect velocity may have caused it to change. Thus, in order to determine whether a policy response is called for, it is necessary to examine the factors that determine velocity.

FACTORS THAT AFFECT VELOCITY

There are a number of factors that can cause velocity to change.[14] Since increased velocity is simply the ratio of nominal GNP to the stock of money, any factor that causes the stock of money to change relative to nominal output, or vice versa, can produce a change in the level of velocity. Likewise, any factor that causes the growth rate of money to change relative to the growth rate of nominal GNP, or vice versa, will cause the growth rate of velocity to change. Furthermore, since the growth rate of velocity is defined as the percentage change in the *level* of velocity per unit of time, factors that affect the level of velocity affect the growth rate if they likewise change through time. Thus, the following discussion will be carried out in terms of the level of velocity, unless otherwise stated.

Many of the factors that affect velocity can be analyzed easily by recognizing that velocity changes whenever people alter their holdings of money relative to their income. Factors that cause people to hold less money relative to their income increase velocity, while factors that cause people to increase their money holdings reduce it. For example, if two households have the same income and monthly expenditure patterns but one receives its income once a month while the other receives it twice a month, the latter, all other things constant, will hold less money on average than the one that receives income once a month. Thus, changes in

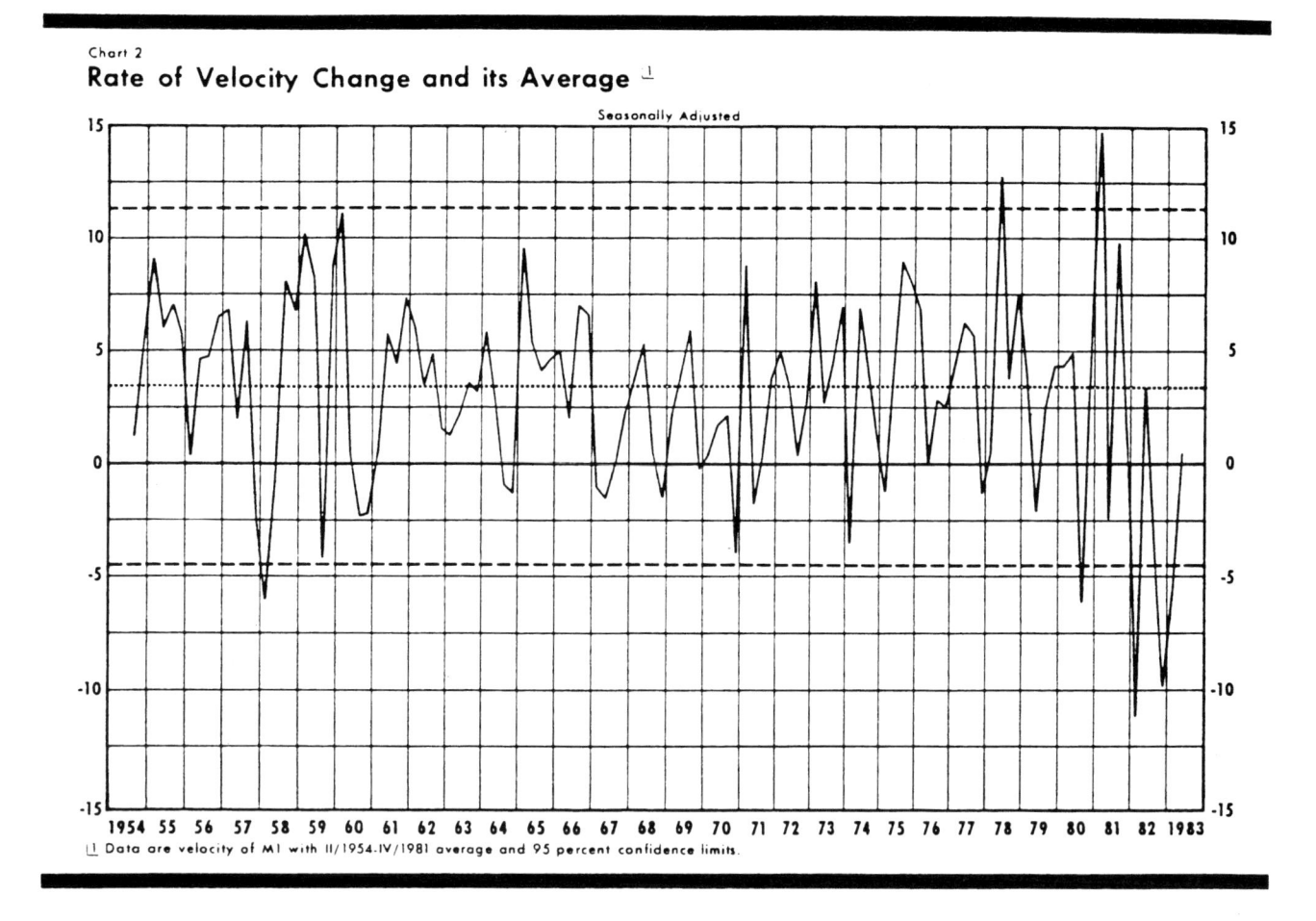

Chart 2
Rate of Velocity Change and its Average [1]

[1] Data are velocity of M1 with II/1954-IV/1981 average and 95 percent confidence limits.

the pattern of receipts and expenditures can produce changes in society's holdings of money relative to income.

Economizing on Money Balances

Other factors that cause individuals to economize on their holdings of money relative to income increase velocity. For example, the increased use of credit cards could reduce individuals' desires to hold money balances and, thus, increase velocity. In particular, these and other lines of credit may lessen individuals' desires to hold money as a contingency against uncertainty.[15]

Two of the most commonly cited factors that can cause changes in velocity are changes in real interest rates and expectations of inflation. Increases in the real interest rate tend to cause individuals to hold less money relative to their real income. The same generally will be true of an increase in the expected rate of inflation. Higher expected inflation will cause individuals to economize on their money holdings, raising velocity.

Financial Innovations

Financial innovations also can produce velocity changes. In general, innovations that reduce the implicit or explicit cost, or both, of transferring funds from non-transaction to transaction forms (perhaps by giving transaction characteristics to assets not included in M1) tend to increase the velocity of M1. Therefore, innovations such as money market deposit accounts and money market mutual funds would increase the velocity of M1 to the extent that they lower these costs.

In contrast, innovations that lower the cost of holding M1 relative to non-M1 assets tend to reduce the velocity of M1. This could be the case with automatic transfer of savings, negotiable order of withdrawal (NOW), and Super-NOW accounts.[16] Such innovations, however, may produce a temporary decline in velocity that lasts only until individuals realign their portfolios.

Cyclical Factors

Finally, there are a number of factors that can cause velocity to change with cyclical movements in real income (see appendix). They suggest that velocity tends to rise during periods of rising real income and fall during periods of declining real income.

Furthermore, there is considerable evidence that a change in money growth affects nominal income with a lag that is distributed over several quarters. Thus, an acceleration in money growth will produce a temporary decline in velocity as nominal output temporarily grows at a slower rate than does money. Thus, a decline in velocity associated with a recession can be exacerbated if the monetary authority expands money rapidly in order to stimulate a sluggish economy.

Permanent Vs. Temporary Effects

While all the factors mentioned above can affect velocity, they need not produce a lasting effect on its level or on its growth rate. For example, it is commonly recognized that, in a noninflationary environment, interest rates tend to be procyclical — rising during the expansion phase of the business cycle and declining during the contraction phase. Although the level of velocity and its growth rate can be affected by movements in interest rates, neither need change permanently; they, like such cyclical movements in interest rates, simply will average out over the course of a business cycle.

Also, financial innovations can have a permanent effect on the level of velocity but, perhaps, only a temporary effect on its growth rate. An innovation that lowers the cost of holding M1 relative to non-M1 assets induces a shift out of non-M1 into M1 assets, permanently lowering M1 velocity but reducing the growth rate only temporarily. Once the portfolios are realigned, the growth rate of velocity simply may resume its previous path.[17] Nevertheless, financial innovations can affect the extent to which velocity responds to changes in some of the other factors mentioned above.[18]

Forecasting Velocity Changes

Indeed, several economists have suggested recently that the seemingly unusual changes in velocity shown in chart 2 can be accounted for by cyclical movements in velocity and by changes in the inflation rate and interest rates.[19] This section does not attempt to evaluate these claims. Instead, the purpose here is to show that even when these factors are accounted for, it is difficult to forecast short-run changes in velocity.

To illustrate this point, the in-sample standard deviation of a model of velocity growth which recently appeared in this *Review* will be used as an estimate of the true one-quarter-ahead forecast error. The in-sample standard deviation is used to be conservative, and this model was selected because it incorporates many of the factors discussed above and because it performs well in forecasting velocity growth.[20] The in-sample standard deviation is about 2.0 percentage points. Thus, after accounting for factors that significantly influence velocity growth, the approximate 95 percent confidence interval for the forecast of velocity growth, $\dot{V}_f$, will be $\dot{V}_f \pm 2(2.0)$ or $\dot{V}_f \pm 4$.[21] This implies a fairly large margin for error. For example, if the forecast for velocity growth is 5 percent, then, loosely interpreted, actual velocity growth can be expected to be between 1 and 9 percent with high probability. This sizable margin for error demonstrates that the monetary authority will generally find it difficult to stabilize nominal output growth in the short run by offsetting short-run changes in velocity.[22]

Furthermore, the sizable error makes it difficult to determine whether a significant change in velocity has taken place. It takes a fairly large change in velocity growth to be significant enough to be considered unusual. Of course, the problems of discriminating between permanent and temporary shifts and between level and growth rate changes remain.

SUMMARY AND CONCLUSIONS

This article outlines the meaning of income velocity and reviews its important role as the link between money growth and nominal GNP growth. It demonstrates the problems that the monetary authority faces if it attempts to offset short-run (quarter-to-quarter) changes in velocity growth. Indeed, it appears that, even if a conservative estimate of the one-quarter-ahead forecast standard deviation is used, the forecast errors are large for policy purposes. Thus, while it might seem desirable for the monetary authority to respond to permanent changes in the level or growth rate of velocity, it is difficult to predict such changes, or to verify them quickly *ex post*.

---

[1]The decline in velocity was a persistent concern of the Federal Open Market Committee (FOMC) in the conduct of monetary policy during 1982 and contributed to the Committee's decision to suspend the use of M1 as an intermediate policy target in October 1982. See Daniel L. Thornton, "The FOMC in 1982: Deemphasizing M1," this *Review* (June/July 1983), pp. 26–35.

[2]Irving Fisher (assisted by Harry G. Brown): *The Publishing Power of Money: Its Determination and Relation to Credit, Interest and Crises* (MacMillan, 1911).

[3]Money was viewed primarily as a medium of exchange necessitated by the lack of synchronization between the sale of one good and the purchase of another. Thus, the proportion of income held (on average) in the form of money balances was determined by institutional factors that determined the pattern of payments and receipts. A discussion of this can be found in most macroeconomics textbooks.

[4]Actually, the classical economists never considered V to be a constant in the sense of unchangeable. Indeed, they recognized

the effects of interest rates and price expectations on velocity; however, they generally believed that such factors would be relatively unimportant over the long run. For a good discussion of these issues, see Laurence Harris, *Monetary Theory* (McGraw-Hill, 1981), chapter 6.

[5]Although they stem from different theoretical approaches, Fisher's equation of exchange is similar to the "Cambridge cash balance equation" of Marshall and Pigou. See Alfred Marshall, *Money, Credit and Commerce* (MacMillan, 1923); and A. C. Pigou, "The Value of Money," *Quarterly Journal of Economics* (November 1917), pp. 38–65.

[6]Money is assumed to be largely exogenous. Both classical and neoclassical writers acknowledged the feedback of prices to money. Modern writers like Friedman and Schwartz consider money to be "for all practical purposes" exogenous in the sense that it can be controlled by the monetary authority. See Milton Friedman and Anna J. Schwartz, *Monetary Statistics of the United States* (National Bureau of Economic Research, 1970), p. 124.

[7]The goals of economic policy as set forth in the Full-Employment Act of 1946 are (1) full employment, (2) price level stability, (3) equilibrium in the balance of payments and (4) a high rate of economic growth. The first two of these are reiterated in the Humphrey-Hawkins Act. Since $Y = P \cdot X$, the first two objectives amount to stabilizing nominal GNP.

[8]This is the "neutrality of money." Also, there was the closely related "classical dichotomy" between money and output. For a discussion of these points, see Harris, *Monetary Theory*, chapters 4 and 6; and Don Patinkin, *Money, Interest and Prices* (Harper and Row, 1965), chapter 8.

[9]Furthermore, full employment does not necessarily mean zero unemployment, but is merely a level consistent with stable prices given the structural characteristics of the labor and output markets, including market imperfections. See Milton Friedman, "The Role of Monetary Policy," *American Economic Review* (March 1968), pp. 1–17, for his concept of the natural rate of unemployment.

[10]This statement and much of the discussion that follows assumes a long-run neutrality of money; that is, changes in the growth rate of money have no lasting effect on the growth rate of real output. If money is not neutral in the long run, both the policy prescriptions and the effects of a failure to respond to velocity changes would differ accordingly.

[11]For example, at its meeting of November 16, 1982, the Federal Open Market Committee anticipated that M1 might grow due to a temporary buildup of balances in M1 components for eventual placement in the new money market deposit accounts (MMDAs), which would become effective on December 14, 1982. Thus, the Committee anticipated a short-run decline in velocity resulting from this potential buildup. See "Record of Policy Actions of the FOMC," *Federal Reserve Bulletin* (January 1983), p. 19.

[12]A ratio scale for the natural log of velocity is presented in figure 1 so that the growth rates can be represented by the slopes of straight lines.

[13]If $\dot{V}$ is normally distributed, then approximately 95 percent of its observed values should fall within ±2 standard deviations.

[14]For discussions of some of these, see John A. Tatom, "Was the 1982 Velocity Decline Unusual?" this *Review* (August/September 1983), pp. 5–15; and William T. Gavin, "Velocity and Monetary Targets," *Economic Commentary*, Federal Reserve Bank of Cleveland (June 6, 1983).

[15]For a more detailed discussion, see Mack Ott, "Money, Credit and Velocity," this *Review* (May 1982), pp. 21–34. To date, however, there is little empirical support for this proposition about credit cards.

[16]John A. Tatom, "Recent Financial Innovations: Have They Distorted the Meaning of M1?" this *Review* (April 1982), pp. 23–35; and John A. Tatom, "Money Market Deposit Accounts, Super-NOWs and Monetary Policy," this *Review* (March 1983), pp. 5–16.

[17]For example, if individuals held expectations of inflation over a long period of time because of, say, excessive money growth, they might attempt to realign their portfolios continually in order to economize on money holdings and, as a result, the growth rate of velocity would be positive over this period.

[18]The availability of more and better substitutes for a commodity tends to increase its own and cross elasticities of demand. Thus, financial innovations affect velocity to the extent that they alter velocity's response to the above factors.

[19]See Tatom, "Was the 1982 Velocity Decline Unusual?"; John P. Judd, "The Recent Decline in Velocity: Instability of Money Demand or Inflation?" Federal Reserve Bank of San Francisco *Economic Review* (Spring 1983), pp. 12–19; and Milton Friedman, "Why a Surge of Inflation is Likely Next Year," *Wall Street Journal*, September 1, 1983. Though these economists generally agree on the factors affecting velocity, they disagree on the relative importance of the factors cited.

[20]The Tatom model has a smaller root-mean-squared error than the best univariate time series model recently reported by Hein and Veugelers, as well as a model which explains velocity growth with movements in real interest rates and the expected rate of inflation alone. See Tatom, "Was the 1982 Velocity Decline Unusual?"; and Scott E. Hein and Paul T. W. M. Veugelers, "Velocity Growth Predictability: A Time Series Perspective," this *Review* (October 1983), pp. 34–43.

[21]That is, approximately 95 percent of the intervals so constructed in one quarter would contain the value of velocity in the next. This simplified interpretation of the forecast interval tends to understate the margin of forecast error. See Robert S. Pindyck and Daniel L. Rubinfeld, *Econometric Models and Economic Forecasts* (McGraw-Hill, 1976), chapter 6.

[22]This result implies that recent suggestions that the Federal Reserve use nominal GNP as an intermediate target are ill-advised.

Appendix: Cyclical Factors That Affect Velocity

The purpose of this appendix is to illustrate four factors that can produce movements in velocity associated with cyclical swings in GNP.

Measured Vs. Theoretical Velocity

Velocity as it is usually measured may differ from its theoretical counterpart. As a result, not all changes in measured velocity indicate true changes in velocity. To illustrate this, consider the common specification of the demand for nominal money,

(A.1) $M^d = f(P, \dot{p}^e, r, r^e, Y_p, Z)$,

where

P = the current price level

$\dot{p}^e$ = the expected future price level

r = the current real interest rate

r^e = the expected future real interest rate

Y_p = current nominal *permanent income*

Z = all other factors that affect money demand.[1]

It is usually assumed that individuals do not suffer from a money illusion (i.e., equation A.1 is homogenous of degree one in P and Y_p) so that equation A.1 can be written as

(A.2) $M^d/P = f(\dot{P}^e, r, r^e, Y_p/P, Z)$

or

(A.3) $m^d = f(\dot{P}^e, r, r^e, y_p, Z)$,

where m^d denotes the demand for *real* money balances and y_p denotes real permanent income. Now assume that A.3 is homogenous of degree s in real permanent income so that A.3 can be written as

(A.4) $m^d/(y_p)^s = f(\dot{P}^e, r, r^e, Z)$.

Further assume that $s = 1$, so that the theoretical measure of velocity, V^*, is

$V^* = Y_p/M = 1/f(\dot{P}^e, r, r^e, Z)$.

Thus, if velocity is measured as Y/M, changes in measured velocity can occur that do not reflect changes in V^*. Of course, estimates of Y_p could be used to get a better estimate of V^*; however, this problem will continue to the extent that there are estimation errors. Moreover, the most commonly watched measure of velocity is Y/M.

Economies of Scale

Another problem arises when $s \neq 1$. It is sometimes argued that the elasticity of the demand for real money balances with respect to real permanent income is less than one. If this is the case, the percentage change in real money balances will be less than the percentage change in real income. An increase in real income will result in a less than proportionate increase in the holding of real money and, hence, an increase in velocity. Thus, if there are cyclical movements in permanent income, velocity would rise during the expansion phase of the cycle and fall during the contraction phase. This would occur even if permanent income were measured precisely. This factor also could account for a secular rise in velocity as real output expands. For example, if real output is growing at a 4 percent rate and the real income elasticity of the demand for real money is about one-half, then velocity would grow secularly at about a 2 percent rate.

Short-Run Adjustments of Money Demand

Another factor that can account for cyclical movements in velocity is the possibility of short-run adjustments of money demand. A change in one of the factors in f(·) alters an individual's demand for real money while leaving his actual holdings of real money unchanged. As a result, the individual must adjust actual money holdings to his new desired holdings. Such an adjustment is costly, so the adjustment may progress (perhaps slowly) over time. Theoretically, the speed at which this portfolio adjustment takes place depends on the cost of moving to the new equilibrium relative to the cost of being out of equilibrium: the higher the former cost relative to the latter, the slower the speed of adjustment.[2] If these adjustment costs are small, the adjustment will be rapid; however, most empirical estimates suggest a very slow adjustment.[3] In any event, if money demand does not adjust immediately, an increase in real income can produce a smaller increase in the demand for money in the short run and, hence, a short-run increase in velocity. As the demand for money adjusts towards the new equilibrium, velocity will approach the level implied in A.4.

The above analysis rests in a disequilibrium between actual and desired money holdings. If such disequilibria exist, they also could be caused by real-side shocks, such as natural disasters, oil price shocks and the like.

Lags in the Effect of Money on Nominal Income

Another possibility is a lag effect from money to income.[4] That is, changes in the current money stock produce changes in nominal income with a lag that is distributed over several quarters. If this is the case, a change in the current money stock produces a less than proportional change in current nominal income and, hence, an initial decline in velocity. Thus, periods of relatively rapid money growth tend to be associated initially with declining velocity, while periods of relatively slow money growth tend to be associated initially with rising velocity. Taking this factor and previously mentioned factors into consideration, it could be argued that the decline in velocity during 1982 was precipitated by the decline in real economic activity and exacerbated by the rapid growth of M1 beginning III/1982.

---

[1] See Milton Friedman, "The Quantity Theory of Money: A Restatement," in *Studies in the Quantity Theory of Money* (University of Chicago Press, 1956).

[2] See Zvi Griliches, "Distributed Lags: A Survey," *Econometrica* (January 1967), pp. 16–49.

[3] For a discussion of this problem and some estimates of the speed of adjustment, see Daniel L. Thornton, "Maximum Likelihood Estimates of A Partial Adjustment-Adaptive Expectations Model of the Demand for Money," *Review of Economics and Statistics* (May 1982), pp. 225–29.

[4] If money were exogenous, then this lag would only result from a lagged response of money demand, such as that discussed above. In this instance, this and the previous factor would be identical.

Daniel L. Thornton is a senior economist at the Federal Reserve Bank of St. Louis. John G. Schulte provided research assistance.

9. Lessons of the German Inflation
Henry Hazlitt

Volumes have been written about the great German hyperinflation. It was, as Henry Hazlitt observes, "the most spectacular in history;" it was not, however, the most extreme. (That dubious honor goes to Hungary, whose post-WWII hyperinflation was short-lived but involved an even more substantial currency depreciation.) —G.S., Ed.

****

We learn from extreme cases, in economic life as in medicine. A moderate inflation, that has been going on for only a short time, may seem like a great boon. It appears to increase incomes and to stimulate trade and employment. Politicians find it profitable to advocate more of it—not under that name, of course, but under the name of "expansionary" or "full-employment" policies. It is regarded as politically suicidal to suggest that it be brought to a halt. Politicians promise to "fight" inflation; but by that they almost never mean slashing government expenditures, balancing the budget, and halting the money-printing presses. They mean denouncing the big corporations and other sellers for raising their prices. They mean imposing price and rent controls.

When the inflation is sufficiently severe and prolonged, however, when it becomes what is called a hyperinflation, people begin at last to recognize it as the catastrophe it really is. There have been scores of hyperinflations in history—in ancient Rome under Diocletian, in the American colonies under the Continental Congress in 1781, in France from 1790 to 1796, in Austria, Hungary, Poland, and Russia after World War I, and in three or four Latin American countries today.

But the most spectacular hyperinflation in history, and also the one for which we have the most adequate statistics, occurred in Germany in the years from 1919 to the end of 1923. That episode repays the most careful study for the light it throws on what happens when an inflation is allowed to run its full course. Like every individual inflation, it had causes or features peculiar to itself—the Treaty of Versailles, with the very heavy reparation payments it laid upon Germany, the occupation of the Ruhr by Allied troops in early 1923, and other developments. But we can ignore these and concentrate on the features that the German hyperinflation shared with other hyperinflations.

At the outbreak of World War I—on July 31, 1914—the German Reichsbank took the first step by suspending the conversion of its notes into gold. Between July 24 and August 7 the bank increased its paper note issue by 2 billion marks. By November 15, 1923, the day the inflation was officially ended, it had issued the incredible sum of 92.8 quintillion (92,800,000,000,000,000,000) paper marks. A few days later (on November 20) a new currency, the rentenmark, was issued. The old marks were made convertible into it at a rate of one trillion to one.

It is instructive to follow in some detail how all this came about, and in what stages. By October 1918, the last full month of World

War I, the quantity of paper marks had been increased fourfold over what it was in the prewar year 1913, yet prices in Germany had increased only 139 percent. Even by October 1919, when the paper money circulation had increased sevenfold over that of 1913, prices had not quite increased sixfold. But by January 1920 this relationship was reversed: money in circulation had increased 8.4 times and the wholesale price index 12.6 times. By November 1921 circulation had increased 18 times and wholesale prices 34 times. By November 1922 circulation had increased 127 times and wholesale prices 1,154 times, and by November 1923 circulation had increased 245 *billion* times and prices 1,380 *billion* times.

These figures discredit the crude or rigid quantity theory of money, according to which prices increase in proportion to the increase in the stock of money—whether the money consists of gold and convertible notes or merely of irredeemable paper.

And what happened in Germany is typical of what happens in every hyperinflation. In what we may call Stage One, prices do not increase nearly as much as the increase in the paper money circulation. This is because the man in the street is hardly aware that the money supply is being increased. He still has confidence in the money and in the preexisting price level. He may even postpone some intended purchases because prices seem to him abnormally high, and he still hopes that they will soon fall back to their old levels.

Then the inflation moves into what we may call Stage Two, when people become aware that the money stock has increased, and is still increasing. Prices then go up approximately as much as the quantity of money is increased. This is the result assumed by the rigid quantity theory of money. But Stage Two, in fact, may last only for a short time. People begin to assume that the government is going to keep increasing the issuance of paper money indefinitely, and even at an accelerating rate. They lose all trust in it. The result is Stage Three, when prices begin to increase far faster than the government increases, or even than it can increase, the stock of money.

(This result follows not because of any proportionate increase in the velocity of circulation of money, but simply because the value that people put upon the monetary unit falls faster than the issuance increases. See chapter 13 for a more detailed discussion of this point.)

Money versus Prices

But throughout the German inflation there was almost no predictable correspondence between the rate of issuance of new paper marks, the rise in internal prices, and the rise in the dollar-exchange rate. Suppose, for example, we assign an index number of 100 to currency circulation, internal prices, and the dollar rate in October 1918. By February 1920 circulation stood at 203.9, internal prices at 506.3, and the dollar rate at 1,503.2. One result was that prices of imported goods then reached an index number of 1,898.5.

But from February 1920 to May 1921 the relationship of these rates of change was reversed. On the basis of an index number of 100 for all of these quantities in February 1920, circulation in May

1921 had increased to 150.1, but internal prices had risen to only 104.6, and the dollar exchange rate had actually fallen to 62.8. The cost of imported goods had dropped to an index number of 37.5.

Between May 1921 and July 1922 the previous tendencies were once more resumed. On the basis of an index number of 100 for May 1921, the circulation in July 1922 was 248.6, internal prices were 734.6, and the dollar rate 792.2.

Again, between July 1922 and June 1923 these tendencies continued, though at enormously increased rates. With an index number of 100 for July 1922, circulation in June 1923 stood at 8,557, internal prices at 18,194, and the dollar rate at 22,301. The prices of imported goods had increased to 22,486.

The amazing divergence between these index numbers gives some idea of the disequilibrium and disorganization that the inflation caused in German economic life. There was a depression of real wages practically throughout the inflation, and a great diminution in the real prices of industrial shares.

How did the German hyperinflation get started? And why was it continued to this fantastic extent?

Its origin is hardly obscure. To pay for the tremendous expenditures called for by a total war, the German government, like others, found it far easier both economically and politically to print money than to raise adequate taxes. In the period from 1914 to October 1923, taxes covered only about 15 percent of expenditures. In the last ten days of October 1923, ordinary taxes were covering less than one percent of expenses.

What was the government's own rationalization for its policies? The thinking of the leaders had become incredibly corrupted. They inverted cause and effect. They even denied that there was any inflation. They blamed the depreciation of the mark on the adverse balance of payments. It was the rise of prices that had made it necessary to increase the money supply so that people would have enough money to pay for goods. One of their most respected monetary economists, Karl Helfferich, held to this rationalization to the end:

> The increase of the circulation has not preceded the rise of prices and the depreciation of the exchange, but it followed slowly and at great distance. The circulation increased from May 1921 to the end of January 1923 by 23 times; it is not possible that this increase had caused the rise in the prices of imported goods and of the dollar, which in that period increased by 344 times.[2]

Of course such reasoning was eagerly embraced by Germany's politicians. In the late stages of the inflation, when prices rose far faster than new money could even be printed, the continuance and even acceleration of inflation seemed unavoidable. The violent rise of prices caused an intense demand for more money to pay the prices. The quantity of money was not sufficient for the volume of transactions. Panic seized manufacturers and business firms. They were not able to fulfill their contracts. The rise of prices kept racing ahead of the volume of money. The thirty paper mills of the government, plus its well-equipped printing plants, plus a hundred private printing presses, could not turn out the money fast enough. The situation was desperate. On October 25, 1923, the Reichsbank issued a statement that during the day it had been able to print only 120 *quadrillion* paper marks, but the demand for the day had been for a *quintillion!*

One reason for the despair that seized the Germans was their conviction that the inflation was caused principally by the reparations burden imposed by the Treaty of Versailles. This of course played a role, but far from the major one. The reparations payments did not account for more than a third of the total discrepancy between expenditure and income in the German budget in the whole four financial years 1920 through 1923.

In the early stages of the inflation German internal prices rose more than the mark fell in the foreign exchange market. But for the greater part of the inflation period—in fact, up to September 1923—the external value of the mark fell much below its internal value. This meant that foreign goods became enormously expensive for Germans while German goods became great bargains for foreigners. As a result, German exports were greatly stimulated, and so was activity and employment in many German industries. But this was later recognized as a false prosperity. Germany was in effect selling its production abroad much below real costs and paying extortionate prices for what it had to buy from abroad.

In the last months of the German inflation, beginning in the summer of 1923, internal prices spurted forward and reached the level of world prices, even allowing for the incredibly depreciated exchange. The exchange rate of the paper mark, calculated in gold marks, was 1,523,809 paper marks to one gold mark on August 28, 1923. It was 28,809,524 on September 25, 15,476,190,475 on October 30, and was "stabilized" finally at one trillion to one on November 20.

One change that brought about these astronomical figures is that merchants had finally decided to price their goods in gold. They fixed their prices in paper marks according to the exchange rate. Wages and salaries also began to be "indexed," based on the official cost-of-living figures. Methods were even devised for basing wages not only on the existing depreciation but on the probable future depreciation of the mark.

Finally, with the mark depreciating every hour, more and more Germans began to deal with each other in foreign currencies, principally dollars.

Experience That Did Not Educate

Viewed in retrospect, one of the most disheartening things about the inflation is that no matter how appalling its consequences became, they failed to educate the German monetary economists, or cause them to reexamine their previous sophisms. The very fact that the paper marks began to depreciate faster than they were printed (because everybody feared still further inflation) led these economists to argue that there was no monetary or credit inflation in Germany at all! They admitted that the stamped value of the paper money issued was enormous, but the "real" value—that is, the gold value according to the exchange rate—was far lower than the total money circulating in Germany before the war. This argument was expounded by Karl Helfferich in official testimony in June 1923. In the summer of 1922 Professor Julius Wolf wrote: "In proportion to the need, less money circulates in Germany now than before the war. This statement may cause surprise, but it is correct. The circulation is now 15–20 times that of pre-war days, while prices have risen 40–50 times." Another economist, Karl Elster, in his book on the German mark, declared: "However enormous may be the apparent rise in the circulation in 1922, actually the figures show a decline"!

Of course all of the bureaucrats and politicians responsible for the inflation tried to put the blame for the soaring prices of everything from eggs to the dollar on to a special class of selfish and wicked people called "speculators"—forgetting that everybody who buys or sells and tries to anticipate future prices is unavoidably a speculator.

The Effect on Production

There is today still an almost universal belief that inflation stimulates trade, employment, and production. For the greater part of the German inflation, most businessmen believed this to be true. The depreciation of the mark stimulated their exports. In February and March 1922, when the dollar was rising, business seemed to reach a maximum of activity. The *Berliner Tageblatt* wrote in March of the Leipzig Fair: "It is no longer simply a zeal for acquiring, or even a rage: it is a madness." In the summer of 1922 unemployment practically disappeared. In 1920 and 1921, on the other hand, every improvement in the mark had been followed by an increase of unemployment.

The real effect of the inflation, however, was peculiarly complex. There were violent alternations of prosperity and depression, feverish activity and disorganization. Yet there were certain dominant tendencies. Inflation directed production, trade, and employment into channels different from those they had previously taken. Production was less efficient. This was partly the result of the inflation itself, and partly of the deterioration and destruction of German plant and equipment during the war. In 1922 (the year of greatest economic expansion after the war) total production seems to have reached no more than 70 to 80 percent of the level of 1913. There was a sharp decline in farm output.

High prices imposed "forced saving" on most of the German population (in the sense that they forced people to reduce the number of things they could consume). High paper-profit margins combined with tax considerations led German manufacturers to increase their investment in new plant and equipment. (Later much of this new investment proved to be almost worthless. As will be shown in chapter 16, this is an inevitable consequence of prolonged inflation.)

There was a great decline in labor efficiency. Part of this was the result of malnutrition brought about by high food prices. Bresciani-Turroni tells us: "In the acutest phase of the inflation Germany offered the grotesque, and at the same time tragic, spectacle of a people which, rather than produce food, clothes, shoes, and milk for its own babies, was exhausting its energies in the manufacture of machines or the building of factories."[3]

There was a great increase in unproductive work. As a result of changing prices and increased speculation, the number of middlemen increased continually. By 1923 the number of banks had multiplied fourfold over 1914. Speculation expanded pathologically. When prices were increasing a hundredfold, a thousandfold, a millionfold, far more people had to be employed to make calculations, and such calculations also took up far more time of old employees and of buyers. With prices racing ahead, the will to work declined. The production of coal in the Ruhr, which in 1913 had been 928 kilograms per miner, had decreased in 1922 to 585 kilograms. The "dollar rate" was the theme of all discussions.

Inefficient and unproductive firms were no longer eliminated. In 1913 there had been, on the average, 815 bankruptcies a month. They had decreased to 13 in August 1923, to 9 in September, to 15 in October, and to 8 in November. The acelerative depreciation of the paper mark kept wiping out everybody's real debt.

The continuous and violent oscillations in the value of money made it all but impossible for manufacturers and merchants to know what their prices and costs of production would be even a few months ahead. Production became a gamble. Instead of concentrating on improving their product or holding down costs, businessmen speculated in goods and the dollar.

Money savings (e.g., in savings bank deposits) practically ceased.

The novelist Thomas Mann has left us a description of the typical experience of a consumer in the late stages of the inflation:

> For instance, you might drop in at the tobacconist's for a cigar. Alarmed by the price, you'd rush to a competitor, find that his price was still higher, and race back to the first shop, which may have doubled or tripled its price in the meantime. There was no help for it, you had to dig into your pocketbook and take out a huge bundle of millions, or even billions, depending on the date.[4]

But this doesn't mean that the shopkeepers were enjoying an economic paradise. On the contrary, in the final months of the inflation, business became demoralized. On the morning of November 1, 1923, for example, retail traders fixed their prices on the basis of a dollar exchange rate of 130 billion paper marks to one dollar. By afternoon the dollar rate had risen to 320 billion. The paper money that shopkeepers had received in the morning had lost 60 percent of its value!

In October and November, in fact, prices became so high that few could pay them. Sales almost stopped. The great shops were deserted. The farmers would not sell their products for a money of vanishing value. Unemployment soared. From a figure of 3.5 percent in July 1923, it rose to 9.9 percent in September, 19.1 percent in October, 23.4 percent in November and 28.2 percent in December. In addition, for these last four months more than 40 percent of union members were employed only part time.

The ability of politicians to profit from manufacturing more inflation had come to an end.

The Effect on Foreign Trade

Because the paper mark usually fell faster and further on the foreign exchange market than German internal prices rose, German goods became a bargain for foreigners, and German exports were stimulated. But the extent of their increase was greatly overestimated at the time. The relationship between the dollar rate and the internal price rise was undependable. When the mark improved on the foreign exchange market, exports fell off sharply. Germans in many trades viewed any improvement of the mark with alarm. The main long-run effect of the inflation was to bring about a continuous instability of both imports and exports. Moreover, the two were tied together. German industry largely worked with foreign raw materials; it had to import in order to export.

Germany did not "flood the world with its exports." It could not increase production fast enough. Its industrial output in 1921 and 1922, in spite of the appearance of feverish activity, was appreciably lower than in 1913. As I have noted before, because of price and foreign exchange distortions, Germany was in effect giving away part of its output.

But this loss had one notable offset. In the earlier stages of the inflation, foreigners could not resist the idea that the depreciated German mark was a tremendous bargain. They bought huge quantities. One German economist calculated that they probably lost seven-eighths of their money, or about 5 billion gold marks, "a sum triple that paid by Germany in foreign exchange on account of reparations."

The Effect on Securities

Those who have lived only in comparatively moderate inflations will find it hard to believe how poor a hedge the holding of shares in private companies provided in the German hyperinflation. The only meaningful way of measuring the fluctuation of German stock prices is as a percentage of changes in their gold (or dollar) value, or as a percentage of German wholesale prices. In terms of the latter, and on the basis of an index number of 100 for 1913, stocks were selling at an average of 35.8 in December 1918, 15.8 in December 1919, 19.1 in December 1920, 21 in December 1921, 6.1 in December 1922, and 21.3 in December 1923.

This lack of responsiveness is accounted for by several factors. Soaring costs in terms of paper marks forced companies continually to offer new shares to raise capital, with the result that what was being priced in the market was continually "diluted" shares. Mounting commodity prices, and speculation in more responsive hedges like the dollar, absorbed so large a proportion of the money supply that not much was left to invest in securities. Companies paid very low dividends. According to one compilation, 120 typical companies in 1922 paid out dividends equal, on the average, to only one-quarter of one percent of the prices of the shares.

The nominal profits of the companies were frequently high, but there seemed no point in holding them for distribution because they would lose so much of their purchasing power in the period between the time they were earned and the day the stockholder got them. They were therefore ploughed back into the business. But people desperately wanted a return, and they could make short-term loans at huge nominal rates of interest. (High interest rates also meant low capitalized values.)

Moreover, investors rightly suspected that there was something wrong with the nominal net profits that the companies were showing. Most firms were still making completely inadequate depreciation and replacement allowances or showing unreal profits on inventories. Many companies that thought they were distributing profits were actually distributing part of their capital and operating at a loss. Finally, over each company hung an "invisible mortgage" — its potential taxes to enable the government to meet the reparations burden. And over the whole market hung, in addition, the fear of Bolshevism.

Yet it must not be concluded that stocks were at all stages a poor hedge against inflation. True, the average of stock prices (in gold value on the basis of an index number of 100 for 1913) fell from 69.3 in October 1918 to 8.5 in February 1920. But most of those who bought at this level made not only immense paper profits but real profits for the next two years. By the autumn of 1921 speculation on the German Bourse reached feverish levels. "Today there is no one—," wrote one financial newspaper, "from lift-boy, typist, and small landlord to the wealthy lady in high society — who does not speculate in industrial securities."

But in 1922 the situation dramatically changed again. When the paper index is converted into gold (or into the exchange rate for the dollar) it fell in October of that year to only 2.72, the lowest level since 1914. The paper prices of a selected number of shares had increased 89 times over 1914, but wholesale prices had increased 945 times and the dollar 1,525 times.

After October 1922, once again, the price of shares rapidly began to catch up, and for the next year not only reflected changes in the dollar exchange rate, but greatly surpassed them. Given an index number in gold of 100 in 1913, the price of shares rose to 16.0 in July 1923, 22.6 in September, 28.5 in October, and 39.4 in November. When the inflation was over, in December 1923, it was 26.9. But this meant that shares ended up at only about one-fourth of their gold value in 1913.

The movement of share prices contributed heavily to the profound changes in the distribution of wealth brought about in the inflation years.

Interest Rates

In an inflation, lenders who wish to protect themselves against the probable further fall in the purchasing power of money by the time their principal is repaid, are forced to add a "price premium" to the normal interest rate. This elementary precaution was ignored for years by the German Reichsbank. From the early days of the war until June 1922 its official discount rate remained unchanged at 5 percent. It was raised to 6 percent in July, to 7 percent in August, 8 percent in September, 10 percent in November, 12 percent in January 1923, 18 percent in April, 30 percent in August, and 90 percent in September.

But even the highest of these rates did nothing to deter borrowing by debtors who expected to pay off in enormously depreciated marks. The result was that the Reichbank's policy kindled an enormous credit inflation, based on commercial bills, on top of the enormous government inflation based on treasury bills. After September 1923, a bank or private individual had to pay at a rate of 900 percent per annum for a loan from the Reichsbank. But even this was no deterrent. At the beginning of November 1923 the market rate for "call money" rose as high as 30 percent per day — equivalent to more than 10,000 percent on an annual basis.

The Monetary Reform

There is not space here for an adequate summary of the redistribution of wealth, the profound social upheaval, and the moral chaos brought about by the German inflation. I must reserve them for separate treatment, and move on to discuss the monetary reform that ended the inflation.

On October 15, 1923, a decree was published establishing a new currency, the rentenmark, to be issued beginning November 15. On November 20 the value of the old paper mark was "stabilized" at the rate of 4,200 billion marks for a dollar, or one trillion old paper marks for a rentenmark or gold mark. The inflation came to a sudden halt.

The result was called "the miracle of the rentenmark." Indeed, many economists find it difficult to this day to explain exactly why the rentenmark held its value. It was ostensibly a mortgage on the entire industrial and agricultural resources of the country. It was provided that 500 rentenmarks could be converted into a bond having a nominal value of 500 gold marks. But neither the rentenmarks nor the bond were actually made convertible into gold.

Moreover, the old paper marks continued to be issued at a fantastic rate. On November 16 their circulation amounted to 93 quintillion; it soared to 496 quintillion on December 31, and continued to rise through July of the following year.

Bresciani-Turroni is inclined to attribute the "miracle" of the rentenmark to the desperate need for cash (more and more people had stopped accepting paper marks), and to the word *wertbeständig* ("constant value") printed on the new money. The public, he thinks, "allowed itself to be hypnotized" by that word.

There is a more convincing explanation. Though paper marks continued to be issued against *commercial* bills, from November 16 on, the discounting of *treasury* bills by the Reichsbank was stopped. This meant that at least no more paper money was being issued on behalf of the government to finance its deficits. In addition, the Reichsbank intervened in the foreign exchange market. In effect it pegged the rentenmark at 4.2 to the dollar and the old marks at 4.2 trillion to the dollar. Germany was now on a dollar exchange standard!

The Stabilization Crisis

The effect was dramatic. In the last months of the inflation the German economy was demoralized. Trade was coming to a standstill, many people were starving in the towns, factories closed. As we have seen, unemployment in the trade unions, which had been 6.3 percent in August, rose to 9.9 percent in September, 19.1 percent in October, 23.4 percent in November, and 28.2 percent in December. (The inflation technically came to an end in mid-November, but its disorganizing effects did not.) But after that confidence quickly revived, and trade, production, and employment with it.

Bresciani-Turroni and other writers refer to the "stabilization crisis" that follows an inflation which has been brought to a halt. But after a hyperinflation has passed beyond a certain point, any so-called stabilization crisis is comparatively mild. This is because the inflation itself has brought so much economic disorganization.

When it is said that unemployment rose after the mark stabilization, the statement is true at best only as applied to a few months. Bresciani-Turroni's month-by-month tables of unemployment end in December 1923. Here is what happened in the nine months from October 1923 through June 1924:[5]

Month	Total Unemployed
October 1923	534,360
November 1923	954,664
December 1923	1,473,688
January 1924	1,533,495
February 1924	1,439,780
March 1924	1,167,785
April 1924	694,559
May 1924	571,783
June 1924	401,958

Thus by June 1924 unemployment had returned to the prestabilization figure.

There was a real stabilization crisis, but it showed itself in a different way. One of the things that happens in an inflation, and especially in a hyperinflation, is that labor is employed in different directions than the normal ones, and when the inflation is over, this abnormal demand disappears. During an inflation labor is drawn into luxury lines — furs, perfumes, jewelry, expensive hotels, nightclubs — and many essentials are comparatively neglected. In Germany labor went particularly into fixed capital, into the erection of new plant, and into the overexpansion of industries making "instrumental" goods. And then, suddenly, as one industrialist bluntly put it, many of these factories were found to be "nothing but *rubbish*." In many cases it was soon found to be a mistake even to keep them closed down in the hope of reopening later. The mere cost of maintenance was excessive. It was cheaper to demolish them.

In brief, when the inflation ended, the distortions and illusions to which it had given rise came to an end with it. Parts of the economy had been overdeveloped at the expense of the rest. The inflation had produced a great lowering of real wages. In the first months of 1924 a big increase took place in the average incomes of individual workers as well as in employment. The index of real incomes rose from 68.1 in January 1924 to 124 in June 1928. This led to a great increase in the demand for consumption goods, and to a corresponding fall in the production of capital or instrumental goods. There was suddenly recognized to have been a great overproduction of coal, iron, and steel. Unemployment set in in these industries. But once more careful attention was paid to production costs, and there was a return to labor efficiency.

There was apparently a great shortage of working capital, if we judge by interest rates. In April and May 1924 the rate for monthly loans rose in Berlin to a level equivalent to 72 percent a year. But a large part of this reflected continuing distrust of the stability of the new currency. At the same time loans in foreign currencies were only 16 percent. And in October 1924, for example, when rates for loans in marks had fallen to 13 percent, loans in foreign currencies were down to 7.2 percent.

It would be difficult to sum up the whole German inflation episode better than Bresciani-Turroni himself did in the concluding paragraph of his great book on the subject:

> At first inflation stimulated production because of the divergence between the internal and external values of the mark, but later it exercised an increasingly disadvantageous influence, disorganizing and limiting production. It annihilated thrift; it made reform of the national budget impossible for years; it obstructed the solution of the Reparations question; it destroyed incalculable moral and intellectual values. It provoked a serious revolution in social classes, a few people accumulating wealth and forming a class of usurpers of national property, whilst millions of individuals were thrown into poverty. It was a distressing preoccupation and constant torment of innumerable families; it poisoned the German people by spreading among all classes the spirit of speculation and by diverting them from proper and regular work, and it was the cause of incessant political and moral disturbance. It is indeed easy enough to understand why the record of the sad years 1919–23 always weighs like a nightmare on the German people.

These lines were first published in 1931. There is only one thing to add. The demoralization that the debasement of the currency left in its wake played a major role in bringing the Nazis and Adolf Hitler into power in 1933.

[1] For most of the statistics and some of the other information in this chapter I am indebted to two books: chiefly to Costantino Bresciani-Turroni, *The Economics of Inflation* (London: George Allen & Unwin, 1937), and partly to Frank D. Graham, *Exchange, Prices, and Production in Hyper-*

Inflation: Germany, 1920–1923 (Princeton: Princeton University Press, 1930; and New York: Russell & Russell, 1967). These authors in turn derived most of their statistics from official sources.

[2] Karl Helfferich, *Das Geld* (sixth edition, Leipzig, 1923).

[3] *Economics of Inflation*, p. 197.

[4] Lecture, 1942; published in *Encounter*, 1975.

[5] The figures do not include part-time workers or employees in public emergency projects, but only unemployed workers eligible for unemployment compensation. I am indebted to Prof. Günther Schmölders for supplying them.

10. The Consequences to Society of Changes in the Value of Money
John Maynard Keynes

> *This chapter from Keynes's famous* Tract on Monetary Reform *is a classic treatment of the disruptive consequences of inflation, written largely in reaction to the post-World War I German hyperinflation. Keynes here emphasizes the tendency of inflation—and unanticipated inflation especially—to redistribute wealth in a way that discourages saving and investment. --G.S., Ed.*

* * *

MONEY is only important for what it will procure. Thus a change in the monetary unit, which is uniform in its operation and affects all transactions equally, has no consequences. If, by a change in the established standard of value, a man received and owned twice as much money as he did before in payment for all rights and for all efforts, and if he also paid out twice as much money for all acquisitions and for all satisfactions, he would be wholly unaffected.

It follows, therefore, that a change in the value of money, that is to say in the level of prices, is important to Society only in so far as its incidence is unequal. Such changes have produced in the past, and are producing now, the vastest social consequences, because, as we all know, when the value of money changes, it does *not* change equally for all persons or for all purposes. A man's receipts and his outgoings are not all modified in one uniform proportion. Thus a change in prices and rewards, as measured in money, generally affects different classes unequally, transfers wealth from one to another, bestows affluence here and embarrassment there, and redistributes Fortune's favours so as to frustrate design and disappoint expectation.

The fluctuations in the value of money since 1914 have been on a scale so great as to constitute, with all that they involve, one of the most significant events in the economic history of the modern world. The fluctuation of the standard, whether gold, silver, or paper, has not only been of unprecedented violence, but has been visited on a society of which the economic organisation is more dependent than that of any earlier epoch on the assumption that the standard of value would be moderately stable.

During the Napoleonic Wars and the period immediately succeeding them the extreme fluctuation of English prices within a single year was 22 per cent; and the highest price level reached during the first quarter of the nineteenth century, which we used to reckon the most disturbed period of our currency history, was less than double the lowest and with an interval of thirteen years. Compare with this the extraordinary movements of the past nine years. To recall the reader's mind to the exact facts, I refer him to the table on the next page.

I have not included those countries—Russia, Poland, and Austria—where the old currency has long been bankrupt. But it will be observed that, even apart from the countries which have suffered revolution or defeat, no quarter of the world has escaped a violent movement. In the United States, where the gold standard has functioned unabated, in Japan, where the war brought with it more profit than liability, in the neutral country of Sweden, the changes in the value of money have been comparable with those in the United Kingdom.

INDEX NUMBERS OF WHOLESALE PRICES EXPRESSED AS A PERCENTAGE OF 1913 (1).

Monthly Average.	United Kingdom (2).	France.	Italy.	Germany.	U.S.A. (3).	Canada.	Japan.	Sweden.	India.
1913	100	100	100	100	100	100	100	100	..
1914	100	102	96	106	98	100	95	116	100
1915	127	140	133	142	101	109	97	145	112
1916	160	189	201	153	127	134	117	185	128
1917	206	262	299	179	177	175	149	244	147
1918	227	340	409	217	194	205	196	339	180
1919	242	357	364	415	206	216	239	330	198
1920	295	510	624	1,486	226	250	260	347	204
1921	182	345	577	1,911	147	182	200	211	181
1922	159	327	562	34,182	149	165	196	162	180
1923*	159	411	582	765,000	157	167	192	166	179

(1) These figures are taken from the *Monthly Bulletin of Statistics* of the League of Nations. (2) *Statist* up to 1919; thereafter the median of the *Economist, Statist,* and Board of Trade Index Numbers. (3) Bureau of Labour Index Number (revised).

* First half-year.

From 1914 to 1920 all these countries experienced an expansion in the supply of money to spend relatively to the supply of things to purchase, that is to say *Inflation*. Since 1920 those countries which have regained control of their financial situation, not content with bringing the Inflation to an end, have contracted their supply of money and have experienced the fruits of *Deflation*. Others have followed inflationary courses more riotously than before. In a few, of which Italy is one, an imprudent desire to deflate has been balanced by the intractability of the financial situation, with the happy result of comparatively stable prices.

Each process, Inflation and Deflation alike, has inflicted great injuries. Each has an effect in altering the *distribution* of wealth between different classes, Inflation in this respect being the worse of the two. Each has also an effect in overstimulating or retarding the *production* of wealth, though here Deflation is the more injurious. The division of our subject thus indicated is the most convenient for us to follow,— examining first the effect of changes in the value of money on the distribution of wealth with most of our attention on Inflation, and next their effect on the production of wealth with most of our attention on Deflation. How have the price changes of the past nine years affected the productivity of the community as a whole, and how have they affected the conflicting interests and mutual relations of its component classes? The answer to these questions will serve to establish the gravity of the evils, into the remedy for which it is the object of this book to inquire.

I.—Changes in the Value of Money, as affecting Distribution

For the purpose of this inquiry a triple classification of Society is convenient—into the Investing Class, the Business Class, and the Earning Class. These classes overlap, and the same individual may earn, deal, and invest; but in the present organisation of society such a division corresponds to a social cleavage and an actual divergence of interest.

1. *The Investing Class.*

Of the various purposes which money serves, some essentially depend upon the assumption that its real value is nearly constant over a period of time. The chief of these are those connected, in a wide sense, with contracts for the *investment of money*. Such contracts—namely, those which provide for the payment of fixed sums of money over a long period of time—are the characteristic of what it is convenient to call the *Investment System,* as distinct from the property system generally.

Under this phase of capitalism, as developed during the nineteenth century, many arrangements were devised for separating the management of property from its ownership. These arrangements were of three leading types: (1) Those in which the proprietor, while parting with the management of his property, retained his ownership of it—*i.e.* of the actual land, buildings, and machinery, or of whatever else it consisted in, this mode of tenure being typified by a holding of ordinary shares in a joint-stock company; (2) those in which he parted with the property temporarily, receiving a fixed sum of *money* annually in the meantime, but regained his property eventually, as typified by a lease; and (3) those in which he parted with his real property permanently, in return either for a perpetual annuity fixed in terms of money, or for a terminable annuity and the repayment of the principal in money at the end of the term, as typified by mortgages, bonds, debentures, and preference shares. This third type represents the full development of *Investment.*

Contracts to receive fixed sums of money at future dates (made without provision for possible changes in the real value of money at those dates) must have existed as long as money has been lent and borrowed. In the form of leases and mortgages, and also of permanent loans to Governments and to a few private bodies, such as the East India Company, they were already frequent in the eighteenth century. But during the nineteenth century they developed a new and increased importance, and had, by the beginning of the twentieth, divided the propertied classes into two groups—the "business men" and the "investors"—with partly divergent interests. The division was not sharp as between individuals; for business men might be investors also, and investors might hold ordinary shares; but the division was nevertheless real, and not the less important because it was seldom noticed.

By this system the active business class could call to the aid of their enterprises not only their own wealth but the savings of the whole community; and the professional and propertied classes, on the other hand, could find an employment for their resources, which involved them in little trouble, no responsibility, and (it was believed) small risk.

For a hundred years the system worked, throughout Europe, with an extraordinary success and facilitated the growth of wealth on an unprecedented scale. To save and to invest became at once the duty and the delight of a large class. The savings were seldom drawn on, and, accumulating at compound interest, made possible the material triumphs which we now all take for granted. The morals, the politics, the literature, and the religion of the age joined in a grand conspiracy for the promotion of saving. God and Mammon were reconciled. Peace on earth to men of good means. A rich man could, after all, enter into the Kingdom of Heaven—if only he saved. A new harmony sounded from the celestial spheres. "It is curious to observe how, through the wise and beneficent arrangement of Providence, men thus do the greatest service to the public, when they are thinking of nothing but their own gain"[1]; so sang the angels.

The atmosphere thus created well harmonised the demands of expanding business and the needs of an expanding population with the growth of a comfortable non-business class. But amidst the general enjoyment of ease and progress, the extent, to which the system depended on the stability of the money to which the investing classes had committed their fortunes, was generally overlooked; and an unquestioning confidence was apparently felt that this matter would look after itself. Investments spread and multiplied, until, for the middle classes of the world, the gilt-edged bond came to typify all that was most permanent and most secure. So rooted in our day has been the conventional belief in the stability and safety of a money contract that, according to English law, trustees have been encouraged to embark their trust funds exclusively in such transactions, and are indeed forbidden,

---

[1] *Easy Lessons on Money Matters for the Use of Young People.* Published by the Society for Promoting Christian Knowledge. Twelfth Edition, 1850.

except in the case of real estate (an exception which is itself a survival of the conditions of an earlier age), to employ them otherwise.[2]

As in other respects, so also in this, the nineteenth century relied on the future permanence of its own happy experiences and disregarded the warning of past misfortunes. It chose to forget that there is no historical warrant for expecting money to be represented even by a constant quantity of a particular metal, far less by a constant purchasing power. Yet Money is simply that which the State declares from time to time to be a good legal discharge of money contracts. In 1914 gold had not been the English standard for a century or the sole standard of any other country for half a century. There is no record of a prolonged war or a great social upheaval which has not been accompanied by a change in the legal tender, but an almost unbroken chronicle in every country which has a history, back to the earliest dawn of economic record, of a progressive deterioration in the real value of the successive legal tenders which have represented money.

Moreover, this progressive deterioration in the value of money through history is not an accident, and has had behind it two great driving forces— the impecuniosity of Governments and the superior political influence of the debtor class.

The power of taxation by currency depreciation is one which has been inherent in the State since Rome discovered it. The creation of legal-tender has been and is a Government's ultimate reserve; and no State or Government is likely to decree its own bankruptcy or its own downfall, so long as this instrument still lies at hand unused.

Besides this, as we shall see below, the benefits of a depreciating currency are not restricted to the Government. Farmers and debtors and all persons liable to pay fixed money dues share in the advantage. As now in the persons of business men, so also in former ages these classes constituted the active and constructive elements in the economic

---

[2] German trustees were not released from a similar obligation until 1923, by which date the value of trust funds invested in titles to money had entirely disappeared.

scheme. Those secular changes, therefore, which in the past have depreciated money, assisted the new men and emancipated them from the dead hand; they benefited new wealth at the expense of old, and armed enterprise against accumulation. The tendency of money to depreciate has been in past times a weighty counterpoise against the cumulative results of compound interest and the inheritance of fortunes. It has been a loosening influence against the rigid distribution of old-won wealth and the separation of ownership from activity. By this means each generation can disinherit in part its predecessors' heirs; and the project of founding a perpetual fortune must be disappointed in this way, unless the community with conscious deliberation provides against it in some other way, more equitable and more expedient.

At any rate, under the influence of these two forces—the financial necessities of Governments and the political influence of the debtor class—sometimes the one and sometimes the other, the progress of inflation has been *continuous*, if we consider long periods, ever since money was first devised in the sixth century B.C. Sometimes the standard of value has depreciated of itself; failing this, debasements have done the work.

Nevertheless it is easy at all times, as a result of the way we use money in daily life, to forget all this and to look on money as itself the absolute standard of value; and when, besides, the actual events of a hundred years have not disturbed his illusions, the average man regards what has been normal for three generations as a part of the permanent social fabric.

The course of events during the nineteenth century favoured such ideas. During its first quarter, the very high prices of the Napoleonic Wars were followed by a somewhat rapid improvement in the value of money. For the next seventy years, with some temporary fluctuations, the tendency of prices continued to be downwards, the lowest point being reached in 1896. But while this was the tendency as regards direction, the remarkable feature of this long period was the relative *stability* of the price level. Approximately the *same* level of price ruled in or about the years 1826, 1841, 1855, 1862, 1867, 1871, and 1915. Prices were also level in the years 1844, 1881, and 1914. If we call the index number of these latter years 100, we find that, for the period of close on a century from 1826 to the outbreak of war, the maximum fluctuation in either direction was 30 points, the index number never rising above 130 and never falling below 70. No wonder that we came to believe in the stability of money contracts over a long period. The metal *gold* might not possess all the theoretical advantages of an artificially regulated standard, but it could not be tampered with and had proved reliable in practice.

At the same time, the investor in Consols in the early part of the century had done very well in three different ways. The "security" of his investment had come to be considered as near absolute perfection as was possible. Its capital value had uniformly appreciated, partly for the reason just stated, but chiefly because the steady fall in the rate of interest increased the number of years' purchase of the annual income which represented the capital.[1] And the annual money income had a purchasing power which on the whole was increasing. If, for example, we consider the seventy years from 1826 to 1896 (and ignore the great improvement immediately after Waterloo), we find that the capital value of Consols rose steadily, with only temporary set-backs, from 79 to 109 (in spite of Goschen's conversion from a 3 per cent rate to a $2\frac{3}{4}$ per cent rate in 1889 and a $2\frac{1}{2}$ per cent rate effective in 1903), while the purchasing power of the annual dividends, even after allowing for the reduced rates of interest, had increased 50 per cent. But Consols, too, had added the virtue of stability to that of improvement. Except in years of crisis Consols never fell below 90 during the reign of Queen Victoria; and even in '48, when thrones were crumbling, the mean price of the year fell but 5 points. Ninety when she ascended the throne, they reached their maximum with her in the year of Diamond

---

[1] If (for example) the rate of interest falls from $4\frac{1}{2}$ per cent to 3 per cent, 3 per cent Consols rise in value from 66 to 100.

Jubilee. What wonder that our parents thought Consols a good investment!

Thus there grew up during the nineteenth century a large, powerful, and greatly respected class of persons, well-to-do individually and very wealthy in the aggregate, who owned neither buildings, nor land, nor businesses, nor precious metals, but titles to an annual income in legal-tender money. In particular, that peculiar creation and pride of the nineteenth century, the savings of the middle class, had been mainly thus embarked. Custom and favourable experience had acquired for such investments an unimpeachable reputation for security.

Before the war these medium fortunes had already begun to suffer some loss (as compared with the summit of their prosperity in the middle 'nineties) from the rise in prices and also in the rate of interest. But the monetary events which have accompanied and have followed the war have taken from them about one-half of their real value in England, seven-eighths in France, eleven-twelfths in Italy, and virtually the whole in Germany and in the succession states of Austria-Hungary and Russia.

The loss to the typical English investor of the pre-war period is sufficiently measured by the loss to the investor in Consols. Such an investor, as we have already seen, was steadily improving his position, apart from temporary fluctuations, up to 1896, and in this and the following year two maxima were reached simultaneously — both the capital value of an annuity and also the purchasing power of money. Between 1896 and 1914, on the other hand, the investor had already suffered a serious loss—the capital value of his annuity had fallen by about a third, and the purchasing power of his income had also fallen by nearly a third. This loss, however, was incurred gradually over a period of nearly twenty years from an exceptional maximum, and did not leave him appreciably worse off than he had been in the early 'eighties or the early 'forties. But upon the top of this came the further swifter loss of the war period. Between 1914 and 1920 the capital value of the investor's annuity again fell by more than a third, and the purchasing power of his income by about two-thirds. In addition, the standard rate of income tax rose from 7½ per cent in 1914 to 30 per cent in 1921.[1] Roughly estimated in round numbers, the change may be represented thus in terms of an index of which the base year is 1914:

	Purchasing Power of the Income of Consols.[1]	Do. after deduction of Income Tax at the standard rate.	Money price of the capital value of Consols.	Purchasing Power of the capital value of Consols.
1815	61	59	92	56
1826	85	90	108	92
1841	85	90	122	104
1869	87	89	127	111
1883	104	108	138	144
1896	139	145	150	208
1914	100	100	100	100
1920	34	26	64	22
1921	53	39	56	34
1922	62	50	76	47

[1] Without allowance for the reduction of the interest from 3 to 2½ per cent

The second column well illustrates what a splendid investment gilt-edged stocks had been through the century from Waterloo to Mons, even if we omit altogether the abnormal values of 1896–97. Our table shows how the epoch of Diamond Jubilee was the culminating moment in the prosperity of the British middle class. But it also exhibits with the precision of figures the familiar bewailed plight of those who try to live on the income of the same trustee investments as before the war. The owner of consols in 1922 had a real income, one half of what he had in 1914 and one third of what he had in 1896. The whole of the improvement of the nineteenth century had been obliterated, and his situation was not quite so good as it had been after Waterloo.

Some mitigating circumstances should not be overlooked. Whilst the war was a period of the dissipation of the community's resources as a whole, it was a period of saving for the individuals of the saving class, who with their larger holdings of the securities

[1] Since 1896 there has been the further burden of the Death Duties.

of the Government now have an increased aggregate money claim on the receipts of the Exchequer. Also, the investing class, which has lost money, overlaps, both socially and by the ties of family, with the business class, which has made money, sufficiently to break in many cases the full severity of the loss. Moreover, in England, there has been a substantial recovery from the low point of 1920.

But these things do not wash away the significance of the facts. The effect of the war, and of the monetary policy which has accompanied and followed it, has been to take away a large part of the real value of the possessions of the investing class. The loss has been so rapid and so intermixed in the time of its occurrence with other worse losses that its full measure is not yet separately apprehended. But it has effected, nevertheless, a far-reaching change in the relative position of different classes. Throughout the Continent the pre-war savings of the middle class, so far as they were invested in bonds, mortgages, or bank deposits, have been largely or entirely wiped out. Nor can it be doubted that this experience must modify social psychology towards the practice of saving and investment. What was deemed most secure has proved least so. He who neither spent nor " speculated," who made " proper provision for his family," who sang hymns to security and observed most straitly the morals of the edified and the respectable injunctions of the worldly-wise,—he, indeed, who gave fewest pledges to Fortune has yet suffered her heaviest visitations.

What moral for our present purpose should we draw from this ? Chiefly, I think, that it is not safe or fair to combine the social organisation developed during the nineteenth century (and still retained) with a *laisser-faire* policy towards the value of money. It is not true that our former arrangements have worked well. If we are to continue to draw the voluntary savings of the community into " investments," we must make it a prime object of deliberate State policy that the standard of value, in terms of which they are expressed, should be kept stable; adjusting in other ways (calculated to touch all forms of wealth equally and not concentrated on the relatively helpless "investors") the redistribution of the national wealth, if, in course of time, the laws of inheritance and the rate of accumulation have drained too great a proportion of the income of the active classes into the spending control of the inactive.

2. *The Business Class*

It has long been recognised, by the business world and by economists alike, that a period of rising prices acts as a stimulus to enterprise and is beneficial to business men.

In the first place there is the advantage which is the counterpart of the loss to the investing class which we have just examined. When the value of money falls, it is evident that those persons who have engaged to pay fixed sums of money yearly out of the profits of active business must benefit, since their fixed money outgoings will bear a smaller proportion than formerly to their money turnover. This benefit persists not only during the transitional period of change, but also, so far as old loans are concerned, when prices have settled down at their new and higher level. For example, the farmers throughout Europe, who had raised by mortgage the funds to purchase the land they farmed, now find themselves almost freed from the burden at the expense of the mortgagees.

But during the period of change, while prices are rising month by month, the business man has a further and greater source of windfall. Whether he is a merchant or a manufacturer, he will generally buy before he sells, and on at least a part of his stock he will run the risk of price changes. If, therefore, month after month his stock appreciates on his hands, he is always selling at a better price than he expected and securing a windfall profit upon which he had not calculated. In such a period the business of trade becomes unduly easy. Any one who can borrow money and is not exceptionally unlucky must make a profit, which he may have done little to deserve. The continuous enjoyment of such profits engenders an expectation of their renewal. The practice of borrowing from banks is extended beyond what is normal. If the market expects prices to rise still further, it is natural that stocks of commodities should be held speculatively for the rise, and for a time the mere expectation of a rise is sufficient, by inducing speculative purchases, to produce one.

Take, for example, the *Statist* index number for raw materials month by month from April, 1919, to March, 1920:

April, 1919 . . . 100	October 127
May 108	November . . . 131
June 112	December . . . 135
July 117	January, 1920 . . 142
August 120	February . . . 150
September . . . 121	March 146

It follows from this table that a man, who borrowed money from his banker and used the proceeds to purchase raw materials selected at random, stood to make a profit in every single month of this period with the exception of the last, and would have cleared 46 per cent on the average of the year. Yet bankers were not charging at this time above 7 per cent for their advances, leaving a clear profit of between 30 and 40 per cent per annum, without the exercise of any particular skill, to any person lucky enough to have embarked on these courses. How much more were the opportunities of persons whose business position and expert knowledge enabled them to exercise intelligent anticipation as to the probable course of prices of particular commodities! Yet any dealer in or user of raw materials on a large scale who knew his trade was thus situated. The profits of certain kinds of business to the man who has a little skill or some luck are certain in such a period to be inordinate. Great fortunes may be made in a few months. But apart from all such, the steady-going business man, who would be pained and insulted at the thought of being designated speculator or profiteer, may find windfall profits dropping into his lap which he has neither sought nor desired.

Economists draw an instructive distinction between what are termed the "money" rate of interest and the "real" rate of interest. If a sum of money worth 100 in terms of commodities at the time when the loan is made is lent for a year at 5 per cent interest, and is only worth 90 in terms of commodities at the end of the year, the lender receives back, including his interest, what is only worth 94½. This is expressed by saying that while the *money* rate of interest was 5 per cent, the *real* rate of interest had actually been negative and equal to *minus* 5½ per cent. In the same way, if at the end of the period the value of money had risen and the capital sum lent had come to be worth 110 in terms of commodities, while the *money* rate of interest would still be 5 per cent the *real* rate of interest would have been 15½ per cent.

Such considerations, even though they are not explicitly present to the minds of the business world, are far from being academic. The business world may speak, and even think, as though the money rate of interest could be considered by itself, without reference to the real rate. But it does not act so. The merchant or manufacturer, who is calculating whether a 7 per cent bank rate is so onerous as to compel him to curtail his operations, is very much influenced by his anticipations about the prospective price of the commodity in which he is interested.

Thus, when prices are rising, the business man who borrows money is able to repay the lender with what, in terms of real value, not only represents no interest, but is even less than the capital originally advanced; that is, the real rate of interest falls to a negative value, and the borrower reaps a corresponding benefit. It is true that, in so far as a rise of prices is foreseen, attempts to get advantage from this by increased borrowing force the money rates of interest to move upwards. It is for this reason, amongst others, that a high bank rate should be associated with a period of rising prices, and a low bank rate with a period of falling prices. The apparent abnormality of the money rate of interest at such times is merely the other side of the attempt of the real rate of interest to steady itself. Nevertheless in a period of rapidly changing prices, the money rate of interest seldom adjusts itself adequately or fast enough to prevent the real rate from becoming abnormal. For it is not the *fact* of a given rise of prices, but the *expectation* of a rise compounded of the various possible price-movements and the estimated probability of each, which affects money rates; and in countries where the currency has not collapsed completely, there has seldom or never existed a sufficient general confidence in a further rise or fall of prices to cause the short-money rate of interest to rise above 10 per cent per annum, or to fall below 1 per cent.[1] A fluctuation of this order is not sufficient to balance a movement of prices, up or down, of more than (say) 5 per cent per annum,—a rate which the actual price movement has frequently exceeded.

Germany has recently provided an illustration of the extraordinary degree in which the money rate of interest can rise in its endeavour to keep up with the real rate, when prices have continued to rise for so long and with such violence that, rightly or wrongly, every one believes that they will continue to rise further. Yet even there the money rate of interest has never risen high enough to keep pace with the rise of prices. In the autumn of 1922, the full effects were just becoming visible of the long preceding period during which the real rate of interest in Germany had reached a high negative figure, that is to say during which any one who could borrow marks and turn them into assets would have found at the end of any given period that the appreciation in the mark-value of the assets was far greater than the interest he had to pay for borrowing them. By this means great fortunes were snatched out of general calamity; and those made most who had seen first, that the right game was to borrow and to borrow and to borrow, and thus secure the difference between the real rate of interest and the money rate. But after this had been good business for many months, every one began to take a hand, with belated results on the money rate of interest. At that time, with a nominal Reichsbank rate of 8 per cent, the effective gilt-edged rate for short loans had risen to 22 per cent per annum. During the first half of 1923, the rate of the Reichsbank itself rose to 24 per cent, and subsequently to 30, and finally 108 per cent, whilst the

[1] The merchant, who borrows money in order to take advantage of a prospective high real rate of interest, has to act in advance of the rise in prices, and is calculating on a probability, not upon a certainty, with the result that he will be deterred by a movement in the money rate of interest of much less magnitude than the contrary movement in the real rate of interest, upon which indeed he is reckoning, yet is not reckoning with certainty.

market rate fluctuated violently at preposterous figures, reaching at times 3 per cent *per week* for certain types of loan. With the final currency collapse of July-September 1923, the open market rate was altogether demoralised, and reached figures of 100 per cent per month. In face, however, of the rate of currency depreciation, even such figures were inadequate, and the bold borrower was still making money.

In Hungary, Poland, and Russia—wherever prices were expected to collapse yet further—the same phenomenon was present, exhibiting as through a microscope what takes place everywhere when prices are expected to rise.

On the other hand, when prices are falling 30 to 40 per cent between the average of one year and that of the next, as they were in Great Britain and in the United States during 1921, even a bank rate of 1 per cent would have been oppressive to business, since it would have corresponded to a very high rate of real interest. Any one who could have foreseen the movement even partially would have done well for himself by selling out his assets and staying out of business for the time being.

But if the depreciation of money is a source of gain to the business man, it is also the occasion of opprobrium. To the consumer the business man's exceptional profits appear as the cause (instead of the consequence) of the hated rise of prices. Amidst the rapid fluctuations of his fortunes he himself loses his conservative instincts, and begins to think more of the large gains of the moment than of the lesser, but permanent, profits of normal business. The welfare of his enterprise in the relatively distant future weighs less with him than before, and thoughts are excited of a quick fortune and clearing out. His excessive gains have come to him unsought and without fault or design on his part, but once acquired he does not lightly surrender them, and will struggle to retain his booty. With such impulses and so placed, the business man is himself not free from a suppressed uneasiness. In his heart he loses his former self-confidence in his relation to society, in his utility and necessity in the economic scheme.

He fears the future of his business and his class, and the less secure he feels his fortune to be the tighter he clings to it. The business man, the prop of society and the builder of the future, to whose activities and rewards there had been accorded, not long ago, an almost religious sanction, he of all men and classes most respectable, praiseworthy and necessary, with whom interference was not only disastrous but almost impious, was now to suffer sidelong glances, to feel himself suspected and attacked, the victim of unjust and injurious laws,—to become, and know himself half-guilty, a profiteer.

No man of spirit will consent to remain poor if he believes his betters to have gained their goods by lucky gambling. To convert the business man into the profiteer is to strike a blow at capitalism, because it destroys the psychological equilibrium which permits the perpetuance of unequal rewards. The economic doctrine of normal profits, vaguely apprehended by every one, is a necessary condition for the justification of capitalism. The business man is only tolerable so long as his gains can be held to bear some relation to what, roughly and in some sense, his activities have contributed to society.

This, then, is the second disturbance to the existing economic order for which the depreciation of money is responsible. If the fall in the value of money discourages investment, it also discredits enterprise.

Not that the business man was allowed, even during the period of boom, to retain the whole of his exceptional profits. A host of popular remedies vainly attempted to cure the evils of the day; which remedies themselves—subsidies, price and rent fixing, profiteer hunting, and excess profits duties—eventually became not the least part of the evils.

In due course came the depression, with falling prices, which operate on those who hold stocks in a manner exactly opposite to rising prices. Excessive losses, bearing no relation to the efficiency of the business, took the place of windfall gains; and the effort of every one to hold as small stocks as possible brought industry to a standstill, just as previously their efforts to accumulate stocks had over-stimulated it. Unemployment succeeded Profiteering as the problem of the hour. But whilst the cyclical movement of trade and credit has, in the good-currency countries, partly reversed, for the time being at least, the great rise of 1920, it has, in the countries of continuing inflation, made no more than a ripple on the rapids of depreciation.

3. *The Earner.*

It has been a commonplace of economic text-books that wages tend to lag behind prices, with the result that the real earnings of the wage-earner are diminished during a period of rising prices. This has often been true in the past, and may be true even now of certain classes of labour which are ill-placed or ill-organised for improving their position. But in Great Britain, at any rate, and in the United States also, some important sections of labour were able to take advantage of the situation not only to obtain money wages equivalent in purchasing power to what they had before, but to secure a real improvement, to combine this with a diminution in their hours of work (and, so far, of the work done), and to accomplish this (in the case of Great Britain) at a time when the total wealth of the community as a whole had suffered a decrease. This reversal of the usual course has not been due to an accident and is traceable to definite causes.

The organisation of certain classes of labour—railwaymen, miners, dockers, and others—for the purpose of securing wage increases is better than it was. Life in the army, perhaps for the first time in the history of wars, raised in many respects the conventional standard of requirements,—the soldier was better clothed, better shod, and often better fed than the labourer, and his wife, adding in war time a separation allowance to new opportunities to earn, had also enlarged her ideas.

But these influences, while they would have supplied the motive, might have lacked the means to the result if it had not been for another factor—the windfalls of the profiteer. The fact that the business man had been gaining, and gaining notoriously, considerable windfall profits in excess of the normal profits of trade, laid him open to pressure, not only from his employees but from public opinion generally; and enabled him to meet this pressure without financial difficulty. In fact, it was worth his while to pay ransom, and to share with his workmen the good fortune of the day.

Thus the working classes improved their *relative* position in the years following the war, as against all other classes except that of the "profiteers." In some important cases they improved their absolute position—that is to say, account being taken of shorter hours, increased money wages, and higher prices, some sections of the working classes secured for themselves a higher real remuneration for each unit of effort or work done. But we cannot estimate the *stability* of this state of affairs, as contrasted with its desirability, unless we know the source from which the increased reward of the working classes was drawn. Was it due to a permanent modification of the economic factors which determine the distribution of the national product between different classes? Or was it due to some temporary and exhaustible influence connected with inflation and with the resulting disturbance in the standard of value?

A violent disturbance of the standard of value obscures the true situation, and for a time one class can benefit at the expense of another surreptitiously and without producing immediately the inevitable reaction. In such conditions a country can without knowing it expend in current consumption those savings which it thinks it is investing for the future; and it can even trench on existing capital or fail to make good its current depreciation. When the value of money is greatly fluctuating, the distinction between capital and income becomes confused. It is one of the evils of a depreciating currency that it enables a community to live on its capital unawares. The increasing *money* value of the community's capital goods obscures temporarily a diminution in the real quantity of the stock.

The period of depression has exacted its penalty from the working classes more in the form of unemployment than by a lowering of real wages, and State assistance to the unemployed has greatly moderated even this penalty. Money wages have followed prices downwards. But the depression of 1921–22 did not reverse or even greatly diminish the relative advantage gained by the working classes over the middle class during the previous years. In 1923 British wage rates stood at an appreciably higher level above the pre-war rates than did the cost of living, if allowance is made for the shorter hours worked.

In Germany and Austria also, but in a far greater degree than in England or in France, the change in the value of money has thrown the burden of hard circumstances on the middle class, and hitherto the labouring class have by no means supported their full proportionate share. If it be true that university professors in Germany have some responsibility for the atmosphere which bred war, their class has paid the penalty. The effects of the impoverishment, throughout Europe, of the middle class, out of which most good things have sprung, must slowly accumulate in a decay of Science and Art.

We conclude that Inflation redistributes wealth in a manner very injurious to the investor, very beneficial to the business man, and probably, in modern industrial conditions, beneficial on the whole to the earner. Its most striking consequence is its *injustice* to those who in good faith have committed their savings to titles to money rather than to things. But injustice on such a scale has further consequences. The above discussion suggests that the diminution in the production of wealth which has taken place in Europe since the war has been, to a certain extent, at the expense, not of the consumption of any class, but of the accumulation of capital. Moreover, Inflation has not only diminished the capacity of the investing class to save but has destroyed the atmosphere of confidence which is a condition of the willingness to save. Yet a growing population requires, for the maintenance of the same standard of life, a proportionate growth of capital. In Great Britain for many years to come, regardless of what the birth-rate may be from now onwards (and at the present time the number of births per day is nearly double the number of deaths), upwards of 250,000 new labourers will enter the labour market annually in excess of those going out of it. To maintain this growing body of labour at the same standard of life as before, we require not merely growing markets but a growing capital equipment. In order to keep our standards from deterioration, the national capital must grow as fast as the national labour supply, which means new savings of at least £250,000,000 [1] per annum at present. The favourable conditions for saving which existed in the nineteenth century, even though we smile at them, provided a proportionate growth between capital and population. The disturbance of the pre-existing balance between classes, which in its origins is largely traceable to the changes in the value of money, may have destroyed these favourable conditions.

On the other hand Deflation, as we shall see in the second section of the next chapter, is liable, in these days of huge national debts expressed in legal-tender money, to overturn the balance so far the other way in the interests of the *rentier*, that the burden of taxation becomes intolerable on the productive classes of the community.

II.—CHANGES IN THE VALUE OF MONEY, AS AFFECTING PRODUCTION.

If, for any reason right or wrong, the business world *expects* that prices will fall, the processes of production tend to be inhibited; and if it expects that prices will rise, they tend to be over-stimulated. A fluctuation in the measuring-rod of value does not alter in the least the wealth of the world, the needs of the world, or the productive capacity of the world. It ought not, therefore, to affect the character or the volume of what is produced. A movement of *relative*

---

[1] That is to say, it costs not less than £1000 in new capital outlay to equip a working man with organisation and appliances, which will render his labour efficient, and to house and supply himself and his family. Indeed this is probably an underestimate.

prices, that is to say of the comparative prices of different commodities, *ought* to influence the character of production, because it is an indication that various commodities are not being produced in the exactly right proportions. But this is not true of a change, as such, in the *general* price level.

The fact that the expectation of changes in the *general* price level affects the processes of production, is deeply rooted in the peculiarities of the existing economic organisation of society, partly in those described in the preceding sections of this chapter, partly in others to be mentioned in a moment. We have already seen that a change in the general level of prices, that is to say a change in the measuring-rod, which fixes the obligation of the borrowers of money (who make the decisions which set production in motion) to the lenders (who are inactive once they have lent their money), effects a redistribution of real wealth between the two groups. Furthermore, the active group can, if they foresee such a change, alter their action in advance in such a way as to minimise their losses to the other group or to increase their gains from it, if and when the expected change in the value of money occurs. If they expect a fall, it may pay them, as a group, to damp production down, although such enforced idleness impoverishes society as a whole. If they expect a rise, it may pay them to increase their borrowings and to swell production beyond the point where the real return is just sufficient to recompense society as a whole for the effort made. Sometimes, of course, a change in the measuring-rod, especially if it is unforeseen, may benefit one group at the expense of the other disproportionately to any influence it exerts on the volume of production; but the tendency, in so far as the active group anticipate a change, will be as I have described it.[1] This is

[1] The interests of the salaried and wage-earning classes will, in so far as their salaries and wages tend to be steadier in money-value than in real-value, coincide with those of the inactive capitalist group. The interests of the consumer will, in so far as he can vary the distribution of his floating resources between cash and goods purchased in advance of consumption, coincide with those of the active capitalist group; and his decisions, made in his own interests, may serve to reinforce the effect of those of the latter. But that the interests of the same individual will often be those of one of the groups in one of his capacities and of the other in another of his capacities, does not save the situation or affect the argument. For his losses in one capacity depend only infinitesimally on him personally refraining from action in his other capacity. The facts, that a man is a cannibal at home and eaten abroad, do not cancel out to render him innocuous and safe.

simply to say that the intensity of production is largely governed in existing conditions by the anticipated real profit of the *entrepreneur*. Yet this criterion is the right one for the community as a whole only when the delicate adjustment of interests is not upset by fluctuations in the standard of value.

But there is a further reason, connected with the above but nevertheless distinct, why modern methods of production require a stable standard,— a reason springing to a certain extent out of the character of the social organisation described above, but aggravated by the technical methods of present-day productive processes. With the development of international trade, involving great distances between the place of original production and the place of final consumption, and with the increased complication of the technical processes of manufacture, the amount of *risk* which attaches to the undertaking of production and the length of time through which this risk must be carried are much greater than they would be in a comparatively small self-contained community. Even in agriculture, whilst the risk to the consumer is diminished by drawing supplies from many different sources, which average the fluctuations of the seasons, the risk to the agricultural producer is increased, since, when his crop falls below his expectations in volume, he may fail to be compensated by a higher price. This increased risk is the price which producers have to pay for the other advantages of a high degree of specialisation and for the variety of their markets and their sources of supply.

The provision of adequate facilities for the carrying of this risk at a moderate cost is one of the greatest of the problems of modern economic life, and one of those which so far have been least satisfactorily solved. The business of keeping the productive machine in continuous operation (and thereby avoiding unemployment) would be greatly simplified if this risk could be diminished or if we could devise a better means of insurance against it for the individual *entrepreneur*.

A considerable part of the risk arises out of fluctuations in the *relative* value of a commodity compared with that of commodities in general during the interval which must elapse between the commencement of production and the time of consumption. This part of the risk is independent of the vagaries of money, and must be tackled by methods with which we are not concerned here. But there is also a considerable risk directly arising out of instability in the value of money. During the lengthy process of production the business world is incurring outgoings in terms of *money*—paying out in money for wages and other expenses of production—in the expectation of recouping this outlay by disposing of the product for *money* at a later date. That is to say, the business world as a whole must always be in a position where it stands to gain by a rise of price and to lose by a fall of price. Whether it likes it or not, the technique of production under a *régime* of money-contract forces the business world always to carry a big speculative position; and if it is reluctant to carry this position, the productive process must be slackened. The argument is not affected by the fact that there is some degree of specialisation of function within the business world, in so far as the professional speculator comes to the assistance of the producer proper by taking over from him a part of his risk.

Now it follows from this, not merely that the *actual occurrence* of price changes profits some classes and injures others (which has been the theme of the first section of this chapter), but that a *general fear* of falling prices may inhibit the productive process altogether. For if prices are expected to fall, not enough risk-takers can be found who are willing to carry a speculative " bull " position, and this means that *entrepreneurs* will be reluctant to embark on lengthy productive processes involving a money outlay long in advance of money recoupment,—whence unemployment. The *fact* of falling prices injures *entrepreneurs*; consequently the *fear* of falling prices causes them to protect themselves by curtailing their operations; yet it is upon the aggregate of their individual estimations of the risk, and their willingness to run the risk, that the activity of production and of employment mainly depends.

There is a further aggravation of the case, in that an expectation about the course of prices tends, if it is widely held, to be cumulative in its results up to a certain point. If prices are expected to rise and the business world acts on this expectation, that very fact causes them to rise for a time and, by verifying the expectation, reinforces it; and similarly, if it expects them to fall. Thus a comparatively weak initial impetus may be adequate to produce a considerable fluctuation.

Three generations of economists have recognised that certain influences produce a progressive and continuing change in the value of money, that others produce in it an oscillatory movement, and that the latter act cumulatively in their initial stages but produce the conditions for a reaction after a certain point. But their investigations into the oscillatory movements have been chiefly confined, until lately, to the question what kind of cause is responsible for the initial impetus. Some have been fascinated by the idea that the initial cause is always the same and is astronomically regular in the times of its appearance. Others have maintained, more plausibly, that sometimes one thing operates and sometimes another.

It is one of the objects of this book to urge that the best way to cure this mortal disease of individualism is to provide that there shall never exist any confident expectation either that prices generally are going to fall or that they are going to rise; and also that there shall be no serious risk that a movement, if it does occur, will be a big one. If, unexpectedly and accidentally, a moderate movement were to occur, wealth, though it might be redistributed, would not be diminished thereby.

To procure this result by removing all possible influences towards an initial movement, whether such influences are to be found in the skies only or everywhere, would seem to be a hopeless enterprise. The remedy would lie, rather, in so controlling the standard of value that, whenever something occurred which, left to itself, would create an expectation of a change in the general level of prices, the controlling authority should take steps to counteract this expectation by setting in motion some factor of a contrary tendency. Even if such a policy were not wholly successful, either in counteracting expectations or in avoiding actual movements, it would be an improvement on the policy of sitting quietly by, whilst a standard of value, governed by chance causes and deliberately removed from central control, produces expectations which paralyse or intoxicate the government of production.

We see, therefore, that rising prices and falling prices each have their characteristic disadvantage. The Inflation which causes the former means Injustice to individuals and to classes,—particularly to investors; and is therefore unfavourable to saving. The Deflation which causes falling prices means Impoverishment to labour and to enterprise by leading *entrepreneurs* to restrict production, in their endeavour to avoid loss to themselves; and is therefore disastrous to employment. The counterparts are, of course, also true,—namely that Deflation means Injustice to borrowers, and that Inflation leads to the over-stimulation of industrial activity. But these results are not so marked as those emphasised above, because borrowers are in a better position to protect themselves from the worst effects of Deflation than lenders are to protect themselves from those of Inflation, and because labour is in a better position to protect itself from over-exertion in good times than from under-employment in bad times.

Thus Inflation is unjust and Deflation is inexpedient. Of the two perhaps Deflation is, if we rule out exaggerated inflations such as that of Germany, the worse; because it is worse, in an impoverished world, to provoke unemployment than to disappoint the *rentier*. But it is not necessary that we should weigh one evil against the other. It is easier to agree that both are evils to be shunned. The Individualistic Capitalism of to-day, precisely because it entrusts saving to the individual investor and production to the individual employer, *presumes* a stable measuring-rod of value, and cannot be efficient —perhaps cannot survive—without one.

For these grave causes we must free ourselves from the deep distrust which exists against allowing the regulation of the standard of value to be the subject of *deliberate decision*. We can no longer afford to leave it in the category of which the distinguishing characteristics are possessed in different degrees by the weather, the birth-rate, and the Constitution,—matters which are settled by natural causes, or are the resultant of the separate action of many individuals acting independently, or require a Revolution to change them.

11. Money and Interest Rates
by William Poole

The bearing of the quantity of money on the level of interest rates is frequently misunderstood: a very naive but nonetheless common view holds that interest is the "price" of money, so that an expansion of the quantity of money tends to <u>lower</u> interest rates. In fact, monetary expansion will tend to lower interest rates in the very short run, if at all. In the long run, one-time changes in the quantity of money have no effect on interest rates, while persistent expansion of the money stocks leads to <u>higher</u> interest rates.–G.S., Ed.
****

In this chapter the relationships between money and interest rates are explored. For the most part these relationships are indirect. Money growth affects the inflation rate and the level of economic activity, both of which in turn are major determinants of the level of interest rates. In addition, when the rate of growth of money changes, but before inflation and economic activity are affected, there may be some direct monetary impact on interest rates, but this impact is probably relatively small.

As the reader is no doubt aware, there is an enormous variety of interest rates—rates on short- and long-term securities, on government bonds and corporate bonds, on savings accounts and home mortgages, and so forth. In the analysis presented here, the focus will be on interest rates on high-grade securities, but for the purposes at hand it is not necessary to be very precise about exactly what interest rates are being analyzed. As Figs. 5.1 and 5.2 make clear, interest rates on various types of securities fluctuate very much together. While much can be said about the determinants of interest rate differentials, our concern will be with the broad movements of interest rates in general.

THE SIMPLE ARITHMETIC OF INTEREST

A thorough understanding of the simple arithmetic of interest is essential to an understanding of the economics of interest. The arithmetic is, fortunately, very simple although calculation is sometimes tedious.

The best place to start is with the concept of *future value*. If $100 is placed in a savings account at five percent interest for one year, then the amount of interest earned will be $5. Assuming the interest is left in the account, at the end of the year the account balance will be $105. Or, in symbols,

$$A_1 = A_0(1 + i),$$

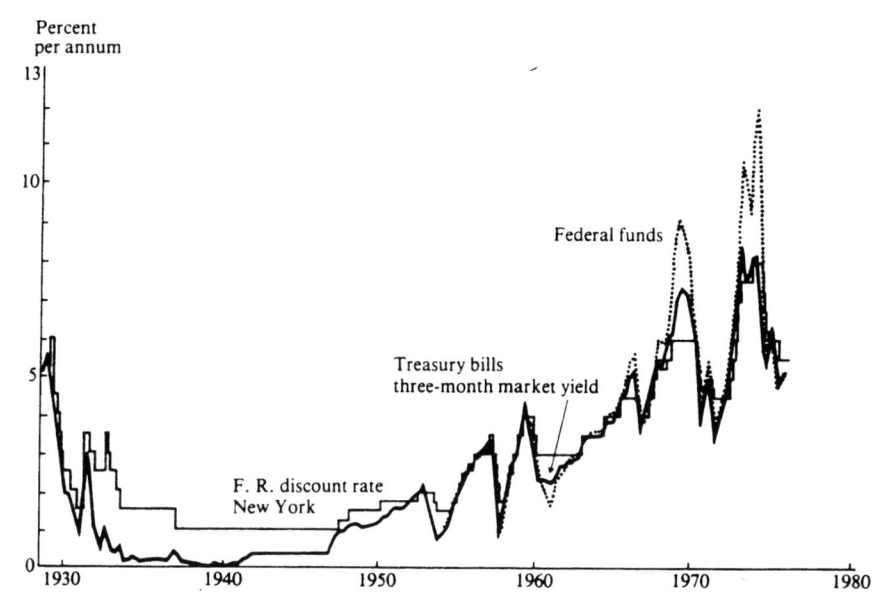

Fig. 5.1 Short-term interest rates. Federal Reserve discount rate, effective date of change; all others, quarterly averages.

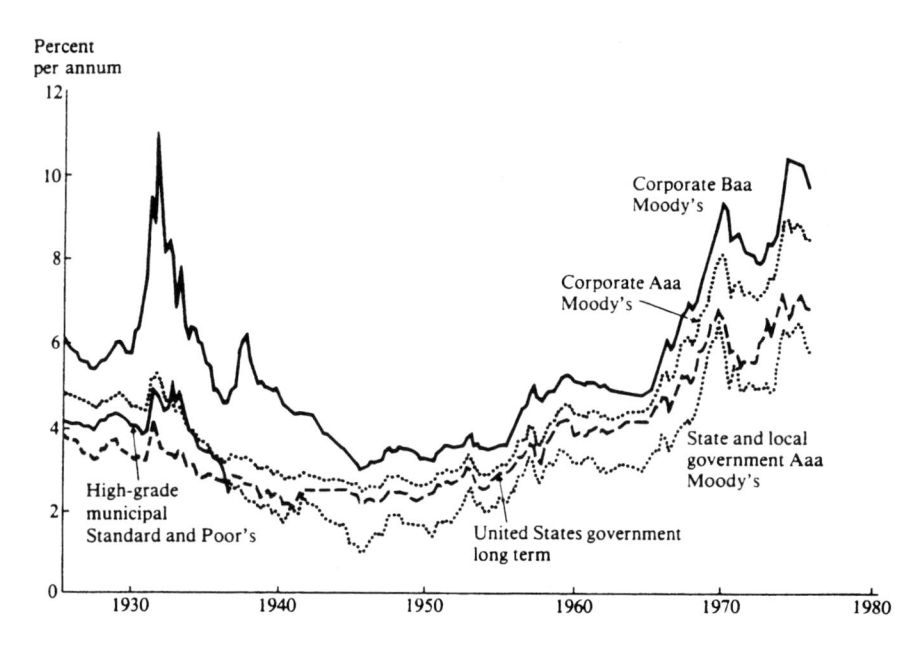

Fig. 5.2 Long-term bond yields, quarterly averages.

where A_1 is the account balance at the end of the year, A_0 the balance at the beginning of the year, and i is the interest rate expressed in decimal rather than percent form. This formula gives the *future value*, A_1, of A_0 dollars invested for one year at the interest rate i.

When funds are invested for more than one year, the same formula may be applied year by year as many times as needed. For example, it is obvious that $A_2 = A_1(1 + i)$. But since $A_1 = A_0(1 + i)$, we have $A_2 = A_0(1 + i)^2$. Thus the formula for the future value of A_0 dollars invested for two years at the same interest rate i is

$$A_2 = A_0(1 + i)^2.$$

Similarly, the future value of A_0 dollars invested for n years is

$$A_n = A_0(1 + i)^n.$$

Now the concept of *present value* may be explained. If the interest rate is five percent, how many dollars are needed *now* in order to have $105 available in one year? The answer, obviously, is $100; $100 is said to be the present value of $105 in one year at five percent interest. In symbols,

$$A_0 = \frac{A_1}{1+i}.$$

This formula can be obtained by simply dividing both sides of the future value formula by $1 + i$. Similarly, the present value of A_n dollars in n years is given by $A_0 = \frac{A_n}{(1+i)^n}$. Another frequently used terminology is that A_0 is obtained by discounting A_n; the *discount factor*, $(1 + i)^n$, is divided into A_n to obtain A_0.

Since the concept of present value so frequently seems confusing, one further comment may prove helpful. Whenever confusion reigns, start with the future value formula: "If I invest A_0 dollars now at i percent for n years, I will end up with $A_n = A_0(1 + i)^n$. If I know A_n, then I can find A_0, the present value of A_n, by dividing both sides of this formula by $(1 + i)^n$."

This discussion has been based on the assumption of *annual compounding*: it was assumed that interest was added to an account at the end of each year. In the analysis below annual compounding will be assumed; no essential difference is made by the fact that in practice a great variety of compounding periods are employed in interest rate calculations.

THE FOUR TYPES OF LOANS

There are four basic types of interest-bearing accounts and securities: the savings account, the bill, the bond, and the mortgage. Most people are familiar with the savings account—interest is added to the account every year (or every quarter, or every month) and if no withdrawals are made the account balance will grow over time according to the future value formula discussed above. Obviously, the higher the rate of interest, the more rapidly the account balance will grow.

The essential characteristic of the savings account is that the account balance is fixed at any moment of time and variations in the rate of interest generate variations in the amount of interest earnings. The present value is certain while the future value is unknown and subject to variation as the interest rate varies.

Unlike the savings account, bills, bonds, and mortgages all have known future values while their present values change when interest rates change. Consider first a one-year bill. The borrower promises to repay $100 in one year. In return, the lender turns over to the borrower the present value of $100 in one year, $100/(1 + i)$. The bill, whether a piece of paper with fancy engraving, an IOU on a scrap of paper, or a computer entry, may then be sold by the original lender to someone else. If the interest rate has gone up (down) between the time the original loan was made and the bill is sold, the present value of the bill goes down (up). The borrower is unaffected; his or her promise is to repay $100 at the maturity of the bill *regardless* of what might happen to the interest rate.

Loans in the form of bills, sometimes called discount loans, are ordinarily limited to relatively short maturities, usually a year or less. Longer term loans take the bond or mortgage form. In a bond the borrower promises to pay a predetermined *dollar* amount of interest every year and then to repay the principal at the maturity date. A mortgage has exactly the same form except that the principal is repaid year by year along with the interest instead of in a lump sum at maturity.

Consider the example of a $100, 20-year, five-percent bond. The annual interest payment is five dollars. This interest payment is fixed at the time the bond is sold and does not change over the life of the bond no matter what happens to market rates of interest. The interest rate written into the bond agreement is frequently called the coupon rate since in most cases the bond owner clips coupons off the bond year by year and sends them to the borrower in order to get the annual interest.

The present value of the bond is nothing more than the sum of the present value of all the coupons and the principal repayment. The first coupon, C, has a present value of $C/(1 + i)$, the second $C/(1 + i)^2$, and so forth out to the last coupon which has a present value of $C/(1 + i)^{20}$ on a 20-year bond. Thus, the present value of a bond maturing in m years

$$PV = \frac{C}{1+i} + \frac{C}{(1+i)^2} + \cdots + \frac{C}{(1+i)^m} + \frac{100}{}$$

This same formula can be used to calculate the except that the annual mortgage payment, in doll the last term representing the lump-sum bond p maturity is deleted.

From the present value formula for a bond (or mortgage), it is clear that the value of a bond will fluctuate if the market rate of interest, i, fluctuates. As emphasized in discussing bills, fluctuations in the market rate of interest do not affect borrowers' obligations on outstanding bonds or mortgages. For example, most readers are aware that the payments on home mortgages are not affected by fluctuations in market interest rates, a consequence of the mortgage form of borrowing.[1] But fluctuations in market rates of interest do affect the market value of the mortgage and therefore affect the lender.

The characteristics of the principal forms of loans have now been outlined along with the simple arithmetic of interest rates. The key point to understand is that when funds are borrowed through issuance of a bill, a bond, or a mortgage, the dollar repayment obligations of the borrower are fixed and do not change over the life of the loan. Changes in market rates of interest do, however, affect the owners of outstanding bills, bonds, and mortgages. An increase (decrease) in the market rate of interest decreases (increases) the present values, and therefore the market values, of these securities.

REAL VERSUS NOMINAL INTEREST RATES

The discussion so far has concerned *nominal* interest rates—interest rates stated in money terms without allowance for changes, if any, in the general price level. But the importance of inflation is obvious; would you rather lend $100 for one year at five percent in the United States today or 100 marks for one year at ten percent in Germany in 1922? Clearly, lending funds in Germany at ten percent in 1922 was essentially equivalent to giving money away since the purchasing power of 110 marks in 1923 was a tiny fraction of the purchasing power of 100 marks in 1922. If the inflation rate is 300 percent per month, then a nominal interest rate of 300 percent per month is required just to stay even, to maintain the *real* value of the funds lent.

The relationships between the real rate of interest, the nominal rate of interest, and the rate of inflation can be seen as follows. First, note that the real rate of interest is five percent if a loan yields enough dollars so that after one year five percent more goods can be purchased even though goods prices have changed. For example, if corn costs $2.00 per bushel, $200 will buy 100 bushels. One year later the price of corn may have changed, but if a $200 loan plus the interest earned will buy 105 bushels, then the real rate of interest, r, is five percent.

Real interest rate calculations are not ordinarily made using the prices of particular goods but, instead, using a general price index. If P is the price

---

[1] The type of mortgage being discussed here is the fixed rate mortgage; variable interest rate mortgages, though not common, do exist.

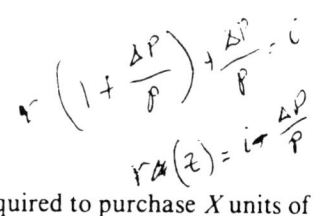

level at a particular time, then PX dollars are required to purchase X units of goods in general at that time. If $P + \Delta P$ is the price level one year later, then $(P + \Delta P) \times (1 + r)$ dollars are required to purchase $X(1 + r)$ units of goods one year later. The dollar *amount* of interest is the difference between $(P + \Delta P) \times (1 + r)$ and PX. The nominal interest rate, i, expressed in decimal rather than percent form, is the dollar amount of interest divided by the loan of PX dollars. Thus,

$$i = \frac{(P + \Delta P) \times (1 + r) - PX}{PX} = r + \frac{\Delta P}{P} + r\frac{\Delta P}{P}$$

As long as the inflation rate and the real rate of interest are both relatively low, the term $r\frac{\Delta P}{P}$ is very small and may be neglected. Thus, the frequently used relationship $i = r + \frac{\Delta P}{P}$ is obtained. This relationship is often written $r = i - \frac{\Delta P}{P}$ to reflect the fact that once a loan has been made at a stated nominal interest rate, i, the real rate of interest actually earned will depend on what the inflation rate turns out to be.

THE EFFECTS OF INFLATION ON INTEREST RATES

Now that interest rate arithmetic and background have been discussed, let us begin the discussion of interest rate economics by examining the effect of long-run inflation once the economy has fully adjusted to inflation. To understand the effect of inflation on the nominal rate of interest, consider the following example: Suppose, first, that the long-run rate of inflation is zero and that the rate of interest charged on a car loan is eight percent. Suppose, further, that the price of the car is $5000 if purchased today and, because there is no inflation, the price of the car is expected to be the same next year. Finally, suppose that you expect to receive a $5000 inheritance next year and that you expect to use $5000 to buy a car. The question is this: Should you borrow $5000 today to buy the car in order to be able to enjoy it for a year, expecting to repay the borrowing in one year with the inheritance, or should you wait and simply buy the car next year?

To examine this question, consider two alternative courses of action. If the car is purchased today and $5000 is borrowed, then with the interest rate of eight percent on the car loan the interest expense is $400. Suppose, for the sake of argument, that $400 sounds fairly costly to you given your current need for a car and you are just on the borderline as to whether you should pay the $400 in order to enjoy the car now or whether you should wait for a year to avoid paying interest. In the language that economists so often use, you are *indifferent* between buying the car now and buying it later.

To make this decision in an inflationary period we need to examine the same kinds of numbers. But in the inflationary period we know that the price of the car will be higher next year by, say, five percent. Thus, the car that can be purchased for $5000 this year is expected to cost $5250 next year.

If the nominal interest rate on the car loan is still eight percent, then it clearly pays to buy the car now if you were indifferent in the situation when there was no inflation. With the eight percent rate of interest you must still pay the $400 of interest but you save the $250 price increase by buying the car this year instead of next year. The net interest cost is only $150 from buying the car now; if you were just indifferent before when it cost you $400, then clearly you will buy the car now when the net interest cost is only $150. This net interest charge of $150 on the $5000 of borrowing works out to an interest rate of three percent instead of eight percent. In other words, the real, or inflation-adjusted, rate of interest is now three percent.

What would the nominal interest rate have to be in the inflationary situation for you to be indifferent between buying the car now and buying it later? Suppose the interest rate on the car loan were 13 percent instead of eight percent. Then, on the $5000 loan the interest expense would be $650 whereas it had been $400 before. However, paying the $650 interest allows you to avoid the $250 price increase, leaving a net of $400, the same as before.

This example conforms to the simple formula derived earlier for calculating the real rate of interest: the real rate is the nominal rate less the rate of inflation. It is quite clear that should you anticipate inflation, you will regard the nominal rate of interest in a different way from the way you would regard it if you do not anticipate inflation.

In this example we have discussed the *demand for borrowed funds* as it depends on the real rate of interest. Now consider a slightly different example. Suppose the $5000 inheritance is received now and the problem is to decide whether to buy the car now or in one year. If the car is bought later, the $5000 can be invested now and can earn interest for a year. Suppose that at a zero rate of inflation you can earn three percent in a savings account. Then in one year you will have $150 of interest earnings and it will still cost you the same amount, $5000, for the car. But in the event of five percent inflation that $150 of interest will not even cover the increased price of the car, the price increase of $250. If, with zero inflation, you had been indifferent between buying the car now and buying the car later when the interest earned is three percent, then you will again be indifferent during an inflationary period if the rate of interest on the savings account has increased by the same amount as the expected rate of inflation. With five percent inflation the savings account would have to earn an eight percent nominal rate of interest, the three percent real plus the five percent expected rate of inflation. Here, it is clear that the *supply of lendable funds* also depends on the real rate of interest.

Thus, in the long run, with a fully anticipated inflation of X percent per year, the nominal rate of interest will be bid up by X percentage points. Borrowers will be willing to pay the higher nominal rate of interest and lenders will demand the higher nominal rate of interest. We in fact observe that countries with high rates of inflation do indeed have high nominal rates of interest and countries with low rates of inflation have relatively low nominal rates of interest. The same is true of a given country at different points in time: when a country has a low rate of inflation it typically has a low nominal rate of interest and vice versa.

The relationship between real and nominal rates for the United States from 1948 through 1976 is shown in Fig. 5.3. In the figure the solid line is the nominal interest rate, represented by the monthly average three-month United States Treasury bill rate for the middle month of each calendar quarter.[2] The points in the figure show the realized real rate of interest on Treasury bills, calculated by subtracting from the bill rate the rate of increase in the Consumer Price Index over the life of the bill.[3] Somewhat surprisingly, the available evidence indicates that the real rate of interest on Treasury bills in the United States since the Korean War has averaged only one to two percent per annum.[4]

Figure 5.3 shows that the higher average level of the nominal interest rate after 1965 was not associated with a higher real rate of interest; in fact, the average real rate for the 1966–1976 period was clearly lower than for the 1955–1965 period. Thus, the higher rates of inflation after 1965 were not associated with commensurately higher nominal rates of interest.

While it is necessary to be cautious in generalizing from the particular case of a higher sustained inflation after 1965, this experience suggests either that a higher rate of inflation reduces the real rate of interest, or that the adjustment to inflation is slow and was far from complete even toward the end of the 1966–1976 period. The latter possibility seems especially likely

---

2 The bill rate plotted in Fig. 5.3 is not quite the same as the rate that appears in government statistics, shown in Fig. 5.1. That rate reflects the market convention of calculating the rate as

$$i = \frac{360}{n}(100 - P_B),$$

where P_B is the price per \$100 of maturity value of a bill with n days to maturity and i is in percent per annum. As can be seen from this formula, the market convention defines the interest rate as if a year had 360 days and as if the amount invested were \$100. To construct Fig. 5.3, the market quotes were adjusted to reflect the facts that a year actually has 365 days and that the amount actually invested is P_B.

3 Actually, the exact expression for the real rate of interest was used:
$$r = (i - \Delta P/P)/(1 + \Delta P/P).$$

4 See Fama 1975.

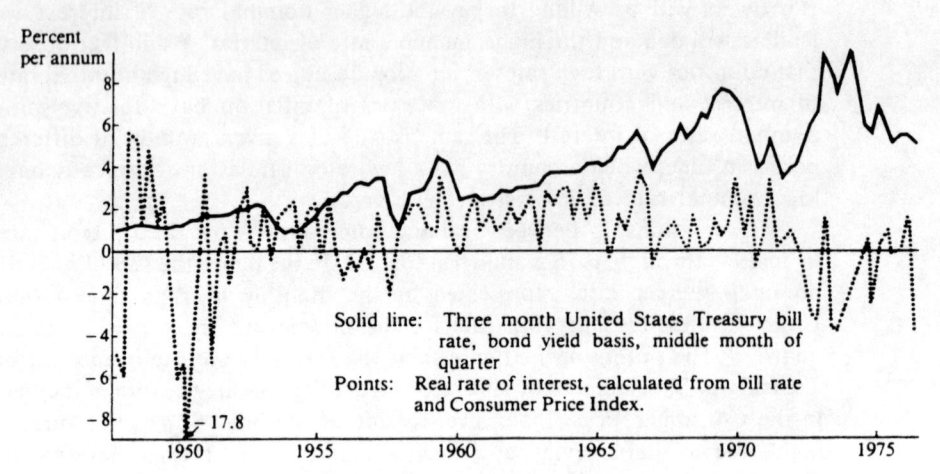

Fig. 5.3 Nominal and real interest rates in the United States, 1948-1976.

Solid line: Three month United States Treasury bill rate, bond yield basis, middle month of quarter
Points: Real rate of interest, calculated from bill rate and Consumer Price Index.

since the period contained three significant accelerations of inflation (in 1965-1966, 1968-1969, and in 1973-1974) that clearly caught people by surprise. In any event, it is clear that over a substantial period of time changes in the nominal rate of interest largely reflect changes in the rate of inflation.

Over short periods of time, however, people ordinarily do not realize what is happening to the rate of inflation, a point that was emphasized in discussing inflation in earlier chapters. It takes time before households and firms understand that the situation has changed and that a previous condition of relative stability in the rate of inflation has ended. As discussed in Chapter 4, when the rate of inflation initially rises and before inflationary expectations develop, business activity is generally strong. With unemployment low, households are borrowing funds to finance new cars, new homes, and so forth, and business firms are borrowing funds to finance the construction of new facilities. Because of these increased demands for funds, interest rates rise. But as the business expansion proceeds, wages and prices come under upward pressure, and the inflation rate begins to rise.

Because a reliable measure of inflationary expectations is not available, it is not possible unambiguously to divide a nominal interest rate change into components reflecting changes in the anticipated real rate and in the anticipated rate of inflation, and so it is not known how much of a nominal interest rate increase at the onset of inflation reflects inflationary anticipations and how much reflects the strong credit demands typical of a period of rising economic activity. What can be learned from examining Fig. 5.3, however, is that in the short run interest rate changes have often been in the correct direction but of insufficient magnitude to stabilize the realized real rate given the inflation rate that actually occurred. The nominal rate is moving in the correct direction, but by an insufficient amount, whenever nominal and real rates move in opposite directions. For some examples of this pattern, note that falling real rates were associated with rising nominal rates in 1956–1957, 1965–1966, and 1972–1973. For examples of the opposite pattern, note that rising real rates were associated with rising nominal rates in 1958 and, on average, from 1961 to 1964.

These observations justify an important general conclusion: No inference about the direction of change of the real interest rate can be drawn from an observed change in the nominal rate per se. Recent experience provides particularly dramatic evidence on this point. The realized real rate fell sharply from February 1972 to May 1973 even though the nominal rate on Treasury bills rose from 3.27 percent to 6.55 percent. And from mid-1974 to early 1975 the real rate rose even though the nominal rate fell sharply from 9.29 percent in August 1974 to 5.65 percent in February 1975. The true cost of borrowing, the real rate of interest, is most decidedly not measured, either in theory or in fact, by the nominal rate of interest.

It seems likely that in the short run a major part of an increased inflation is typically unanticipated, and so there is a wealth transfer from creditors to debtors. The wealth transfer occurs because people who had lent money expecting to receive, say, a two percent real rate of interest in fact receive a real rate of interest lower than anticipated. At the same time, of course, this lower real rate of interest is an unexpected bargain for those who have borrowed.

Expectations of inflation develop, however, as people observe the continuing inflation. And as these expectations develop, interest rates on new loans will adjust. But many long-term bonds, issued at the earlier rates, are still outstanding. As emphasized before, these bonds have fixed coupons that do not adjust as interest rates change. Therefore, as inflationary expectations rise, the prices of outstanding bonds are bid down. Thus this period is an especially painful one for bondholders. Not only are their fixed bond coupons worth less and less over time as the price level rises but also the market value of their bonds drops sharply. High quality long-term corporate bonds originally sold in the early 1960s with coupons about five percent were selling at only 60 to 70 percent of face value by the early 1970s.

THE BUSINESS CYCLE PATTERN OF INTEREST RATES

This discussion has emphasized that there are two principal factors over the business cycle that affect interest rates. One is the development of inflationary expectations and the other is the change in the demand for funds in order to finance business and consumer spending. Rising inflationary expectations generally accompany a business cycle expansion because as business booms, prices tend to rise and individuals come to believe that price increases will continue. Conversely, as business activity recedes, the rate of inflation generally falls and people come to realize that the weak markets do not afford a good opportunity to put through the same prices increases as before.

The effects of demands for durable goods were alluded to earlier and may now be discussed somewhat more fully. Much business and household spending is obviously financed by borrowing. Business firms float long-term bonds, and they borrow short term as well, in order to finance purchases of equipment, factory buildings, inventories, and so forth. Similarly, households borrow funds to finance purchases of houses, cars, TV sets, and so forth. When the economy moves into a recession and incomes fall, households reduce their purchases of these goods as they find themselves squeezed because of periods of unemployment, and business firms find that the demand for their output has fallen and therefore they have less need to expand their plants and equipment. For both reasons the demands for funds fall and therefore interest rates fall.

We may now tie together the effects of changes in the money stock on interest rates. When money growth first expands it tends to generate a business boom, as discussed in Chapter 4, and this boom adds to demand for borrowed funds by households and business firms. By the same token the business expansion tends to increase prices as people bid for goods; this process, if continued long enough, will degenerate into an ongoing inflation. As the inflation comes to be anticipated investors will demand higher nominal interest rates and borrowers will be willing to pay the higher interest rates. Money affects interest rates, therefore, because money affects both business activity and the rate of inflation.

In addition to the effects discussed above, money growth has a direct temporary impact on interest rates, though this impact is relatively unimportant quantitatively. Suppose the economy is fully adjusted to a particular rate of growth of money. Now assume that money growth suddenly rises. The higher money growth initially appears as an extra supply of loanable funds, and interest rates may tend to fall a bit. Of course, once the extra money growth begins to stimulate business activity, and later on inflation and inflationary expectations, interest rates will rise.

The tendency of higher money growth temporarily to depress interest rates temporarily is limited, and perhaps eliminated, by market anticipations of the eventual implications of higher money growth. If bond market participants expect the higher money growth to continue, they know that interest rates will shortly be higher and bond prices lower. No one wants to buy bonds when bond prices are expected to fall. Thus, higher money growth may immediately *depress* bond prices (raise interest rates) to the level expected to be implied in the future by the monetary policy being followed.

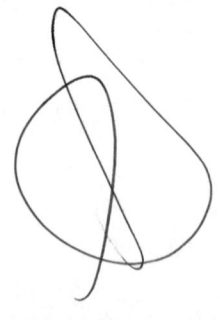

SUMMARY OF MONETARY EFFECTS ON INTEREST RATES

We may summarize the basic argument as follows: First, an increase in money growth tends to cause business to expand; the higher demand for cars, TV sets, factories, and so forth, adds to the demand for borrowed funds and raises interest rates. Second, the higher rate of money growth tends to raise the rate of inflation and inflationary anticipations, and the level of nominal interest rates is bid up accordingly. Third, in the very short run the process may go somewhat the other way. When the money stock is expanded, an extra supply of loanable funds is introduced into the credit markets and interest rates may fall temporarily.

If this very short-run effect is to operate, however, it must be that investors do not fully understand what is happening. If investors see the central bank buying large amounts of securities and believe that an inflationary monetary expansion will ensue, then they will not be eager to hold onto their bonds at higher prices. Therefore the very short-run effect of money on interest rates can occur only to the extent that investors do not realize that money growth is expanding, do not fully understand the implications of a higher rate of money growth, or believe that the extra money creation is temporary and will be reversed. Especially given the experience of recent years, the inflationary implications of excessive money growth probably are understood by most investors; however, it is quite difficult to figure out exactly when a higher rate of money growth is a temporary phenomenon and when it is a more permanent feature of central bank policy.

This point is an extremely important one. Interest rates, and indeed many other aspects of economic behavior, will depend in part on the interpretation that people give to the actions of the monetary authorities and of government policymakers in general. Thus whatever may be predicted under the assumption that people's expectations have not changed, the prediction must be regarded warily because expectations cannot be assumed to be independent of policy actions. Expectations of inflation are not formed only from looking at the past rate of inflation; anyone who is attempting to get one step ahead of the game will not wait for the inflation to develop but will look directly at the underlying causes of inflation. For this reason, in assessing the impact of changes in the money stock on interest rates and other variables, it is always extremely important to take into account the way in which the monetary changes affect the expectations of households and business firms.

REFERENCE

Fama, Eugene F., 1975. Short-term interest rates as predictors of inflation, *American Economic Review* **65** (June): 269-282.

12. The Natural Rate of Unemployment: Concepts and Issues

Stuart E. Weiner

The monetarist notion of a "natural" rate of unemployment is closely related to Wicksell's idea of a "natural" rate of interest. Both refer to "ideal" magnitudes that would exist in an economy free of monetary disequilibrium, i.e., one where the general price level has adjusted to the point where money supply and money demand are equal. But the fact that "natural" rate of unemployment is "ideal" in this particular sense does not mean that it is necessarily an optimal or desirable rate of unemployment. As Stuart Weiner makes clear in the following essay, a "natural" rate of unemployment may be higher than is desirable, so that policymakers may legitimately aim at its reduction. The point of calling it "natural" is merely to indicate that the rate cannot be reduced through monetary expansion. —G.S., Ed.

****

The unemployment rate in the United States currently stands at 6.9 percent. That translates to 8 million workers out of work. How should policymakers respond?

In the past, policymakers might have responded by aggressively pursuing expansionary monetary and fiscal policies in an attempt to substantially lower the unemployment rate, perhaps to the 4 percent target established by the Council of Economic Advisors in the 1960s or the identical target established by the Humphrey-Hawkins Act of 1978. Today, however, with the emergence of the "natural rate" theory of unemployment, it is generally believed that there is an unemployment limit below which aggregate policies cannot go. And that limiting natural rate of unemployment is currently thought to be in the 5 to 7 percent range. Attempts to lower unemployment below this natural rate will only result in accelerating inflation. Thus, where 15 years ago a 6.9 percent unemployment rate would have elicited a highly stimulative aggregate policy response, today such a response is unlikely.

But while macroeconomic policymakers' hands are tied, microeconomic policymakers' hands need not be tied. Several labor market imperfections underlie the natural rate. And microeconomic policies can be used to eliminate these imperfections. The natural rate of unemployment is not necessarily full-employment unemployment, nor is it necessarily optimal unemployment. It changes over time and can be changed at any time.

This article examines these and other issues relating to the natural rate of unemployment concept. It echoes the sentiment that large-scale macroeconomic policies cannot be used to permanently lower unemployment below its natural rate. But it also stresses that the natural rate itself can be lowered with microeconomic policies designed to remove labor market imperfections.

The first section of the article provides an overview of the natural rate concept. How is the natural rate defined, and in what sense is it a barrier to macroeconomic policy? The second section reviews estimates of the natural rate of unemployment. How is the natural rate measured, and what is its value today? The third section examines the underlying sources of the natural rate. Why is the natural rate of unemployment so high, and what can be done to lower it? The article closes by emphasizing that a lowering of the natural rate of unemployment is an essential ingredient to a successful long-run anti-inflation strategy.

The natural rate: a barrier to macroeconomic policy

The natural rate of unemployment is defined as that rate of unemployment at which there is no tendency for inflation to accelerate or decelerate. When the economy is at the natural rate, inflation is constant from one year to the next. Workers and firms come to expect this inflation rate and base their decisions on it. For this reason, the natural rate of unemployment is also sometimes called the constant inflation rate of unemployment or the nonaccelerating inflation rate of unemployment.[1]

To gain a better understanding of how and why the economy eventually settles at the natural rate of unemployment, consider the hypothetical example depicted in Figure 1. In this diagram, the inflation rate is measured along the vertical axis and the unemployment rate is measured along the horizontal axis. Suppose the economy is initially at point A. At that point, the inflation rate is 3 percent and the unemployment rate is at its assumed natural rate of 6 percent. Because the unemployment rate is at its natural rate—with workers and

FIGURE 1
The natural rate hypothesis: hypothetical example

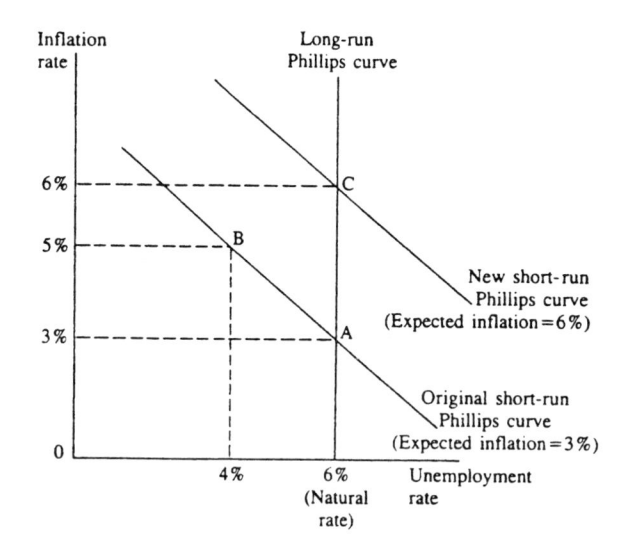

firms expecting and getting 3 percent inflation—there is no pressure for change. Consequently, the economy will stay at point A.

Now suppose policymakers increase aggregate demand in an attempt to lower the unemployment rate below 6 percent. They could do so, for example, by running a larger budget deficit or by pursuing a more expansionary monetary policy. In either case, with the increase in aggregate spending, firms will want to hire more workers. And to get those types of workers in short supply, firms will have to bid up wages. These higher wages, in turn, will likely be passed on into higher prices.[2] Thus, the initial effect of the expansionary policy will be a decline in the unemployment rate and a rise in inflation. The economy will move to a position like point B.

Point B might be preferable to point A. Although inflation is higher (5 percent instead of 3 percent), unemployment is lower (4 percent instead of 6 percent). The issue is moot, however, because point B is not sustainable. The economy will not stay at point B but will move to point C.

Why will the economy not stay at point B? Recall that at point A workers were expecting inflation of 3 percent. With the increase in aggregate demand and the subsequent move to point B, inflation rises to 5 percent. But workers are still expecting 3 percent. While some workers are receiving higher wages at B, others are not so that, on average, workers' real wages (wages adjusted for inflation) are lower than expected. As a result, as labor contracts expire and new ones are negotiated, workers will update their inflation expectations and demand higher wages. These higher wages will cause prices to climb even higher. And as wages rise—with no further increase in aggregate demand—firms will cut back on their hiring. This means that the unemployment rate will rise. Eventually, the economy will settle at point C, with an unemployment rate of 6 percent and an inflation rate of 6 percent.[3]

Point C is a sustainable position for the economy. At point C, the unemployment rate is once again at its natural rate. Workers and firms are expecting and getting an inflation rate of 6 percent. There is no pressure for change. Thus, the sole long-run impact of the expansionary macroeconomic policy has been a doubling of the inflation rate.

The hypothetical example in Figure 1 illustrates the limitations of large-scale aggregate demand policies. In the short run, lower unemployment may be "bought" with higher inflation, as in moving from A to B. But in the long run, there is no tradeoff between inflation and unemployment. The economy will simply move from A to C. Efforts to reduce the unemployment rate below its natural rate will only result in accelerating inflation.

This "natural rate hypothesis" has only come to the fore in recent years. Throughout the 1960s and early 1970s, it was generally believed that there was a long-run tradeoff between inflation and unemployment. Possible combinations of inflation and unemployment, it was thought, could be represented by a "Phillips curve" (named after the British economist who popularized it) and policymakers could maintain the economy at any point on that curve. As the inflationary 1970s and early 1980s unfolded, however, it became increasingly clear that a permanent tradeoff did not exist. The Phillips curve was not stable, but rather shifted over time as workers and firms adjusted their inflation expectations. An inflation-unemployment tradeoff might exist in the short run along a given short-run Phillips curve, but as expectations adjusted and the short-run curve shifted, the tradeoff disappeared, resulting in a vertical long-run Phillips curve. Such short-run and long-run Phillips curves are incorporated in Figure 1.[4]

Estimating the natural rate

Because the natural rate of unemployment is a theoretical concept, it is not directly observable and thus has to be estimated. Chart 1 shows one such estimated series, calculated by Robert J. Gordon, and compares it with the actual unemployment rate over the postwar period.

Three features stand out. First, the actual unemployment rate has rarely equaled the natural unemployment rate. Second, the natural rate is at a relatively high-level. And third, the natural rate has trended upward over time.

The divergence of the actual and natural rates of unemployment reflects the vagaries of the business cycle. The economy does not grow at a smooth, constant rate, but rather starts and stalls as cyclical forces take the economy first into an expansion, then a recession, then another expansion.[5] Along the way, the actual unemployment rate will deviate from the natural unemployment rate. As workers and firms adapt to changing conditions, however, adjusting their inflation expectations, the economy will gravitate back toward its natural position. At that point, the actual unemployment rate and the natural unemployment rate will coincide.

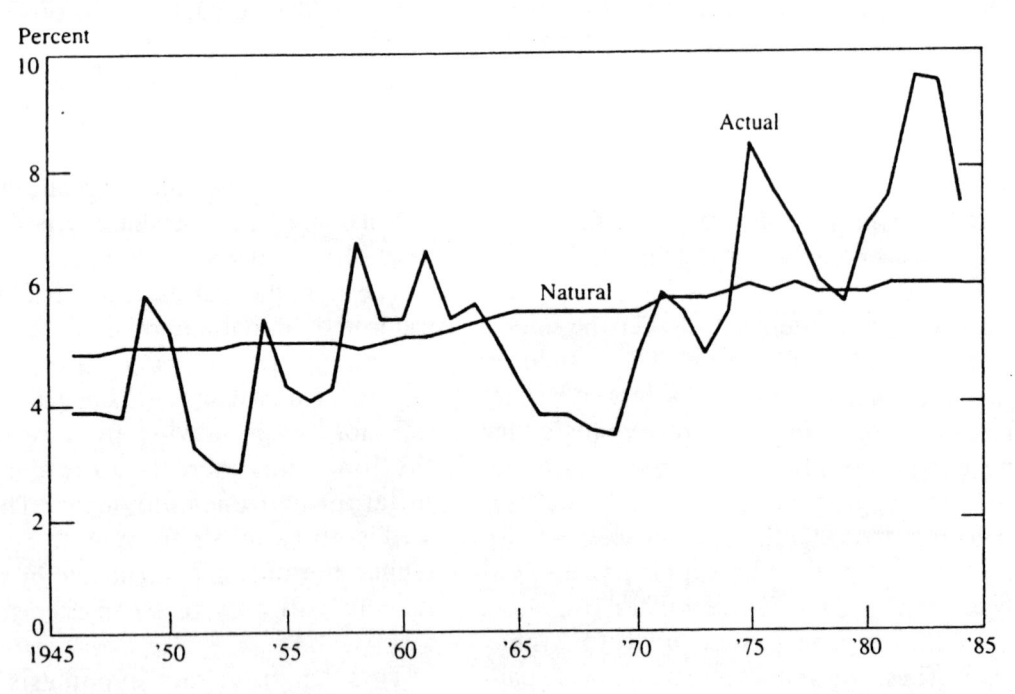

CHART 1
Unemployment rate: actual and natural

Source: *Actual*. U.S. Department of Labor.
Natural. Robert J. Gordon, *Macroeconomics*, 3rd edition, Table B-1, and Robert J. Gordon, "Unemployment and Potential Output in the 1980's," *Brookings Papers on Economic Activity*, 1984:2, Table A-1 (value for 1984:Q4 taken to be 6.0 percent by author). For description of Gordon's methodology, see Robert J. Gordon, "Inflation, Flexible Exchange Rates, and the Natural Rate of Unemployment," in *Workers, Jobs, and Inflation*, Martin Neil Baily, editor, Brookings Institution, 1982.

CHART 2
Natural rate of unemployment: divergence of estimates

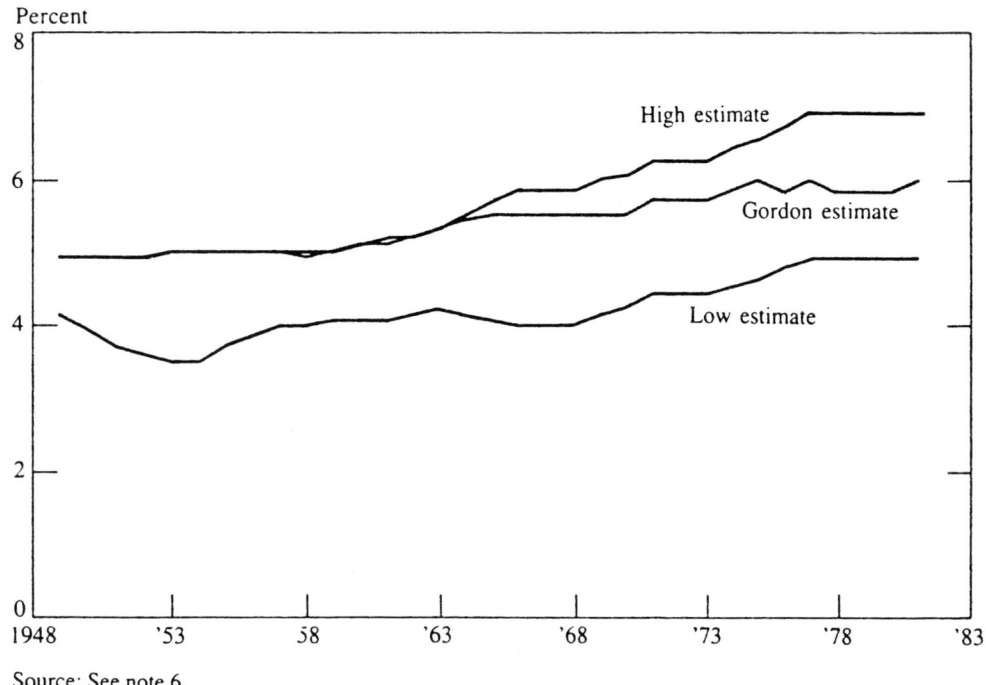

Source: See note 6.

The relatively high level of the natural rate reflects imperfections in labor markets, imperfections that exist regardless of the overall state of the economy. For this reason, unemployment at the natural rate is often referred to as structural unemployment to distinguish it from cyclical unemployment. Structurally unemployed individuals may be unemployed for a variety of reasons. They may have the wrong skills, live in the wrong areas, face institutional barriers, be inefficient in job search, or have little incentive to accept the jobs they are offered. Some portion of this structural unemployment is nevertheless beneficial because it represents normal turnover and job search, two key ingredients in a dynamic, thriving economy. This portion of structural unemployment is usually referred to as frictional unemployment.

The gradual rise in the natural rate over the years is generally attributed to the changing composition of the U.S. labor force. Thirty years ago, the labor force was dominated by men. Today, the labor force contains a large share of women and teenagers as well. Since women and teenagers typically have higher unemployment rates than men—experiencing more structural (and frictional) unemployment—the overall unemployment rate consistent with constant inflation has risen.

Divergence of estimates

The natural rate series plotted in Chart 1 is only one of many that have been advanced in recent years. Other series based on other estimation techniques have been generated for part or all of the postwar period. All of the series tend to show the natural rate rising over time. But individual estimates vary widely.

Chart 2 gives some idea of this divergence. Surrounding the Gordon series of Chart 1 is an uncertainty band for the natural rate, the boundaries of which have been constructed from the upper and lower estimates of eight additional series.[6] The band has averaged about one and a half percentage points in width. This divergence reflects the inherent difficulty of obtaining a precise estimate of the natural rate.[7]

There are two principal techniques for estimating the natural rate. The first follows an aggregated approach and is used by Gordon and some others. A statistical equation relating inflation and aggregate unemployment is estimated. A natural rate series is then generated by solving for that unemployment rate for which inflation is not changing.[8] The second estimation technique follows a disaggregated approach. Natural rates are estimated for several demographic groups based on historical relationships between their unemployment rates and the unemployment rate of a reference group, where the reference group's natural rate is assumed known and constant. These disaggregated series are then weighted by labor force shares to construct an aggregate natural rate series.[9] Neither technique is necessarily superior to the other. Both are inherently imprecise.

Benefits of accurately estimating the natural rate

The inherent imprecision in estimating the natural rate is unfortunate. The more uncertainty there is about the natural rate—that is, the wider the uncertainty band of Chart 2—the more cautious aggregate policymakers have to be. If they are not careful, they can temporarily push the actual unemployment rate below the natural unemployment rate, causing a permanent increase in inflation. And because of this self-imposed caution, potential output will be foregone. Suppose, for example, that there is some belief that the natural rate could be 7 percent when in fact it is 6 percent. And further suppose that, to be safe, policymakers keep the actual unemployment rate at 7 percent. According to recent estimates of Okun's Law, this extra percentage point in the actual unemployment rate would result in roughly $40 billion of lost output per year.[10]

This pure economic loss understates the total social cost, of course, because an additional percentage point of unemployment means additional personal stress for some one million individuals, stress that some researchers have linked to increased health and crime problems.[11] Foregone output also means a larger federal budget deficit than necessary. Adding one million people to the employment rolls would increase the tax base and, therefore, revenues and lower expenditures on such social assistance items as unemployment insurance and welfare. Given the numerous benefits of accurately estimating the natural rate, further research in this area is clearly warranted.

Lowering the natural rate

The natural rate hypothesis asserts that large-scale fiscal and monetary policies cannot be used to permanently lower the unemployment rate below its natural rate. But the natural rate itself can be lowered through microeconomic policies aimed at its many sources.

This point is illustrated in the hypothetical example in Figure 2. Here, points A, B, and C have been recast from Figure 1. Suppose the economy is initially at point A. At that point, the inflation rate is 3 percent and the unemployment rate is at its assumed natural rate of 6 percent. Now suppose policymakers desire a lower unemployment rate, say 4 percent. They could stimulate aggregate demand, taking the economy to point B. But as discussed earlier, point B cannot be sustained. The economy will not stay at B but will move on to point C, with no improvement in unemployment and an

FIGURE 2
Lowering the natural rate: hypothetical example

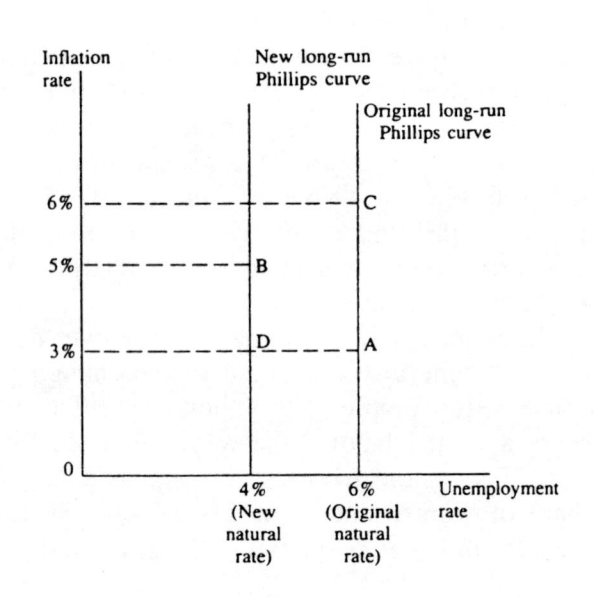

even higher inflation rate. Alternatively, policymakers could try to lower the natural rate to 4 percent, taking the economy to point D.[12] Such a reduction is possible in principle, provided the underlying sources of the natural rate have been identified and appropriate actions taken.

Underlying sources of the natural rate

Five types of labor market imperfections underlie the natural rate of unemployment, that is, are sources of structural unemployment. These include skill mismatches, location mismatches, institutional barriers, imperfect information flows, and transfer payment disincentives. For each, microeconomic policies exist that could potentially serve as remedies. Of course, a given policy would be advisable only to the extent that its incremental benefits exceeded its incremental costs.

The first type of labor market imperfection is the mismatch between the skills possessed by available workers and the skills required for available jobs.[13] Job openings and unemployed individuals can coexist because the individuals do not have the requisite qualifications for the jobs. New entrants into the labor force, reentrants into the labor force, and workers displaced from dying industries often confront this type of unemployment. So, too, do chronically low-skilled individuals who for one reason or another never acquire the skills that would widen their employment opportunities.

Skill mismatch unemployment would decline if available workers were better educated and better trained. Consequently, any policies that furthered those ends would serve as partial remedies to the high natural rate. Better elementary and secondary educational programs, of course, would constitute a basic first step. In addition, vocational training loan programs, similar in design to present college loan programs, could be instituted to assist low and middle-income youths in acquiring training at technical schools. And wage subsidy programs designed to encourage on-the-job training might be even more effective in augmenting the skills of the labor force.[14]

The second type of labor market imperfection is the mismatch between the location of available jobs and the location of available workers. Locational mismatch unemployment can be said to exist when job seekers living in one location could qualify for vacancies in another location.

Locational mismatch can arise when one region of the country grows more quickly than another. One example that has received considerable publicity in recent years is the movement of jobs and people to the Sunbelt. Rapid industrial growth in the South and Southwest has come partly at the expense of the Northeast and Midwest, with the result that some of the unemployment in these northern regions is locationally derived. Potential remedies for regional locational mismatch unemployment include worker relocation subsidies and an extensive and more efficient national employment service.[15]

Locational mismatch can also arise in the same metropolitan area. Such intrametropolitan mismatch occurs when vacancies exist in the suburbs but available workers in the central city are unable to reach them, either because of high commuting costs or because such individuals do not learn about the vacancies due to high search costs or distance-related deterioration of job information flows. This type of mismatch has also come to the fore in recent years. Firms have increasingly abandoned central cities for sites in the suburbs, with possible adverse effects on the employment prospects of inner-city residents. One possible solution to this intrametropolitan locational mismatch is to encourage firms to stay in the inner cities. Several states have established enterprise zone programs in an attempt to do just that.[16] Alternatively, rapid transit routes from the inner city to surrounding suburbs could be improved.

The third type of labor market imperfection is the existence of institutional barriers. Various laws and social practices prevent labor markets from working as efficiently as possible. Minimum wage laws, union membership restrictions, and racial and sexual discrimination provide three examples.

Minimum wage laws, despite their good intentions, have a deleterious impact on the employment prospects of low-skilled, low-wage individuals. Wages are not permitted to fall below an artificial floor even when market conditions dictate such a decline. Consequently, wages are higher than they otherwise would be, causing employers to hire fewer workers and causing more individuals to enter the labor force. The net result is an excess supply of low-skilled, low-wage individuals, which increases unemployment. If wages were free to settle at market-clearing levels, unemployment among such individuals would decline.[17]

Union membership restrictions are another type of institutional barrier. Individuals excluded for one reason or another from joining a union are unable to work at union shops and unable to take advantage of union training programs. Such restrictions reduce employment opportunities, both now and in the future. Racial and sexual discrimination in hiring has a similar impact. Qualified individuals are shut out of potential positions, losing valuable on-the-job training in the process. Like minimum wage laws and union membership restrictions, discriminatory hiring obstructs the smooth functioning of labor markets.

The remedy for unemployment resulting from institutional barriers is, of course, to remove the barriers. Abolishing minimum wage laws, banning union membership restrictions, and prohibiting discriminatory hiring would all serve to lower the natural rate.

The fourth type of labor market imperfection is imperfect information flows. Job vacancies may exist but go unfilled simply because job seekers are unaware of the vacancies.

Individuals can search for employment in several ways. They can apply directly to employers, place and answer classified ads, use public and private employment agencies, and exchange information through word of mouth. Some methods of job search may not be as efficient as others. Sole reliance on public employment agencies, for example, may be ineffective because of a large number of applicants per vacancy. Alternatively, some methods of job search may be inefficient for certain groups only. For example, word of mouth is likely to be ineffective for inner-city residents because a large percentage of such individuals' peers are unemployed.

Establishing a more efficient and extensive public employment service would be one way to improve the flow of information to job seekers. Beyond that, however, policy options appear limited. It is difficult, and perhaps undesirable, to develop measures that would influence how individuals search for work.

The fifth type of labor market imperfection relates to the disincentives associated with various public transfer programs. An individual receiving unemployment compensation or welfare payments has little incentive to search for or accept a job paying only a marginally higher income. Public transfer payments clearly serve a useful purpose in providing some measure of income security to individuals facing adversity. However, they also tend to lengthen the duration of unemployment spells.

Several proposals have been made for reducing this type of incentive-based unemployment. Suggestions range from reducing benefit levels or eligibility to establishing a voucher system in which transfer payment recipients could in effect buy employment from employers. The issue continues to generate a great deal of debate.

While all unemployment at the natural rate inherently reflects imperfections in labor markets, some of this unemployment may nevertheless be beneficial from a personal standpoint. This component of structural unemployment, the frictional component, mirrors a healthy search process. When an individual quits a job to look for a better one or enters the labor force after a spell of nonparticipation, the time spent in job search represents in part an investment in the future. (This unemployment is structural because if job information networks were perfect, job search would be unnecessary.) An individual entering the labor force from college, for example, would probably not want to accept the first job offered. Instead, the new entrant would want to "shop around," talking to a number of potential employers and weighing the alternatives. Similarly, a woman reentering the labor force after several years in the home would probably want to take some time to explore her employment opportunities. In a world of imperfect sequential information, such a strategy is optimal.[18]

Society also profits from this extended job search. A dynamic economy generates a continuum of jobs requiring a continuum of skills. The better matched workers and jobs are, the more productive workers will be. An economy without frictional unemployment is either an economy with perfect information—an unlikely event—or an economy with little vitality and diversity. From a societal as well as a personal standpoint, therefore, some unemployment at the natural rate is beneficial.

Past and future trends in the natural rate

Charts 1 and 2 indicate that the natural rate of unemployment has been gradually rising. As noted earlier, this rise is generally attributed to the influx of women and young adults into the U.S. labor force. Chart 3 shows the growing prominence of women and young adults in the work force. In 1955, men aged 25 and older made up nearly 60 percent of the labor force. By 1984, their share had fallen to 45 percent. Women, meanwhile, increased their share of the labor force from 25 percent to 34 percent.

And young people—combining males and females—watched their share grow from 15 percent to 21 percent. Because women and young adults traditionally have higher unemployment rates than men, the overall unemployment rate consistent with constant inflation has risen.

Part of the reason that women and young adults tend to have higher unemployment rates than men is that their frictional unemployment rates tend to be higher. Young adults are more likely to be entering the labor force for the first time. Women are more likely to be entering after an extended absence. As discussed earlier, such entry and reentry imply a higher normal level of frictional unemployment. But women and young adults may also be more vulnerable to some of the underlying labor market imperfections. Newly entering teenagers, for example, are more likely to face minimum wage barriers and, because they have not had an opportunity to receive on-the-job training, are more likely to face skill mismatch problems. Similarly, reentering women are more likely to face skill mismatch problems because the skills they acquired years ago may

CHART 3
Labor force shares

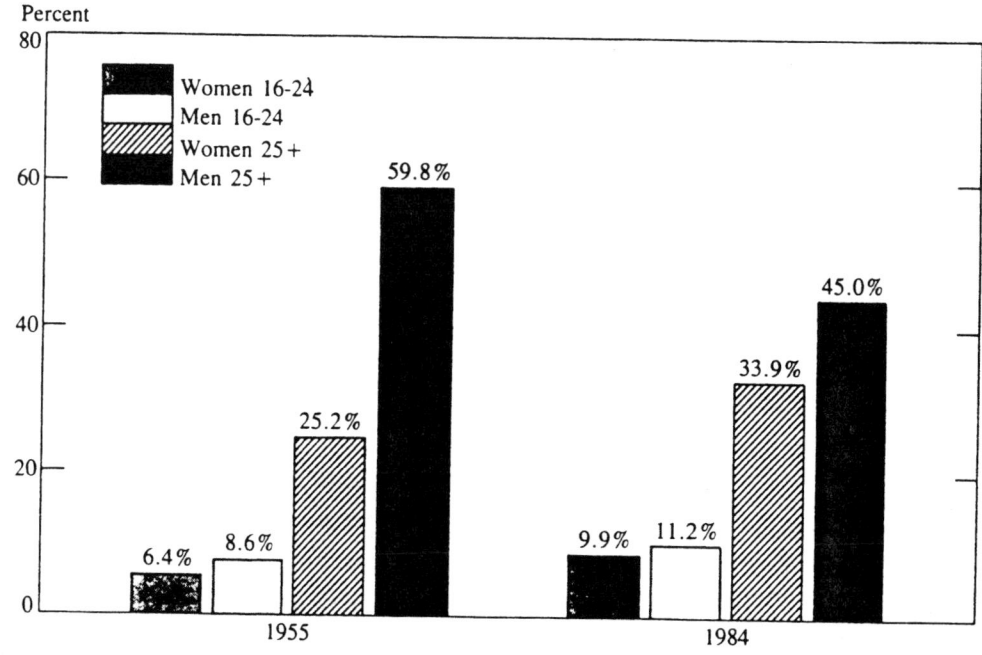

Source: U.S. Department of Labor

have become obsolete. It is not enough, therefore, to categorically dismiss higher unemployment rates among women and young adults as simply reflecting higher levels of frictional unemployment. More serious underlying problems may also be present.

Another potential source of the rise in the natural rate is secular demand shifts, that is, fundamental changes in the composition of demand for domestically produced goods and services. Some authors believe, for example, that the rise in the U.S. natural rate since the early 1970s partly reflects a demand shift from durable goods to services.[19] Long-term employees, it is argued, have increasingly been displaced from shrinking manufacturing industries, their skills no longer needed or needed only in other parts of the country. As a result, skill and locational mismatch unemployment may have increased, particularly among adult men.[20,21]

Under the assumption that the natural rate is in the 5 to 7 percent range today, where is it likely headed? There appears to be some consensus that it will decline a bit because of demographic trends. The baby boomers, who entered and swelled the ranks of the labor force in the 1960s and 1970s, are now mature workers. Accordingly, the young adult share of the labor force, which peaked in 1978, should continue to fall off. Women's share of the labor force, which climbed to new highs in the 1970s and early 1980s, might also be expected to level off. Thus, one can probably look for a mild decline in the natural rate in the years ahead.[22]

The natural rate will still be high, however, representing potential waste and hardship. Policymakers will still have to decide whether to continue to tolerate a high natural rate or to take steps to lower it with microeconomic policies.

Desirability of reducing the natural rate

A legitimate question to ask is how low, if at all, should the natural rate be lowered? Clearly, as previously noted, cost-benefit analysis would be in order before adopting any or a combination of the corrective microeconomic policies outlined above. A more extensive national employment service, for example, would not come cheap. Nor would a vocational loan program or improvements in rapid transit. But abstracting from these cost considerations, how low should the natural rate be pushed? What is an appropriate target for the natural rate?

Lowering the natural rate would produce several clear benefits. For one thing, more output would be generated. More persons working would mean more product produced. Second, the federal budget deficit would narrow. Tax revenues would expand while social assistance expenditures would contract. Third, less personal hardship would be endured. And fourth, the Federal Reserve and other policy authorities would be under far less pressure to use large-scale macroeconomic policies to maintain a potentially unsustainable and inflationary actual unemployment rate.

But it is very difficult, perhaps impossible, to say what the target natural rate should be. Economists have debated the meaning of "full employment" unemployment and "optimal" unemployment for decades. No consensus has emerged. It is generally acknowledged that some unemployment—frictional unemployment—is useful. But while some positive unemployment rate may be advantageous, a rate in the 5 to 7 percent range—reflecting, as it does, numerous labor market imperfections—is probably too high. Removing some of these imperfections would appear beneficial.[23]

Summary

The natural rate of unemployment concept has emerged in the past 15 years to become the dominant guide for macroeconomic policy. According to this theory, there is an unemployment limit below which aggregate demand policies cannot go. This limiting "natural rate of unemployment" is thought to be currently in the 5 to 7 percent range. Attempts to lower unemployment below this natural rate with large-scale monetary and fiscal policy, it is believed, will only result in accelerating inflation.

But the natural rate itself can be lowered

with microeconomic policies designed to remove labor market imperfections. And such policies would likely pay large social dividends. As Anthony Solomon, past president of the Federal Reserve Bank of New York, recently observed:

> Obviously labor market issues are not part of monetary policy. But to me, the other side of a successful long-run anti-inflation strategy would have to do with the functioning of our labor markets. The level of unemployment rates consistent with nonaccelerating inflation has been too high in recent years given the social costs. If I were to name the single most important issue in domestic macro-economic policy, I would say it is the need to lower the average unemployment rate consistent with price stability.[24]

---

[1] It is also sometimes referred to as the equilibrium unemployment rate or, perhaps misleadingly, as the full-employment unemployment rate.

[2] Prices would generally be rising anyway because of the aggregate demand pressures.

[3] How long this process will take is a matter of considerable debate. Some authors believe the return to the natural rate will be quite rapid; models incorporating "rational expectations" and perfect wage and price flexibility yield such a result. Others believe the return to the natural rate will be less rapid; models rejecting rational expectations or, more frequently, the perfect wage and price flexibility assumption, yield this result. For discussion, see Robert J. Gordon, "Price Inertia and Policy Ineffectiveness in the United States, 1890-1980," *Journal of Political Economy*, Vol. 90, December 1982, pp. 1087-1117.

[4] The seminal articles on the natural rate hypothesis are Milton Friedman, "The Role of Monetary Policy," *American Economic Review*, March 1968, pp. 1-17, and Edmund S. Phelps, "Phillips Curves, Expectations of Inflation, and Optimal Unemployment Over Time," *Economica*, August 1967, pp. 254-281. Other highly readable accounts include Robert J. Gordon, "Recent Developments in the Theory of Inflation and Unemployment," *Journal of Monetary Economics*, Vol. 2, 1976, pp. 185-219, and Thomas M. Humphrey, "The Evolution and Policy Implications of Phillips Curve Analysis," *Economic Review*, Federal Reserve Bank of Richmond, March/April 1985, pp. 3-22. Friedman, who coined the term "natural rate of unemployment," makes the point that the natural rate of unemployment is natural only in the sense that it reflects real forces as opposed to monetary forces. See Friedman, "The Role of Monetary Policy," pp. 7-9.

[5] These cyclical forces emanate from a variety of sources, including private aggregate demand shocks (such as investment booms and consumption booms), public aggregate demand shocks (such as wartime defense buildups), and exogenous supply shocks (such as crop failures and OPEC price rises). Countercyclical monetary and fiscal policies attempt to offset such cyclical disturbances, mitigating movements away from the natural rate.

[6] The boundaries have been smoothed by means of a three-year symmetric moving average. The series considered, in addition to the Gordon series referenced in Chart 1, are as follows: the U_1^* and U_2^* series (1955-77) from Jeffrey M. Perloff and Michael L. Wachter, "A Production Function—Nonaccelerating Inflation Approach to Potential Output," in *Three Aspects of Policy and Policymaking: Knowledge, Data, and Institutions*, Carnegie-Rochester Conference Series on Public Policy, Vol. 10, Karl Brunner and Allan H. Meltzer, eds., pp. 113-163, supplemented by the U_N series (1948-54) from Michael L. Wachter, "The Changing Cyclical Responsiveness of Wage Inflation," *Brookings Papers on Economic Activity*, 1976:1, pp. 115-159; the UNAT series (1946-78) from Robert J. Barro, "Unanticipated Money Growth and Unemployment in the United States," *American Economic Review*, March 1977, pp. 101-115; the U1, U2, and U3 series (1948-82) from Peter K. Clark, "Okun's Law and Potential GNP," unpublished manuscript, Board of governors of the Federal Reserve System, June 1983; the "potential" series (1950-76) from George L. Perry, "Potential Output and Productivity," *Brookings Papers on Economic Activity*, 1977:1, pp. 11-47; and the estimated natural rate range (1965-82) from Stanley Fischer and Rudiger Dornbusch, *Economics*, McGraw-Hill, New York, 1983, p. 731. Some of these authors, reluctant to explicitly recognize their series as natural rate series, elect instead to call them normalized, potential, or benchmark series.

[7] The difficulty of estimating the natural rate has long been acknowledged, from Friedman's early lament that "we have as yet devised no method to estimate accurately and readily the natural rate of ... unemployment" ("The Role of Monetary Policy," p. 10), to Robert J. Gordon's contention that "the exact value of the natural rate will always be uncertain" ("The Welfare Cost of Higher Unemployment," *Brookings Papers on Economic Activity*, 1973:1, p. 135), to Fischer and Dornbusch's observation that "no one knows for sure what the natural rate is" (*Economics*, p. 731).

[8] Gordon's natural rate series and Barro's UNAT series are based on this methodology. Such methods usually proceed in one of two ways: (1) estimating a series of short-run Phillips curves and then inverting them, solving for the unemployment rate that keeps inflation constant, or (2) estimating unemployment equations in which unemployment is made a function of unexpected inflation and then solving for that unemployment rate that arises when there are no inflationary surprises—that is, when actual inflation equals expected inflation. Although these procedures have the advantage of solving directly for the natural rate, specification of the relevant equation is rarely clearcut.

[9] Perloff and Wachter's U_1^* series, Wachter's U_N series, and Clark's U1 series are based on this methodology. A variant is Perry's "potential" series. The principal shortcoming of this demographic normalization method is its assumption that the reference group's (typically prime-aged men, aged 25-54) relation to inflation has not changed. There is no guarantee, for example, that a 3 percent unemployment rate among prime-aged men is necessarily consistent with constant inflation in 1985 even though it might have been in an earlier base year. Demographic normalization is only an indirect method for estimating the natural rate, a point its practitioners readily concede.

[10] This estimate is based on Table 4 of Douglas M. Woodham, "Potential Output Growth and the Long-Term Inflation Outlook," *Quarterly Review*, Federal Reserve Bank of New York, Summer 1984, pp. 16-23.

[11] Robert J. Gordon surveys some of this literature in *Macroeconomics*, 3rd edition, Little, Brown, and Co., Boston, 1984, pp.

353-354. See also Kay Lehman Schlozman and Sidney Verba, "The New Unemployment: Does It Hurt?" *Public Policy*, Vol. 26, no. 3, Summer 1978, pp. 333-358, and James Q. Wilson and Philip J. Cook, "Unemployment and Crime—What is the Connection?" *The Public Interest*, Spring 1985, pp. 3-8.

[12] Any other point along the new long-run Phillips curve would also be possible, provided an appropriate aggregate demand policy was followed. For example, an inflation rate of less than 3 percent (that is, a point below point D) could eventually be realized if a contractionary aggregate demand policy were adopted. An inflation rate of higher than 3 percent, say the 5 percent at point B, could eventually be realized if an expansionary aggregate demand policy was adopted. (The desirability of a higher inflation rate is, of course, dubious.) In all cases, the actual unemployment rate would settle at the now-lower natural unemployment rate of 4 percent.

[13] This discussion of labor market imperfections draws heavily from Stuart E. Weiner, "Enterprise Zones as a Means of Reducing Structural Unemployment," *Economic Review*, Federal Reserve Bank of Kansas City, March 1984, pp. 4-8.

[14] A wage subsidy program, the Targeted Jobs Tax Credit (TJTC) program, was part of federal law from 1978 to 1985. Its provisions were somewhat modest, however, and it applied to a limited set of individuals. See Weiner, "Enterprise Zones," footnote 25, p. 16, for further discussion. For a general discussion of wage subsidy programs, see Robert H. Haveman, "The Potential of Targeted Marginal Employment Subsidies," in *Marginal Employment Subsidies*, OECD, Paris, 1982.

[15] National relocation subsidies already exist to some degree through the deductibility of moving expenses in the federal income tax.

[16] See Weiner, "Enterprise Zones," pp. 3-16, for an analysis of enterprise zones.

[17] Charles Brown, Curtis Gilroy, and Andrew Cohen survey the empirical evidence on minimum wage effects in "The Effect of Minimum Wage on Employment and Unemployment," *Journal of Economic Literature*, Vol. 20, no. 2, June 1982, pp. 487-528.

[18] Robert J. Gordon develops this argument in *Macroeconomics*, 3rd edition, pp. 342-344.

[19] David M. Lilien, "Sectoral Shifts and Cyclical Unemployment," *Journal of Political Economy*, August 1982, pp. 777-793, and Robert J. Barro, *Macroeconomics*, John Wiley & Sons, New York, 1984, pp. 212, 229-30, share this view. Michael Podgursky also examines this issue in "Sources of Secular Increases in the Unemployment Rate," *Monthly Labor Review*, July 1984, pp. 19-25.

[20] As noted in the text, potential policies exist for alleviating this mismatch, policies that demand serious consideration. But it is highly doubtful whether policymakers should try to head off demand shifts before they occur. Such shifts are symptomatic of a dynamic economy responding to changing tastes and technologies. Resisting such shifts appears ill advised.

[21] A third potential source of the rising natural rate is aggregate supply shocks. OPEC price increases in the mid and late 1970s and slower productivity growth throughout the decade may have contributed to the natural rate's ascent. When such supply shocks occur, the cost of producing a given amount of output increases, with the result that firms desire to produce less and to hire fewer workers. To the extent that these workers stay in the labor force, unwilling to work at the now-lower equilibrium real wage, the natural rate rises. Such a rise is presumably temporary, however, since reservation wages would eventually be expected to decline. Offsetting policies may sometimes be possible, for example, encouraging productivity-enhancing investment in the face of a productivity decline. In other cases, such as an oil shock, little can be done.

[22] For further discussion, see Henry F. Myers, "High Unemployment Is Likely to Linger On," *Wall Street Journal*, February 25, 1985, p. 1, and William C. Freund and Mel Colchoniro, "The Boon of Shrinking Jobless Rolls," *Wall Street Journal*, November 28, 1984, p. 26.

[23] For a far-ranging discussion of such notions as full employment unemployment, optimal unemployment, and voluntary unemployment, see James Tobin, "Inflation and Unemployment," *American Economic Review*, March 1972, pp. 1-18. Formal models that imply that the natural rate is always, in some sense, efficient or optimal include Edward C. Prescott, "Efficiency of the Natural Rate," *Journal of Political Economy*, Vol. 83, no. 6, 1975, and Robert E. Hall, "A Theory of the Natural Unemployment Rate and the Duration of Employment," *Journal of Monetary Economics*, April 1979, pp. 153-170. A model implying the opposite, that the natural rate can contain involuntary unemployment, is Steven C. Salop, "A Model of the Natural Rate of Unemployment," *American Economic Review*, March 1979, pp. 117-125. Robert J. Gordon examines the factors involved in determining the "optimal" unemployment rate in "The Welfare Cost," pp. 133-195.

[24] Anthony M. Solomon, "Some Problems and Prospects for Monetary Policy in 1985," *Quarterly Review*, Federal Reserve Bank of New York, Winter 1984-85, p. 5.

Stuart E. Weiner is a senior economist at the Federal Reserve Bank of Kansas City. Kermit Daniel and Tom Dean, research associates at the bank, helped in the preparation of the article.

13. Inflation, the Misdirection of Labour, and Unemployment
F.A. Hayek

According to the Monetarist "natural rate" hypothesis, every economy possesses some underlying rate of unemployment stemming from "frictional" and "structural" causes, which no monetary stimulus can undo. This view contradicts the Keynesian notion, popular in the 1960s and 70s, that more rapid monetary growth can always achieve a lower rate of unemployment at the cost of a higher rate of inflation. In "Inflation, the Misdirection of Labour, and Unemployment," Austrian economist F.A. Hayek takes the Monetarist idea one step further. According to Hayek, inflation does not just fail to reduce unemployment in the long-run, but actually serves to increase unemployment by distorting relative prices. According to this view, higher rates of inflation will be associated with higher "natural" rates of unemployment, due to increased numbers of "frictionally" and "structurally" unemployed persons. —G.S., Ed.

****

I
Inflation and Unemployment

AFTER A unique 25-year period of great prosperity the economy of the Western world has arrived at a critical point. I expect that the experience of the period will enter history under the name of The Great Prosperity as the 1930s are known as The Great Depression. We have indeed succeeded, by eliminating all the automatic brakes which operated in the past, namely the gold standard and fixed rates of exchange, in maintaining the full and even over-employment which was created by an expansion of credit and in the end prolonged by open inflation, for a much longer time than I should have thought possible. But the inevitable end is now near, if it has not already arrived.

I find myself in an unpleasant situation. I had preached for forty years that the time to prevent the coming of a depression is the boom. During the boom nobody listened to me. Now people again turn to me and ask how the consequences of a policy of which I had constantly warned can be avoided. I must witness the heads of the governments of all the Western industrial countries promising their people that they will stop the inflation *and* preserve full employment. But I know that they *cannot* do this. I even fear that such attempts, as President Ford has just announced, to postpone the inevitable crisis by a new inflationary push, may temporarily succeed and make the eventual breakdown even worse.

Three choices in policy
The disquieting but unalterable truth is that a false monetary and credit policy, pursued through almost the whole period since the last war, has placed the economic systems of all the Western industrial countries in a highly unstable position in which *anything* we can do will produce most unpleasant consequences. We have a choice between only three possibilities:

– to allow a rapidly accelerating open inflation to continue until it has brought about a complete disorganisation of all economic activity;

– to impose controls of wages and prices which will for a time conceal the effects of a continued inflation but would inevitably lead to a centrally-directed totalitarian economic system; and

– finally, to terminate resolutely the increase of the quantity of money which would soon, through the appearance of substantial unemployment, make manifest all the misdirections of labour which the inflation of the past years has caused and which the two other procedures would further increase.

Lessons of the Great Inflation
To understand why the whole Western world allowed itself to be led into this frightful dilemma, it is necessary to glance briefly back at two events soon after the First World War which have largely determined the views that have governed the policy of the post-war years. I want first to recall an experience which has unfortunately been largely forgotten. In Austria and Germany the Great Inflation had directed our attention to the connection between changes in the quantity of money and changes in the degree of employment. It especially showed us that the employment created by inflation diminished as soon as the inflation slowed down, and that the termination of the inflation always produced what came to be called a 'stabilisation crisis' with substantial unemployment. It was the insight into this connection which made me and some of my contemporaries from the outset reject and oppose the kind of full employment policy propagated by Lord Keynes and his followers.

I do not want to leave this recollection of the Great Inflation without adding that I have probably learnt at least as much if not more than I learnt from personally observing it by being taught to see – then largely by my teacher, the late Ludwig von Mises – the utter stupidity of the arguments then propounded, especially in Germany, to explain and justify the increases in the quantity of money. Most of these arguments I am now encountering again in countries, not least Britain and the USA, which then seemed economically better trained and whose economists rather looked down at the foolishness of the German economists. None of these apologists of the inflationary policy was able to propose or apply measures to terminate the inflation, which was finally ended by a man, Hjalmar Schacht, who firmly believed in a crude and primitive version of the quantity theory.

British origin of inflation as cure for unemployment
The policy of the recent decades, or the theory which underlies it, had its origin, however, in the specific experiences of Great Britain during the 1920s and 1930s. Great Britain had after what now seems the very modest inflation of the First World War, returned to the gold standard in 1925, in my opinion very sensibly and honestly, but unfortunately and unwisely at the former parity. This had in no way been required by classical doctrine: David Ricardo had in 1821 written to a friend[1] that 'I never should advise a government to restore a currency, which was depreciated 30 per cent, to par'. I ask myself often how different the economic history of the world might have been if, in the discussion of the years preceding 1925, even only one English economist had remembered and pointed out this long-published passage from Ricardo.

In the event, the unfortunate decision taken in 1925 made a prolonged process of deflation inevitable, which process might

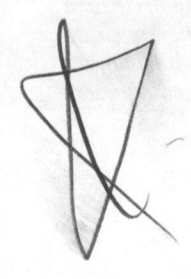

---

[1] David Ricardo to John Wheatley, 18 September, 1821, reprinted in *The Works of David Ricardo*, ed. Piero Sraffa, Cambridge University Press, Vol. IX, 1952, p. 73.

have been successful in maintaining the gold standard if it had been continued until a large part of the wages had been reduced. I believe this attempt was near success when in the world crisis of 1931 Britain abandoned it together with the gold standard, which was greatly discredited by this event.

II

Keynes' Political 'Cure' for Unemployment

Development of Keynesian ideas

It was during the period of extensive unemployment in Great Britain preceding the world-wide economic crisis of 1929–31 that John Maynard Keynes developed his basic ideas. It is important to note that this development of his economic thought happened in a very exceptional and almost unique position of his country. It was a period when, as a result of the big appreciation of the international value of the pound sterling, the real wages of practically all British workers had been substantially increased compared with the rest of the world, and British exporters had in consequence become substantially unable successfully to compete with other countries. In order to give employment to the unemployed it would therefore have been necessary either to reduce practically *all* wages or to raise the sterling prices of most commodities.

In the development of Keynes' thought it is possible to distinguish three distinct phases. First, he began with the recognition that it was necessary to reduce real wages. Second, he arrived at the conclusion that this was *politically* impossible. Third, he convinced himself that it would be vain and even harmful. The Keynes of 1919 had still understood that:

> 'There is no subtler, no surer means of overturning the existing basis of society than to debauch the currency. The process engages all the hidden forces of economic law on the side of destruction, and does it in a manner which not one man in a million is able to diagnose.'[1]

His political judgement made him the inflationist, or at least avid anti-deflationist, of the 1930s. I have, however, good reason to believe that he would have disapproved of what his followers did in the post-war period. If he had not died so soon, he would have become one of the leaders in the fight against inflation.

'The fatal idea'

It was in that unfortunate episode of English monetary history in which he became the intellectual leader that he gained acceptance for the fatal idea: that unemployment is predominantly due to an insufficiency of aggregate demand compared with the total of wages which would have to be paid if all workers were employed at current rates.

This formula of employment as a direct function of total demand proved so extraordinarily effective because it seemed to be confirmed in some degree by the results of quantitative empirical data. In contrast, the alternative explanations of unemployment which I regard as correct could make no such claims. The dan-

---

[1] *The Economic Consequences of the Peace* (1919), reprinted in *The Collected Writings of John Maynard Keynes*, Macmillan for the Royal Economic Society, Vol. II, 1971, p. 149.

gerous effects which the 'scientific' prejudice has had in this diagnosis is the subject of my Nobel lecture at Stockholm (Part II). Briefly, we find the curious situation that the (Keynesian) theory, which is comparatively best confirmed by statistics because it happens to be the only one which can be tested quantitatively, is nevertheless false. Yet it is widely accepted only because the explanation earlier regarded as true, and which I still regard as true, cannot *by its very nature* be tested by statistics.

III
THE TRUE THEORY OF UNEMPLOYMENT

THE TRUE, though untestable, explanation of extensive unemployment ascribes it to a discrepancy between the distribution of labour (and the other factors of production) between industries (and localities) and the distribution of demand among their products. This discrepancy is caused by a distortion of the system of *relative* prices and wages. And it can be corrected only by a change in these relations, that is, by the establishment in each sector of the economy of those prices and wages at which supply will equal demand.

The cause of unemployment, in other words, is a deviation from the equilibrium prices and wages which would establish themselves with a free market and stable money. But we can never know beforehand at what structure of relative prices and wages such an equilibrium would establish itself. We are therefore unable to measure the deviation of current prices from the equilibrium prices which make it impossible to sell part of the labour supply. We are therefore also unable to demonstrate a statistical correlation between the distortion of relative prices and the volume of unemployment. Yet, although not measurable, causes may be very effective. The current superstition that only the measurable can be important has done much to mislead economists and the world in general.

Keynes' temptations to the politicians
Probably even more important than the fashionable prejudices concerning scientific method which made the Keynesian theory attractive to professional economists were the temptations it held out for politicians. It offered them not only a cheap and quick method of removing a chief source of real human suffering. It also promised them release from the most confining restrictions that had impeded them in their striving for popularity. Spending money and budget deficits were suddenly represented as virtues. It was even argued persuasively that increased government expenditure was wholly meritorious, since it led to the utilisation of hitherto unused resources and thus cost the community nothing but brought it a net gain.

These beliefs led in particular to the gradual removal of all effective barriers to an increase in the quantity of money by the monetary authorities. The Bretton Woods agreement had tried to place the burden of international adjustment exclusively on the surplus countries, that is, to require them to expand but not to require the deficit countries to contract. It thus laid the foundation for a world inflation. But this was at least done in the laudable endeavour to secure fixed rates of exchange. Yet when the criticism of the inflation-minded majority of economists succeeded in removing this last obstacle to national inflation, no effective brake remained, as the experience of Britain since the late 1960s illustrates.

Floating exchanges, full employment, stable currency
It is, I believe, undeniable that the demand for flexible rates of exchange originated wholly from countries such as Britain some of whose economists wanted a wider margin for inflationary expansion (called 'full employment policy'). They have, unfortunately, later received support also from other economists who were not inspired by the desire for inflation but who seem to me to have overlooked the strongest argument in favour of fixed rates of exchange: that they constitute the practically irreplaceable curb we need to *compel* the politicians, and the monetary authorities responsible to them, to maintain a stable currency.

The maintenance of the value of money and the avoidance of inflation constantly demand from the politicians highly unpopular measures which they can justify to people adversely affected only by showing that government was compelled to take them. So long as the preservation of the external value of the national currency is regarded as an indisputable necessity, as it is with fixed exchange rates, politicians can resist the constant demands for cheaper credits, avoidance of a rise in interest rates, more expenditure on 'public works', and so on. With fixed exchanges a fall in the foreign value of the currency or an outflow of gold or foreign exchange reserves acted as a signal requiring prompt government action. With flexible exchange rates, the effect of an increase in the quantity of money on the internal price level is much too slow to be generally recognised or to be charged to those ultimately responsible for it. Moreover, the inflation of prices is usually preceded by a welcome increase in employment, and it may therefore even be welcomed because its harmful effects are not visible until later.

It is therefore easy to understand why, in the hope of restraining countries all too inclined towards inflation, others like Germany, even while noticeably suffering from imported inflation, hesitated in the post-war period to destroy altogether the system of fixed rates of exchange. For a time it seemed likely to restrain the temptation further to speed up inflation. But now that the system of fixed rates of exchange appears to have totally collapsed, and there is scarcely any hope that self-discipline might induce some countries to restrain themselves, little reason is left to adhere to a system that is no longer effective. In retrospect one may even ask whether, out of a mistaken hope, the German Bundesbank or the Swiss National Bank have not waited too long, and then raised the value of their currency too little. But in the long run I do not believe we shall regain a system of international stability without returning to a system of fixed exchange rates which imposes upon the national central banks the restraint essential if they are successfully to resist the pressure of the inflation-minded forces of their countries – usually including Ministers of Finance.

IV
Inflation Ultimately Increases Unemployment

But why all this fear of inflation? Should we not try to learn to live with it, as some South American States seem to have done, particularly if, as some believe, this is necessary to secure full employment? If this were true and the harm done by inflation were only that which many people emphasise, we would have to consider this possibility seriously.

Why we cannot live with inflation

The answer, however, is twofold. *First*, such inflation, in order to achieve the goal aimed at, would have constantly to *accelerate*, and accelerating inflation would sooner or later reach a degree which makes all effective order of a market economy impossible. *Second*, and most important, in the long run such inflation makes much *more* unemployment inevitable than that which it was originally designed to prevent.

The argument often advanced that inflation produces merely a *redistribution* of the social product, while unemployment *reduces* it and therefore represents a worse evil, is thus false, because *inflation becomes the cause of increased unemployment*.

Harmful effects of inflation

I certainly do not wish to under-estimate the other harmful effects of inflation. They are much worse than anyone can conceive who has not himself lived through a great inflation. I count my first eight months in a job during which my salary rose to 200 times the initial amount as such an experience. I am indeed convinced that such a mismanagement of the currency is tolerated by the people only because, while the inflation proceeds, nobody has the time or energy to organise a popular rebellion.

What I want to say is that even the effects which every citizen experiences are not the worst consequence of inflation, which is usually not understood because *it becomes visible only when the inflation is past*. This must particularly be said to economists, politicians or others who like to point to the South American countries which have had inflations lasting through several generations and seem to have learnt to live with them. In these predominantly agrarian countries the effects of inflation are chiefly limited to those mentioned. The most serious effects that inflation produces in the labour markets of industrial countries are of minor importance in South America.

The attempts made in some of these countries, in particular Brazil, to deal with the problems of inflation by some method of indexing can, at best, remedy some of the consequences but certainly not the chief causes or the most harmful effects. They could not prevent the worst damage which inflation causes, that misdirection of labour which I must now consider more fully.

The misdirection of labour

Inflation makes certain jobs *temporarily* attractive. They will disappear when it stops or even when it ceases to accelerate at a sufficient rate. This result follows because inflation

(a) changes the distribution of the money stream between the

various sectors and stages of the process of production, and
(b) creates expectation of a further rise of prices.

The defenders of a monetary full employment policy often represent the position as if a *single* increase of total demand were sufficient to secure full employment for an indefinite but fairly long period. This argument overlooks both the inevitable effects of such a policy on the distribution of labour between industries and those on the wage policy of the trade unions.

As soon as government assumes the responsibility to maintain full employment at whatever wages the trade unions succeed in obtaining, they no longer have any reason to take account of the unemployment their wage demands might have caused. In this situation every rise of wages which exceeds the increase in productivity will make necessary an increase in total demand if unemployment is not to ensue. The increase in the quantity of money made necessary by the upward movement of wages thus released becomes a *continuous* process requiring a constant influx of additional quantities of money. The additional money supply must lead to changes in the relative strength of demand for various kinds of goods and services. And these changes in relative demand must lead to further changes in relative prices and consequent changes in the direction of production and the allocation of the factors of production, including labour. I must leave aside here all the other reasons why the prices of different goods – and the quantities produced – will react differently to changes in the demand (such as elasticities – the speed with which supply can respond to demand).

The chief conclusion I want to demonstrate is that the longer the inflation lasts, the larger will be the number of the workers whose jobs depend on a *continuation* of the inflation, often even on a continuing *acceleration* of the rate of inflation – not because they would not have found employment without the inflation, but because they were drawn by the inflation into *temporarily* attractive jobs which after a slowing down or cessation of the inflation will again disappear.

The consequences are unavoidable
We ought to have no illusion that we can escape the consequences of the mistakes we have made.[1] Any attempt to preserve the jobs made profitable by inflation would lead to a complete destruction of the market order. *We have once again in the post-war period missed the opportunity to forestall a depression while there was still time to do so.* We have indeed used our emancipation from institutional restraints – the gold standard and fixed exchange rates – to act more stupidly than ever before.

But if we cannot escape the re-appearance of substantial unemployment, this is not the effect of a failure of 'capitalism' or the market economy, but exclusively due to our own errors which past experience and available knowledge ought to have enabled us to avoid. It is unfortunately only too true that the disappointment of expectations they have created may lead to serious social

---

[1] I should make it clear that, although I was addressing an audience in Italy, what I am saying certainly also applies to Britain and most other Western countries. There is little sign so far of this truth being understood in Britain. – F.A.H.

unrest. But this does not mean that we can avoid it. The most serious danger now is certainly that attempts, so attractive for the politicians, to postpone the evil day and thereby make things in the long run even worse, may still succeed. I must confess I have been wishing for some time that the inescapable crisis may come soon. And I hope now that any attempts made promptly to restart the process of monetary expansion will not succeed, and that we shall now be forced to face the choice of a new policy.

Temporary, not mass, unemployment
Let me, however, emphasise at once that, although I regard a period of some months, perhaps even more than a year, of considerable unemployment as unavoidable, this does not mean that we must expect another long period of mass unemployment comparable with the Great Depression of the 1930s, provided we do not commit very bad mistakes of policy. Such a development can be prevented by a sensible policy which does not repeat the errors responsible for the duration of the Great Depression.

But before I turn to what our future policy ought to be I want to reject emphatically a misrepresentation of my point of view. I certainly do not recommend unemployment as a *means* to combat inflation. But I have to advise in a situation in which *the choice open to us is solely between some unemployment in the near future and more unemployment at a later date*. What I fear above all is the *apres nous la deluge* attitude of the politicians who in their concern about the next elections are likely to choose more unemployment later. Unfortunately even some commentators, such as the writers of the *Economist*, argue in a similar manner and have called for 'reflation' when the increase in the quantity of money is still continuing.

V

WHAT CAN BE DONE NOW?

The first step
THE FIRST necessity now is to stop the increase of the quantity of money – or at least to reduce it to the rate of the real growth of production – and this cannot happen soon enough. Moreover, *I can see no advantage in a gradual deceleration*, although for purely technical reasons it may prove all we can achieve.

It does not follow that we should not endeavour to stop a real deflation when it threatens to set in. Although I do not regard deflation as the original cause of a decline in business activity, a disappointment of expectations has unquestionably tended to induce a process of deflation – what more than 40 years ago I called a 'secondary deflation'[1] – the effect of which may be worse, and in the 1930s certainly was worse, than what the original cause of the reaction made necessary, and which has no steering function to perform.

I have to confess that 40 years ago I argued differently. I have since altered my opinion – not about the theoretical explanation of the events but about the practical possibility of removing the obstacles to the functioning of the system by allowing deflation to proceed for a while.

[1] Defined and discussed in Part III, p. 44. I recall that the phrase was frequently used in the LSE Seminar from the 1930s.

I then believed that a short process of deflation might break the rigidity of money wages (what economists have since come to call their 'rigidity downwards') or the resistance to the reduction of some particular money wages, and that in this way we could restore relative wages determined by the market. This seems to me still an indispensable condition if the market mechanism is to function satisfactorily. But I no longer believe it is in practice possible to achieve it in this manner. I probably should have seen then that the last chance was lost after the British government in 1931 abandoned the attempt to bring costs down by deflation just when it seemed near success.

Prevent recession degenerating into depression
If I were today responsible for the monetary policy of a country I would certainly try to prevent a threatening deflation, that is, an absolute decrease of the stream of incomes, by all suitable means, and would announce that I intended to do so. This alone would probably be sufficient to prevent a degeneration of the recession into a long-lasting depression. The re-establishment of a properly functioning market would however still require a re-structuring of the whole system of relative prices and wages and a re-adjustment to the expectation of stable prices, which presupposes a much greater flexibility of wages than exists now. What chance we have to achieve such a determination of relative wage-rates by the market and how long it may take I dare not predict. But, although I recognise that a *general* reduction of money wages is politically unachievable, I am still convinced that the required adjustment of the structure of *relative* wages can be achieved without inflation only through the reduction of the money wages of some groups of workers, and therefore must be thus achieved.

From a longer point of view it is obvious that, once we have got over the immediate difficulties, we must not avail ourselves again of the seemingly cheap and easy method of achieving full employment by aiming at the maximum of employment which in the short run can be achieved by monetary pressure.

The Keynesian dream
The Keynesian dream is gone even if its ghost will continue to plague politics for decades. It is to be wished, though this is clearly too much to hope for, that the term 'full employment' itself, which has become so closely associated with the inflationist policy, should be abandoned – or that we should at least remember that it was the aim of classical economists long before Keynes. John Stuart Mill reports in his autobiography[1] how 'full employment with high wages' appeared to him in his youth as the chief *desideratum* of economic policy.

The primary aim: stable money, not unstable 'full' employment
What we must now be clear about is that our aim must be, not the maximum of employment which can be achieved in the short run, but a 'high and stable [i.e. *continuing*] level of employment', as one of the wartime British White Papers on employment policy phrased it.[2] This however we can achieve only through the re-

---

[1] *Autobiography and other Writings*, ed. J. Stillinger, Houghton Mifflin, Boston, 1969.
[2] *Employment Policy*, Cmd. 6527, HMSO, May 1944, Foreword.

establishment of a properly functioning market which, by the free play of prices and wages, establishes for each sector the correspondence of supply and demand.

Though it must remain one of the chief tasks of monetary policy to prevent wide fluctuations in the quantity of money or the volume of the income stream, the effect on employment must not be the dominating consideration guiding it. *The primary aim must again become the stability of the value of money.* The currency authorities must again be effectively protected against the political pressure which today forces them so often to take measures that are politically advantageous in the short run but harmful to the community in the long run.

Disciplining the monetary authorities
I wish I could share the confidence of my friend Milton Friedman who thinks that one could deprive the monetary authorities, in order to prevent the abuse of their powers for political purposes, of all discretionary powers by prescribing the amount of money they may and should add to circulation in any one year. It seems to me that he regards this as practicable because he has become used for statistical purposes to draw a sharp distinction between what is to be regarded as money and what is not. This distinction does not exist in the real world. I believe that, to ensure the convertibility of all kinds of near-money into real money, which is necessary if we are to avoid severe liquidity crises or panics, the monetary authorities must be given some discretion. But I agree with Friedman that we will have to try and get back to a more or less automatic system for regulating the quantity of money in ordinary times. His principle is one that monetary authorities ought to aim at, not one to which they ought to be tied by law. The necessity of 'suspending' Sir Robert Peel's Bank Act of 1844 three times within 25 years after it was passed ought to have taught us this once and for all.

And although I am not as optimistic as the Editor of the London *Times*, Mr William Rees-Mogg, who in a sensational article[1] (and now in a book)[2] has proposed the return to the gold standard, it does make me feel somewhat more optimistic when I see such a proposal coming from so influential a source. I would even agree that among the feasible monetary systems the international gold standard is the best, if I could believe that the most important countries could be trusted to obey the rules of the game necessary for its preservation. But this seems to me exceedingly unlikely, and no single country can have an effective gold standard: by its nature it is an international system and can function only as an international system.

It is, however, a big step in the direction of a return to reason when at the end of his book Mr Rees-Mogg argues that

> 'We should be tearing up the full employment commitment of the 1944 White Paper, a great political and economic revolution.
>
> 'This would until very recently have seemed a high price to

---

[1] 'Crisis of Paper Currencies: Has the Time Come for Britain to Return to the Gold Standard?', *The Times*, 1 May, 1974.

[2] *The Reigning Error. The Crisis of World Inflation*, Hamish Hamilton, London, 1974.

pay; now it is no great price at all. There is little or no prospect of maintaining full employment with the present inflation, in Britain or in the world. The full employment standard became a commitment to inflation, but the inflation has now accelerated past the point at which it is compatible with full employment.'[1]

Equally encouraging is a statement of the British Chancellor of the Exchequer, Mr Denis Healey, who is reported to have said:

'It is far better that more people should be in work, *even if that means accepting lower wages on average*, than that those lucky enough to keep their jobs should scoop the pool while millions are living on the dole'.[2] (My italics.)

It would almost seem as if in Britain, the country in which the harmful doctrines originated, a reversal of opinion were now under way. Let us hope it will rapidly spread over the world.

---

[1] *Ibid.*, p. 112.

[2] Speech at East Leeds Labour Club reported in *The Times*, 11 January, 1975.

14. A Cash-Balance Interpretation of Depression
Leland Yeager

> *Unlike the Austrian theory of the business cycle, the monetarist view links depression to an inadequacy of money or "cash balances." Leland Yeager's essay, though less well-known than the writings of Milton Friedman, is perhaps the best available summary of the monetarist view. Yeager sees deflation both as a symptom and as a potential long-run cure for depression, but argues that a deflationary cure may be slow and costly owing to the "stickiness" of prices. --G.S., Ed.*

* * *

I. THE CASH-BALANCE APPROACH

The usual account of inflation or depression stresses too much or too little demand for goods and services. It is enlightening to reverse this emphasis by focussing on the demand for and supply of money. The present paper views depression as an excess demand for money, in the sense that people want to hold more money than exists. It views an inflationary boom as an excess supply of money, in the sense that more money exists than people want to hold.

This interpretation has advantages:

1. It provides a unifying framework into which various strands of theory—the saving-investment relation, the alleged Keynesian underemployment equilibrium, the Pigou effect, an interpretation of Say's Law, a clarification of the terms "inflation" and "deflation," and the relation between price levels and production-and-employment levels—fit neatly as special aspects. It avoids some pitfalls of partial-equilibrium analysis of individual markets by focussing on the one thing—money—exchanged on all markets.

2. The cash-balance approach achieves this unity by tying macro- and microeconomics together, by handling depression and inflation with the familiar concepts of supply of and demand for a particular thing. In focussing on the cash-balance decisions of individual firms and households, it draws on a leading source of empirical generalizations in economics—economists' "inside" knowledge of human motives and decision-making.

3. Viewed as dealing with imbalance between the demand for and supply of money, business-cycle theory sheds some ambitions tending to lead it astray. Actually, there is no more reason to search for one universally valid explanation of such imbalance than there is to search for one universally valid explanation of an excess demand for or excess supply of any ordinary commodity—or than to search for a one-and-only cause of broken legs.

4. An account of the relation between the total money stock and people's efforts to build up, cut, or maintain their cash balances can be presented as a logical translation of the more familiar effective-demand and saving-and-investment theories. Thus nonmonetary theorists will have a hard time showing that the cash-balance approach is wrong, even though they may object to its dragging hidden assumptions about money out into the open.[1]

5. The cash-balance approach helps distinguish between treatment of unemployment due to general deficiency of effective demand and treatment of unemployment due to other troubles. It shows how a policy of price-level stabilization through monetary and fiscal action would coincide with preventing unemployment of the first type while not misusing expansion of demand as an inappropriate weapon against unemployment of the second type.

6. The cash-balance approach need not, surprisingly, presuppose any precise dividing line between money and near-moneys.

II. SAY'S LAW AND MONEY

Say's Law, or a crude version of it, rules out general overproduction: an excess supply of some things in relation to the demand for them necessarily constitutes an excess demand for some other things in relation to their supply.[2] This seems an unassailable truism. Apparent overproduction in some industries shows not general overproduction but only disharmony between the relative outputs of various industries and the pattern of consumers' and investors' preferences. Subnormal profit opportunities in some industries must be matched by above-normal profit opportunities elsewhere. *General* depression is impossible.

The catch is this: While an excess supply of some things does necessarily mean an excess demand for others, those other things may, unhappily, be money. If so, depression in some industries no longer entails boom in others. Say's Law assumed a peculiar kind of demand for money: people, taken together, were always satisfied with the existing quantity of money and never wanted to change their total cash balances except to adapt them passively to changes in the total quantity of money available.[3]

Actually, the quantity of money people desire to hold does not always just equal the quantity they possess. Equality of the two is an equilibrium condition, not an identity. Only in what Oscar Lange calls *monetary equilibrium*[4] are they equal. Only then are the total values of goods and labor supplied and demanded equal, so that a deficient demand for some kinds entails an excess demand for others.

Say's Law overlooked monetary disequilibrium. If people on the whole are trying to add more money to their total cash balances than is being added to the total money stock (or are trying to maintain their cash balances when the money stock is shrinking), they are trying to sell more goods and labor than are being bought. If people on the whole are unwilling to add as much money to their total cash balances as is being added to the total money stock (or are trying to reduce their cash balances when the money stock is not shrinking), they are trying to buy more goods and labor than are being offered.

The most striking characteristic of depression is not overproduction of some things and underproduction of others but, rather, a general "buyers' market," in which sellers have special trouble finding people willing to pay money for goods and labor. Even a slight depression shows itself in the price and output statistics of a wide range of consumer-goods and investment-goods industries. Clearly some very general imbalance must exist, involving the one thing—money—traded on *all* markets. In inflation, an opposite kind of monetary imbalance is even more obvious.

III. DEMAND FOR AND SUPPLY OF MONEY

Whether we regard the quantities of money supplied and demanded as stocks or as flows is a matter of convenience rather than of principle.[5] Equilibrium in the stock sense coincides with equilibrium in the flow sense. When people on the whole want to hold exactly the quantity of money in existence, they cannot be wanting to change their cash balances at a rate different from the rate at which this quantity is changing. Similarly, disequilibria in the stock and flow senses coincide. People on the whole cannot keep on trying to adjust their cash balances to equal more or less than the total money supply unless they are at the same time trying to change their cash balances at a rate different from the actual rate of change in the money supply. That is, if people demand cash balances totalling more or less at some particular instant than the existing money supply, then the demanded rate of change in cash balances is infinite (a finite change in zero time). The demanded infinite rate of change in cash balances cannot be equal to any actual rate of change in the money supply.[6]

Households and businesses demand cash balances for what are usually classified as transactions, precautionary, speculative, and investment motives.[7] Consideration of these motives shows that the total of cash balances demanded tends to be positively associated with the physical volume of transactions paid for in money (which depends in turn on payment practices and other institutional conditions, on the human and business population, and on the level of production or real income) and with the level of prices and wages. Interest rates and expectations of future price levels and business conditions also presumably have some effect on the demand for money. The supply of money can conveniently be regarded at any one moment as a definite quantity, which government and banking operations change over time.

As just implied, the number of money units that people demand to hold in their cash balances varies inversely with the purchasing power, or value, of the unit. (A person wants to hold fewer dollars in America than francs in France.) The similarity between the demands for money and for any ordinary commodity is clear.

For any ordinary commodity, there is some price at which the amounts demanded and supplied would be equal. And so with money: there is some value of the money unit that would equate the amounts demanded and supplied. But—again as is true of any ordinary commodity—the equilibrium value at one particular time might be a *dis*equilibrium value later. Supply and demand schedules are always shifting.

Since the prices of many goods and services are notoriously "sticky," the value of money does not adjust readily enough to keep the amounts of money supplied and demanded always equal as schedules shift. The value of money is often "wrong." Depression is such a disequilibrium: given the existing levels of prices, wages, and interest rates, people are on balance more eager to get money by selling goods and labor than to give up money in buying goods and labor.

This interpretation harmonizes with the Keynesian theory, which attributes a cyclical fall in income to an excess of intended saving over intended investment. The very fact of oversaving implies the existence of some form other than goods in which people can accumulate savings: if people are trying to save more money than they or others are willing to spend on "real" investment, people on the whole must be trying to acquire larger cash balances than are available in the aggregate. Conversely, if people are trying to spend more money on "real" investment than they or others are willing to save, then people on the whole are trying in vain to reduce their cash balances. (Or, if the money supply is growing, people are demanding additions to their cash balances that are smaller than the additions to the money supply.) It follows that an excess of intended saving over intended investment *is* an excess demand for money and that an excess of intended investment over intended saving *is* an excess supply of money.

Decisions about saving and investment are largely decisions about the holding of cash balances. Some factors affecting businessmen's willingness to make investments—price expectations and the state of business "confidence," for example—coincide with factors affecting the amounts of money that businessmen wish to hold. Keynes himself devotes chapter 17 of his *General Theory* to an analysis of the "essential properties" of money which at times make people prefer so strongly to hold money rather than capital goods that investment is insufficient. He explains that the liquidity-premium and low carrying cost of money may keep the demand for it from being readily choked off, that the money supply is inexpansible in a depression (apart from official action), and that the elasticity of substitution of other assets for money is slight. Keynes continues:

> The first condition means that demand may be predominantly directed to money, the second that when this occurs labour cannot be employed in producing more money, and the third that there is no mitigation at any point through some other factor being capable, if it is sufficiently cheap, of doing money's duty equally well. The only relief—apart from changes in the marginal efficiency of capital—can come (so long as the propensity towards liquidity is unchanged) from an increase in the quantity of money, or—which is formally the same thing—a rise in the value of money which enables a given quantity to provide increased money-services.

. . .

> Unemployment develops, that is to say, because people want the moon;—men cannot be employed when the object of desire (*i.e.* money) is something which cannot be produced and the demand for which cannot be readily choked off. There is no remedy but to persuade the public that green cheese is practically the same thing and to have a green cheese factory (*i.e.* a central bank) under public control.[8]

In the Keynesian theory, intended saving and intended investment are made equal by fluctuations not so much in interest rates as in income. Excess intended saving cuts income until intended saving falls to the level of intended investment. The cash-balance theory accounts for something equivalent. Excess demand for money means deficient demand for goods and labor, which brings on cutbacks in production and employment. The resulting drop in income reduces the demand for cash balances on account of the transactions motive[9] and probably on account of other motives also. When poverty had cut the total quantity of money demanded down to the quantity in existence, it would no longer be strictly correct, I suppose, to speak of an excess demand for money. The excess demand would be virtual, not actual. Poverty would be suppressing it. The situation would correspond to the somewhat misnamed Keynesian "underemployment equilibrium," in which excess intended saving is being suppressed by the low level of income.

In this situation, any monetary expansion would begin to replace poverty as the means of working off an actual excess demand for money. So would any fall or further fall in prices and wages—at least, so says the theory of the Pigou effect.[10] While stickily fall*ing* prices and wages are a symptom of an excess demand for money, a sufficient *fall* in prices and wages would be a cure. Homeopathy could conceivably work. A rise in the value of money would tend to cut the number of money units demanded and so stimulate spending. Whether reliance on the Pigou effect is a *practical* road out of depression, however, requires some comment later.

The concept of stickiness in the value of money as an obstacle to restoring monetary equilibrium brings out a direct contrast between depression and suppressed inflation. A. P. Lerner has emphasized this contrast by renaming suppressed inflation "suppression."[11] Suppression is the condition of a "sellers' market," general shortages, and impairment of allocation by prices that develops when prices are kept from fully adjusting to monetary inflation. Depression is the opposite condition that develops when prices are kept from fully adjusting to monetary deflation. As Lerner shrewdly remarks, depression is the name for (monetary) deflation with prices kept from falling.

Now we can understand the paradox that either "deflation" or "inflation" would cure depression, and that either "inflation" or "deflation" would cure suppression. The kind of deflation that would cure depression is *price-and-wage* deflation—a big enough rise in the value of money to cut the quantity of money demanded down to the quantity in existence. The kind of inflation that would cure depression is *monetary* inflation—a big enough increase in the money supply (or fall in the demand schedule for cash balances) to relieve the excess demand.

The kind of inflation that would cure suppression is price-and-wage inflation—a big enough fall in the value of money to raise the quantity of money demanded up to the quantity in existence. Here is the sense in the quip that the best cure for (suppressed) inflation is inflation. The kind of deflation that would cure suppression is monetary deflation—a big enough cut in the money supply (or rise in the demand schedule for cash balances) to wipe out the excess supply. (Confusion between price-and-wage and monetary "inflation" and "deflation" has sometimes bedeviled theory and policy. NRA, with its price-raising codes of "fair competition," seems to have been an example. In the absence of sufficient monetary inflation, price-and-wage *de*flation is a better treatment for depression than price-and-wage *in*flation.)

One more paradox is now understandable. Depression could conceivably be prevented either by maintaining wages and prices or—barring transitional difficulties—by cutting wages and prices. Wage-price maintenance would be salutary only if accomplished by just enough monetary expansion to avoid an excess demand for money and the symptomatic sticky sag in wages and prices. But barring monetary action, swift reduction of wages and prices to a new equilibrium level would be needed to forestall the excess demand for money that, as we are supposing, would otherwise persist.

Returning to the question whether the Pigou effect is a practical depression cure, we must first note the problem posed by a money supply made up mainly of private debt. Encouragement to money holders through a rise in the real value of their cash balances would be largely offset by discouragement to private money issuers, even though the existence of some commodity money or government-issued money suffices, in principle, for the Pigou effect to work.[12] A second difficulty stems from perverse shrinkage of the money supply, so well emphasized by advocates of 100 per cent reserve banking. Third, prices and wages will not in practice go down readily enough for a prompt Pigou effect; and besides, since prices and wages are not all equally flexible or inflexible, a major change in their general level would distort the structure of *relative* prices and so transitionally worsen maladjustments in production and trade. Fourth, a sticky downward sag of prices and wages would cause expectations that worsened the excess demand for money in the meanwhile. Fifth, even if prices and wages could somehow fall suddenly and completely enough to forestall such expectations, the increased real burden of carrying and repaying outstanding debt would discourage business and consumer debtors. (Defaults and so forth would rule out offsetting benefits to creditors, as distinct from holders of actual money.) Sixth, such a rapid change in the purchasing power of money would subvert money's usefulness as a standard of value. Seventh, inertia would add to transitional difficulties. A person's cash balance is partly a matter of habit and is not adjusted fully and promptly to changes in the value of the money unit. When prices are falling rapidly, people may for a while thus unintentionally hold more purchasing power than usual in money.[13] Finally, fears of default by customers and of demands for early repayment of borrowings, together with worsened chances of borrowing in case of need, tend to increase businessmen's precautionary demands for cash balances when prices are falling. Banks, also, take customers' defaults, bankruptcies, and cash withdrawals as warnings to build up their own liquidity by reducing loans and investments.[14] Even households have reasons for trying to strengthen their cash positions.

Despite all these obstacles, monetary equilibrium would theoretically be restored in the long run at a new and higher value of the money unit; but "in the long run...."

The impracticality of waiting for a rise in the value of money to cure an excess demand for it in no way impairs our interpretation of depression as just such an excess demand. Certainly it does not discredit the idea of deliberately managing money to keep its supply and demand always in equilibrium.

IV. NEAR-MONEYS

One worry about the cash-balance interpretation of depression arises at first sight. Demand for current output might conceivably be slack in a depression because people preferred to hold liquid assets in general rather than actual money in particular. For instance, could not depression consist in an excess demand for bonds rather than for actual money? No: an excess demand for bonds (or for short-term bills, savings accounts, savings and loan shares, and other interest-bearing obligations to pay money) cannot persist unaccompanied by an excess demand for money itself. Given the prevailing prices, wages, and interest rates, the total value of goods and services that people want to exchange for bonds, directly or indirectly, will not exceed the total value of bonds that people want to exchange for goods and services—that is, people will not want to hold more bonds than exist—unless they also want to hold more money than exists.

The reason can be made clear by supposing, for the sake of argument, that people's preferences do shift away from goods and services and in favor of bonds without also shifting away from goods and services in favor of money. That would mean a shift toward bonds in people's preferences as between bonds and money, which would tend to raise the money prices of outstanding bonds. Bond prices—that is, interest rates—would adjust so as to maintain equilibrium between the desire to hold bonds and the desire to hold money and so prevent an excess demand for bonds relative to goods and services from existing in the absence of a similar excess demand for money. (Bond prices would so rise unless official intervention prevented it. If transactions at prices above the legal maximum were simply forbidden, this very prevention of equilibrium bond prices would be the straightforward explanation of any excess demand for bonds. Such a case would not show that business depressions are typified by an excess demand for bonds but not for money. If, on the other hand, the government used open-market sales to keep bond prices from rising, that very addition to the bond supply and subtraction from the money supply would prevent an excess demand for bonds relative to money and so prevent an excess demand for bonds relative to goods and services in the absence of an excess demand for money relative to goods and services.)

Furthermore, as Hicks's theory of the cost, bother, and risk of security transactions[15] and Keynes's liquidity-preference theory explain, there is some floor below which the interest rate on any particular kind of debt will not go. At this floor rate, the reward for holding bonds is so small that people no longer prefer to hold additional wealth as bonds rather than as cash. Any further strengthening of desires to refrain from buying current output and instead to hold liquid assets must increase the excess demand for actual money along with—or even instead of—the excess demand for bonds.

A rephrasing of this complicated argument is in order. Even if the deficient spending on current output that constitutes a depression is due to an excess demand relative to goods and services for money-plus-bonds rather than for money alone, we may properly focus attention on the excess demand for money. Whatever else may characterize it, a depression must involve an excess demand for money; an excess demand for bonds could not exist alone. People could not behave in a way that would tend (barring price stickiness) to raise the purchasing power of the dollars in which bonds are expressed and yet not also tend to raise the purchasing power of the dollars in which checking accounts and currency are expressed. Furthermore, money is a very good substitute for bonds in satisfying the demand for liquid assets. When bond prices have been bid up to where bonds yield no more interest than the floor rate explained by Keynes and Hicks, then money proper is a perfect substitute for bonds. Anything that would tend to relieve the excess demand for money proper would also tend to relieve the excess demand for liquid assets in general and so would tend to relieve the deficiency in spending on current output.

Even more obviously, depression is not an excess demand for shares of stock in preference to both bonds and money as well as to current output. Actually, the demand for stocks depends on profit or dividend prospects, which are poorer than usual in depression. If depression were an excess demand for stocks and not for money, then the money prices of stocks would tend to rise. This, of course, is the reverse of what actually happens in depressions.

Depression certainly cannot be explained as an excess demand for nonreproducible assets in preference to current output. We know that depressions are not characterized by special eagerness to acquire Old Masters and the like.

In summary, the argument still stands that depression is an excess demand for *money* in preference to current output. The cash-balance interpretation does not depend on any clear dividing line between money and near-moneys. If there is an excess demand for money as broadly defined, there must also be an excess demand for money as narrowly defined.

V. POLICY

We have interpreted changes in the general price level as symptoms of the excess demand for money that constitutes a depression and of the excess supply of money that constitutes an inflationary sellers' market. The symptom tends in the long run to be a cure, but only imperfectly. Money management to prevent the symptom would coincide with management to prevent the disease.

To clinch our understanding of this point, let us visualize a graph measuring the volume of cash balances demanded and supplied along the x-axis and an index of the purchasing power of money along the y-axis. For familiar reasons, the curve showing the demand for money slopes downward from left to right. The supply curve can be regarded as a vertical line. Now, if either schedule shifted in such a way as to cause an excess supply of money at the old level of money's purchasing power, there would be a tendency for the purchasing power to fall. An opposite shift would tend to make the purchasing power rise. Such changes in the value of money would work towards a new equilibrium, but, as explained near the end of section III, only after delay and transitional troubles. If, however, monetary policy always kept adjusting the money supply so as to keep the supply-and-demand intersection at the same level, the value of money would not tend to change. Clearly, then, stability in the value of money is a criterion for continued equality between the quantities of money supplied and demanded. A policy of stabilizing the value of money apparently coincides pretty well with avoiding depressions and inflationary booms.

It does not coincide, however, with a guarantee of permanent full employment. Not all unemployment is due to a general deficiency of effective demand. Some "frictional" unemployment is normal. "Structural" unemployment might prevail if technology and the pattern of consumer demand required use of various factors of production in fairly rigid proportions: if the factors were in fact available in *other* proportions, some would unavoidably be in excess supply.[16] More plausibly, perhaps, price and wage rigidities might block attainment of the relative price structure needed to make businessmen and consumers choose the production techniques and consumption patterns compatible with full employment. A related difficulty could arise if an autonomous upward push on wages and prices (by union pressure, for instance) kept tending to make the existing money supply inadequate for a full-employment level of business activity. The question would arise whether to "support" a creeping inflation of wages and prices by continually expanding the money supply.

The cash-balance approach, with its emphasis on price-level movements as symptoms of excess demand for or supply of money, makes it clear why money management aimed at price-level stability coincides with preventing unemployment due to general lack of effective demand while not overdoing monetary expansion in a futile attempt to cure the kinds of unemployment that require other treatment.

A possible objection to monetary stabilization is that price-level changes could be measured in many different ways; nobody could say just how much the value of money had changed over a certain period, or even, perhaps, whether the value had gone up or down or held steady. Granting all this, there is still a great difference between a clear change in the value of money as shown by *any* reasonable indicator and, on the other hand, real doubt whether the value had risen or fallen. Maintenance of such doubt would be successful stabilization and would coincide with avoiding any considerable disequilibrium.

One qualification should be made. Constancy in the value of money indicates continued equilibrium only if individual prices and wages are flexible enough so that disequilibrium *would* show itself in a price-level movement. If incipient price-level changes are to give signals for necessary adjustments in a tentatively chosen rate of money-supply growth, then individual prices and wages must be free. Ceilings and floors on individual prices and wages bring to mind Wilhelm Röpke's aphorism, "The more stabilization, the less stability."[17] Röpke's wise insight calls for overall stabilization measures rather than for myriad special interventions.

In short, it is more appropriate for the value of money to be stable than sticky.[18] Stickiness in the value of money is poor responsiveness to forces trying to change it; stability is steadiness through avoidance of forces trying to change it.[19]

This paper says nothing about *how* the quantity of money might best be regulated. Nothing said here necessarily provides a case for (or against) traditional monetary policy proper in preference to regulating the money supply through government budget surpluses and deficits. The cash-balance approach does, however, clarify the case for deliberately regulating the money supply somehow. An understanding of this case should help overcome superstitious qualms about creating money outright to pay for deliberate anti-depression open-market operations or government budget deficits.

[*] The author thanks Mr. Norman Lombard and Professor Dudley Dillard for helpful comments on a much earlier and longer draft.

[1] Even ostensibly "nonmonetary" business-cycle theories must, at least tacitly, allow changes in the flow of money. Cf. D. Hamberg, *Business Cycles* (New York, °1951), pp. 193, 216, 217, 220, 372. As Hamberg says on pages 113-114 and as Gottfried Haberler says in *Prosperity and Depression*, 3rd ed. (Geneva, 1941), p. 101, the acceleration principle cannot dominate the whole economic system rather than just particular sectors unless the money or credit supply is elastic.

[2] Oscar Lange, "Say's Law: A Restatement and Criticism," in O. Lange and others, eds., *Studies in Mathematical Economics and Econometrics* (In Memory of Henry Schultz) (Chicago, 1942), pp. 49, 53, 57-58.

[3] *Ibid.*, p. 53.

[4] *Ibid.*, p. 52.

[5] Edwin Cannan, "The Application of the Theoretical Apparatus of Supply and Demand to Units of Currency," *Economic Journal*, Dec. 1921, XXXI, pp. 453-54.

[6] For another demonstration that excess demand for and excess supply of money in the flow sense coincide respectively with excess demand and excess supply in the stock sense, see Don Patinkin, "The Indeterminacy of Absolute Prices in Classical Economic Theory," *Econometrica*, Jan. 1949, XVII, pp. 5, 7-9.

[7] Albert Gailord Hart, *Money, Debt and Economic Activity* (New York, 1948), pp. 195-208, 523-25.

[8] John Maynard Keynes, *The General Theory of Employment, Interest and Money* (New York, 1936), pp. 234-35. For an enlightening interpretation of Keynes' chapter 17, see Abba P. Lerner, "The Essential Properties of Interest and Money," *Quarterly Journal of Economics*, May 1952, LXVI, pp. 172-193.

[9] Emil Küng, *Die Selbstregulierung der Zahlungsbilanz* (St. Gallen, 1948), pp. 50-51. J. M. Keynes also recognized that a drop in income would lessen the quantity of money demanded on account of the transactions motive. However, his main emphasis (which to my mind is mistaken) was on how this effect lowers the interest rate and so stimulates investment. "The General Theory of Employment," *Quarterly Journal of Economics*, Feb. 1937, LI, p. 218.

[10] See, for example, A. C. Pigou, "Economic Progress in a Stable Environment," *Economica*, Aug. 1947, n.s. XIV, pp. 180-88. Surprisingly, Keynes himself hints at the Pigou effect in his passages quoted above.

[11] "The Inflationary Process: Some Theoretical Aspects," *Review of Economic Statistics*, Aug. 1949, XXXI, p. 195.

[12] Don Patinkin, "Price Flexibility and Full Employment," *American Economic Review*, Sept. 1948, XXXVIII, pp. 547-52. Patinkin stresses also the rise in the real value of government securities.

[13] In times of inflation, a comparable inertia may worsen the excess supply of money by delaying one's decision to increase one's cash balance. James Harvey Rogers, *The Process of Inflation in France, 1914–1927* (New York, 1929), pp. 132, 134, 318–20.

[14] Hamberg, *Business Cycles*, pp. 140, 183, 389.

[15] J. R. Hicks, *Value and Capital*, 2nd ed. (Oxford, 1946), pp. 163–67.

[16] Masao Fukuoka, "Full Employment and Constant Coefficients of Production," *Quarterly Journal of Economics*, Feb. 1955, LXIX, pp. 23–44. For a broader discussion of nonmonetary unemployment, see Lloyd W. Mints, *Monetary Policy for a Competitive Society* (New York, 1950), pp. 15–28.

[17] *Die Lehre von der Wirtschaft*, 4th ed. (Erlenbach-Zürich, 1946), p. 268.

[18] A. P. Lerner makes a suggestive distinction between stickiness and stability of an ordinary price. *Quarterly Journal of Economics*, May 1952, p. 186.

[19] George L. Bach has argued that stabilization of a flexible price level coincides with anti-depression and anti-inflation policy. "Monetary-Fiscal Policy, Debt Policy, and the Price Level," *American Economic Review*, May 1947, XXXVII, pp. 232, 236.

15. The Genesis of the Depression
Lionel Robbins

Lionel Robbins was an economist at the London School of Economics who was heavily influenced by both Friedrich Hayek and Ludwig von Mises. According to their "Austrian" theory of the business cycle, depressions are the inevitable result of previous booms, where booms themselves are caused by excessive monetary expansion. Robbins' presentation of the Austrian view is especially clear and persuasive. Students may therefore be surprised to learn that Robbins himself eventually repudiated the Mises-Hayek theory. --G.S., Ed.

* * *

1. So far, the various explanations of the depression which we have examined have all proved to be defective; some because they were not explanations at all but merely restatements of the problem; some because the assumptions on which they rested were in obvious conflict with fact. Where then are we to turn?

2. Let us go back a little to a point which was raised in the last chapter when we were discussing over-production. We saw there that one way of describing the slump was to depict it as a simultaneous breakdown of the profitability of many different lines of industry. It is well known, in fact, that this breakdown is most serious in the industries producing what are known as producers' goods; that is to say, the so-called constructional industries and the industries producing raw materials.[1] In these industries the depression shows itself as a condition of over-production, a condition in which costs are higher than prices, a condition in which the supply coming forward is not taken up at profitable prices, a condition in which the businesses engaged in these lines of industry find that their earlier expectations are not justified by the state of the market, a condition in which earlier errors of anticipation are revealed.

One way of putting our problem, therefore, is to ask why the errors thus revealed were originally committed, why they occurred in this peculiar form. It is quite clear that the leaders of business are at no time equipped with perfect foresight. We should always expect some mistakes to be made somewhere. But in the absence of special information we should expect a random distribution. We should not expect this peculiar cluster of errors. Why should the leaders of business in the various industries producing producers' goods make errors of judgement at the same time and in the same direction?

Now it seems probable, as was hinted in the last chapter, that a dislocation which is common to many industries, if it does not actually originate on the side of money, will at least be transmitted and enlarged though the monetary medium. This provides a clue

---
[1] See Tables 8 and 9, Statistical Appendix, for evidence on this point.

of a kind to the solution of our problem. But it does not, in itself, explain the peculiar distribution of error. Money is spent on everything. Why do not fluctuations in the supply of or the demand for money affect all lines of production equally? Are there any reasons for supposing that monetary changes will bring about the kind of error we are contemplating?

3. Let us first see if such a thing is theoretically conceivable. If this proves to be the case, we can then proceed to discover whether the assumptions on which our theory is based have a counterpart in the reality of the fluctuation we are examining.

Our problem relates to demand expressed in terms of money. It is necessary, therefore, to be quite clear wherein money demand consists.

If we take a cross-section of the industrial system at any moment of time, the activities of supply there discernible fall quite naturally into two groups. On the one hand we have the supply of goods and services ready for immediate consumption—bread, fuel, domestic service, etc. On the other hand we have the supply of things which directly or indirectly contribute chiefly to the consumption of the future. In this group fall raw materials, semi-manufactures, machines, factories, and all those durable consumption-goods like houses whose consumptive uses stretch out over long periods ahead. This division corresponds more or less to the familiar statistical division between consumers' goods and producers' goods save that with the producers' goods we must here include durable consumption-goods such as houses. In conception, this distinction between production for present and future consumption is quite clear and definite. In practice we have to be content with rough classification. A suit of clothes is a durable consumption-good. But we usually class it with consumption-goods. If we like, we may make a distinction between the supply of income-goods and the supply of capital-goods, remembering that the use of a house for which rent is paid will be an income-good and the house itself considered as an object of ownership will be a capital-good.

Corresponding to these activities of supply there will be streams of money demand. On the one hand, there will be streams of money being spent on goods for immediate consumption. On the other hand, business men and others will be spending money on goods and services whose fruits will only be available in the future. The housewife will be spending money on bread, fuel, etc. The baker will be spending money on the labour he employs to make bread, on replenishing his stocks of flour, perhaps on repairing his oven, and so on and so forth. The distinction here is roughly the same as the distinction between expenditure out of income and capital expenditure. The sums of money spent by consumers, in normal times at any rate, will be part or the whole of their money-incomes, moneys which have accrued to them as a result of the labour which they do as producers or the property which, in one way or another, they lend out. The business men will be using their capital—money released by the sale of stock or new funds borrowed in one way or another from the capital market. Corresponding to our distinction relating to supply we may distinguish between the demand for income-goods and the demand for capital-goods.

The minute circumstances determining expenditure on income-goods need not concern us here. But the direction of capital expenditure deserves a little further attention. As we have seen, at any moment of time business men must be conceived as spending money on particular objects—re-investing capital which has been freed by previous sales, or investing new sums which they have saved themselves or borrowed from the capital market. What determines the direction of their expenditure? In the capitalist system, within the limits prescribed by law, free capital can be spent on anything. A business man who has capital free may re-invest it in his business, doing the same sort of thing he has done before. Or he may put it elsewhere. What in fact are the considerations governing the direction of his expenditure?

Clearly in particular instances there may be all sorts of non-pecuniary considerations. But, speaking broadly, it is not misleading to say that the main considerations are anticipations of profit. Money goes where, taking everything into account, the profits are expected to be highest. The business man considers costs on the one side and prices on the other, and tries to put his money where the margin of profit is greatest. If therefore the return on capital in different lines of industry is not equal (and it never actually becomes equal) there is a tendency for capital to shift from those branches and methods of production where it is relatively lower to those where it is relatively higher. The rate of return on capital is, as it were, the governor of the system.

One further point before we utilise these elementary notions in examining the effects of monetary changes. It should be clear that at any moment there must exist possibilities of production which might be utilised if the profitability of other lines of industry were not so high. When the rate of interest drops from 4 to 3 per cent, a whole range of enterprises, which were not worth while when 4 per cent was the rule, now become attractive. Factories can be built, machines constructed, transport facilities extended, housing provided, which, when the higher rate prevailed, were out of the question. The owners of free capital would not undertake these things themselves if a higher return could be obtained elsewhere. They could not profitably have been undertaken on borrowed money, since the cost of borrowing was too high. The anticipated rate of return on capital, therefore, performs the double function of guiding the direction of existing investment and confining it to enterprise yielding a return above a certain margin.

4. So far we have supposed that money spent at any moment, either by business men or consumers, is money which has been released either by sales of stock, the rendering of services, or the hiring out of property. We have assumed the total supply of currency and credit to be constant. We have tacitly excluded the possibility of an augmentation of money demand either by way of an increase of currency, or by an increase in the rate at which currency and credit are used. We must now examine what happens if this occurs. We must examine the effects on production of monetary changes.

Let us suppose, for the sake of simplicity, an increase in the supply of money.

Now it is very important, from our point of view, to be clear how this increase actually comes about. Suppose that by a governmental decree all money holdings were to be doubled; that is to say, suppose that all balances at the banks were multiplied by two and all holders of cash were entitled to treat each note and coin in their possession as double its previous face value. In such circumstances, in a free economy with fairly full employment, there is no reason to suppose that great disturbances would follow. The competition of buyers would lead to the fairly quick marking up of all prices to something like double their original level. Some distributive changes there would be as a result of the existence of long-term contracts. *Rentiers* would continue at the old level of income. Profit-makers and possibly wage-earners would benefit correspondingly. These distributive changes would possibly lead to shifts in demand for particular commodities.

But there seems no reason to expect that a general oscillation of any importance would be generated.

But, in the real world, new money is not made available in this way. In normal times, expansion and contraction of the money supply comes, not *via* the printing press and government decree, but *via* an expansion of credit through the banks. The rate of discount of the Central Bank is the main regulator of money supply. This involves a mode of diffusion of new money radically different from the case we have just examined—a mode of diffusion which may have important effects on the nature and direction of production. Let us see how this happens.

Let us suppose that, for reasons which for the moment we will leave uninvestigated, the Central Banks of the world make their rates of discount lower than would be justified by the volume of voluntary saving coming into the system. (We shall return later on to a discussion of the possible reasons for such a policy.) What are likely to be the effects on production?

Let us ignore, for the time being, the rather intricate mechanism by which the initial change will transmit itself through the capital market. The fundamental fact on which we must concentrate our attention is that borrowing is cheaper. The structure of interest rates has fallen. This means that the profitability of all forms of production which involve making things which only yield services at a later date, or over a long period of time, is increased. Consider the position of a speculative builder when the rate at which he borrows falls by one per cent, say from 6 per cent to 5. Suppose he has been paying £1000 for a certain collection of materials. Interest on that at 6 per cent is £60. When the rate falls to 5 per cent and the price of existing house property rises accordingly, he will be making an increased profit until the price rises to something a little less than £1200. Clearly it will pay to borrow more.

We can perhaps see this even more clearly if we use the language of the real-estate market. A fall in the rate of interest implies an increase in the number of years' income which it is worth while to pay for the possession of land outright. When the rate of interest is 5 per cent the corresponding number of years' purchase is 20. When it is 4 per cent it is 25. Now this applies not merely to land and houses but to all kinds of capital instruments. The longer-lived the capital instrument, or the greater its distance from consumption, the more its value is affected by the change in the rate of interest. The shorter-lived it is, or the less its distance from consumption, the less is it affected. The value of flour in the baker's shop is hardly affected at all by a cheapening of the cost of borrowing. The value of mines, forests, houses and heavy factory equipment is enormously affected.

It follows, therefore, that the bulk of the new borrowing will be undertaken by those who propose to engage in enterprises of this nature. The new money will flow to those parts of the economic system most affected by the rate of interest. There will be an increased demand for what we have called capital-goods. There will be a boom in the constructional industries and the industries producing raw materials. Producers in these industries, on the strength of the new demands, will be able to bid away from other industries factors of production common to both. The new labour supply will go into these industries rather than elsewhere. Raw materials, such as coal, pig iron and timber, will tend to be used in greater proportions in these parts of the economic system. The production of "producers' goods" and durable consumption-goods, such as houses, will increase.

So far, the phenomena we have described are almost exactly similar to the phenomena we should expect to accompany a fall in the rate of interest which was due to an increase in voluntary saving. But there is this very important difference. An increase in voluntary saving which is made effective in the investment market, means a spontaneous change in the proportion of money spent on income-goods and capital-goods—a change in favour of the latter. It is of the essence of saving that it involves a proportionate slackening of expenditure on present consumption, and a proportionate increase of expenditure on making things which will only be consumable in the future. But the change we have been describing involves a change in the amount spent on capital-goods without any diminution, on the part of the recipients of income, of expenditure on consumption-goods. The business men who have borrowed the new money from the banks compete with the demands which come from those whose money has been secured by the sale of stocks, the performance of work or the hiring out of their property.

But these sums of new money which come from the banks do not remain at the stage of demand for raw materials and the products of the constructional industries. Gradually, as they filter through the economic system, they become ultimate income. Now there is nothing which justifies us in assuming that the recipients of income will necessarily increase the proportion of their incomes that they save. It follows, therefore, that as the new money becomes income we must expect a strengthening of the demand, not for capital-goods, but for income-goods. The old proportion between demand for income-goods and demand for capital-goods tends to be re-established.

But what does this mean in terms of the relative profitability of different lines of industry? Surely that the producers making for immediate consumption will now be in a stronger position to bid against the producers of capital-goods for the factors of production which they use in common and for new loans from the banks. And what does this mean? A tendency to a rise in costs and a hardening of market rates of interest. Wages rise. Interest rates in the short-loan market rise still more. But this means that the anticipations on which the producers of capital-goods planned their extensions of production are frustrated. What do they do? Probably they try to obtain new credits at the banks. For a time this may be possible. The initial prospects of profitability will in all probability have tempted both banks and individuals to reduce their margin of liquidity. But eventually the rise in costs and in the rate of interest becomes too great. The error of the initial anticipations becomes revealed. Investment in the lines of industry most affected by the rate of interest is seen to be unprofitable. The supply of capital-goods coming forward encounters a slackening demand. There ensues depression in the constructional industries and the industries producing raw materials.

5. So much by way of bare essential outline of the manner in which an inflationary extension of credit may generate collective error on the part of the producers of capital-goods. It is not difficult to fill in sufficient detail as regards the actual movement of the capital markets to give the picture a much more familiar appearance.

Let us start, as before, from a state of affairs in which the rate of discount of the Central Banks has moved downwards. We may assume that the Central Banks are in a position to make this rate effective either in virtue of the actual market situation or of "management" in the shape of purchases of securities in the open market. What happens as a result of this movement?

It is probable that the effect will at first be confined to the short-loan market. Bill rates and call-loan rates will be low. There will be a condition of ease and liquidity in the inner circle of financial institutions.

If such a state of affairs continues for long, however, it will begin to spread to the long-term market. It will be profitable to borrow from the banks to hold long-dated securities. There will be an upward movement in the market for bonds and debentures. There is no need to suppose that all this is financed by new credit. As the upward movement proceeds, people who have had money lying idle in the banks will be drawn into the movement. The existing supply of money will commence to circulate more rapidly.

It is not possible for a movement of this sort to proceed very far before it begins to affect other branches of the market. The fall in the yield of bonds and debentures, which is the obverse of the rise in their value, will lead the more adventurous spirits in the market to begin to look elsewhere for a higher return on their investment. The market in common stocks will rise. It will not be long before a stock exchange boom is in progress. If it is a country where development is expected, there will be extensive speculation too in real estate.

But a boom of this sort is not a thing which can be confined in its effects to the money market. The idea that a boom on the Stock Exchange keeps money from industry is of course the exact reverse of the truth. The rise in security prices makes it easier for existing undertakings to secure overdrafts from the banks. At the same time it is a direct incentive to the flotation of new issues. If the centre is financially important, part of this will probably take the form of foreign lending.

All this will be reflected in the various commodity markets. As the money raised in these different ways is spent, it will tend to drive up (or to prevent from falling) the prices of raw materials. The heavy industries will begin to make larger profits. This in turn will react on the market for securities. Prices will be marked up to reflect the higher expectations of profit. More money will be borrowed from the banks to finance speculative operations. The rapidity with which deposits are used will increase still further. The yield of gilt-edged securities will begin to rise. The opportunity for speculative gain will be such that short-loan rates will be driven above long. By this time the banks will have become alarmed and will be making various attempts to put the brake on. For some time, however, the wave of optimism may carry the boom along.

But it cannot go on. As it proceeds, the technical strain on the credit structure becomes greater and greater. At the same time, the rise in wage rates, reinforced probably by the expenditure of speculative gains for consumptive purposes, diminishes the prospects of profitability of the industries producing capital-goods, both by raising their costs and by stimulating the competition of the consumption-good industries, thus raising the rate at which they can borrow. Usually it is some accident which is actually responsible for a reversal of the process—a conspicuous business failure, the rumour of a bad crop, or something fortuitous of that kind. But the end is certain. Once costs have begun to rise it would require a continuous increase in the rate of increase of credit to prevent the thing coming to disaster. But that itself, as we have seen in the great post-war inflations, would eventually generate panic. Sooner or later the initial errors are discovered. And then starts a reverse rush for liquidity. The Stock Exchange collapses. There is a stoppage of new issues. Production in the industries producing capital-goods slows down. The boom is at an end.

6. Finally, one more word about the origin of such movements. So far, for the sake of expository convenience, we have assumed that the expansion of credit was directly initiated by the banks. This is not unlikely. Indeed, as we shall see, there is strong reason to suppose that such was the origin of at least one important phase of the fluctuation we are discussing. But it is not at all necessary. The downward movement of the discount rate may be the result of the flow of new gold from the mines. It is equally possible that the expansion may originate on the "goods side". The conditions for credit expansion of the sort we have been discussing are present when, the structure of money rates remaining constant, there occurs some change in the sphere of production, some invention, some opening up of new markets, some discovery of new natural resources, which makes borrowing more profitable—to use a technical term, some change which tends to raise the "natural rate" of interest. If in such circumstances money rates are not raised, then there are present the conditions for an extension of borrowing, an introduction into circulation of new money, which brings it about that investment is in excess of saving.

Recognition of this point should do much to remove the misgivings which are often entertained with regard to "purely monetary" theories of the trade cycle. A purely monetary theory of the trade cycle—a theory which explained the ups and downs of trade solely in terms of movements of the general level of prices brought about by the arbitrary changes in monetary conditions—is quite rightly regarded with suspicion by most people who have had some experience of the working of the economic machine. If it were all as easy as that the trade cycle would have been eliminated already. If a mistake were made in one direction, it would be enough to reverse it by the converse monetary measures. The world we live in is not of this degree of simplicity.

But the theory we have been developing does not make this assumption. It allows for the impulse to expansion to come either from the condition of real investment or from changes in monetary policy. It exhibits at every point the changes in the world of productive activity which follow these initial impulses, and it shows them proceeding *via* changes in anticipation of the future of business men and investors. It explains the real over-production in certain lines of industry which arises as a result of these changes. It shows how, when the boom has collapsed, there exist dislocations and disproportionalities in the world of industry, the wreckage of false expectations, which monetary manipulation is not likely to remove. Only in its emphasis on the importance of demand in terms of money and the influence of money rates of interest as transmitted through investment markets can it be described as a monetary theory of the trade cycle. But in this form surely emphasis on monetary factors is only in accordance with common knowledge of the facts of business.

7. So far we have simply discovered how a general fluctuation of trade is logically possible. We have seen how an inflation which operates through the mechanism of the money market may breed errors of anticipation among the capital-producing industries which lead first to the phenomena of a boom and then, when these errors are revealed, to a consequential collapse. How does this theory fit the facts of the present depression?

At this point it is necessary to proceed with great caution. Whatever be the ultimate truth with regard to the origin of this depression, one thing is certain, that no one explanation is capable of explaining all its different aspects. As we shall see in more detail in the next chapter, the fundamental causes, whatever they may be, have operated in a *milieu* more than usually disturbed by external changes and secondary oscillations, and their manifestations are thus inevitably complicated. It will take years of careful scrutiny of the available material before we can hope to be in a position to pronounce with complete confidence on these matters, and it is not certain that we shall ever reach this stage. Nevertheless, even now, there is a considerable body of evidence which seems to afford a presumption that causes, not dissimilar from the causes outlined above, have actually been in operation.

The big collapse came in America, and it is to America, and the centres most intimately associated with America, that we must turn if we are to discover the antecedents of the depression.

If we look in this direction we do certainly find movements remarkably similar to the movements we should expect from our theory. We saw in the last chapter what a very considerable expansion of credit took place in the Federal Reserve System from 1925 onwards. The following chart, which exhibits bank debits divided by bank deposits, gives a rough indication of the changes in the velocity of circulation during the same period:[1]

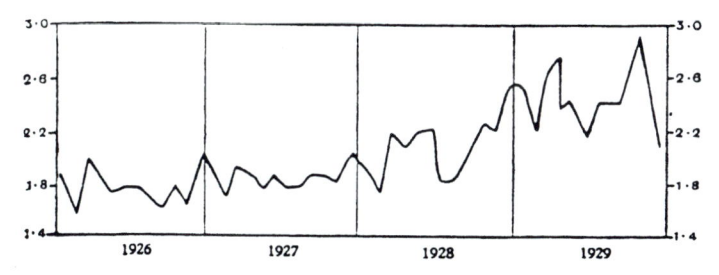

UNITED STATES—VELOCITY OF CIRCULATION OF BANK DEPOSITS

No doubt some of this was restricted to a very narrow field of speculative operations—though it should be observed that the index for the banks outside New York moves in the same direction as the New York index itself. But even when this has been fully discounted, it is evident, if we take both the increase in credit and the increase in velocity into account, that the increase in the effective volume of money was very great indeed—that there was undoubtedly a most considerable inflationary movement.

The effects of this are quite evident in the market for common stocks. The following chart shows the movement of the prices of such securities during the period under consideration.[2]

[1] For the figures on which it is based see Statistical Appendix, Table 15.
[2] For the figures see Statistical Appendix, Table 2.

It is not necessary to labour the point that this was one of the most remarkable Stock Exchange booms in modern economic history.

Expectations are not disappointed when we turn

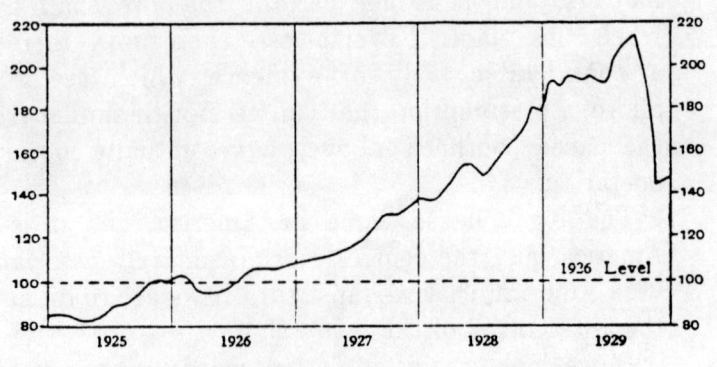

UNITED STATES—INDEX OF SECURITY PRICES

to the sphere of production. The following chart[1] shows the movement of the production of producers' goods and consumers' goods at this time. The indices from which it is constructed are not by any means all that could be desired from the point of view of statistical purity, but the general direction of movement is unmistakeable.

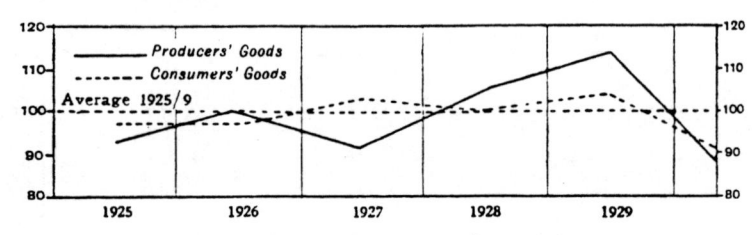

UNITED STATES—INDICES OF PRODUCTION

The construction of durable consumers' goods too shows a similar movement. The index of the value of residential building contracts awarded rises from 117 in 1927 to 126 in 1928. It then falls off as money rates become higher. In general we find all the characteristic evidences of a boom in the constructional and raw material producing industries.

Similarly, when we turn to interest rates and costs we find movements which conform to the expectations

---

[1] For the figures see Statistical Appendix, Table 9.

of theory. The following chart shows movements of short-loan rates of interest in New York City:[1]

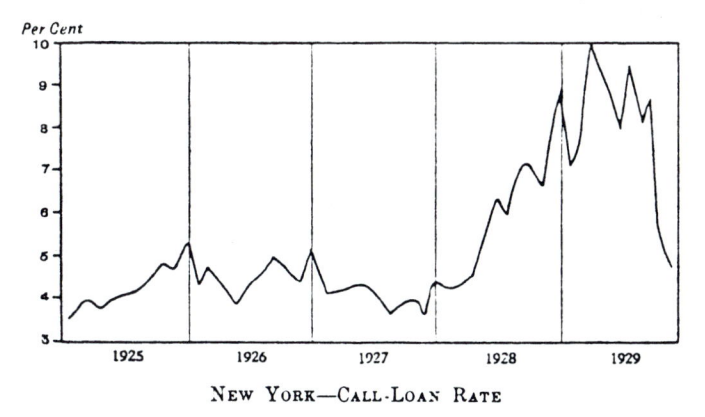

NEW YORK—CALL-LOAN RATE

Statistics of costs are hard to obtain. The wage index, however, which stood at 212 in January 1925 and 221 in January 1927, had risen to 227 in September 1929. Here we have just those directions of movement which have been explained.

It is sometimes said that the movement of wage rates is too small to have played the part here ascribed to them. This objection is reinforced by appeal to the comparatively small increase in the figures of national income recorded during this period ($79 billions to $85 billions). This seems to have little weight. This for two reasons. In so far as the wage index is an index of costs, it probably considerably under-estimates the movement. All the evidence on trade fluctuation seems to show that, during the later phases of a cycle, costs rise faster than the movement of wage rates would suggest. On the other hand, in so far as it is an index of increased pressure at the consumption end, it must be remembered that it again clearly errs on the side of under-estimation. During the later stages of the boom there seems reason to suppose that among many classes of consumers speculative gains were treated as income and spent accordingly. Moreover, statistics of national income are misleading here, since they include agricultural incomes which were actually falling during the period under consideration. So far as manufacturing industry is concerned there seems no reason to doubt that, towards the end of the boom, there occurred an increase in costs and a considerable increase of spending for consumptive purposes.

The one element which at first sight appears to be incompatible with the explanation we have offered is the movement of prices. In June 1924 the level of

[1] For the figures see Statistical Appendix, Table 21.

wholesale prices in the United States stood at 95.[1] In June 1927 it stood at 94. In June 1929 it stood at 95. The price-level was almost stationary—if anything, tending to fall slightly. At first sight this appears to be incompatible with the suggestion of an inflationary boom, and there can be no doubt that it was the more or less stable condition of the price-level which blinded contemporary observers to the real nature of what was going on at the time. So long as the price-level remains stationary, they urged, there can be no fear of inflation. A little reflection, however, should show that this belief is fallacious. A stationary price-level shows an absence of inflation only when production is stationary. When productivity is increasing, then, in the absence of inflation, we should expect prices to fall. Now the period we are examining was a period of rapidly increasing productivity. The comparative stability of prices, therefore, so far from being a proof of the absence of inflation, is a proof of its presence.

On this point the verdict of Mr. J. M. Keynes is particularly interesting. Mr. Keynes, it will be remembered, was not one of those who expressed alarm at the abundance of cheap money during the days of the expansion. On the contrary, he was one of the chief influences in the world calling for more and more cheap money. In the *Treatise on Money*, however, with customary candour, he admits having misapprehended the situation:

Anyone who looked only at the index of prices would see no reason to suspect any material degree of inflation, whilst anyone who looked only at the total volume of bank credit and the prices of common stocks would have been convinced of the presence of an inflation actual or impending. For my part I took the view at the time that there was no inflation in the sense in which I use this term. Looking back in the light of fuller statistical information than was then available, I believe that whilst there was probably no material inflation up to the end of 1927, a genuine profit inflation developed some time between that date and the summer of 1929.[1]

On the existence of inflation in America during these years, therefore, there would appear to be substantial agreement. Would that this had been so then.

8. The inflation was not confined to America, although it was in that part of the world that some of its most characteristic manifestations were witnessed. An enormous volume of foreign loans spread out

---

[1] For the figures see Statistical Appendix, Table 6.
[1] *A Treatise on Money*, vol. ii. p. 190.

to other centres and generated expansion there. The following chart shows the movement of capital into Germany and the resulting credit expansion:[2]

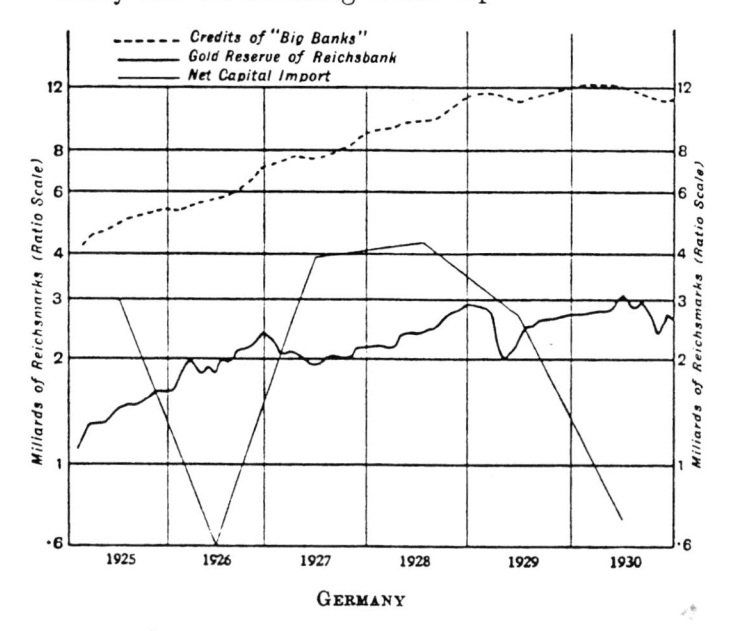

```
------ Credits of "Big Banks"
—————— Gold Reserve of Reichsbank
—————— Net Capital Import
```

GERMANY

Security prices had reached a peak in the early part of 1927 from which they were shaken by efforts on the part of the Reichsbank to control the situation. But the inflowing tide of credit from the United States overbore this tendency to recession. In the later part of the year they revived and remained active until the end of 1928, when the inflow of foreign lending began to slacken. The discount rate which was 5 per cent in the early part of 1927 reached $7\frac{1}{2}$ per cent in the spring of 1929. Wages rose. The index of skilled wages, for instance, which was 96 in the first quarter of 1927, by October 1929 had reached a level of 104. Other series show a similar movement. Here surely are characteristic symptoms of the effects of credit expansion.[1]

But the expansion did not stop here. It was almost world-wide in extent. It is difficult to compile an index of world expansion. The following table, based on statistics furnished by the League of Nations, gives

---

[2] For the figures see Statistical Appendix, Tables 23, 24 and 25.

[1] For further figures see Statistical Appendix, Tables 26, 27 and 28.

some idea of the extent to which even not predominantly industrial countries were affected:

Loans, Discounts and Advances of Commercial Banks

Country	1924	1929
Canada	100	162
Argentine	100	134
Brazil	100	151 (1928)
Australia	100	146
New Zealand	100	122
Union of South Africa	100	181

These figures probably a little exaggerate the expansion for they are "corrected" for changes in the price-level, which fell slightly during the period. But it is difficult to understand the frame of mind of those who deny the existence of a very considerable degree of inflation.

9. But why did inflation take place?

It is clear that the effects of the war and the post-war inflation, which caused so large a proportion of the world's gold supply to be concentrated in New York, laid the foundations for the expansion. It has sometimes been said that these gold imports were sterilised. But, as we have seen, this is a complete misapprehension. They were made the basis of a very considerable expansion.

But clearly this is not the end of the story. If we look back at the chart of credit movements in the States which we were examining in the last chapter we shall see, as indeed we noticed then, that the system continued to expand in 1927-28, even when gold was flowing out. It is clear, too, from the velocity chart that it was during this period that the situation got really out of hand. Why did this take place?

The answer seems to be that it was the direct outcome of misdirected management on the part of the Federal Reserve authorities—an error of management, however, which Englishmen at any rate have no right to speak of with reproach, for it seems almost certain that it was carried out very largely with the intent to ease our position.

The situation seems to have been roughly as follows. By the spring of 1927 the upward movement of business in the United States, which started in 1925, showed signs of coming to a conclusion. A moderate depression was in sight. There is no reason to suppose that this depression would have been of very great duration or of unusual severity. It was a normal cyclical movement.

Meantime, however, events in England had produced a position of unusual difficulty and uncertainty. In 1925 the British authorities had restored the Gold Standard at a parity which, in the light of subsequent events, is now generally admitted to have been too high. The consequences were not long in appearing. Exports fell off. Imports increased. The Gold Standard was in peril. The effects of the over-valued exchange made themselves felt with greatest severity in the coal trade. Throughout 1926 there raged labour disputes, which were the direct consequence of these troubles—first the general strike, then a strike in the coal-fields which dragged out for over six months, still further endangering the trade balance. By 1927 the position was one of great danger. International assistance was sought. And in the summer of that year, partly in order to help us, partly in order to ease the domestic position, the authorities of the Federal Reserve System took the momentous step of forcing a régime of cheap money. A vigorous policy of purchasing securities was initiated.

On this point the evidence of Mr. A. C. Miller, the most experienced member of the Federal Reserve Board, before the Senate Committee on Banking and Currency, seems decisive:

In the year 1927 ... you will note the pronounced increase in these holdings [Federal Reserve holdings of United States securities] in the second half of the year. Coupled with the heavy purchases of acceptances it was the greatest and boldest operation ever undertaken by the Federal Reserve System, and, in my judgement, resulted in one of the most costly errors committed by it or any other banking system in the last 75 years! ...[1]

What was the object of Federal Reserve Policy in 1927? It was to bring down money rates, the call rate among them, because of the international importance the call rate had come to acquire. The purpose was to start an outflow of gold—to reverse the previous inflow of gold into this country.[2]

The policy succeeded. The impending recession was averted. The London position was eased. The reflation succeeded. Production and the Stock Exchange took on a new lease of life. But from that date, according to all the evidence, the situation got completely out of control. By 1928 the authorities were thoroughly frightened. But now the forces they had released were

[1] *Senate Hearings pursuant to S.R. 71*, 1931, p. 134.
[2] *Ibid.* p. 154.

too strong for them. In vain they issued secret warnings. In vain they pushed up their own rates of discount. Velocity of circulation, the frenzied anticipation of speculators and company promoters, had now taken control. With resignation the best men in the system looked forward to the inevitable smash.

Thus, in the last analysis, it was deliberate co-operation between Central bankers, deliberate "reflation" on the part of the Federal Reserve authorities, which produced the worst phase of this stupendous fluctuation. Far from showing the indifference to prevalent trends of opinion, of which they have so often been accused, it seems that they had learnt the lesson only too well. It was not old-fashioned practice but new-fashioned theory which was responsible for the excesses of the American disaster.

16. Are Banking Crises Free-Market Phenomena?
George Selgin

The conventional view of banking crises sees them as a problem inherent in insufficiently regulated fractional-reserve banking systems. But a look at the historical evidence suggests that relatively heavily-regulated banking systems have been especially crisis-prone, while relatively unregulated ones have often been close to crisis-free. The evidence supports the view that banking crises are caused by over-regulation. --G.S., Ed.

* * *

What causes banking crises, involving a general loss of confidence in banks? Practically everyone believes that they are an inherent part of fractional reserve banking, and that government agencies alone are capable of preventing them. Even many persons who otherwise believe in free markets and who are critical of government regulation of banks generally accept the need for some kind of government intervention to prevent or otherwise deal with occasional banking crises. This conventional view of banking crises is so generally accepted that its truth is often simply taken for granted by policy makers, who seldom bother to examine it critically. Nevertheless, a close look at the theory underlying it highlights certain empirical implications that turn out to be quite at odds with reality.

The Conventional Theory of Banking Crises

A banking crisis erupts when many or all banks in a banking system are confronted by large-scale demands to redeem their liabilities in cash, which demands the banks are unable to satisfy. In attempting to satisfy the demands, banks in a fractional-reserve banking system must undertake large-scale reductions in their balance sheets, shrinking available supplies of money and credit.

If banks held 100 percent reserves, they could redeem all their liabilities at once if they had to without precipitating a crisis. A 100-percent reserve banking crisis is an impossibility. Some conservative thinkers, including past Chicago-school economists Henry Simons and Lloyd Mints,[1] view this fact as reason enough for condemning fractional-reserve banking and for recommending its replacement with some 100-percent-reserve alternative. Such a stance takes for granted not only that fractional-reserve banking systems are inherently unstable, but also that fractional-reserve banking is not a source of potential welfare gains to society. Both claims are of doubtful validity, the first for reasons to be made clear in the text, and the second because it overlooks the benefits fractional-reserve banking provides in harnessing money holdings as a vehicle for funding investment. Under competitive conditions the latter benefits are partly enjoyed by money holders themselves, whose gain takes the form of explicit interest payments, lowered bank service charges, or some combination of each.

A second feature of the banking system upon which the conventional theory relies is that bank deposit contracts are serviced on a "first-come-first-served" basis: when persons come to redeem their deposits in cash, their banks pay them in the order of their arrival. Those who are first in line therefore face the highest probability of getting their deposits cashed, while those who are last in line face the lowest probability. This assumption is important, because it serves to motivate runs on individual banks. Such runs play a crucial part in the conventional theory of systemwide banking crises.

Granting these basic assumptions, how does a crisis occur? According to the conventional theory, the crisis is triggered by some "shock" to the banking system. This shock may exist only in the minds of some depositors, making the crisis a kind of self-deflating financial "bubble," or it may be a real event.[2] In either case, the shock must be assumed to threaten at least one bank's liquidity or solvency and, hence, its ability to satisfy its customers' demands for cash. The perception that any bank is having difficulties by itself is sufficient to trigger a run on the bank, for reasons that are obvious enough in light of the "first-come-first-served" way in which withdrawals are handled.

This conventional explanation of how a run against a single bank might occur is still a long way from a plausible story about a banking *crisis* involving simultaneous runs on all or many of a nation's banks. Clearly it is such a crisis, and not runs on single banks or small numbers of banks, that matters: if only a small number of banks is affected by runs, then persons running on those banks would have no reason to abandon the banking system altogether by hoarding cash. Such persons would instead merely transfer their savings (or as much of them as they have been fortunate enough to recover) to other, unaffected banks. Such limited runs, unlike a true banking crisis, do not end in a collapse of money and credit, and so are really no more important than a loss of market share by some limited group of firms in any industry.

How, then, may individual bank runs and failures be transformed into a true banking crisis? One possibility is an external shock that threatens to undermine the solvency of most or all banks simultaneously. It is difficult, though, to imagine a shock that could have such an effect on a large and heterogeneous banking system. Assuming that the banking system as a whole, if not individual banks within that system, is well diversified, it would seem that only a foreign invasion, a civil war, or some massive monetary shock not originating in the private banking system itself could have such a devastating effect. The conventional theory of crises does not, however, portray banking crises as a wartime phenomenon only or as one linked to any particular monetary policies. The theory must, therefore, rely on some mechanism other than wars and monetary policy shocks to account for "typical" crises.

It is here that the conventional view resorts to a "contagion effect" hypothesis, which holds that a run on any bank is likely to spread like an infectious disease to other banks, eventually undermining confidence in all. Why are bank runs contagious? The most popular explanation appeals to what are technically referred to as "information asymmetries" in the market for bank deposits. Although each banker knows the contents of his asset portfolio, most depositors do not, so they are inclined to assume that all banks are more or less alike. Because of this assumption, whenever any one bank is seen to be in difficulty, either because it has already failed or because it is being run upon by its customers, other ill-informed depositors immediately begin to worry that their own banks may also be in trouble. Rather than take a chance, and realizing that if they are to recover their deposits, they must redeem them before others have received all the cash, they run on their banks. A crisis thus ensues, with the shadow of distrust cast simultaneously upon all banks.

It is important to realize that, according to the conventional view, contagions are not extraordinary events but are likely to take place in any banking system unprotected by deposit insurance or a vigilant and dependable central bank. A presumption exists, therefore, that the authorities must guard against each and every bank failure if they are to succeed in avoiding banking crises, or must otherwise insulate the banking system from contagions by offering comprehensive insurance to depositors. Otherwise, individual bank runs or failures will occasionally lead to breakdowns of the whole system of money and credit.

Some Evidence against the Conventional Theory

The conventional theory of banking crises has guided banking policy in the United States and elsewhere for many decades. It has been used to rationalize many kinds of restrictions on banking, ranging from minimum reserve and capital requirements to various interest rate and bank portfolio restrictions. It has also led to the proliferation of government-run deposit insurance schemes, despite the well-known hazards associated with them. Finally, it has helped justify the extension and consolidation of central bank powers and privileges, encouraging those few nations still lacking their own central banks to view their arrangements as inherently unsafe and economically backward.

Yet for all its wide-ranging influence, the conventional theory of banking crises appears to fail the most elementary kind of empirical test. The theory implies not only that crises are likely in any fractional-reserve banking system, but that they are especially likely in systems lacking any public lender of last resort or government deposit insurance. Readily available historical evidence, however, contradicts both claims. Tables 1 and 2, derived from the only international surveys of banking crises of which I am aware, suggest that genuine banking crises have been rare in most well-studied fractional-reserve banking systems and entirely absent in several. Moreover, many of those systems that appear to have had few or no banking crises also lacked both deposit insurance and a lender of last resort.

I am not aware, furthermore, of any reason for suspecting that these relatively crisis-free banking systems were subject to fewer or less severe shocks than relatively crisis-prone ones. For example, it appears that in most respects Canada was just as "shocked" as the United States was by the post-1929 collapse of prices and incomes. Yet while the United States banking system soon suffered its worst banking crisis ever, Canada suffered no banking crisis—indeed, no bank failures—at all. Likewise, while the English banking system was battered by numerous shocks throughout the nineteenth century, Scottish banks seemed relatively immune. Because it can account for cross-country differences in the incidence of crises only by appealing to corresponding differences in the incidence of fundamental shocks (or perceptions of shocks), the conventional theory of crises seems hard-pressed to explain the actual incidence of crises in various times and places.

Faced with this evidence of the conventional theory's failure, one cannot help wondering how it managed to become so popular in the first place. Another look at the historical incidence of banking crises suggests an explanation. As the tables show

Table 1: Banking Panics, 1793–1933: "Unfree" Banking Systems

Year of Panic	United States	England	France	Germany	Italy
1793	x	x	—	—	—
1797	x	x	—	—	—
1810	x	x	—	—	—
1815	x		—	—	—
1819	x		—	—	—
1825	x	x	—	—	—
1833	x		—	—	—
1837	x	x	—	—	—
1839	x		—	—	—
1847	x	x	x	—	—
1848			■	—	—
1857	x	x	x	x	—
1864			x		—
1866		x			—
1873	x			x	—
1875				■	—
1882			x[a]		—
1884					—
1889			x		—
1890					—
1891					x
1893	x				x
1894					■
1901				x	
1907	x				
1913				x	
1914	x ■				x
1921					x
1930	x		x		
1931	x			x	
1933	x				

Sources: Bordo, "Financial Crises," n4 below; Schuler, "World History," n6 below; and Schwartz, "Financial Stability," n4 below.

Note: [a]Large bank failure.

clearly, banking crises appear to have been a U.S. specialty, with England earning second place in the banking crisis marathon. Most of our economic theories, including the conventional theory of banking crises, come from British and especially American economists, who know much more about the economic histories of their own countries than they know about experiences elsewhere. It is no wonder, therefore, that the received theory of banking crises appears, superficially at least, to fit the historical record of the United States and England, while bearing little connection to the experiences of many other nations. Even critics of the received theory have played into the hands of its proponents

Table 2: Banking Panics, 1793–1933: "Free" Banking Systems

Year of Panic	Canada	Scotland	Sweden	Australia	China	South Africa
1793	—		—	—	—	—
1797	—	x[a]	—	—	—	—
1810	—		—	—	—	—
1815	—		—	—	—	—
1819			—		—	—
1825			—[b]		—	—
1833					—	—[c]
1837	x[d]				—	
1839					—	
1845		■				
1847					—	
1857					—	
1864					—	
1866					—	
1873					—	
1882					—	
1884					—	
1889					—	
1890					—	
1891						
1893				x		
1901			■			
1907			x			
1911				■		
1914	x[e] ■					
1920						x[f] ■
1923	x[g]					
1930						
1931						
1933						

Sources: Same as Table 1; also Lars Jonung, "The Economics of Private Money: The Experience of Private Notes in Sweden, 1831–1902," unpublished working paper, Stockholm School of Economics, 1989; and Lawrence H. White, *Free Banking in Britain: Theory, Experience and Debate, 1800–1845* (Cambridge: Cambridge University Press, 1984).

Notes: [a]Restriction of payments. [b]Swedish free-banking era begins. [c]South-African free-banking era begins. [d]Listed as a crisis year by Schuler, but not by Schwartz. [e]Minor runs caused by binding capital requirements for note issuance. [f]Inflation follows abandonment of gold standard during World War I. [g]Major bank failure accompanied by minor runs on other banks.

by relying solely on U.S. experience to refute conventional assumptions, when evidence from other nations would make their task much easier.[3] On the other hand, the few writers who have actually surveyed international experience tend to focus too much on comparing the United States with the "United Kingdom" (meaning England) in drawing general conclusions from their surveys.[4] These writers are thus led to credit the presence of an "effective" or "dependable" public lender of last resort as the most important reason for the relative infrequency of panics in certain countries during certain periods, ignoring the more numerous cases (including those shown in Table 2) in which panics were avoided despite the absence of a public lender of last resort.

Behind our first empirical observation—that banking crises have not been equally frequent everywhere—lies another: that bank failures typically have not been contagious, or have been only mildly contagious. All banking systems have seen individual banks fail, but such failures have only rarely led to runs on most other banks. (Even in the United States, whose banking system has suffered more bank failures and experienced more crises than any other, wide-ranging bank contagions have been few and far between.)[5] This observation is supported both by direct evidence concerning the extent of bank runs and by statistics on the demand for legal tender, which should, other things being equal, increase whenever panic becomes general.

In fact, of well-studied episodes, only the U.S. crisis of 1933 appears to have involved a truly systemwide panic. Apparently this single episode has inspired the conventional view of banking crises. Yet I shall argue later that even it does not lend any real support to conventional views concerning the nature of banking crises.

These considerations suggest that the conventional theory of banking crises is seriously inadequate. Yes, banking crises do occasionally occur, and at least one appears to have involved a nation's entire banking system. But far from being a typical or likely consequence of isolated bank failures or runs, genuine banking crises appear to be relatively unusual events, and events that are more unusual in some banking systems than in others. Clearly, there is a need for some alternative theory capable of shedding light on why banking crises have occurred in certain times and places, but not in others, despite the common ingredient of individual bank failures.

Another casual look at the evidence suggests the basic outlines of such an alternative theory by revealing, perhaps counterintuitively, that banking crises have been *more* frequent in heavily regulated banking systems than in relatively unregulated ones. Drawing on a survey by Kurt Schuler,[6] Table 1 lists banking systems which, throughout their histories, have been subject to at least two "major" regulatory restrictions, while Table 2 lists systems that were, for a time at least, characterized by no more than one major restriction. Although "free" for a while, the Table 2 systems were all eventually rendered unfree by additional major restrictions, usually consisting of restrictions on competitive note issuance anticipating or inaugurating the establishment of central banks.[7] Such restrictions are indicated in the table by black boxes showing dates when the new restrictions were imposed. Similar boxes in Table 1 mark dates when privileged banks of issue capable of serving as "lenders of last resort" were established in previously "unfree" (but nonetheless decentralized) banking systems. No box appears in the column for England because the Bank of England already possessed unique note issue privileges there before 1793 — the first crisis date recorded on the table.

This grouping of banking systems reveals clearly the positive connection between the extent of legal restrictions on various banking systems on one hand and the number of banking crises experienced by those systems on the other. Of forty-eight recorded crises, all but seven (one of which is listed as a crisis in only one of two surveys employed) occurred in unfree systems. Furthermore, nearly half of the crises took place in systems having privileged banks of issue that might, in principle, have served as lenders of last resort. This suggests that the presence of a public lender of last resort has, after all, been neither necessary nor sufficient to prevent the occurrence of banking crises. Of course, defenders of central banking might still insist that the presence of an "effective" or "dependable" lender of last resort is sufficient to prevent crises. Such a stance appears, however, to require an overly convenient definition of "effectiveness" or "dependability."

That is the big picture. Underlying it are smaller portraits of individual crises connecting them to particular institutional and legal circumstances. The common features present in these portraits can be summed up by observing that it is quite difficult, if not impossible, to give a coherent account of any single banking crisis anywhere without acknowledging a crucial role for some form of government interference or "legal restriction" in helping to make the crisis come about.[8]

A "Legal Restrictions" Theory of Banking Crises

An alternative theory of crises, based on the last observation, would hold that banking crises are not free-market phenomena, but are rather consequences of government intervention in banking and currency systems.

Many kinds of "legal restrictions" have played a role in historical banking crises, so that it is not possible to treat all crises as having identical causes: unlike the conventional theory of crises, the "legal restrictions" theory proposed here is multicausal rather than unicausal. The conventional theory's unicausal view of crises is, indeed, one of its clear weaknesses. Unicausal explanations of complex though recurrent economic events may be elegant and neat, but they are often also simplistic and wrong. While the conventional theory of banking crises accounts only for a "typical" crisis that has no historical counterpart, the legal restrictions theory is really a collection of distinct explanations for particular crises — all of which, however, share a common basis in misguided government policies.

Although one cannot construct a "general theory" of banking crises based on legal restrictions, one can present a catalogue of legal restrictions, showing how each may help bring about a banking crisis and offering illustrations from the United States and elsewhere. George Benston and I have already offered partial catalogues, so I will not do more than summarize their contents here.[9] The kinds of legal restrictions that have made past banking crises possible are those that (1) increased individual banks' vulnerability to shocks of various kinds; (2) have themselves been sources of important shocks; (3) have created an environment conducive to "contagion" effects, so that individual bank failures are more likely to lead to systemwide runs; and (4) have obstructed private market mechanisms for avoiding or averting crises.

(1) Restrictions rendering banks more vulnerable to shocks include regulations artificially limiting banks' ability to diversify their assets and liabilities against relative price shocks. The most important examples of such restrictions are those artificially limiting the size of private banking firms, either by restricting branching or by limiting access to capital. Direct portfolio restrictions (like those once embodied in many bank charters) also limit diversification, exposing banks to unnecessary risks. Restrictions on interest rates like those once enforced by Regulation Q have exposed banks unnecessarily to interest-rate shocks.

Some legal restrictions increase individual banks' exposure to risk by actually subsidizing risky undertakings while allowing banks to reduce their own capital holdings. Examples of this include government deposit insurance and the presence of any lender of last resort willing to rescue insolvent banks.

(2) Among restrictions that provide a basis for shocks that would otherwise not occur, the most important are laws supporting discretionary money-supply management by central banks. These laws—including both legal tender laws that enable the issuance of fiat money, and legal restrictions on private note issuance—are the fundamental basis for major interest-rate and price-level swings which, according to Anna Schwartz,[10] have been the root causes of both past and recent waves of financial firm insolvencies.

(3) Restrictions have also made contagion effects more likely. As noted previously, contagion effects have been the exception rather than the rule in economic history. That in itself contradicts the conventional theory of banking crises. But there is more: where contagions have taken hold in the past, they too have been encouraged by government interference. For example, government-erected barriers to branch banking in the United States have sponsored the artificial growth of correspondent relationships among banks, making confidence in banks a function of confidence in their correspondents. Another, more widely practiced form of legal interference—interference with private note issuance—has obstructed an important "secondary" market for bank liabilities. This market might otherwise have served to price bank-specific risks efficiently, eliminating information asymmetries. Other forms of interference, including bank holidays and manipulations of the monetary standard, have also helped produce contagions of panic, as will be seen below in reviewing the crisis of 1933.

(4) Perhaps the worst way in which governments have helped expose banking systems to crises has been by interfering with

banks' own devices for avoiding or otherwise dealing with such crises. By restricting private note issuance, governments have made it impossible for private banks to accommodate even routine changes in the demand for currency.[11] Governments have also prevented banks from undertaking "restrictions" of payments as a private means for coping with major shocks.[12] Finally, governments have artificially encouraged reliance on central bank lending in place of private interbank lending: all too often, central banks have functioned, not as lenders of last resort, but as lenders of *first* resort. This makes them appear more essential in rescuing illiquid but solvent banks than they really are. Central bankers are loath to pass up any opportunity to present themselves as white knights coming to the rescue of an illiquid private bank—the damsel in distress.

Of course, branching restrictions and other devices that discourage the development of large, private banks also undermine opportunities for private assistance, for the simple reason that it is much more difficult for a clearinghouse or other private bankers' "club" to put together a large emergency loan package that relies on many small banks than it is to put together a similar package involving fewer, large banks. Restrictions on mergers, finally, rule out other potential private rescue efforts, and thereby increase the likelihood of depositors suffering losses and staging runs.

The Role of Currency Monopoly

One legal restriction seldom discussed in the literature—the inability of private banks to issue their own notes—enhances the likelihood of banking crises in at least three important ways. First, it prevents banks from relying on their own resources to accommodate routine changes in the public's demand for currency. Second, it eliminates the secondary note market that could otherwise do away with information asymmetries in the market for bank money. Finally, monopolization of the supply of currency has been the basis for central banks' discretionary control of the stock of bank reserves. Through such control, central banks have been able to expand their own balance sheets recklessly, causing otherwise impossible gyrations in the price level, interest rates, and exchange rates—the most severe shocks to which private banks have ever been subjected.

That currency monopoly is the basis for central banks' discretionary manipulations of the money stock is, I trust, obvious enough: As long as all banks have equal rights to issue notes, none ever thinks of holding a rival's notes as reserves. Instead, rivals' notes are actively returned for redemption in some basic money. Historically, this was gold.

The awarding of monopoly privileges in note issuance changes all this. Suddenly one bank becomes the system's sole source of convenient paper currency. Other banks begin to covet its notes, which (being, at first, still redeemable in gold) are in widespread demand. Soon these notes are being treated as a reserve in place of gold—which is, in turn, placed on deposit with the privileged bank. At this point the privileged bank no longer has to worry about its own issues being redeemed by rivals. Its sole concern becomes the balance of international gold payments, which eventually turns against it if it expands too much, as it is inevitably tempted to do. (Under free banking, in contrast, it is simply not possible to have a balance of payments crisis initiated by excessive domestic money creation.) But there is a way around the balance of payments constraint that limits even monopoly bank expansion under a gold standard: the suspension of gold payments. What no bank would have dared to do in a system in which all banks enjoyed equal rights is now done with impunity by the privileged bank of issue, thereby making its notes a fiat money, first temporarily, then for good.

The establishment of fiat money, in turn, means unlimited scope for a privileged bank to further abuse its powers in pursuit of narrow political and financial ends. Such was, broadly speaking, the history of the growth of central banks and fiat money throughout much of the world during the present century. This history has set the stage for price level, interest rate, and exchange rate movements such as were never seen under the gold standard. These fluctuations have spelled doom to thousands of private banks. The link between central banking and the abandonment of commodity money is particularly worth stressing, because so many past economists wrongly perceived central banks as devices for securing monetary stability. The evidence presented here suggests, on the contrary, that central banking is incompatible with monetary stability. Free banking grounded in strict rules of contract and bankruptcy law would have provided a much stronger bulwark against the flood of paper money.

One lesson in this is, to use the language of game theory, that the central banking "game" does not have a positive sum: the unique powers enjoyed by central banks have not been costlessly acquired. They are, rather, powers that would, under free-market circumstances, have been more widely shared among all private banks. The consequence of regulations concentrating these powers in a single, government-favored bank has been to make other banks weaklings dependent on central banks for their protection. Today, unfortunately, few observers (banking experts included) appreciate how the rise of central banking has served to weaken private banks.

The Banking Crisis of 1933

It is of course impossible, within the confines of a short article, to offer a "legal restrictions" theory of every historical banking crisis, or even of the forty-one crises listed in Table 1. I will attempt, however, to apply the theory to one important banking crisis, namely, the U.S. crisis of 1933. That crisis is particularly important because, of all crises, it best appears to fit the conventional view. That is not surprising as the conventional view was, to a large extent, shaped by the events of 1933.

The basic features of the crisis, consistent with the conventional view, were as follows. Large numbers of bank failures in the early 1930s triggered massive withdrawals of currency from the banking system which, in turn, led to the system's failure in March 1933. That failure might have been avoided had the Fed played the part of lender of last resort, either in the traditional manner (by making loans to solvent though illiquid banks), or by otherwise expanding the monetary base to compensate for changes in the currency-deposit ratio.

Whereas the conventional view blames government for failing to respond appropriately to the crisis, treating the crisis itself as originating in market conditions, the legal-restrictions approach identifies a more fundamental role of government interference. To begin, consider the large numbers of bank failures preceding the systemwide failure of March 1933. Although bank failures accelerated in the early 1930s, they had been common during the 1920s, when nearly 6000 U.S. banks failed. Most of the failures, both then and throughout the first two years of the Great Depression, were of small-unit banks in agricultural regions. These banks suffered from a decline in the relative price of agricultural products that predated the crash. Had the United States enjoyed nationwide branch banking, it might have avoided many or most of these relative-price-induced bank failures. Canada, which had branch banking, did avoid bank failures both before and after 1929, except for a single failure in 1923 involving fraud.

U.S. bank failures rose after 1929 in part because of an increase in the public's desired currency-to-deposit ratio, which tends to move inversely with changes in real income.[13] Had U.S. banks been free to issue their own notes, as Canadian banks still could, they might have accommodated much of this initial increase in the currency ratio by issuing more of their own notes in exchange for deposits. Indeed, national banks did manage to increase their note issues, from $691 million in February 1932 to $922 million in May 1933, thanks to a minor relaxation in otherwise binding note issuance restrictions.[14] This increase was, however, only a fraction of what was needed to accommodate the wants of the public. The remaining adjustment had to be provided through greater issues of Federal Reserve Notes and clearinghouse certificates and, in the absence of either, by means of a depletion of bank reserves.

Clearinghouse authorities in New York and elsewhere sought the Treasury's permission to issue clearinghouse certificates as substitutes for bank notes, as they had done during earlier crises. But they were refused permission on the grounds that such a private response was no longer needed: the Fed was capable of issuing "plenty of money that looks like real money."[15] In the event, of course, the Fed's response proved far from adequate.

Despite large numbers of bank failures, and legal restrictions precluding a secondary market in bank notes, bank runs prior to 1933 appear to have been confined to banks that either were insolvent before the runs or, owing to branching restrictions, were correspondents of insolvent banks. Even the dramatic run against the Bank of United States in December 1930 was not contagious.[16] Widespread panic did not become a feature of the U.S. banking crisis until February 1933, when it was provoked by two ill-conceived government policies. These policies were the state-declared bank holidays, commencing with Michigan's on February

14; and the federal government's plan to devalue the dollar, which became a subject of widespread rumors around the same time.

Bank holidays became a potent cause of contagion effects by encouraging currency withdrawals by depositors in nearby states, who feared the holidays themselves might spread. Holidays therefore exacerbated the very problem of bank runs they were intended to forestall.[17] Bank holidays were also unnecessary: as bankers urged at the time, mere "restrictions" of payments of reserve money, such as were undertaken during previous panics in 1893 and 1907, could have served the purpose of protecting banks' liquidity without closing the banks and thereby entirely depriving depositors and borrowers of access to funds.[18]

Rumors that gold would be devalued led to a run on the dollar, the burden of which was felt mainly by the Federal Reserve Bank of New York. According to Barry Wigmore, it was the Federal Reserve, rather than commercial banks, that needed and pleaded for a bank holiday, which was finally declared by New York's Governor Lehrman on March 4, precipitating the national bank holiday on March 6. Gold was, in fact, devalued soon afterwards. Although by the time of its accomplishment this devaluation may have appeared necessary as a means for restoring monetary stability, devaluation was certainly *not* necessary earlier in the year, when it was first proposed as a means of supporting the prices of farm commodities to placate the farm lobby.[19]

Other federal policies, including increased postal rates and a two-cent tax on checks, both adopted in mid-1932, also contributed to the banking crisis by encouraging public withdrawals of currency from the banking system. Such errors of commission, rather than the Federal Reserve's equally destructive errors of omission, warrant calling the crisis of 1933 a product of legal restrictions rather than a free-market phenomenon. This seems to be the case with banking crises in general.

NOTES

1. Henry C. Simons, *Economic Policy for a Free Society* (Chicago: University of Chicago Press, 1948); Lloyd W. Mints, *Monetary Policy for a Competitive Society* (New York: McGraw-Hill, 1950).
2. Several recent studies favor the real-shock or information-based view of crises over the "bubble" alternative. See, for example, Frederic S. Mishkin, "Asymmetric Information and Financial Crises: A Historical Perspective," in R. Glen Hubbard, ed., *Financial Markets and Financial Crises* (Chicago: University of Chicago Press, 1991), 69–108; and Charles W. Calomiris and Gary Gorton, "The Origins of Banking Panics: Models, Facts, and Bank Regulation," in ibid., 109–73.
3. See, for example, George Kaufman, "Bank Contagion: A Review of the Theory and Evidence," *Journal of Financial Services Research* 8, no. 2 (April 1994): 123–50.
4. See Michael D. Bordo, "Financial Crises, Banking Crises, Stock Market Crashes and the Money Supply: Some International Evidence, 1870–1933," in Forrest Capie and Geoffrey E. Wood, eds., *Financial Crises and the World Banking System* (London: Macmillan, 1986), 190–248; and Anna J. Schwartz, "Financial Stability and the Federal Saftey Net," in William S. Haraf and Rose Marie Kushmeider, eds., *Restructuring Banking and Financial Services in America* (Washington: American Enterprise Institute, 1988), 34–62.

5. Kaufman, n3 above.
6. Kurt Schuler, "The World History of Free Banking: An Overview," in Kevin Dowd, ed., *The Experience of Free Banking* (London: Routledge, 1992), 7-47.
7. In most cases the major change marking the transition from free to unfree banking was the establishment of a central bank enjoying exclusive note-issue privileges.
8. This conclusion relies soles on readily available secondary accounts of the incidence of banking crises. Regrettably the extent of such evidence, especially for "free" banking systems, is quite limited. Ideally, one would want to have detailed survey evidence from a larger sample of both free and unfree systems. The conclusions reached here are, therefore, tentative ones. They do, nonetheless, at least attempt to come to grips with the evidence already at hand.
9. George Benston, "Does Bank Regulation Produce Stability? Lessons for the United States," in Forrest Capie and Geoffrey E. Woods, eds., *Unregulated Banking: Chaos or Order?* (London: Macmillan, 1991), 207-32; George Selgin, "Legal Restrictions, Financial Weakening, and the Lender of Last Resort," *Cato Journal* 9, no. 2 (Fall 1989): 429-59.
10. Schwartz, n4 above.
11. George Selgin, "Accommodating Changes in the Relative Demand for Currency: Free Banking vs. Central Banking," *Cato Journal* 6, no. 2 (Fall 1986): 617-34.
12. Hugh Rockoff, "Institutional Requirement for Stable Free Banking," *Cato Journal* 6, no. 2 (Fall 1986): 617-34.
13. Phillip Cagan, "The Demand for Currency Relative to Total Money Supply" *Journal of Political Economy* 66, no. 1 (August 1958): 303-28.
14. Benjamin Anderson, *Economics and the Public Welfare* (Indianapolis: Liberty Press, 1979), 289.
15. Helen M. Burns, *The American Banking Community and New Deal Banking Reforms, 1933-1935* (Westport, Conn.: Greenwood, 1974), 75.
16. Elmus Wicker, "A Reconsideration of the Banking Panic of 1930," *Journal of Economic History* 40, no. 3 (September 1980): 571-83.
17. George Benston et al., *Perspectives on Safe and Sound Banking* (Cambridge, Mass.: MIT Press, 1986), 52; E. C. Colt and N. S. Keith, *28 Days: A History of the Banking Crisis* (New York: Greenburg, 1933). Nevada was actually the first state to declare a banking holiday, in November 1932.
18. Gerald P. Dwyer, Jr. and R. Anton Gilbert, "Bank Runs and Private Remedies," Reserve Bank of St. Louis *Review* 71, no. 93 (May/June 1989): 43-61; see also Rockoff, n2 above. The success of restriction would have depended on banks' (or clearinghouses') ability to issue notes (or clearinghouse certificates) as substitutes for legal-tender currency and bond-based national bank notes. As noted, the Federal government refused to give banks or clearinghouses permission to issue such substitute currencies.
19. Barry A. Wigmore, "Was the Bank Holiday of 1933 Caused by a Run on the Dollar?" *Journal of Economic History* 47, no. 3 (September 1987): 739-55.

17. The Biggest Scam in History
James Ring Adams

A common view of the savings and loan crisis is that it has been a consequence of excessive deregulation. The article that follows, taken from James Ring Adams' book, The Big Fix, *tells a different story. According to Adams, it was not too little but too much regulation, especially in the form of mandatory government deposit insurance, that helped bring about the crisis.* —G.S., Ed.

****

1

THE DOWNHILL SLIDE to the $300 billion savings and loan disaster began one night in mid-1980 in a high-ceilinged conference room in the United States Capitol. The push came from one man, the slick and not overly scrupulous chairman of the House Banking Committee, Fernand St Germain. A congressman from Woonsocket, Rhode Island, since 1960, St Germain vigorously enjoyed the perquisites of office, including frequent nights on the town with the lobbyists of the United States League of Savings Institutions. Once handsome, his features now drooped in jowly dissipation, and his evening meetings sometimes ended with the arrival of hard and beautiful young women whose expertise lay elsewhere than banking.

St Germain had other business in hand at this conference committee. In time-honored congressional routine, members of the House and Senate had come together to produce a bill that compromised between versions passed by each chamber. On this night, they were thrashing out the first major attempt to revise the New Deal banking regulations. Over the years, deposit insurance had inched up to cover accounts of $40,000. The Senate bill had raised the limit to $50,000. The House hadn't voted on the issue. In the conference, St Germain pulled off a fateful coup. He proposed a "compromise" limit of $100,000. "It was a United States League [of Savings Institutions] special," says one thrift regulator. "But they were surprised they got it." Adds Tim McNamar, then a Deputy Secretary of the Treasury, "We were lucky they didn't get a million."

What was so bad about raising the deposit guarantee? For starters, it changed the nature of the program. Roosevelt's compromise in 1933 had focused deposit insurance on the small saver. It seemed reasonable to protect a middle-class nest egg, to cover the necessaries of life, but why guarantee the affluence of the rich? Besides, the depositor with an uninsured balance would be forced to take a keen interest in the soundness of his bank. Money would drain from the poorly run banks and wind up in safe ones. This market discipline would help limit the losses that might be charged to the insurance funds.

St Germain's coup more than doubled the guarantee, changed the incentives to banks and thrifts, and created a new subsidy for the rich. Bankers quickly figured out how to market the subsidy. Even in the midst of the S&L debacle, when the perversion of deposit insurance was widely discussed, Citibank mailed a brochure to its customers showing how to stretch FDIC coverage to $1.4 million. (Both FDIC and FSLIC offered separate guarantees not only for individual accounts but for trust accounts, joint accounts and the like. So the trick was to split deposits into individual accounts for each family member and use all the available permutations to set up joint and trust accounts. By creating joint accounts for husband and wife, husband and child, wife and child, child and child, each could be insured to $100,000.)

An even greater perversion of deposit insurance was underway in the sales rooms of the big brokerage houses. National firms such as Merrill Lynch and Drexel Burnham were turning the populist program of Steagall and Vandenberg into a new fixed-income investment vehicle. They were pioneering the national market in "jumbo CDs." The brokers packaged funds to buy certificates of deposit in amounts just under the federal guarantee; they shopped thrifts across the country for the highest interest rates, then sold their clients shares in the CD as an absolutely safe, high return, federally guaranteed investment. Some experts trace the origin of this market to St Germain's coup. The increase to $100,000, they say, made the jumbo CD feasible. Others think the scheme would have developed anyway. In either case, St Germain helped turn deposit insurance on its head.

It took one more element to convert this program from just another haywire government subsidy into the most costly scam in history. With the increased guarantee, thrift owners soon realized that no matter what they did, they had access to almost unlimited deposits. Buyers of jumbo CDs cared only about the interest rate, which was almost always highest at the weakest thrifts. "Hot money" flowed into the hands of the worst managers at a phenomenal rate. Their thrifts grew a thousandfold and more in just four years and kept growing as their losses mounted.

By mid-1983, the regulators were finding brokered deposits in their problem cases. An excited Edwin Gray, chairman of the Home Loan Bank Board, later complained to the Senate Banking Committee, "It was the easy, instantaneous access to very willing money brokers, willing to provide high-priced federally insured money to any institutions which sought it—in virtually unlimited amounts—which fueled the rapidly made investments and loans that have become very bad assets in some of the most significant thrift failures we have seen." William Isaac, Gray's counterpart at the FDIC, added that more than a third of the brokered funds in his system had gone to troubled banks. In some of his basket cases, "hot money" made up almost half of their deposits. Many depositors taking advantage of these jumbo CDs were themselves federally insured banks, thrifts and credit unions.

The broker business was a ready-made scam, and some took full advantage. As regulators pored over the books of failed banks, one name kept popping up. The FDIC surveyed all 80 of the banks that closed from 1982 to 1985 and found that 25 of them had drawn funds from the First United Fund, Ltd. of Garden City, Long Island. This outfit was the brainchild of Mario Renda, a New Yorker who pioneered the technique of linking his deposits to a reciprocal favor. In Kansas, according to the indictment in a later case, he pumped deposits into a failing bank on the condition that it funnel loans to the people he named. Renda pleaded guilty in that case, as well as in a separate case in the Federal District Court in Brooklyn, where he was charged with receiving kickbacks for providing deposits from two union welfare funds.

Monies provided by people like Renda were the elixir of life for insolvent thrifts which miraculously stayed open, institutions regulators were beginning to call the "living dead" or the "zombies." By the mid-1980s, the S&L industry had begun to defy the elemental laws of business. Any other business that lost more than it made would quickly fold. But a thrift in the hole not only stayed open, it thrived. Even stranger, its deposits grew faster than in the rest of the industry. According to one study, sick thrifts in 1986 held $315 billion in liabilities (deposits and borrowings), about 40 percent of the amount held in the well thrifts; by the second quarter of 1988, holdings of the sick thrifts had grown to 50 percent of their healthy competitors' total. How to explain this phenomenon, where the bankrupt not only survived but outcompeted the solvent? Answered one critic, "a zombie has transcended its natural death from accumulated losses by the black magic of federal guarantees."

The deposit brokers had become agents of a Ponzi scheme. This device, named after a Boston businessman of the 1920s, paid off early investors with the funds from later investors, creating the illusion of high profits. Of course, nothing was left for the last people enticed into the scheme. The brokers provided the new money that covered the zombies' operating losses and paid off their old depositors. But when the scam collapsed, the new depositors weren't penniless; they merely collected their money from FSLIC and ultimately from the taxpayer. The zombies had to pay high interest to stay alive; federal insurance took care of all the risk; so for the brokers, jumbo CDs were a legitimate business. And in fact the largest broker of all was Merrill Lynch, whose former chairman Donald Regan became Chief of Staff in the White House.

Renda was an extreme case, but he merely drove the logic of deposit insurance to its extreme conclusion. As FDR had warned, the program became a subsidy for bank fraud. Why did this happen when it did? The answer is that the early 1980s produced the worst possible combination of pressures. The increase in deposit insurance coincided with the first major effort to revise the depression era structure of bank law. Some circles try to blame the thrift crisis on this movement or, more polemically, on Reagan deregulation. This scapegoating misses the point. Market pressures dating from the Carter administration and earlier had forced some damaging changes, but the problem lay in the failure to deregulate enough. Congress reacted to a series of crises by enacting piecemeal reforms that created even more severe crises. Each change left the industry ever more exposed to the baleful effects of deposit insurance.

For example, consider the fate of the federal ceiling on bankbook rates, Regulation Q. Since the depression, banks and thrifts had been permitted to offer only a fixed interest rate. The rule was ultimately untenable, but it did prevent depositors from shopping around for the highest rate. In principle, competition was based on reputations for safety and sound management. The depositor could not get maximum return on his dollar, but there was no national hot money market.

By 1980, pressure had been building for years to eliminate Regulation Q. Depositors could not shop among the thrifts for higher interest rates, but as soon as the choice of uncontrolled (and uninsured) money market funds became available, money flowed away from the traditional savings institutions. This money flight was called "disintermediation," which became one of the buzz words of the 1970s. Regulation Q, like all price controls, produced a shortage of the controlled product, namely deposits. Reacting to pleas from the thrifts and banks, Congress in 1980 created a commission to phase it out. (This bill was also the vehicle for St Germain's coup on deposit insurance.)

This reform put the thrifts in another bind. They could now hold on to their depositors by offering higher interest rates, but they couldn't change the return they were earning on most of their mortgages. The combination of high cost of money and low earnings put a deadly squeeze on their profitability. As profits vanished, thrifts began dipping into their capital, the money originally put up by investors and owners when the thrift was formed. This nest egg provided the first line of defense against losses. By 1982, on an industrywide average, capital was nearly exhausted. Some 50 S&Ls had failed, a shocking number for the time. The crisis produced another deregulation bill, the Garn-St Germain Act of 1982.

Garn-St Germain shifted the focus to rebuilding capital. Reasoning that thrifts couldn't profit on their traditional mortgages, the bill greatly expanded the types of investments they could make. A new breed of owner was invited in, aggressive risk-takers who presumably would help the thrifts earn their way out of their hole. States such as Texas, California, and Florida went even further in broadening investment powers for state-chartered thrifts. California led the way with the 1983 Nolan Act, which has been called the "most liberal banking law ever passed anywhere." As a means of rebuilding capital, these acts resembled calling in a fox to repopulate a chicken coop.

Garn-St Germain unleashed a horde of habitual risk-takers without subjecting them to any risk. The Bank Board compounded the problem by relaxing capital requirements almost to nonexistence. With expanded deposit insurance and reductions in the amount of capital thrifts were required to keep on hand, the new owners had every incentive to be as reckless as possible. They would reap the benefits of a long-shot business deal but bear none of the cost. In the words of one regulator, "Heads, they win. Tails, FSLIC loses." Insurance professionals have a term for it, "moral hazard." The policy offers too much temptation to cheat.

As fraud ran rampant in the system, some argued that officers at failing thrifts had been corrupted by the perverse incentives, that they had taken one desperate gamble too many in the attempt to recoup their fortunes. In Brooklyn Federal Court, Judge Jack Weinstein dismissed a criminal case against a thrift president on the grounds that the government had encouraged his high-risk lending. Yet it's more likely that thrifts in 1982 had become a juicy target for those who knew a scam when they saw one and wanted to get in on it.

Consider the unhappy careers of two men we'll name Jack Tieg and Wilmer Strait. This is the only fiction in the book. Tieg and Strait are composites; we'll see enough of their real-life equivalents later on.

□ 2 □

JACK TIEG, graying and a bit heavy around the middle, was still proud of his condition for a 55-year-old. His great passion was golf, although he hadn't had much chance to play recently. Jack was president and majority stockholder of a small thrift in the small city of Westward, commercial center for the dairy farms in the valley and the vacation towns in the hills. His father had started the Westward Savings and Loan Association with friends from his country club, a doctor, several lawyers, the head of the local sprocket factory. When Jack took it over in 1976, it gave him an easy life. He made mortgage loans to local farmers and the town shopkeepers, many of whom he'd grown up with. He took in deposits at 5.5 percent, the limit set by the Federal Reserve under Regulation Q. He could count on a spread of two percentage points between his fixed rate mortgages and the interest he paid to depositors. It gave him a steady profit but not a spectacular rate of return on his stock. On Wednesday afternoons, he headed to the club in the foothills for a brisk 18 holes. He participated in his trade association, the United States League of Savings Institutions, calling his congressman when the League put out the word. The representative always answered the call, since Jack's father had helped arrange his nomination.

Jack took pride in his position. Every December, he invited friends over to watch Jimmy Stewart in "It's a Wonderful Life." He always choked up when the guardian angel showed the suicidal thrift executive the tract houses that had been built because he had made the loans. But around 1978, life stopped being so wonderful. Interest rates on government securities surged as they had before, but this time small investors tapped into the market. The druggist, the lawyer, and several of the larger dairy farmers had withdrawn several thousand to put into the new money market accounts advertised by the broker in the big city across the river. For the first time he could remember, deposits in Westward S&L declined.

Jack went to Washington with the state trade group to complain about disintermediation, a fancy word their congressman always mangled. Jack preferred to say that the thrifts just couldn't compete for depositors with Regulation Q tying their hands behind their backs. The Home Loan Bank Board gave them some relief, allowing the S&Ls to offer an experimental Small Savers Certificate at money market rates. Jack called it the "Super-Thrift," and it attracted funds at an alarming rate. By the end of the year, these accounts amounted to one-third of his deposits. Congress promised help too. By mid-1980, Jack was hearing about the Diddymac, a jabberwockian acronym for the Depository Institutions Deregulation and Monetary Control Act.

The Diddymac was definitely going to change the business. It signalled the beginning of the end for Reg Q, although a federal commission was supposed to supervise a gradual phase-out. The act gave Jack another lure for customers, interest-bearing checking accounts. (Actually, the state regulator had let him try that a year before, but now the rest of the country could follow suit.) Jack could now make consumer loans and even offer credit cards if he wanted to. And he had to change all his stationary to reflect the increase in the FSLIC deposit guarantee. Jack's life was becoming more interesting, and he wasn't sure he liked it.

He soon realized what was bothering him. He began paying more to his depositors, a lot more as the national prime interest rates hit 20 percent. But his income still came from the fixed-rate mortgages he had been making since he started out as his father's loan officer 20 years ago. His "spread" narrowed to the vanishing point. One day as he sat in his wood-panelled office lined with sporting trophies, his chief financial officer came in with a worried expression. Westward S&L was now running a loss and starting to dip into its capital for operating expenses. Westward S&L wasn't alone. Jack had been reading that the negative interest rate spread, or as he put it, paying out more than you take in, was sinking thrifts around the country. Washington had solved his old problem, declining deposits, but it left him with a bigger and potentially fatal crisis. It was time to lobby Congress again.

The legislators that Jack and his colleagues talked to weren't just politely concerned; they were frightened. The thrifts faced a widespread collapse. Who knew what could happen to the entire financial system? Just two years after the Diddymac, the House and Senate Banking Committee chairmen put their names on a bill designed mainly to rescue the savings and loan industry. The Garn-St Germain Act of 1982 expanded on the Diddymac. Jack could offer a true money market account, indistinguishable from the product of the mutual fund broker. He could expand his NOW accounts, the interest-bearing checking. He no longer had to worry about Regulation Q. These measures didn't lower his cost of doing business, however, so Garn and St Germain gave him the means of increasing his earnings—or so they thought—as they greatly expanded the kinds of investments Jack could make. Jack found that he was no longer simply in the mortgage business. He could invest up to 55 percent of his assets in commercial real estate and other loans. He could make consumer loans of up to 30 percent of assets. (His counterparts in Texas and California were thoroughly liberated. State-chartered thrifts there could plunge 100 percent of their assets into practically anything.) A lawyer at the Bank Board told Jack that its legal staff had drafted Garn-St Germain to make a federal thrift charter "the best charter in the world." But Jack didn't feel comfortable. He understood home mortgages, but commercial real estate was a new and tricky field. Besides, he had some problems with the regulators.

The cash position at Westward S&L had declined sharply during the interest rate squeeze. On top of that, a drought hit the dairy farmers and some were behind on their mortgage payments. Jack was willing to carry them, but his balance sheet suffered. His regulatory capital, his treasurer reminded him, had fallen from 5 percent to 2 percent of assets. Jack understood that the first buffer against bad loans was his tangible capital (the money put up by investors plus the part of the thrift's earnings that it kept for itself rather than paying to stockholders). When that buffer was exhausted, FSLIC would have to step in. As part of its response to the interest rate squeeze, the Bank Board lowered the minimum capital requirement from 5 percent to 3 percent, but that still didn't help Westward. Jack had an unpleasant choice. He could try to raise fresh capital in a new stock issue or he could sell the thrift.

Jack wanted to get out of this business, and his decision was sealed when he found a buyer. Actually, the buyer found him. "The name is Wilmer Strait," said the hearty voice on the telephone. "I hear you have a thrift for sale." Strait made a generous offer, a good price for Jack's stock and recapitalization of Westward. Jack would stay on the board for the transition. The regulators said Strait was okay, and the directors voted for the sale with relief. Only Jack's wife, Sally, had reservations.

"Something about him isn't right," she said to Jack one afternoon as she dressed for dinner at the club. Sally had been a reporter when she married Jack ten years earlier. Jack respected her judgment, but she was touching a sore spot. "Don't worry about it," he snapped. "He'll do fine."

□ 3 □

WILMER STRAIT was born 40 years ago in one of the hardscrabble hill towns, to a poor Yankee family that had settled there 200 years ago and had not done much since. The valley establishment—Jack Tieg's world—was an alien place. His main contact with it had been to work in the kitchen of Jack's country club as a teenager; he had not been left with endearing memories. He went to business school in the Southwest and stayed there to make his fortune. Folks in Westward hadn't heard much from him until he returned, dressed in cowboy boots and a guayabera shirt and apparently flush with success.

Jack might have shared Sally's concern if he had known more about Strait's career. Wilmer achieved moderate success in real estate in Texas until he met a gentleman from Louisiana. This benefactor owned a pyramid of banks and insurance companies and always seemed willing to back Wilmer's riskiest ventures. One day he took Wilmer aside and explained that he was taking control of a new bank. "I have a happy family of borrowers," he said, "And I expect they'll show their gratitude by purchasing some of this stock."

"How much?" Wilmer replied.

The Louisiana backer had strange friends from New Orleans. One of Wilmer's partners, a transplanted New Yorker, called them the "bent noses." Wilmer noticed that the banks his benefactor bought made loans in Arizona, Nevada, and California, and they invariably wound up in trouble. One chain of Texas banks collapsed in the mid-1970s, inspiring a congressional investigation, but the Louisianan emerged unscathed. The Louisianan passed on ideas about exploiting thrifts to Wilmer and suggested that he might want to try the business. The regulators for Westward would have shuddered if they knew the source of Strait's financing.

Strait promised to recapitalize Westward, and he did inject about $5 million. But he did better with intangibles. As the buyer of a troubled thrift, he had permission from the Bank Board to book "goodwill" as capital. He announced that he planned to get the thrift out of its hole by "growing" it out. Once he was in control, he began breakneck lending in the areas Jack had avoided. He liked real estate loans in Florida and Texas. Even though they were well out of the Westward market area, they seemed highly profitable. Wilmer used his own appraiser for the Sunbelt shopping malls and condos. The appraised value would be the starting point for the loan. Wilmer then added enough to cover interest payments for two years. The loan also included a reserve for fees, which were substantial. So the loans looked highly profitable. Westward controlled the interest reserve and booked the payments when they were due. As long as the reserve lasted, the loans would be current, no matter what happened.

The treasurer came in Wilmer's office to complain about these loans. As a veteran of 35 years with Westward, and a good friend of Jack's father, he usually carried weight in setting policy. "We're not really earning money from these interest reserves," he said. "We're just paying ourselves back our own money and calling it profit. The loan could go bad, and we wouldn't know it for two years."

"The fees are good money," chuckled Wilmer from behind his huge desk. "Some of these developers pay us 4 percent each time we renew the loan, and they have six-month renewals." He toyed with a brass model of a condominium that a friend of the Louisianan had sent up from Dallas. "Who says the loans will go bad, anyway? We have good appraisals."

"That's another thing," the treasurer plunged on. "We don't really know these appraisers. The loans are way out of our area. What if the land is only worth $4 million instead of $10 million?"

"Let me worry about that," said Wilmer. "I'll be going down there myself." At the next board meeting, Wilmer suggested that the treasurer was out of touch with the rapid changes in the industry. He announced the treasurer's resignation with great appreciation for his long service. Jack was away with Sally on a cruise.

True to his word, Wilmer starting touring his far-flung investments. To save time, he told the board, he ordered a Lear jet for the company. Soon Westward had its own hangar at the municipal airport. Wilmer incorporated Westward Aviation to hold the jet and the hangar, and using the broad new investment powers of the Garn-St Germain Act, bought the company with Westward S&L money.

Wilmer started setting up other corporations as well, making them subsidiaries, or subsidiaries of subsidiaries of Westward. The thrift, now Westward Service Corporation, found itself the owner of entities such as ArgEquine, a stud farm for Argentine racehorses; Westward Cycles and Ascensions, Ltd., devoted to Strait's passions of motorcycling and ballooning; and WestInvest, S.A., a money-management office in Geneva, Switzerland, that no one at the thrift seemed to know much about. The thrift made frequent loans for deals handled by these subsidiaries, although it soon became hard to keep track of the money. Some of the old directors quietly left the board. Others took generous loans and bought into Wilmer's multitude of deals. Strait recruited new directors from among his friends. One, a carpenter, became a major builder, filling the river basin with his Westward-financed condos. Driving by one day, Jack Tieg remembered how four feet of water had covered that plain in the hurricane of 1955.

Strait was going far afield for his other banking business. Every once in a while, a loan participation from Florida, Texas or Louisiana would show up on his books. "It's a way of sharing the risk," he explained to his junior officers. "They make a loan for $30 million and sell parts of it to five other thrifts, so we all have a $5 million asset in a region with a different economic cycle." He began to shuffle his own loans through this network, although he didn't have an economic theory to explain why he and several trusted officers would work late to send them out in batches just days before the FSLIC examiners were due.

Westward grew by leaps and bounds. From a modest $25 million in assets under Jack Teig, it swelled to $300 million in Strait's first year. In his second, it broke $500 million, and by the end of his third it passed $1 billion. The community didn't have the economy to provide these deposits. They came from all across the country, attracted by the high interest on the jumbo CDs. Strait spent much of his time on the phone with deposit brokers in New York, Miami and Beverly Hills. Instead of adding tellers, he hired a fax and telex operator and installed a state-of-the art wire room. By the end of his fourth year, more than half of his deposits came from just four brokers. At the same time, local mortgages had fallen to less than one-third of his portfolio. One week, while Wilmer frenetically closed deals in Florida and Texas, a local dairy farmer came in for a loan to rebuild his herd. Wilmer turned him down.

As Westward grew, so did Wilmer's influence. He devoted a lot of energy to cultivating the district congressman, who had enough seniority to be in line for a committee chair. The two flew to Texas to shoot deer with Wilmer's business buddies or to Florida to fish. Strait started raising money for campaigns and helped the congressman set up his own PAC to channel funds to his House allies. The representative began to think about a leadership position. Strait gave him free use of the company jet for speaking engagements in his House colleagues' districts. Strait even began to handle his finances, cutting him in on some of the sounder condo projects.

A national horizon was opening before Wilmer Strait, and he decided to cut back his daily involvement in Westward. He resigned as chairman and brought in a well-known former thrift president from the large city to the east. The new chairman, whom we'll call Parker Ritwire, had just completed a term as president of the state savings and loan trade group. With Wilmer's backing, he had been elected to the board of the regional Federal Home Loan Bank. But Ritwire wasn't the buttoned-down stuffed shirt that Westward employees expected. Recently divorced, he drove a fancy Porsche, dated elegant women and did whatever Strait told him to. Ritwire was a handy acquisition, because Westward was heading towards a major crisis.

FSLIC had started its annual examination of Westward. The man in charge was one of the agency's few veterans; in fact, he was the regulator who had pushed Jack Tieg to recapitalize five years ago. He ran into Jack at the dingy café on Main Street and over coffee started to ask him just what was going on. "We're seeing loan participations from some of our real problem cases in the Southwest," he said. "How did they get up here? You know, a lot of the condos down there don't have anyone living in them. There's no rental money, no cash stream, nothing. And whatever happened to your old treasurer?" These were questions Jack had tried not to ask over the years. Although he'd stayed on as director, he hadn't had the heart to pay close attention. It was time, as he had known it eventually would be, to have a searching talk with Wilmer Strait.

After a walk around the block, he entered the marbled lobby of Westward's new building and stood outside Strait's southwestern style office. In the anteroom, several examiners were pulling loan files. When Strait ushered him in, Jack had the feeling he had been expected. "Hell, yes, I took risks," Strait said, interrupting Jack's questions. "Some paid off; some didn't. That's what happens when you throw the long bomb. But this examination won't stop us. I want you to stay on, Jack, to reassure the locals. Tell them their money's safe. It's all insured."

Jack left the building, expecting to see it padlocked the next day. But the morning came with no news. When he checked in later, the examiners had left the anteroom and Ritwire was sitting in Strait's office. Ritwire handed Jack a paper, his gold chains jingling as he reached across the desk. It was a Memorandum of Understanding with the Bank Board in Washington. The agreement said that Westward would slow down its growth and improve its lending procedures, and Ritwire would replace Strait as the chief executive.

"This is a wrist-slap," said Tieg. Ritwire smiled seraphically. Jack called the chief examiner to compare notes.

"I can't talk about it," his friend replied. "Washington took the case away from us and closed it. I'm being transferred."

□ 4 □

SO THE STORY ENDS with the good guys frustrated, the bad guys unpunished, and the system in the throes of corruption. Eventually Westward will collapse, and the FSLIC will take responsibility for nearly $1 billion in deposits, most of them from money brokers. Most of the loans will be found worthless. The Justice Department will charge Wilmer Strait and his associates with nearly $200 million in bank fraud and embezzlement. FSLIC will sue Jack Tieg and the other directors for failing to perform their fiduciary duty, but the suit will be quietly settled when Jack's lawyers subpoena the Bank Board's records on the decision to transfer the examination to Washington.

The elements of this case show up in nearly every major thrift disaster and in many of the bank failures. A strong personality with strange national connections comes into control of a sleepy institution and makes it grow geometrically. He twists the thrift's investment policy away from traditional family homes into a bizarre array of corporate gambles and real estate schemes. The perverse incentives of deposit insurance make this growth possible. They encourage the reckless plunge for the big payoff. The Westward S&Ls of the industry attract jumbo CDs but not searching scrutiny because the federal insurance funds bear the risk. But the saga of Wilmer Strait raises the ultimate question: What happened to the federal scrutiny? Why weren't the insurance funds able to protect themselves?

All the history, all the economic theory and all the criminal investigations ultimately bring us to this question: What went wrong with the regulators? The framers of deposit insurance showed some awareness of its temptations and tried to build restraints into the system. Chief of these restraints were the bank and thrift examiners and their powers to discipline. It may be a second-best solution to have the defects of one government program ameliorated by another, but the checks and balances can make a difference. The failure of supervision was the fatal blow to the system.

To see its importance, compare the performance of the thrifts and of the commercial banks. Both presumably fell under the same perverse influence of deposit insurance. But the clients of FSLIC ran wild while those of the FDIC remained under some restraint. The difference is that in the thrift industry, the check of federal supervision almost totally collapsed. Also, as Treasury officials argue, capital standards were much stricter in banking. Many factors contributed to this breakdown, including confusion in the early Reagan administration about the meaning of deregulation. But FSLIC's problems aren't unique either.

Five years ago, the FDIC suffered its own disasters. The failures of the FDIC are less well known and their cost dwindles to insignificance next to a debacle measured in terms of the gross national product. But at the time, $1 billion seemed a lot of money to lose to fraud. Even worse, one saw the shadow over the FDIC that later took shape and substance as the nemesis of FSLIC. The suspicion of political interference emerged well before the crude extortions of Speaker of the House Jim Wright.

Wilmer Strait and dozens of real-life counterparts had discovered a simple secret. The best way to steal is to share a portion of the proceeds with those in a position to provide protection. The protectors may be in Congress or the White House or a governor's mansion. They may not understand just what they are doing, and their cut can be incredibly small. But they have stripped the defenses from the financial system, weakened banking and allowed the destruction of the savings and loan industry. The cost is $1200 and rising for every man, woman, and child in the United States.

Part III: POLICY

18. The Necessary and the Desirable Range of Discretion to be Allowed to a Monetary Authority
Jacob Viner

Should the monetary authorities be put on a "tight leash," so as to restrict their ability to manipulate the money stock in ways that may be harmful to consumers, or should the authorities be put on a "loose leash" so that they are free to offset short-run changes in the demand for money? Here Chicago economist Jacob Viner offers a classic statement of the "rules versus discretion" controversy. --G.S., Ed.

* * *

I undertake in this paper to explore the extent to which it is possible and desirable to limit the discretionary activity of a monetary authority by subjecting it, by statute or otherwise, to conform in its operations to a precise rule. I take for granted that some limitations of consequence in the monetary field can be effectively imposed on a monetary authority in the form of an obligation to follow an explicit code of general "principles," and more explicitly, in the negative form of prohibition, from pursuing some specified goals and from engaging in some specified types of activity. Beyond this it does not seem possible to limit the discretion of a monetary authority unless one can impose on it adherence to a single rule which is fairly simple, objective, and operationally workable. Otherwise, "discretion" can be freely exercised by variable interpretation of an ambiguous or elastic rule or by choosing between alternative rules when adherence to both simultaneously is or can be made to seem impossible.

Advocacy of replacement of "authorities" by "rules" is usually associated with a strong belief in the desirability of "economic freedom," and this is conspicuously the case in academic discussion of monetary policy. There is no inherent association, however, logical or historical, between freedom from governmental restraint and the issue as to whether when governmental restraint is present and perhaps is inevitable it is preferable that the restraint should be applied through the imposition of a rigid rule or through the exercise of discretionary authority.

In the monetary field advocates of economic freedom have in the past demanded freedom from both rules and discretionary authority with respect to the minting of coin, the issue of paper money, and the creation of deposits transferable by check. The limitation of the creation of money to government, or the regulation of its private creation, instead of leaving it free to be determined by the accidents of gold or silver mining, or by market competition in the banking industry, is already a major interference by government with free enterprise. Depending on the character of the rule and on the quality and objectives of the discretionary authority, the rule can be an instrument of tyranny, and discretion can be the means whereby economic freedom is promoted to the utmost extent possible consistent with respect for other values. As between the tyranny of an oppressive rule and the misery which could result from an authority which by using its discretionary power to do nothing permits anarchy to reign, even the zealots for economic freedom might find that the choice lay between comparable evils.

The enthusiasm of "liberals" for rules in preference to other modes of economic regulation nevertheless has an obvious and logical source; a government limited to operating through simple and inflexible rules would inevitably be a government tightly limited in the scale and range of its operations. Whether this is in itself desirable or undesirable is an appropriate matter for reasoned debate, or for expression of one's value judgments, prejudices, and emotions. In any case, it is a matter with which I have no concern for present purposes,[1] and my special concern here is with the narrower question of the suitability of "rules" as the major instrument of monetary regulation. I will assume throughout that where there is discretionary authority it will be exercised in accordance with some set of publicly approved principles and by men with the measure of good faith, intelligence, judgment, and skill which it is reasonable to expect them to possess.

I concede at once to rules certain advantages in principle over discretionary authority as rival instruments for the execution of public policy. On purely a priori grounds, not needing to extend beyond the obligation to avoid self-contradictory argument, it can be said for an unambiguous rule, provided it is enforceable and enforced, that it is a complete protection within the area of its immediate subject matter against arbitrary, malicious, capricious, stupid, clumsy, or other manipulation of that subject matter by an "authority." It can be said for a rule rigid through time, if it works and is counted on to work, that it provides absolute certainty and predictability, with respect to the behavior prescribed by the rule. It can also be said for- or against-limitation of government to the choice between action by imposition of rules or inaction that it will in all probability choose inaction more often than if discretionary action by itself and by its agencies were an adopted or permitted alternative. These are all considerations of substantial weight.

On the other hand, it can be said that within the area of its application a rule *ipso facto* shuts out the possibility of adaptation of regulation by well-intentioned, wise, and skillful exercise of discretionary authority to the relevant differences in circumstance. A rule doubtfully or irregularly enforced, and a rule subject at any time to revision, may involve less certainty and predictability than a control operated by a discretionary authority which follows a known set of principles. The particular certainty which the best rule conceivable provides, moreover, may be a certainty which no one in his right mind would want, and may involve the accentuation of uncertainties in a wide range of other matters. A particular rule may accomplish its objective, but it may have undesired side-effects which will drive the government, in order to cope with them, to widen the range of its other activities, whether in a discretionary manner or by adopting additional rules. It may even be a general principle that the attempt to deal by simple rules with complex phenomena will lead to a proliferation of rules, or of authorities, or of rules *and* authorities. Even, therefore, if we accept the minimization of interference by government with the economic behavior of its citizens as a major objective, to substitute rules for discretionary authority can be to move away from rather than towards "economic freedom."

Even if it were conceded, therefore, that, where the objective consequences would be the same, regulation by rule would involve less impairment of economic freedom than regulation by discretionary methods, this would not suffice to settle the general issue in favor of rules. Particular freedoms, moreover, precious values though they may be, need to be limited and qualified so that they may be fitted into a complex value system in which there is conflict and rivalry of values.

There are in consequence of all these factors important limitations on the extent to which it is operationally practicable and psychologically and politically feasible to substitute rule by rule for government by discretionary authority. In the economic field important rules affecting important social issues have in fact been extremely scarce, and to the extent that they have had a substantial degree of durability this has been largely explicable either by the fact that they evolved into taboos, or ends in themselves, and were thus removed from the area of open discussion and rational appraisal, or by the tolerance of widespread evasion. The most conspicuous instances of economic rules with a substantial degree of durability were the prohibition of lending at interest and the maintenance of fixed monetary standards in terms of the precious metals. The most enthusiastic advocate of rules can derive little comfort from the availability of these historical precedents. Aside from the questionability of the ends which these rules were in their origin intended to serve and of the suitability of these rules as means to serve their ends, their durability was largely specious. In the case of the prohibition of usury, both widespread evasion and the promulgation of an elaborate set of exemptions or valid "titles" to the charge of interest on loans resulted in unequal and erratic enforcement and in the development of an elaborate, highly discretionary, and unstable casuistry, which made the rule a generator of uncertainty rather than of certainty. In the case of the metallic monetary standard, the degree of certainty and of genuine durability of the rule was made much less in fact than in appearance by discretionary and often arbitrary debasements and devaluations, by illegal corruptions of the legal coinage, by discretionary alterations in the laws and regulations affecting the nonmonetary uses of the precious metals and their export and import, and by the operation of Gresham's law, where more than one precious metal had legal tender privileges. In both instances there was much to be said for the social usefulness of the breaches of the rules which occurred, whether these were legal or illegal.

The obstacles in principle and in practice to the substitution of rules for discretionary authority can be summarized in a compact set of propositions.

(1) If there is plurality of ends and if several ends are in complex and unstable rivalry or conflict with each other, no rule can be devised which will dispense with the need of exercise of flexible discretionary authority.

(2) If there is a single end but plurality of means, the most appropriate combination, in kind and degree, of means to be used will vary with time, circumstances, and available information and insight, and will therefore need to be determined by more or less *ad hoc* judgment rather than be susceptible of determination by a fixed rule.

(3) If authority is diffused among a number of substantially independent agencies, decision-making will need to be carried out by resort to a continuous or intermittent process of negotiation and mutual accommodation, to the exclusion of fixed and stable rules.

(4) Even if there are a single end, a single authority, and a single means, but the end is a quantity of some kind which is a function of several variables, all of which are important and are in unstable relation to each other, there will be no fixed rule available which will be both practicable and appropriate to its objective.

I will now attempt to explore the significance of these rather abstract propositions for the more concrete field of decision-making in the monetary policy area. In this area there are a multiplicity of objectives, a multiplicity of available tools, a multiplicity of authorities, a multiplicity of governmental agencies whose activities infringe on monetary phenomena; these agencies may be substantially independent of external authority and may be unaware of and unconcerned about these impacts. All of this increases the difficulty of the task of formulating and administering monetary policy. The task would admittedly be facilitated if there could be reduction of the list of objectives, preferably to a single one, reduction of the list of authorities, preferably to a single one, reduction of the list of tools, if it is a long list, and the imposition on other governmental agencies of the requirement that they avoid actions which have undesired monetary impacts.

All of this, however, is easier said than done. Our monetary authorities may perhaps be attempting to serve too wide a range of objectives. Authority in the monetary field may be too widely diffused, as

I am certain it is. A host of miscellaneous agencies of the federal government may have mandates from Congress which are inconsistent with our monetary policy, and may within the limits of the discretion allowed to them act irresponsibly with respect to monetary policy.

Things are as they are, however, for historical and constitutional and political reasons, which in many cases carry great weight with Congress and with the public. It is a useful service to speculate on the improvements which could be made in the operation of our monetary system if we could rearrange and reconstruct at will our existing political institutions and our banking and financial system. It is defeatist to confine oneself to the assumption that we must take the existing institutional complex as fixed and unalterable in making policy recommendations. Where between these extremes is the most profitable point from which to start in making one's policy recommendations will be answered differently by different economists, according to their judgment and temperament. I will operate throughout on the assumption that institutional changes are almost always difficult to attain, even when the case in their favor is strong, and that the chances of obtaining a desired improvement in the mode of operation of our monetary system are much greater if the improvement does not involve any substantial change in the institutional framework of our government or of our financial structure.

I will start with a grossly unrealistic model, in which Congress has assigned exclusively to the Federal Reserve the task of promoting price-level stability, has assigned it no other task, and has confined it to the use of a single tool, open-market operations, so that no questions as to choice of authorities, choice of goals, or choice of tools can arise. I will assume also that whatever happens in the nongovernmental economy and whatever Congress or other agencies of the government may do, there will always be some pattern of open-market operations which will in form and degree suffice to prevent a significant deviation, either short-run and long-run, or only long-run, from the desired price level. Unless it is a fact, and a believed fact, that there is a simple and stable relation between a particular pattern and degree of open-market operations and the general course of prices, the Federal Reserve will still not be able to operate on the basis of a rule, but will have to exercise discretion as to when, in what degree, and in what direction to carry out open-market operations, and also as to what securities and in what relative proportions to buy or sell.

There would also remain the question as to how to define the "price level" and how to obtain a reasonably precise measure of its behavior, so defined. Some "authority" would have to decide this, and it could make its decision only by exercising a substantial degree of "discretion," which would inevitably involve some measure of judgment and some measure of arbitrariness. Let this problem be resolved, or evaded, by the assumption that Congress prescribes the "price level" which is to be stabilized and the precise procedure which is to be followed in measuring it. Further, let it be assumed that a constitutional amendment authorizes Congress to make decisions which neither that Congress nor its successors shall have the power, for a stated and substantial period of time, to change. This would relieve the Federal Reserve of the necessity of exercising discretion in the definition of its single goal. There would still remain the need, however, of deciding the pattern and degree of open-market operations required to maintain a stable price level. No one, as far as I know, has ever claimed that the relation to the price level of the scale of open-market operations of a given pattern, or with a pattern changeable at will, has been, is, or could be simple enough and stable enough to make it possible to find a quantitative rule of open-market operations which could be counted on to maintain approximate stability in the price level, either in the cyclical short run or in the long run. Even, therefore, if price stability were the sole goal and if the Federal Reserve were the sole monetary authority and open-market operations the sole tool it was permitted to use, we would still not have escaped from the necessity of leaving to the discretionary judgment of the Federal Reserve the decision at least of the scale of its open-market obligations.

If with price stabilization as the sole goal it is not possible, analytically or on the basis of past experience, to frame a rule prescribing the scale of open-market operations which could be expected to serve that goal with a tolerable degree of approximation, is any other suitable rule available? Professor Milton Friedman claims that a suitable rule is available as far as long-run stabilization of the price level is concerned—provided a number of important changes are made in the structure and functions of our monetary institutions. The monetary authority should so conduct open-market operations as to result in a constant monthly rate of increase in the stock of money, the rate to be either 3 or 4 per cent, depending on whether "money" is defined as including or excluding time deposits.

Friedman acknowledges that "there is little to be said in theory for the rule that the money supply should grow at a constant rate,"[2] does not indicate what that "little" consists of, and does not seriously expound what can be said "in theory" against commitment to a constant rate of growth in money supply in a world which in most of its economic respects, and perhaps in all, has not grown at a constant rate in the past and offers no ground for expectation that it will do so in the future, near or far. He is concerned, and rightly so, about the ill-behavior of the money supply in the past as judged by any arguable standards, and is concerned, and rightly so, lest its future behavior be as bad as in the past, or at least be not considerably better. What he claims on behalf of his proposed rule is that it is objective, unambiguous, precise, and therefore would leave no significant scope for the exercise of discretion to the monetary authority as far as the supply of money was concerned, that if it had been followed over the past century, or since 1920, our monetary system would have worked much better than it has in fact, and that if it had been in effect since 1948, it would have worked about as well as it has in fact.

I raise no question about the validity of Friedman's statistical report of what our past experience has been because I am neither informed nor competent enough to do so, and because I have great respect for his statistical skill, and also because the statistical record does not seem to me to be of much relevance for the present issue. We are asked to prescribe for the future, and not for a distant past. If we look to past experience for guidance, as we of course should, the most relevant period is the period since 1951, after the Korean War and after the Treasury-Federal Reserve "Accord" of 1951, which restored to the Federal Reserve the power to use its controls in support of price stabilization. It seems to me that our experience during this period was by Friedman's own standards superior to what his rule would have achieved. With the gains which one can reasonably expect time to bring in available statistical data, skills, and insights, the Federal Reserve will be able to perform even better in the future, if it is given adequate authority.

Friedman presents stabilization of the price level as the single appropriate and practicable objective of monetary policy and stabilization of the rate of growth of the money supply merely as a means, though presumably the only effective one available, of attaining that end. The question arises: Why could not the Federal Reserve be given, as the "rule" to follow, the maintenance of the stock of money at whatever level appears necessary to keep stable a particular index number of prices? Friedman raises against this the "technical problem" of choice of a particular index number. But the technical problem of definition of "money" is at least as difficult. If it is the case that different reputable index numbers of prices vary substantially in their behavior through time and that choice between them is difficult, acceptance of the rule that the rate of increase in the money supply should be kept constant at some specified rate becomes the equivalent not of accepting a stable price level as the goal of monetary policy but of accepting whatever price-level trend the rule would happen to produce. The rule thus becomes the end, and the original end is more or less abandoned.

As far as cyclical price movements are concerned, Friedman explicitly abandons price stabilization as a practicable goal. "The link between price changes and monetary changes over short periods is too loose and too imperfectly known to make [short-run] price level stability an objective and reasonably unambiguous guide to policy."[3] To justify faith in a close enough linkage of secular price-level changes to money-supply changes to qualify the money-supply rule as a satisfactory rule for long-run price-level stabilization, he appeals to the statistical record, as he has presented it, both of the behavior of the money supply and of the behavior of the price level as reflected in a particular series of index numbers. Without raising any question about either his money-supply data or his price-level data, I reject that faith on the basis of another article of faith which I hold, but which I concede is not fashionable today in the profession. I believe that the nature of the economic universe is such, and the degree of mutual independence of the money supply and the price level is so substantial as far as logic by itself can determine, that any empirical constancy of relations that is discovered must be suspected of being either fortuitous or the consequence of the particular selection of series, from among those available, subjected to comparison, and that routine extrapolation into the future of such constancy of relations is consequently a highly hazardous basis for prediction. I suggest also that even if we accept an empirical constancy of relations discovered in the past as demonstrating a logical relation in that period, the introduction into the economic universe of a specific rule of behavior for the money supply would constitute an alteration of potential significance in the nature of that universe, and that we must not take for granted that the relation of the price level to the supply of money will be even approximately the same after such a rule is adopted and effectively enforced as it was before. The transformation of a hitherto unpredictable economic variable to one which everyone can predict with certainty is almost certain to have some effect, though one unpredictable in advance, on the pattern of its relations to other economic variables.

Friedman's proposed 3 per cent constant-rate-of-growth-of-the-money-supply rule is compounded of two elements: the assumption, or prediction, of a secular rate of growth of the economy at 2 per cent per annum and of a secular rate of shift of 1 per cent per annum from demand deposits to bank and non-bank time deposits, based on the average experience of the past ten years. This second element is a recognition that the impact of a given stock of "money" on the price level depends upon its velocity of use, and that shifts from one kind of "money" to another, or from money to near-money, will tend to affect the velocity of use of the money supply. It seems to me inadequate recognition, however, of the potential variability in extent and kind of these shifts through time, and to give too much weight to a particular average rate of shift as between an arbitrarily restricted range of the moneys and near-moneys in one decade of past history whose peculiarities of circumstance may not be repeated in any succeeding decade. Here once more an improbable constancy is being projected into the future.

To prescribe a formula which makes a stated percentage of allowance for the influence on the velocity of the stock of money, however defined, of shifts in the relative proportions of money and of one kind of near-money is to predict in effect the net results on velocity of a wide range of unpredictable changes. Such are changes in the relative proportions of currency, demand deposits freely drawable by depositors, "demand deposits" which are required to be maintained as a condition of the grant of loans or as compensation for services rendered, and time deposits with commercial or noncommercial banks or with non-banks. Such also are shifts in the holdings of deposits as between different categories of depositors with different patterns of rate of use of their deposits. Such also are changes in the relative proportions of securities and other more or less liquid assets held by the public to their holdings of money, and shifts in the maturity pattern of these securities. Such also are changes in subjective appraisal by the public of the degree of liquidity of their assets, induced by changes in interest rates, or by changes in the character or in the mode of operation of financial institutions or in the mechanics of payment transfers.

For purposes of academic theorizing, one is free to assume that in the absence of special information these various factors will be mutually offsetting, or will have net effects on the velocity of "money," defined in a particular way, corresponding to their average effects over some preceding period more or less arbitrarily selected. The only logical basis for such assumptions, however, even for purposes of theoretical analysis, rests on convenience and the absence of superior alternatives. But what is under consideration here is not theorizing for its own sake but the adoption of a rule of practice. Staking our future on present prophesying seems a high price to pay for escaping from the bondage of a discretionary authority, especially if one considers how dismal has been the past record of success and failure in economic prophesying on the basis of the projection into the future of past trends.

The choice in practice, of course, need not be between, on the one hand, the grant to the monetary authority of complete discretion, subject presumably to a Congressional mandate to follow some specified general principle or principles, and, on the other hand, its subjection to a precise rule not subject to change, even if it obviously was working badly. Congress could, for example, require the Federal Reserve each year to bring into being such rate of increase (or decrease) in the stock of money, as specifically defined, as in the judgment of the Federal Reserve would if it had prevailed in the preceding five-year period have resulted in a secularly stable price level during that period. This would not require the Federal Reserve to engage in forecasting, would call for annual adjustment of the planned rate of increase in the stock of money in strict conformity with the price-stabilization goal, and would at least weaken any tendency of the price-level trend to deviate cumulatively from stability. This more flexible rule would have the advantage also over a more rigid one that by lessening the risk of a marked discrepancy between the goal of the rule and its actual results it would increase its acceptability and durability. Since the public interest is presumed to be in price stability and in the behavior of the stock of money only as it bears on price stability, substitution of the flexible for the rigid rule would give the public a greater measure of certainty with respect to something it cares about, the trend of the price level, at the cost of introducing a measure of uncertainty about something it cares nothing about for its own sake.

I have been assuming so far that the Federal Reserve has only one goal: stabilization of the price level. This is, of course, not the case. The Federal Reserve states its principal functions to be those of fostering price level stability, high-level employment, and economic growth. It also acknowledges as a subordinate function the damping of cyclical instability, and it at times talks and operates as if it had some additional, though minor, functions. It presents these functions as not of its own choosing but as dictated to it by Congressional mandate and by its understanding of the intent of Congress.

If the Federal Reserve had a single objective, let us say secular price-level stability, the possibility of finding a precise rule or a simple set of rules which would serve this objective with an acceptable degree of efficiency would, other things being equal, be at a maximum. This would be equally true if it were a fact, and were believed to be a fact, that maintaining price-level stability was all that it was feasible to do in the monetary field to promote high-level employment and economic growth. If, however, it is a fact, and recognized by the Federal Reserve to be a fact, that the causal relations between the behavior of the price level, the level of employment, and the rate of economic growth are, as I believe them to be, highly complex, unstable through time, and in large measure unpredictable, there would seem to be only two alternatives open: either to plead uncertainty as to what the effect of its actions would be as a justification for not taking any action specifically directed towards promoting high-level employment and economic growth, or to use its best judgment each time that a decision of some sort is called for as to the relative weight to be given to the three objectives and as to the effect on the three objectives of any specific action available to it. The first would mean, in effect, abandonment by the Federal Reserve of these goals as part of its responsibilities. The second would mean that the Federal Reserve had no choice but to use its authority in a discretionary manner.

This states somewhat too sharply the issue between accepting plural goals and accepting only a single goal. All three goals could be *nationally* accepted, but with the Federal Reserve being assigned responsibility only for the maintenance of price-level stability and with other agencies being assigned the specific tasks of promoting high-level employment and economic growth by the use of other than monetary measures. If the other agencies thereby exercised an influence on the price level which was from the point of view of price-level stabilization wrong in direction or in degree, it would be the duty of the Federal Reserve, in fulfillment of its own obligation, to take compensatory measures with respect to the money supply. If it should prove in practice that there was basic incompatibility between the goals such that a satisfactory level of employment and a satisfactory rate of economic growth required—or seemed to require—some degree of inflation, the decision would have to be made somewhere as to which goal or goals must be given precedence, and wherever the decision was made, "discretion" would have to be exercised both in reaching that decision and in carrying it into effect.

A fourth goal has as a result of the developments of the past few years been brought into the forefront of official and public consciousness: the goal of restoring equilibrium in the American balance of payments, or of maintaining the present dollar price of gold. As in the case of the level of employment and of the rate of growth of the American economy, there could be basic incompatibility between the balance-of-payments-equilibrium goal and the stable-price-level goal. It is, moreover, a characteristic of the stable dollar price of gold as a goal which is perhaps unique to it that the virtues that it possesses or that are claimed for it are such that they vanish if there are recurrent casual, seasonal, or cyclical intermissions in its fulfillment. Like Caesar's wife, the gold standard in any of its variants, to accomplish its purposes, must remain above suspicion of its integrity, without dispensation even for momentary deviations. If there is conflict between the fixed dollar price of gold and the price-level-stabilization goals, or between the former and a rule adopted in the service of the latter, one or the other must give way, and in the absence of a rule for breaking rules I do not see how that can be brought about in an orderly way, except through the decision-making of a discretionary authority.

The price-stabilization goal could itself be regarded as a sort of multiple goal if what was sought was not merely secular stability but also cyclical stability. Friedman's rule disregards this latter goal, except as the maintenance of a constant monthly rate of increase of the money supply might as an incidental by-product make a greater contribution to cyclical price stability than would any other available procedure for regulating the money supply. Friedman in fact claims that our understanding of the cycle is so meager and the lags between the taking of corrective measures in the monetary field and their impact on the economy so long and so uncertainly known that we are justified in concluding that deviations from the rule of maintaining a constant monthly rate of increase of the money supply which are intended to lessen cyclical instability would more often hinder than help. I hold in low regard the state of my knowledge with respect to the intricacies of the business cycle, and therefore cheerfully hand this problem over to the experts. I cannot, however, exorcise from my mind the question as to whether Friedman's verdict that attempts to dampen the business cycle by use of countercyclical monetary measures would tend rather to accentuate it would remain unaltered if such attempts did not necessarily involve departure from a fixed rule of constant growth in the money supply. I venture also to suggest that the "announcement effects" of countercyclical monetary actions may be important, and that the lags associated with them may be very short.

It seems to me that from all this one must conclude that even if a simple rule were practicable if there was only a single objective of monetary policy, plurality of goals makes resort to discretionary management unavoidable. It may be demonstrable that some goals are ill-chosen and that the country should abandon them, and that other goals can be best served by other means than monetary controls or can be only damaged, not helped, if the attempt is made to serve them through the control of the money supply. All of this is open to discussion. The more extreme position that interference of an otherwise valid goal with the practicability of resort to a simple rule for the determination of the money supply can ever be a sufficient or even a strong argument for abandonment of that goal appears rational only if one's enthusiasm for simple rules goes beyond mere faith in their efficiency as means to economic ends. The commitment to an ascetic limitation of goals in order to establish the possibility of the substitution of rules for discretionary authorities can be logically supported only on the basis of a personal set of value premises, unlikely to be widely shared.

I readily concede, however, that a monetary authority, in this instance the Federal Reserve, should seek within reason to practice parsimony of goals, and should not permit its decision-making to become confused and its operations cluttered by accepting an unlimited array of goals, ranging from major ones to relatively trivial ones. Multiplicity of goals may serve as a screen, moreover, for not having any well-defined goals, for operating in a haze of uncertain and volatile objectives, and for using as an alibi for failure to operate vigorously in support of major objectives the need to serve other unspecified or trivial objectives. I, for one, would not absolve the Federal Reserve—or the Treasury—from the charge that at times in the past this plea has been used in defense of failure to formulate clear-cut and rational policy.

Multiplicity of agencies with independent powers of control in the monetary field also constitutes a formidable obstacle to resort to simple rules. A more important drawback of multiplicity of agencies is that it can constitute a formidable obstacle to any effective pattern of monetary control.

In the United States the degree of decentralization of direct and indirect control over the quantity and velocity of money, as well as of official power to influence the supply of near-moneys and their velocities, is nothing short of fantastic, and is unquestionably without parallel anywhere else in the world. Within the Federal Reserve System, control over the supply of money would on a functional organization chart be shown to be divided among the Board of Governors, the Open Market Committee, and, with respect to the administration of the "discount window" and the determination of discount rates, the twelve district banks. Non-member banks, which hold about 16 per cent of the total bank deposits of the country, are regulated by fifty state agencies. Bank supervision and bank examination, which can so operate as to affect directly the quantity of money, are divided among the Federal Reserve, the Controller of the Currency, the F.D.I.C., and state agencies. Federal debt management, which influences the liquidity of the banking system and of the economy, is a function solely of the Treasury, especially since the adoption by the Federal Reserve of the "bills-only" policy for its open-market operations. (In England the Bank of England is to a large extent the debt manager; it determines what kind of national securities the public shall hold by releasing for public sale varying proportions of its subscriptions to Treasury loan issues as well as by carrying out its open-market transactions in securities of an unlimited range of maturities.) There is also a great mass of credit-creating and velocity- and liquidity-influencing activity which is carried on by private financial institutions other than commercial banks, and over these activities the Federal Reserve has as a rule no direct regulatory power, the one significant exception being its control over margin requirements for lending on securities.

The multiplicity of monetary control agencies in the United States is primarily a historical product, with limited correspondence to the needs of an efficient system of monetary and banking controls. In large part it derives its durability and finds such justification as is available to it in loyalties to "states' rights" and in the special features of a unit-banking system. It is thus partly the result of the existence of a multiplicity of objectives, but it also leads naturally to the multiplying of objectives. Multiplicity of tools or instrumentalities of control is also in part a by-product of the multiplicity of agencies. It should be said, however, that the degree of diffusion of control is much greater in appearance than in reality. Within the Federal Reserve System there has been a strong trend toward effective concentration of power in the Board of Governors, even when the formal allocation of power has been left unaltered. As between the Federal Reserve and other agencies there is a substantial amount of formal and informal coordination of policies. The banking resources of the country are quantitatively overwhelmingly within the Federal Reserve System and are thus subject to control, although this exaggerates the degree of control over the banking system as a whole which the Federal Reserve can exercise. As long as entry into and surrender of membership in the Federal Reserve System is at the free will of the individual banks, the Federal Reserve has to give consideration, in applying restrictive control measures, lest they lead to transfers of banks from Federal Reserve membership to non-member state-bank status.

I would in general approve of any move toward concentration of regulatory power over credit-creating agencies, both within the Federal Reserve itself and with respect to the banking system as a whole. But as long as decentralization of authority persists in anything like its present dimensions, the impracticality of regulating the national money supply by means of a simple and rigid rule is for this reason alone complete and unqualified.

The multiplicity of tools used by official agencies which have as their purpose influencing the national supply of money, its velocity, and the liquidity of the economy, or which, while having other primary objectives, have or can have significant influence, direct or indirect, on the quantity of money or its velocity, or on the general liquidity of the economy, provides a further obstacle to the resort to a rigid rule for control of the money supply, especially if price stabilization is accepted as a major goal. Within the Federal Reserve System, the tools available include open-market operations, changes in reserve requirements, changes in the discount rate, the administration of the discount window, changes in the rigor of bank supervision and examination, and the use of selective credit controls. Outside the Federal Reserve System, but within the federal orbit, there are Treasury management of its debt and its cash balance procedures, fiscal policy, the lending, guaranteeing, and credit-insurance activities of federal agencies, and the possible interventions of the President and of Congress. There are also the instruments of control of the state regulatory agencies, which may differ in mode of operation or even in kind from the related federal ones. I am sure that I have failed to make my list of tools used, or available for potential use on a stand-by basis, long as it is, a complete one.

This multiplicity of tools is, I have no doubt, excessive and an obstacle to the efficient pursuit of the major objectives of monetary control. It is, however, in large part a by-product of the multiplicity of authorities and the plurality of objectives. Without concentration of monetary authority and some measure of reduction of the range of objectives for which the controlling agencies are assigned responsibility, the possibility of substantially reducing the number of tools is small. Multiplicity of tools is obviously a barrier to operation by simple rule, since it creates the necessity at all times of discretionary choice as to which tools shall be used and in what proportions.

It does not follow, however, that even if there were a single authority, say, the Federal Reserve, and a single objective, the ideal would be a single tool, unless operation by a simple rule is made the single objective, and perhaps not even then. On the number of tools which should be used, Friedman says: "Retaining defective instruments of control which interfere with the operation of more efficient instruments does not mean retaining power any more than a marksman's ability to hit a distant target with a rifle would be enhanced by requiring him to shoot a blunderbuss at the same time with his left hand."[4]

Quite true. But I can easily picture the Federal Reserve replying that it has more than one target, that it has several hands, none of them left hands, that all its rifles are good instruments for their respective purposes, and that it is sometimes desirable to shoot at more than one target at a time, or to shoot at a single target with more than one rifle.

The Federal Reserve insists on its need of a wide range of tools, but not apparently as wide as is now available to it for use, and, as far as I know, it is not desirous of acquiring the authority to use the many new tools which the younger central banks have invented and are using to their own satisfaction. It does not approve of the use of the discount window as a means of regulating either the stock of money or its velocity, and makes use of it chiefly as a means of supervision over individual banks, to soften the impact of its credit-restriction moves on individual banks which are particularly hard hit thereby, and to provide "last-resort" money to individual banks or to localities which do not have adequate and quick resort to money-market supplies of cash. As long as we have a unit-banking system, there is genuine need of these services, and their absence in countries with branch-banking systems has little if any relevance. If ours was a branch-banking system on a national scale, all of the banks could reasonably be expected either not to need external facilities to meet such exigencies or to have adequate connections with private money-market institutions to be assured of adequate facilities for meeting them without recourse to the Federal Reserve.

The Federal Reserve also finds merit in *changes* in the rediscount rate as a "signaling" device and of occasional use of the discount window to ease adjustment to change in reserve requirements. I see no advantage, however, in signaling in an obscure manner which will be differently interpreted by various sections of the public over signaling in language which is clear and unambiguous to all whenever it takes a restrictive or a relaxing move. In this latter way it would give greater leverage to the "announcement effect" of its moves, and thus lessen the lag between the action and its effect on the economy. I have never been able to see what advantage the Federal Reserve, or the public, derives from permitting all its moves to be surrounded by an aura of mystery, instead of endeavoring to make the objectives of such moves at least as clear to the public as they are to itself. If the Federal Reserve made its changes in reserve requirements more frequent and smaller, as would seem to me to be preferable on other grounds as well if the purpose of such changes was to serve as a flexible instrument of monetary control supplementing open-market operations, there would not be obvious need to lessen their impact through the discount window. I see no other need for rediscounting than that associated with the prevalence of unit banking, which involves the existence of small banks with limited resources and limited access to money-market facilities and makes more significant local differences in the demand for credit and regional differences in the seasonal pattern of demand for and availability of bank credit. But as long as unit banking continues to prevail, rediscounting facilities are needed and should be retained; and their operation as an attraction to small banks to enter the Federal Reserve System also deserves consideration.

If confined to these purposes, rediscounting would always be limited in its over-all dimensions. It is ordinarily so limited in fact. Only a small fraction of the member banks ever rediscount, and only a still smaller fraction are in debt to the Federal Reserve banks at any one time. With the possible exception of one year, the year-to-year and cyclical fluctuations in the indebtedness of member banks to the Federal Reserve have been too small to have been an appreciable influence, for good or ill, on the size of the national stock of money. The temptation to abuse access to the discount window should be thwarted, however, by making the discount rate always a penalty rate, higher than the prevailing rates charged on commercial loans by banks in the relevant Federal Reserve district.

The Federal Reserve does not hold a brief for the use bank supervision and examination as an instrument of control of the stock of money or its velocity. It defends its retention of supervisory and examining authority over member banks only as a needed control over the potential aberrations of unit banks, in the interest of depositors, of the solidity of the banking system as a whole, and of the individual banks themselves where they are weak or badly managed.

Under its "bills-only" policy, the Federal Reserve, in effect, abstained from any participation in debt management, whether for purposes of price-level stabilization or for any other purpose. I believe that debt management is probably too serviceable a tool of monetary policy to justify such abstention, although the same purpose could be served if the Treasury would, in the interest of monetary management, seek and accept the advice of the Federal Reserve with respect to the maturity and other terms of its issues, while the Federal Reserve confined its own operations on the debt holdings of the public to purchases and sales of bills only in the open market. In either case, the immediate objective would be that as far as practicable in the light of other considerations changes in the maturity and rate structure of the federal debt should be such as support instead of working against the monetary objectives of the Federal Reserve. The minimum of coordination of Treasury policy and Federal Reserve policy that can reasonably be demanded is that prior to any major issue the Treasury should invite the Federal Reserve to submit to it the monetary-management considerations which should play a part in Treasury decision-making.

I have little to say that is relevant to the issues dealt with in this paper with respect to the much-debated question as to whether selective controls of lending operations by banks or non-bank financial institutions should be used. From the point of view of monetary management alone, the case for their use rests on the belief that some important classes of loan operations have a wider amplitude of cyclical fluctuation than other classes, so that they constitute "strategic" sectors for control;

that the cyclical pattern of these fluctuations, if left uncontrolled, increases the difficulty of damping the cycle through indirect monetary control over banking operations in general; and that selective direct controls take hold more quickly and therefore have shorter lags in their effects than over-all indirect monetary controls. It is here that the issue of "economic freedom" is most widely raised, and I think most justifiably, in connection with discussion of the appropriate tools for monetary and credit control. The behavior of the stock market during the late 1920's, for which "mass mania" would not be too derogatory a label, suggests at least that there is something to be said against the proposition that the aggregate of atomistically motivated economic decisions of the public at large in a strategic sector should always be accepted by Congress, or by individuals acting in their political role as voters, or by a monetary authority, or by philosophers and economists, as valid collective or social decisions, and should therefore not be interfered with. This raises some questions of practice rather than of principle: If selective controls are to be sanctioned, should they be used as routine measures or only as stand-by power to be applied only in emergencies? Or if their purpose is to serve as a tool of monetary management, should only the decisions as to their mode of use be assigned to the monetary authority, or should it also operate and administer the controls? Presentation of the issues involved suffices for present purposes, and what I would recommend as the appropriate answers in any given situation I neither clearly foresee nor see much reason why anyone, including myself, should regard as a matter of consequence. But they would have to be discretionary decisions.

I am not attempting to write a monetary-management manual, and I am using the availability of a variety of alternative tools of monetary control only as providing illustrative material both for the obstacles which the necessity of choice between tools and of choice as to the combinations in kind and degree in which they are to be used presents to resort to a simple rule. It should suffice for present purposes, therefore, if I conclude my discussion of the problem always present to the Federal Reserve of making the proper choice between the tools which it is authorized to use by a glance at the problems presented by the availability as major instruments of monetary control of both open-market operations and changes in reserve requirements for member banks.

In the modern world at large a wide range of methods of changing reserve requirements in the interest of monetary management is employed or has been proposed. I have been wrongly charged with—or credited with—the invention and advocacy of one particular method: the application of reserve ratio requirements to the cash-to-assets ratio, with different minimum ratios applied for different categories of assets, thus facilitating "selective controls" of credit. Other methods which are used or have been proposed are: variable special deposits with central banks, on which interest is paid; minimum reserve ratios of cash to deposits which rise or fall automatically as the volume of deposits rises or falls; and minimum "liquidity" ratios, where cash and near-moneys are lumped together as reserve assets and compared with the volume of deposits. In the United States the minimum ratio required of cash against demand deposits is the sole important tool of monetary control falling within this class.

The only question I will discuss here is: What are the advantages in the availability to the Federal Reserve of the choice between the use of open-market operations and changes in reserve requirements as against its being restricted to the use of open-market operations?

If, as has happened in the past but is not relevant now and is unlikely to be relevant in the foreseeable future, the Federal Reserve at a time of inflationary pressure is not in possession of sufficient securities of an appropriate kind to conduct large-scale open-market selling operations, availability of a substitute method of reducing the cash holdings of the member banks would be essential. This need not be, however, the power to raise reserve requirements. One alternative would be for the Federal Reserve to borrow from the market or, what amounts to the same thing, to sell its own debentures.

A change in reserve requirements has an immediate impact on the entire Federal Reserve bank membership, whereas the impact of open-market operations is at first concentrated on the great financial centers and its spread through the economy as a whole may be slow. This would ordinarily be regarded as a point in favor of the use of changes in reserve requirements rather than of open-market operations as the instrument of control.

The incidence of the cost of restrictive control operations differs as between open-market operations and changes in reserve requirements. The former affect member and nonmember banks alike, other things being equal, whereas the latter put member banks at a competitive disadvantage as compared to non-member banks. Open-market sales reduce the revenues of the Federal Reserve Banks and purchases increase them, whereas changes in reserve requirements do not directly affect their income. Open-market sales affect the market status of federal securities for operations of corresponding scale more than a rise in minimum reserve requirements.

If at a time when restrictive action is indicated the member banks have surplus reserves, increases in reserve requirements will make it possible for the Federal Reserve to make the member banks illiquid without recourse to massive open-market sales.

Appraisals of the significance of these differences in the mode of operation of the two tools will differ from person to person, and perhaps from time to time, as circumstances change. From the point of view of the Federal Reserve, I have no doubt that it welcomes the availability of choice between the two tools, and that it can cite advantages arising from such availability which I have overlooked. The Federal Reserve claims that at the appropriate times recourse to changes in reserve-ratio requirements provides a more conspicuous indication to the banks and the public of Federal Reserve objectives or appraisal of the situation than would open-market operations. I am not sure, however, that this would be true if the open-market operations and the changes in reserve requirements were of corresponding dimensions, and that this judgment is not based on a misreading of past experience resulting from the fact that the Federal Reserve carries on its open-market operations in small doses, whereas its changes in reserve requirements are infrequent and greater in their scale. In any case, it seems to me that the Federal Reserve can indicate its intentions and its appraisal of an existing situation more clearly and less ambiguously if it uses ordinary language as its means of transmitting information to the public instead of symbolic acts whose significance will be variously interpreted even by experts—and perhaps also by itself.

With respect to the activities which have impacts on the monetary field of federal agencies other than Congress, the Federal Reserve, or the Treasury, the ideal situation from the single point of view of monetary management would be that the Federal Reserve should have some kind of veto power over operations of those agencies which go counter to its objectives. This is, however, impracticable, and the best that can be hoped for is that these other agencies should be instructed by the President or by Congress that as far as is consistent with the performance of the functions assigned to them they should endeavor to avoid acts which do not conform to Federal Reserve policy. Beyond this, the Federal Reserve must accept as part of the facts of life the activities of these agencies which make more difficult its attainment of its own objectives and must endeavor to offset these activities by appropriate measures of its own, in accordance with its best judgment. This also applies to the activities of Congress and the Treasury, although these can be of great enough dimensions to make impossible the full achievement of the Federal Reserve's goals.

I have argued that the nature of economic process, the plurality of goals, the plurality of authorities, the plurality of tools, all of these operate to make impracticable the conduct of monetary management in conformity with a "rule." Consideration of monetary management from the point of view of the possibility of reducing its operations to conformity to the requirements of a single rule has the merit, however, of forcing a re-examination of the validity of its objectives, of the possibility of concentrating authority, and of the inadvisability of extending indefinitely the range of tools used by the controlling agencies. This by-product of the advocacy of reducing monetary management to the application of a single rule can be of great service to the better understanding of how monetary problems can be best handled. But with respect to the issue as between a rule and a discretionary monetary authority, I must close as I began, but now in Aristotle's words rather than my own, substituting only "monetary policy" where Aristotle says "morality":

> Monetary policy lives on details, like all that is practicable and real. Its rules are like the rule of lead of the Lesbians which follows all the turns and contours. Of things which are indeterminate, the rule also needs to be indeterminate.

---

[1] I have recently presented my views on the logical flaws of some "libertarian" argument in "The Intellectual History of Laissez Faire," *Journal of Law and Economics*, 3:45-69 (1960), and in "Hayek on Freedom and Coercion," *Southern Economic Journal*, 27:230-236 (1961). I intend in the near future to subject to similar examination the arguments commonly used by the "interventionists" and "planners." I have no interest and see no profit, however, in attempting to reach a definite position with respect to the merits of the two positions in the general, abstracted from particular conjunctures of time, place, and circumstance, and my biases, insofar as I am aware of them, are perhaps equally strong against what seem to me extreme positions in either direction.

[2] *A Program for Monetary Stability* (New York: Fordham University Press, 1959), p. 98.

[3] *A Program for Monetary Stability*, p. 87.

[4] *A Program for Monetary Stability*, p. 51.

19. The Gold Standard: Myths and Realities
Michael David Bordo

Economists have criticized the gold standard for being both costly and inconsistent with economic stability. Just how true is the latter charge? In the essay that follows, Michael D. Bordo takes a close look at the actual historical record. He concludes that the historical gold standard succeeded in preserving long-run price stability, but at the cost of considerable short-run instability. —G.S., Ed.

****

Recently, there has been considerable interest in the United States' returning to some form of gold standard or at least restoring some role for gold in the U.S. monetary system. Proponents of a return to a gold standard argued that such an action would quickly restore price stability both by providing an effective brake on monetary expansion and by reducing inflationary expectations.[1] Indeed, Congress even established a commission to examine the role of gold in the U.S. monetary system.[2]

In considering the case for a return to some form of gold standard, three important questions must be answered. First, what type of gold standard should we return to? Second, and more fundamentally, what can and what cannot a gold standard do to maintain overall economic stability? An answer to this question would involve understanding both the theory of the gold standard and evidence on the actual performance of the economy under various forms of the gold standard in the past. Third, would returning to some form of a gold standard be a feasible option for the future?

In this paper, we attempt to provide answers to these questions. The first section presents a brief classification of types of gold standards (and other monetary standards). The second section summarizes the theory of the gold standard as a form of commodity money, as a national monetary standard, and as an international monetary standard. The third section discusses the operation of a managed gold standard—the system that has prevailed over much of the period since the Napoleonic Wars. The fourth section presents a brief chronology of the gold standard from 1821 to 1971. The fifth presents empirical evidence for the economies of the United States and the United Kingdom on the price and output stabilization properties of the classical gold standard compared to those of "managed fiduciary money." The sixth examines some of the issues connected with a possible return to gold. Finally, the seventh section presents a brief conclusion assessing the costs and benefits of the gold standard.

TYPES OF GOLD STANDARDS

We can discuss a number of variants of the gold standard in its long history. Under a gold standard, of whatever type, the monetary authority must maintain a fixed price of gold by purchase and sale.

That price must rule not only in transactions by the monetary authority, but also in market transactions in which private participants are free to engage.

The types of gold standard are:

1. A gold coin standard with 100 percent gold cover for nongold money and no central bank.

2. A gold coin standard with fractional reserves held by the government against its note issues and by commercial banks against their deposits, with or without a central bank, with convertibility for all holders of nongold money in gold coin.

3. A gold bullion standard with fractional reserves against the central bank's monetary base (currency plus bank reserves), with no gold coin circulation, and with convertibility for all holders of nongold money limited to large amounts.

4. A gold exchange standard with fractional reserves and with a central bank tied to a currency of a center country that has a gold-coin or gold-bullion standard.

5. The Bretton Woods dollar-gold exchange standard, with convertibility limited to official institution dollar assets "for the settlement of international balances or for other legitimate monetary purposes."[3]

The first type of gold standard existed only in premodern times; as we argue below, the classical gold standard that held sway before 1914 was a combination of types 2 to 4 and is frequently referred to as a managed gold standard.[4]

These various gold standards must be contrasted with the type of standard in use today: an inconvertible paper standard, with a central bank free to exercise discretion or else subject to a prescribed rule with respect to the quantity of money outstanding.[5]

THE THEORY OF THE GOLD STANDARD: THE STYLIZED FACTS

Economists from Cantillon to Keynes have formulated a theory of the gold standard with three dimensions: the gold standard as a commodity money standard, ensuring long-run price stability; the gold standard as a national monetary standard, regulating the quantity and growth of a nation's money supply; and the gold standard as an international monetary standard, ensuring the external value of a nation's currency.[6]

The Gold Standard as a Commodity Money Standard

The gold standard is a form of commodity money standard. Of the numerous commodities that served as money in world history, gold emerged as the most widely accepted. Gold has the desirable properties of money that have been stressed by early writers in economics. It is durable, easily recognizable, storable, portable, divisible, and easily standardized. Especially important, changes in the stock are limited, at least in the short run, by high costs of production, making it costly for governments to manipulate.[7] Because of these physical attributes, it emerged as one of the earliest forms of money.

Through the operation of the competitive market mechanism, a commodity money standard, regardless of the commodity involved, ensures a tendency toward long-run price stability.[8] Under any commodity money standard, the purchasing power of a unit of commodity money, or what it will buy in terms of all other goods and services, will always tend toward equality with its long-run cost of production.

The simplest example of a gold standard is a pure gold coin standard with gold coins serving as the only money. Under such a standard, government's role in the money system is restricted to certifying coins of a fixed weight in gold or, to put it another way, to maintaining a fixed price of its currency in terms of gold. Thus the government would be committed to purchasing gold from the public on demand at a fixed price and to converting it into gold coin. Similarly, the government would sell gold to the public at the fixed price.[9]

The supply of money and the prices of goods in terms of that money would be determined in the market by the demand for gold for monetary and nonmonetary uses and by the supply of gold, which would be governed by the opportunity cost of producing gold. The demand for gold for nonmonetary use would be governed by the relative price of gold and all other commodities. The demand for monetary gold would be governed by (1) total wealth available to hold in asset form, (2) the total amount of goods and services produced, (3) the average price of these goods and services, (4) the return on holding monetary gold relative to the return available on alternative assets, and (6) the tastes and preferences of holders of money.

In such a system, the money supply would vary automatically with the profitability of producing gold. A rapid increase in the output of gold due to gold discoveries or technological improvements in gold mining would raise the prices of all other goods in terms of gold, making them more profitable to produce than gold and thus ultimately leading to a reduction in gold output. Moreover, the initial reduction in the purchasing power of gold would lead to a shift in the demand for gold from monetary to nonmonetary use, thus reinforcing the output effects. Conversely, a decline in prices of goods and services due to technological improvement in the nongold sector would increase the profitability of gold production, encouraging increased gold output, and this would ultimately tend to return prices to their initial level. The initial increase in the purchasing power of gold would also lead to a shift in the demand for gold from nonmonetary to monetary use, thus reinforcing the output effects. This would ensure long-run price stability.

The Gold Standard as a National Monetary Standard

In a closed economy, the free convertibility of gold coin into bullion would ensure a limit to the money supply, since any divergence of the real price or purchasing power of gold from its fixed official value would lead to conversion of coin into bullion or vice versa and would also affect gold production.

The Gold Standard as an International Monetary Standard

The international gold standard is a mechanism to ensure uniformity of price level movements between countries and hence to constrain the money supply of any one country. Under an international gold standard, each country defines the monetary unit as a specific physical quantity of gold, fixing the value of all national monetary units to each other and thus establishing fixed exchange rates. The fixed exchange rate determined by the gold weight in each country is referred to as the par exchange rate. The costs of shipping, packing, and insuring gold set the gold points—the upper and lower limits to fluctuations around the par exchange rate.

Thus, for example, before World War I, the dollar was defined as 23.22 grains of fine gold and a pound sterling as 113.0011 grains of fine gold; hence the par exchange rate of 4.8166 was the multiple of the weight of gold in a pound sterling compared with the weight of gold in a dollar. This represented a fixed exchange rate because the gold weight of each currency was fixed or, equivalently, the price of gold per ounce was fixed.[10]

In addition, countries under the gold standard allow both unlimited convertibility of their currencies at the fixed price and the free export and import of gold.[11] Under the gold standard, in addition to serving as domestic currency, gold is the international medium of exchange, providing the means for setting imbalances in international payments. If the demand for and supply of a national currency do not balance, gold flows are activated. Thus, whenever the dollar price of a British pound at the official or par exchange rate of $4.86 deviated by more than 1 or 2 percent above or below par, it paid either to convert U.S. dollars into gold and transfer it abroad or else to convert British pounds into gold and transfer it here. If U.S. demand increased, for example, for cheaper British goods, this raised the dollar price of the pound. Once the dollar price of the pound reached $4.92, referred to as the U.S. gold export point, it paid to convert U.S. dollars into gold, ship the gold to England, and purchase pounds at $4.86. Conversely, at the U.S. gold import point of $4.83, it paid to convert pounds sterling into gold, ship the gold to the United States, and purchase dollars. Gold shipments in either direction then acted to restore the price of foreign exchange to parity.

Gold flows require internal adjustments under the gold standard. Thus, a deficit in the balance of payments is paid in gold; the outflow reduces the country's domestic money supply and ultimately its price level, hence enhancing the country's appeal as a source of goods and services to foreigners and reducing the domestic demand for foreign goods and services. The surplus country experiences an inflow of gold that raises its domestic money supply and ultimately its price level, hence diminishing that country's appeal as a source of goods and services to foreigners and increasing domestic demand for foreign goods and services. As a consequence of this automatic adjustment process, the duration and size of imbalances is self-limiting.

Under the gold standard, a fixed price of gold acts to constrain the ability of any one country to allow its price level to differ markedly from the price level in the rest of the gold standard world so that price increases in excess of the world average or price declines below the world average are reversed in response to movements in the country's monetary gold stock. The worldwide movement might be deflationary, as it was from 1879 to 1896, or inflationary, as it was from 1896 to 1913. Adherence to the gold standard imposes the requirement that each country accept the world price level.

By the same token, the gold standard fixed exchange rate system makes individual countries vulnerable to disturbances in economic activity that are transmitted from one country to another. A country can ultimately protect itself from a foreign disturbance or from deflationary or inflationary effects on its domestic prices only by cutting the gold link.

THE MANAGED GOLD STANDARD

The simple theory of the gold standard just described was seldom followed in practice. The pure gold coin standard had two features that caused most countries to modify its operation: Very high resource costs were required to maintain a full commodity money standard, and strict adherence to the "iron discipline" of the gold standard required each country to subsume its internal balance (domestic price and real output stability) to its external balance (balance of payments equilibrium). Thus, if a country was running a balance of payments deficit, the "rules of the game" required it to deflate the economy until "purchasing power parity" was restored at the par exchange rate. Such deflation was often accompanied by a reduction in real output and employment. Consequently, a meaningful discussion of how the gold standard actually operated requires a discussion of the ways in which nations modified the gold standard to economize on gold and to shield domestic economic activity from external disturbances.

The Use of Fiduciary Money

As mentioned above, very high resource costs are required to maintain a full commodity money standard. Discovering, mining, and minting gold are extremely costly activities.[12] Consequently, as nations developed, they evolved substitutes for pure commodity money. These substitutes encompassed both government-provided paper money, referred to as fiat money, and privately produced fiduciary money—bank notes and bank deposits. As long as governments maintained a fixed ratio of their notes to gold, and commercial banks kept a fixed ratio of their liabilities to gold (or to government notes and gold), a gold standard could still be maintained. This type of standard prevailed throughout the world before World War I.

One aspect of this "mixed" gold standard system was that one unit of a country's gold reserves could support a number of units of domestic money; for example, the U.S. ratio of money to the monetary gold stock was 8.5 in the 1880-1913 period. This meant that gold flows had powerful effects, in the short run, on the domestic money supply, spending, and prices.[13]

International Capital Flows

In the pre-World War I gold standard era, most international trade was financed by credit—the issuing of short-term claims in the London money market.[14] In addition, economic projects in the less developed economies were generally financed by long-term loans from investors in England, France, and other advanced countries.[15] The influence of these capital flows significantly reduced the burden of gold flows in the adjustment mechanism.

Thus, for example, if a gold discovery raised the domestic quantity of money, interest rates would tend to decline in the short-run, inducing investors to shift short-term capital to foreign money markets. The size of the change in export prices relative to import prices that would otherwise have occurred would be reduced by the resulting gold outflow. Also, to the extent that short-term capital substituted for gold as an international reserve asset and domestic financial intermediaries held balances with correspondents abroad, smaller gold flows would be required to settle international imbalances of payments.

Finally, long-term capital flows enabled developing countries to borrow real resources from developed countries by running a persistent excess of imports of goods and services over exports of goods and services without entailing gold flows.

The Role of Central Banks in the Gold Standard

Under a strict gold standard, there is no need for a central bank. All that is required is for some governmental authority to maintain the fixed domestic currency price of gold by buying and selling gold freely. Indeed, many countries on the gold standard prior to World War I (such as the United States and Canada) did not have central banks. Most European countries, on the other hand, have had central banks that predated the gold standard. These institutions, in most cases, evolved from large commercial banks serving as bankers to the government (for example, the Bank of England was founded in 1697) to institutions serving as lenders of last resort to the banking community.

Under the classical gold standard, central banks were supposed to follow the rules of the game—to speed up the adjustment of the domestic money supply and price level to external gold flows. Whenever a country was faced with a balance of payments deficit and the central bank saw its gold reserves declining, it would raise its discount rate. By causing other interest rates to rise, the rise in the discount rate was supposed to produce a reduction in holdings of inventories and a curtailment of other investment expenditure. The reduction in investment expenditure would then lead to a reduction in overall domestic spending and a fall in the price level. At the same time, the rise in bank rates would stem any short-term capital outflow and attract short-term funds from abroad.

For most countries on the pre-World War I gold standard, with the possible exception of Great Britain, there is evidence that interest rates were never allowed to rise enough to contract the domestic price level—in other words, that they did not follow the rules.[16] Also, many countries frequently followed policies of sterilization of gold flows—of attempting to neutralize the effects of gold flows on the domestic money supply by open-market purchase or sales of domestic securities.[17]

Reserve Currencies and the Role of Sterling

Many countries under the pre-World War I gold standard held their international reserves in the form of gold and in the currencies of several major countries—key currencies.[18] The center of the international payments mechanism was Britain, with the Bank of England maintaining its international reserves primarily in gold. Most other countries kept reserves in the form of gold and sterling assets. Two other major European capitals also served as reserve centers in the period between 1900 and 1914: Paris and Berlin, each of which held reserves in gold, sterling, and each of the other country's currency, while a number of smaller European countries held reserves in the form of francs and marks. Thus, by 1914, for many countries the gold standard was a gold exchange standard.

In addition to the use of other currencies as reserve assets, an elaborate network of short-term financial arrangements developed between private financial institutions centered in the London money market. This extensive network of reserve currencies and short-term international finance had two important results. First, the Bank of England could act as manager of the world's gold standard system without having to hold excessive gold reserves.[19] By altering its bank rate, the Bank of England produced major repercussions around the world.[20]

Second, much of the balance of payments adjustment mechanism before World War I did not require actual gold flows. Instead, the adjustment consisted primarily of transfers of sterling and other currency balances in the London, Paris, Berlin, and New York money markets.[21] In addition, short-term capital flows accommodated the balance of payments adjustment mechanism in this period.[22] Indeed, the pre-World War I gold standard has often been described as a sterling standard.[23]

In sum, the gold standard that emerged before World War I was very different from the pure gold coin standard outlined earlier. Unlike the pure gold coin standard, countries economized on the use of gold both in their domestic money supplies and as a means of settling international payments imbalances. In addition, to avoid the iron discipline of the gold standard, central banks in some countries did not follow the rules of the game, and some countries even abandoned the gold standard periodically.[24] The final modification of the pure gold standard was the key role the Bank of England played as manager of the system. The result was a "managed gold standard." Indeed, most of the characteristics of this managed standard were carried forward to the post–World War I gold exchange standard.

CHRONOLOGY OF THE GOLD STANDARD, 1821-1971

This section briefly sketches the chronology of the gold standard from the end of the Napoleonic Wars to the collapse of Bretton Woods.

The Classical Gold Standard, 1821-1914

In the eighteenth century, England and most countries were on a bimetallic standard based primarily on silver.[25] When Great Britain restored specie payments in 1821 after the inflation episode of Napoleonic Wars, the gold standard was restored. From 1821 to 1880, the gold standard steadily expanded as more and more countries ceased using silver.[26] By 1880, the majority of countries in the world were on some form of a gold standard.

The period from 1880 to 1914, known as the heyday of the gold standard, was a remarkable period in world economic history. It was characterized by rapid economic growth, free flow of labor and capital across political borders, virtually free trade, and, in general, world peace. These external conditions, coupled with the elaborate financial network centered in London and the role of the Bank of England as manager of the system, are believed to be the sine qua non of the effective operation of the gold standard.[27]

The Gold Exchange Standard, 1925-1931

The gold standard broke down during World War I,[28] was succeeded by a period of managed fiduciary money, and then was briefly reinstated from 1925 to 1931 as the gold exchange standard. Under the gold exchange standard, the United States and Great Britain held reserves only in gold, whereas other countries could hold both gold and dollars or pounds as reserves. In addition, most countries engaged in active sterilization policies to protect their domestic money supplies from gold flows.

Following Britain's departure from gold in the face of massive gold and capital flows, the gold exchange standard broke down in 1931 and was again succeeded by managed fiduciary money. The reasons usually cited for the failure of the gold exchange standard include (1) the general unwillingness of countries to subsume internal economic conditions to the external discipline of the gold standard and to frequently sterilize gold flows; (2) an imbalance in the world's distribution of gold caused by Britain's decision to return to gold at an overvalued exchange rate, which led to a chronic gold outflow, France's decision to return to gold at an undervalued exchange rate, which led to persistent gold inflows, and the frequent sterilization of gold inflows by the Federal Reserve System; (3) the inability of London and the unwillingness of New York to act as manager of the system; and (4) German reparations, which disrupted the international payments mechanism.[29]

The Bretton Woods System, 1946-1971

The Bretton Woods system was an attempt to return to a modified gold standard using the U.S. dollar as the world's key reserve currency. All countries other than the sterling bloc settled their international balances in dollars. The United States maintained the fixed price of gold at $35 per ounce, maintained substantial gold reserves, and settled external accounts with gold bullion payments and receipts.

After World War II, persistent U.S. balance of payments deficits helped finance the recovery of world trade from depression and war. However, the steady growth in the use of U.S. dollars as international reserves and persistent U.S. balance of payments deficits steadily reduced U.S. gold reserves and the gold reserve ratio, reducing public confidence in the ability of the U.S. to redeem its currency in gold.[30] This confidence problem, coupled with many nations' aversion to paying both seigniorage and an "inflation tax" to the United States after 1965, led ultimately to the breakdown of the Bretton Woods system in 1971. The U.S. decision in 1971 to stop pegging the price of gold represented the final demise of the gold standard.

THE RECORD OF THE GOLD STANDARD

This section briefly examines some evidence for the United Kingdom and the United States over the period 1800-1979 on the stability of the price level and of real output under both gold and managed fiduciary money standards.[31] Figures 8-1 and 8-2 portray the behavior of the wholesale price index from 1800 to 1979 for both countries.

From 1797 to 1821, during and immediately following the Napoleonic Wars, the United Kingdom was on a fiat (or paper) standard; it officially joined the gold standard in 1821 and maintained a fixed price of gold until 1914. There is very little difference in the U.K. price level between the first year of the gold standard and the last, but over the whole period there was a very slight downward trend in prices averaging 0.4 percent per year. Within that approximate one hundred-year span, however, periods of declining price levels alter-

Figure 8-1. Wholesale Price Index, United Kingdom, 1800-1979.

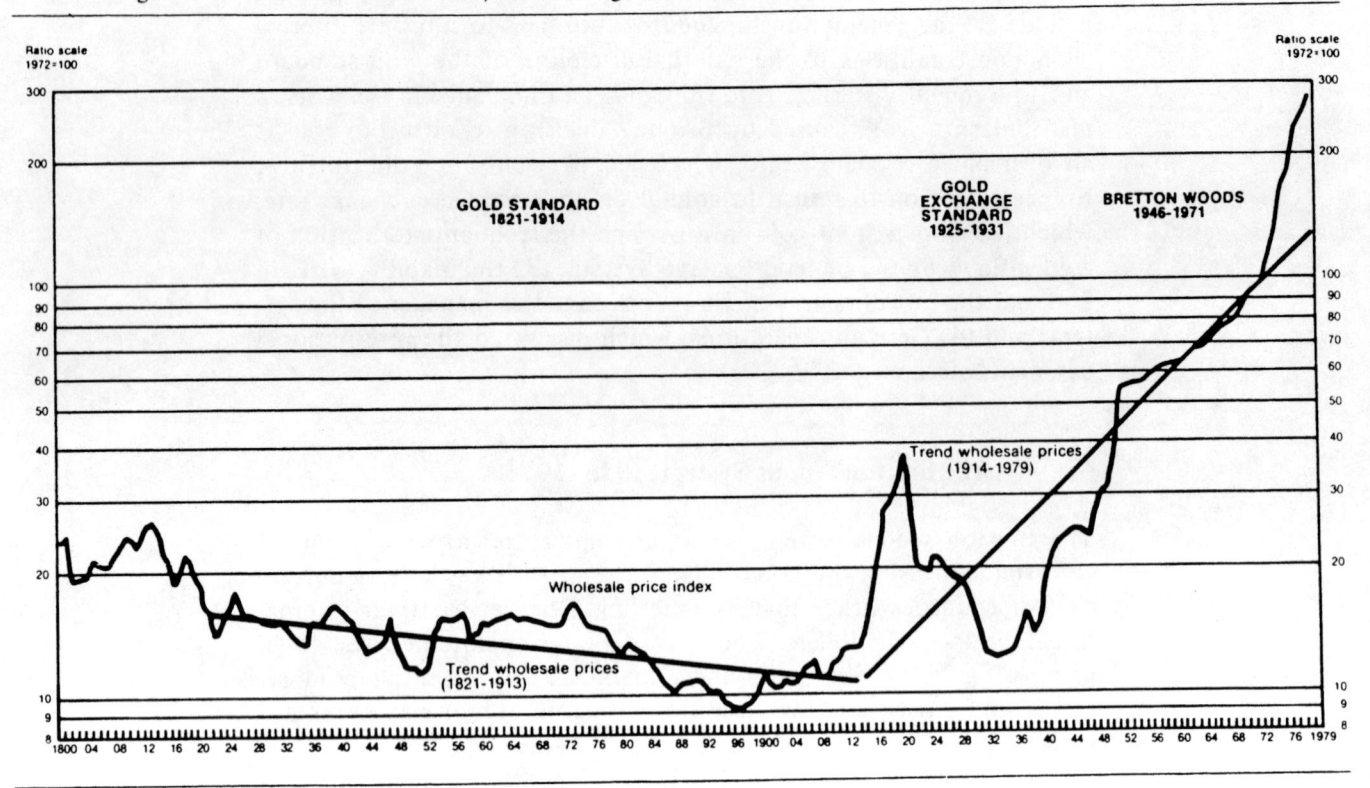

Figure 8-2. Wholesale Price Index, United States, 1800-1979.

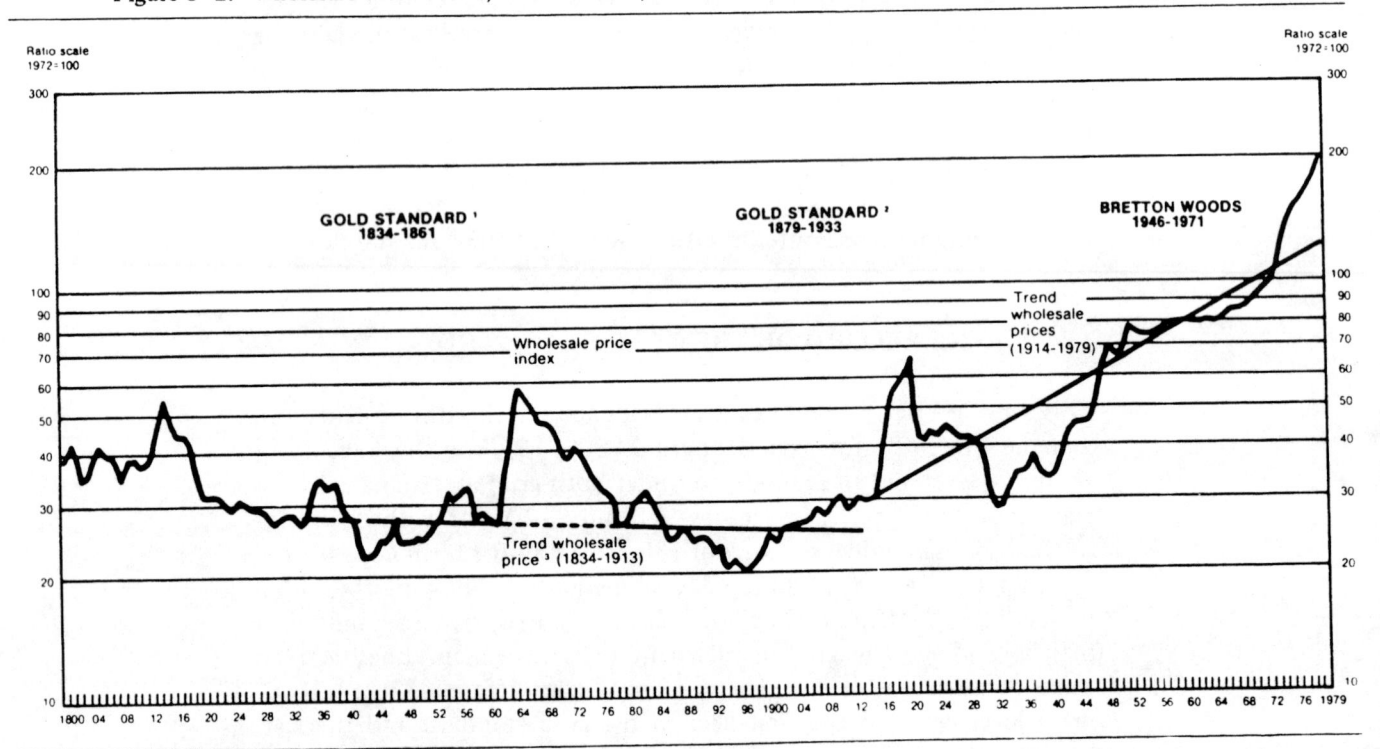

1. Excludes 1838-1843 when spacie payments were suspended.
2. United States imposes gold export embargo from September 1917 to June 1919.
3. Broken line indicates years excluded in computing trend.

Note: Prepared by Federal Reserve Bank of St. Louis.

nated with periods of rising price levels—a pattern consistent with the commodity theory of money. Prices fell until the mid-1840s, reflecting the pressure of rising real incomes on the limited stock of gold. Following the California and Australian gold discoveries of the late 1840s and early 1850s, prices turned around and kept rising until the late 1860s. This was followed by a twenty-five-year period of declining prices, again reflecting both rising real income and an expanding number of countries on the gold standard. This deflation ended after technical advances in gold processing and major gold discoveries in the late 1880s and 1890s increased world gold supplies.

The United States followed a similar pattern to the United Kingdom, experiencing a very slight downward trend in the price level averaging 0.14 percent per year from 1834 to 1913. The country adopted the gold standard in 1834 (it had been on silver for the preceding thirty-five years) and remained on it at the same price of gold until World War I, with the noted exception of the greenback episode from 1861 to 1878.[32] During that period, the country abandoned the gold standard, and prices increased rapidly until 1866. To restore convertibility to gold, prices had to fall sufficiently to restore the prewar purchasing power parity. This occurred in the rapid deflation of 1869 to 1879.

The period since World War I has not been characterized by price stability except for the 1920s, under the gold exchange standard, and the 1950s and early 1960s, under the Bretton Woods system. Indeed, since the end of the gold standard, price levels in both countries have on average been rising. The U.K. price level increased at an average annual rate of 3.81 percent form 1914 to 1979, whereas the U.S. price level increased by an average of 2.2 percent. Figures 8-3 and 8-4 present further evidence of the operation of a commodity money standard and of the long-run price stability characteristic of the gold standard. Figure 8-3 compares the purchasing power of gold in the world (measured by the ratio of an index of the price of gold to the wholesale price index for the United Kingdom) in relation to trend, to the world monetary gold stock in relation to trend, over the period 1821–1914.[33] The index of the purchasing power of gold presented here varies inversely with the wholesale price index presented in Figure 8-1. This inverse association between the two series reflects the fixed price of gold over this period.[34] The trends of both series were rising over the whole period. The upward trend in the purchasing power of gold series reflects a more rapid growth of world real output and, hence, of the demand for monetary gold than could be accommodated by growth in the world's monetary gold stock.

In comparing deviations from trend in the purchasing power of gold to deviations from trend in the world monetary gold stock, one would expect the latter to produce corresponding changes in the price level and, for a given nominal price of gold, to affect inversely the purchasing power of gold. A comparison of deviations from trend of both series reveals this negative association, with deviations from trend in the world monetary gold stock leading deviations from trend in the purchasing power of gold.[35]

Figure 8-3. Monetary Gold Stock and Purchasing Power of Gold Index, World, 1821-1914.

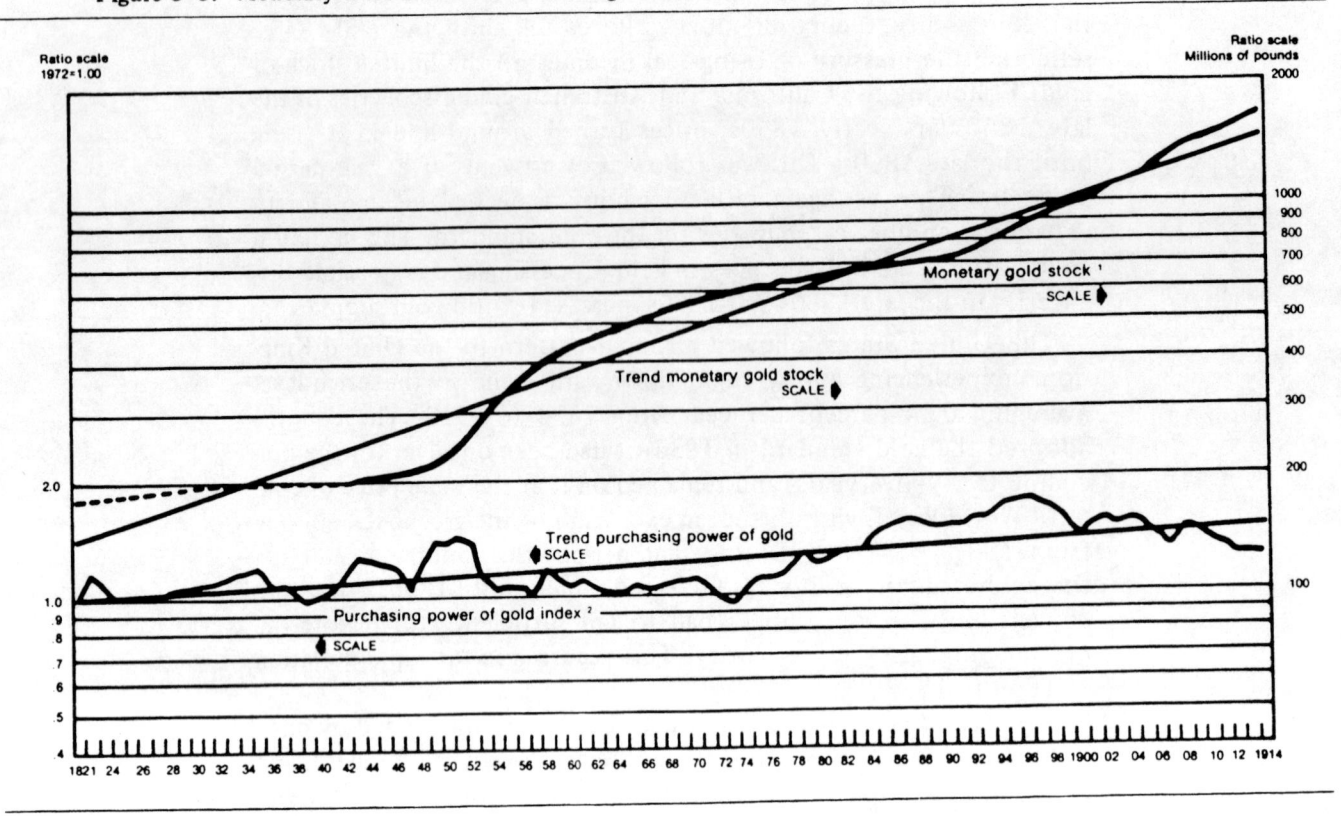

1. Broken line indicates interpolated data.
2. Measured by the ratio of an index of the price of gold to the wholesale price index for the United Kingdom.

Figure 8-4. Monetary Gold Stock and Purchasing Power of Gold Index, United States, 1879-1914.

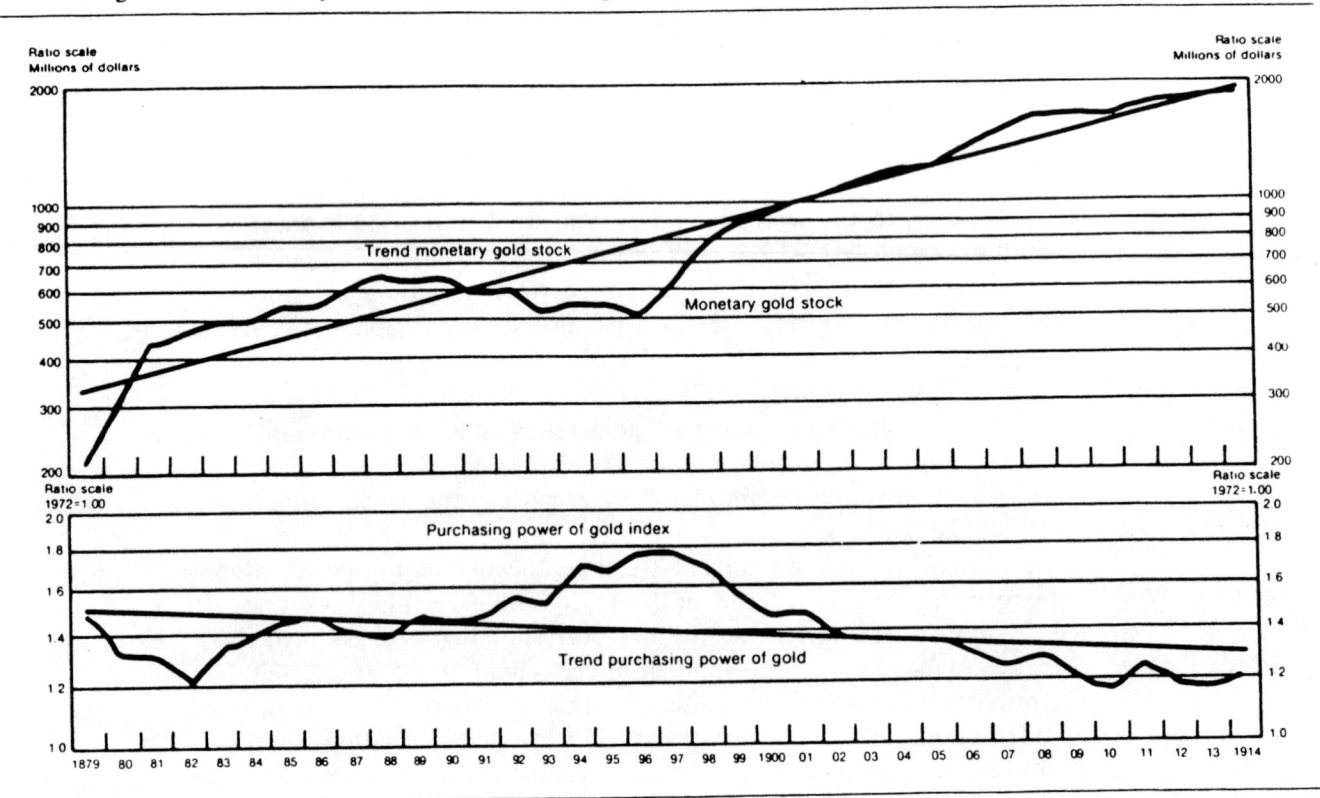

Note: Prepared by Federal Reserve Bank of St. Louis.

In addition, according to the operations of a commodity money standard, movements in the purchasing power of gold would be expected to precede movements in the monetary gold stock, since a rising purchasing power of gold would induce both a shift from nonmonetary to monetary uses of gold and increased gold production. Such a positive association between deviations from trend of the two series is observed.[36] Thus, during the 1830s and 1840s the purchasing power of gold largely exceeded its long-run trend. This was followed by a rapid increase in the world monetary gold stock after 1848 as the output of the new California and Australian mines was added to the existing world's stock. Subsequently, the purchasing power of gold declined from its peak above trend in the mid-1850s and was succeeded by a marked deceleration in the monetary gold stock after 1860. The same pattern arises when comparing the rise in the purchasing power of gold in the 1870s and 1880s with the subsequent increase in the monetary gold stock in the mid-1890s.

Table 8-4 compares the United States' purchasing power of gold with the U.S. monetary gold stock over the 1879 to 1914 gold standard period.[37] In this period the trends of the two series moved in opposite directions. The declining trend in the purchasing power of gold series reflects the more rapid growth in the U.S. monetary gold stock than in real output over the whole period: This rapid growth resulted from (1) the accumulation of monetary gold from the rest of the world early in the period after the resumption of specie payments and (2) the effects of gold discoveries in the 1890s.

As in Figure 8-3, Figure 8-4 shows a negative association between concurrent deviations from trend in the monetary gold stock and in the purchasing power of gold.[38] Also as in Figure 8-3, deviations from trend in the purchasing power of gold preceded deviations from trend in the monetary gold stock.[39] Thus declines in the purchasing power of gold from 1879 to 1882 preceded declines in the monetary gold stock below trend in the late 1880s and early 1890s, whereas rises in the purchasing power of gold after 1882 can be associated with a rising monetary gold stock after 1896. Finally, the declining purchasing power of gold in the mid-1890s can be associated with the declining growth of the monetary gold stock after 1903.

One important implication of the tendency for price levels to revert to a long-run stable value under the gold standard is that it ensured a measure of predictability with respect to the value of money: Though prices would rise or fall for a few years, inflation or deflation would not persist.[40] Such belief in long-run price stability would encourage economic agents to engage in contracts with the expectation that, should prices of commodities or factor services change, the change would reflect real forces rather than changes in the value of money.

Belief in long-term price level stability has apparently disappeared in recent years, since people now realize that the long-run constraint of the gold standard has vanished.[41] As a consequence, it has become more difficult for people to distinguish between changes in relative prices and changes in the price level. Such absolute vs. relative price confusion has increased the possibility of major economic losses, since people fail to respond to market signals.[42]

Finally, we present evidence on real output stability for the United Kingdom and the United States. It is frequently argued that under the gold standard, when countries had to subordinate internal balance considerations to the gold standard's discipline, real output would be less stable than under a regime of managed fiduciary money. Figures 8-5 and 8-6 show the deviations of real per capita income from its long-run trend over the period 1870-1979.

For the United Kingdom, Figure 8-5 shows both a single trend line for the 1870-1979 period as a whole and separate trend lines for each of the pre- and post-World War I subperiods. The U.K. data were split into two subperiods because the trend line for the entire period puts real output after 1919 virtually always below trend. World War I drastically reduced the level of real per capita income and was followed by a lengthy period of recovery. This suggests that the two periods should be handled separately. Examining the deviations from trend (using the subperiod trends) suggests that real per capita income was less variable in the pre-World War I period than subsequently. The mean absolute value of the percentage deviations of real per capita income from trend was 2.14 percent from 1870 to 1913 and 3.75 percent from 1919 to 1979 (excluding 1939-45).

As in the U.K. case, U.S. real per capita income was more stable under the gold standard from 1879 to 1913 than during the entire post-World War I period. The mean absolute values of the percentage deviations of real per capita income from trend were 6.64 percent from 1879 to 1913 and 8.51 percent from 1919 to 1979 (excluding 1941-45).

Moreover, unemployment was on average lower in the pre-1914 period in both countries than in the post-World War I period. For the United Kingdom, the average unemployment rate over the 1888-1913 period was 4.30 percent, whereas over the period 1919-79 (excluding 1939-45) it was 6.52 percent. For the United States, average unemployment rates by subperiod were 6.78 percent from 1890 to 1913 and 7.46 percent from 1919 to 1979 (excluding 1941-45).

Thus, the evidence for the two countries suggests that the managed fiduciary money system superseding the gold standard generally has been associated with less real economic stability.

One dominant feature of the classical gold standard period was long-run price stability. This contrasts favorably with the behavior of the price level under the managed fiduciary money standard for much of the period since World War I. Also, though real output varied considerably from year to year under the gold standard, it did not vary discernibly more than it has in the entire period since World War I.[43]

One problem with comparing the pre-World War I gold standard with the managed fiduciary money standard over the entire post-World War I period is that the latter period includes the turbulent interwar years, and including such a period may bias the case against managed fiduciary money. To account for this, Table 8-1 presents a

Figure 8-5. Real Per Capita Income, United Kingdom, 1870-1979.

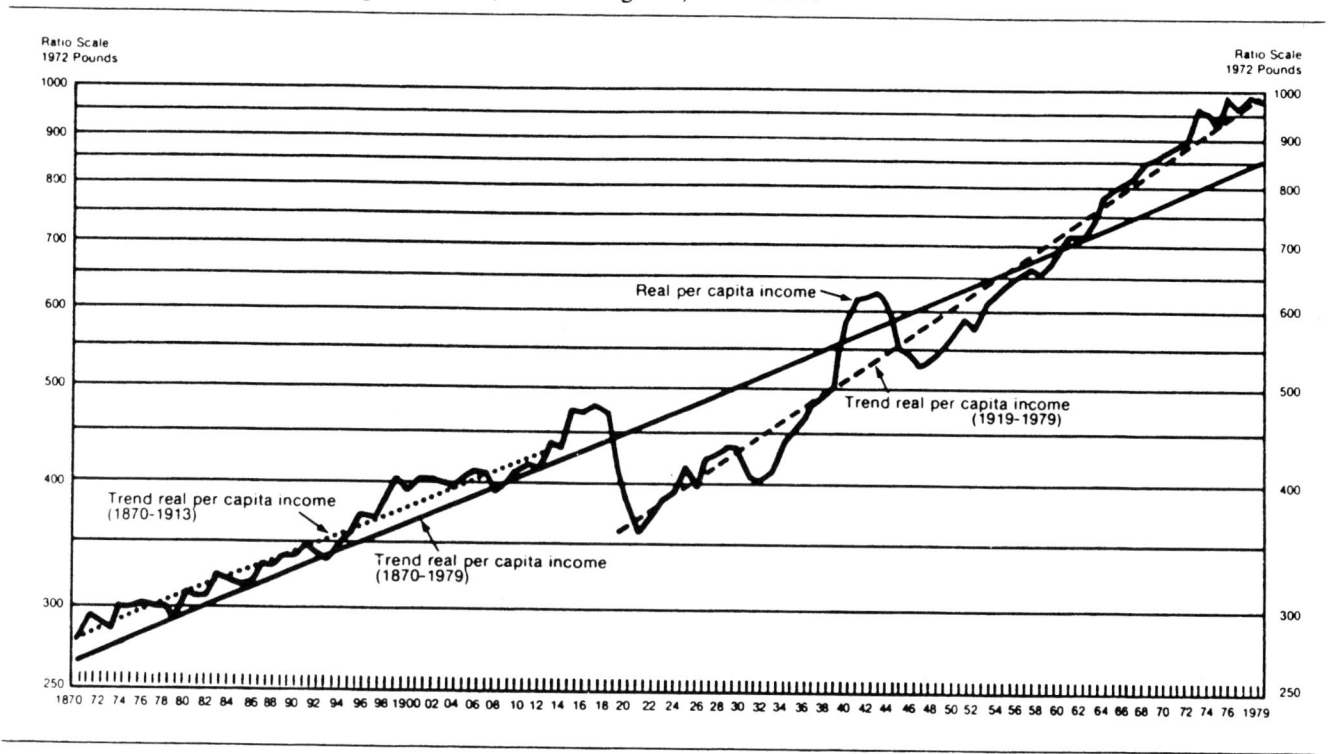

Figure 8-6. Real Per Capita Income, United States, 1870-1979.

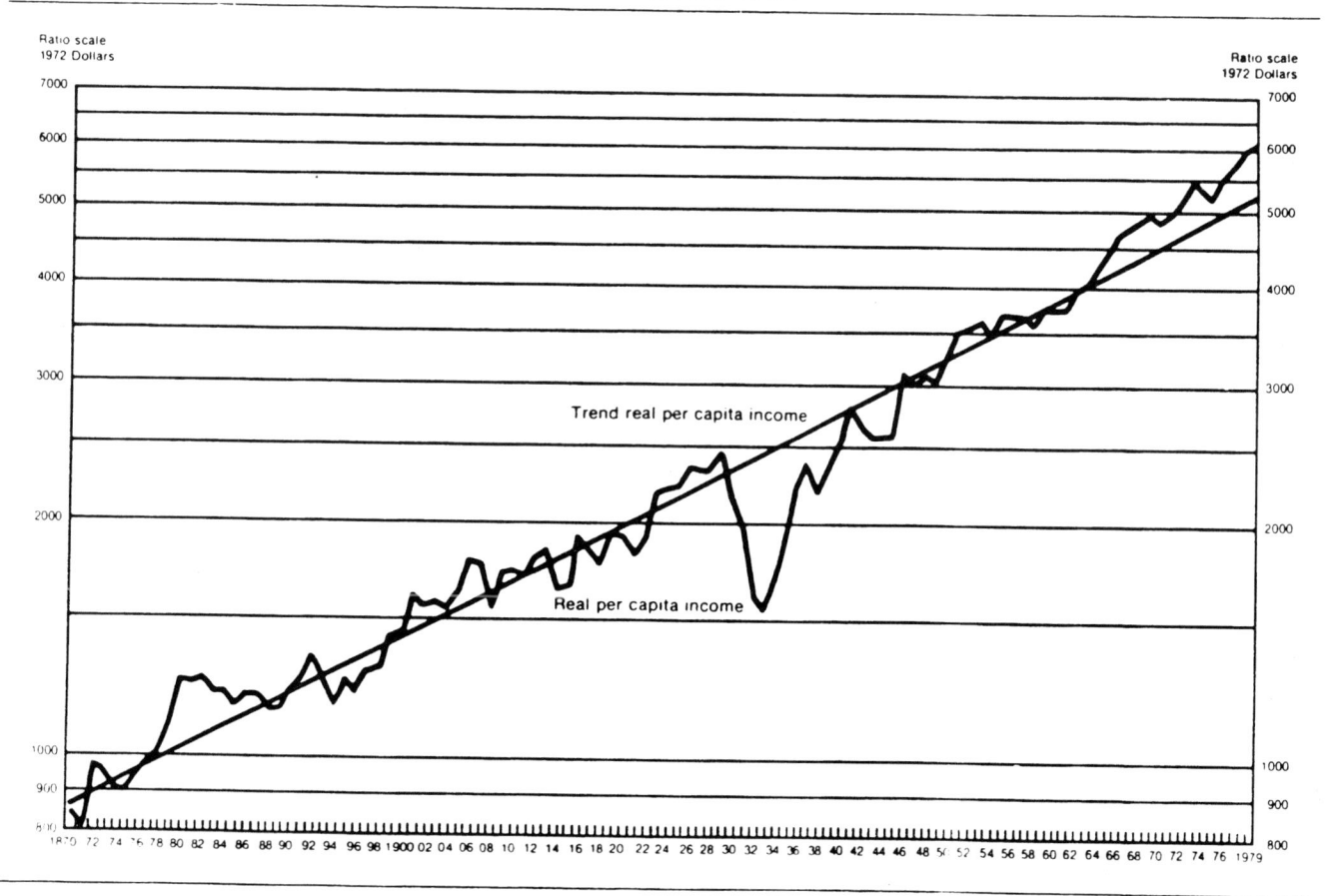

Note: Prepared by Federal Reserve Bank of St. Louis.

Table 8-1. A Comparison of Three Major Periods: the Gold Standard, the Interwar Period, and the Post-World War II Period.

	Gold Standard[a]		Interwar Period		Post-World War II	
	U.K.	U.S.	U.K.	U.S.	U.K.	U.S.
	1870-1913 (1821-1913)	1879-1913 (1834-1913)	1919-39	1919-41	1946-79	1946-79
1. The average annual percentage change in the price level	-0.7 (-0.4)	0.1 (-0.1)	-4.6	-2.5	5.6	2.8
2. The coefficient of variation of annual percentage changes in the price level (ratio)	-14.9 (-16.3)	17.0 (6.5)	-3.8	-5.2	1.2	1.3
3. The coefficient of variation of annual percentage changes in real per capita income (ratio)	2.5	3.5	4.9	5.5	1.4	1.8
4. The average percentage level of unemployment	4.3[b]	6.8[c]	13.3	11.3	2.5	5.0
5. The average annual percentage change in the money supply	1.5	6.1	0.9	1.5	5.9	5.7
6. The coefficient of variation of annual percentage changes in the money supply (ratio)	1.6	0.8	3.6	2.4	1.0	0.5

a. Data for the longer periods were available only for the price level.
b. 1888-1913.
c. 1890-1913.

Notes by row: Rows 1 and 5 were calculated as the regression coefficient of a regression of the log of the variable on a time trend. Rows 2, 3, and 6 were calculated as the ratio of the standard deviation of annual percentage changes in the variable to its means.

Sources: See Michael D. Bordo, "The Classical Gold Standard: Some Lessons for Today," *Federal Reserve Bank of St. Louis Review* 62, no. 5 (May 1981): Appendix pp. 16-17.

comparison for both countries of several measures of performance of the price level, real output, and money growth for three time periods: the pre-World War I gold standard, the interwar period, and the post-World War II period.[44]

First, evidence is presented in row 1 on long-run price level stability measured by the average annual rate of change in the price level over the period. This shows that the interwar period in both countries was characterized by substantial deflation, whereas the post-World War II period has been characterized by inflation. This performance is in marked contrast to the near price stability of the gold standard period. However, price variability, measured in row 2 by the coefficient of variation of percentage year-to-year changes in the price level, reveals a slightly different picture. Prices were more variable under the gold standard than during both post-gold standard periods, with the least variability occurring in the post-World War II period.

Second, evidence is presented in row 3 on real output stability measured by the coefficient of variation of year-to-year percentage changes in real per capita output. Real output was considerably less stable in both countries in the interwar period than it was either under the gold standard or in the post-World War II period, with the latter period having the best record. In addition, the evidence on average unemployment rates presented in row 4 agrees with the evidence on real output stability: Unemployment was by far the highest in the interwar period,[45] and by far the lowest in the post-World War II period in both countries.

Finally, comparisons are made across periods in the average annual rate of monetary growth in row 6, and in the variability in monetary growth (measured by the coefficient of variation of percentage year-to-year changes in the money supply) in row 7. According to monetary theory, a reduction in monetary growth below the long-run trend of real output growth will produce deflation, whereas a rise in monetary growth above the long-run trend of real output growth will lead to inflation. In the transition between different rates of monetary growth, both the levels and growth rates of real output will deviate considerably from long-run trends. Thus, monetary variability will lead to real output variability.[46]

The rate of monetary growth was lower in both countries in the interwar period than in both the post-World War II and the gold standard periods. In the case of the United Kingdom, the post-World War II period exhibits more rapid monetary growth than under the gold standard, whereas for the United States, monetary growth rates are very similar in both the post-war and gold standard periods. Finally, monetary growth was more variable in both countries in the interwar period than in the other two periods, with the post-World War II period displaying the least variability in monetary growth.

The poor economic performance of the interwar period compared to either the preceding gold standard period or the post-World War II period has been attributed to the failure of monetary policy. Indeed, the Bank of England's attempt to restore convertibility to gold at the prewar parity has often been blamed for British deflation and unemployment in the 1920s.[47] The failure of the Federal Reserve System to prevent the drastic decline in the U.S. money supply from 1929 to 1933 has likewise been blamed for the severity of the Great Depression in the United States.[48] One could argue that the greatly improved performance of monetary policy and the economic stability in the two countries in the post-World War II period reflects learning from past mistakes. This suggests that in weighing the historical evidence in favor of a return to the gold standard, a meaningful comparison should be made between the post-World War II period and the gold standard. In such a comparison, the gold standard did provide greater *long-run* price stability, but at the expense of both short-run real output and short-run price stability. The higher rates of inflation, lower variability of real output, and lower unemployment in the two countries in the recent period compared to the preceding periods probably reflects a shift of policy preferences away from the goal of long-run price stability and toward that of full employment. Indeed, the strong commitment to full employment in both countries probably explains the worsening of inflation in the postwar period.[49]

A RETURN TO THE GOLD STANDARD: SOME UNRESOLVED ISSUES

Before seriously considering a return to a gold standard, we must resolve a number of important issues.

The Type of Gold Standard

The issue of the type of gold standard raises a number of questions. First, does the United States want a national or an international standard? It is conceivable for the United States to return unilaterally to a gold standard, that is, to determine its domestic money supply by a gold standard rule of a fixed price of gold. This would be equivalent to having a flexible exchange rate with all countries not on the gold standard. Indeed, a historical precedent for such a standard was the silver standard maintained by China until 1935 in a world where most countries were on a gold standard. However, like China in the period 1933-35, the United States would run the risk of a major external disturbance, which could produce an unwanted inflation or deflation equivalent to the disturbance China suffered following the U.S. silver purchase policy of 1933.[50] However, if other industrialized countries returned to gold along with the United States, then the effect of random disturbances in the gold market would be dissipated across all countries, reducing its impact on any one country.

Thus, ultimately we would want an international gold standard, which would require an international agreement and an amendment to the IMF rules.[51] However, for an international gold standard to be reestablished, the first requirement would be the removal of the forces that caused it to break down. Disparate inflation rates among the industrialized countries led to the collapse of the Bretton Woods system. The gold standard compels countries adhering to it to adjust their price levels to the world level through the operation of the fixed exchange rate. The unwillingness of low inflation countries to subordinate their domestic monetary policies to the requirements of the fixed exchange rate system led to the breakdown of the Bretton Woods arrangement. This means that before the restoration of an international gold standard could be seriously contemplated, the disparity among rates of inflation would need to be reduced, if not eliminated.

Second, what type of gold standard is wanted? A gold coin standard with free convertibility of fiduciary money? A gold bullion standard with free export and import of gold but without a gold coinage? A return to Bretton Woods? As discussed above, all these options in the past led to serious difficulties and were ultimately abandoned. However, this is not to say that feasible arrangements are impossible.

Restoring a Gold Standard

Holding in abeyance the issues just raised, two key issues remain: choosing the right price and determining whether there is sufficient gold to maintain long-run price stability.

Choosing the Right Price. In the past, when the United States and other countries decided to return to a gold standard, they returned to a standard that still existed, and they invariably attempted to restore payments at the old price.[52] However there is no comparable old price today. The last official price of an ounce of gold, $42.23, is so out of line with current market prices that it provides no guidance. The risk involved in choosing the wrong price is considerable. If the price were set too high, it would produce a massive gold inflow and inflation; if too low, a massive gold outflow and deflation.

Since 1968, the price of gold has been determined in the free market.[53] Hence, a solution to the question of the right price may lie in isolating the determinants of supply and demand for gold. The total supply of gold consists of gold production in market economies, the flow from centrally planned economies, official sales (net), jewelry sales by developing countries, and dishoarding of private bullion holdings. The total demand for gold consists of two components: industrial demand (the fabrication demand for gold for jewelry, electronics, and dentistry), and investment or asset demand (the holding of gold in portfolios as a hedge against both inflation and uncertainty).

Table 8-2 displays the components of the supply and demand for gold as well as the behavior of the price of gold and the real price of gold from 1968 to 1980. On the supply side, production in market economies, representing the largest component of total supply, declined steadily throughout the period, whereas both the flow from centrally planned economies and net official sales varied considerably over the period. The flow from centrally planned economies does not seem to be related to either the nominal or the real price of gold over the period, whereas official sales increased with rising gold prices in the 1976-79 period.

On the demand side, both components are highly variable, with asset demand the more variable component. Also, as theory would predict, industrial demand varied inversely with movements in the real price, whereas asset demand varied directly.[54]

Finally, both nominal and real price series are dominated by two major increases, the first running from 1972 to 1975 and the second from 1977 to 1980, both likely reflecting expectations of a rise in world inflation.

The price of gold at any given moment is determined by total demand and supply; however, it is important in the short run to distinguish between the influence of stocks and flows. It has been argued that in the short run, conditions in the stock (asset) market prevail, since within short periods the effects of net additions to the gold stock on the total stock are small. Thus, the key determinant of price would be factors shifting the asset demand for gold. As the time period lengthens, flow factors become more important until in the long run the key determinants of price would be the independent variables in the flow demand and supply functions.[55]

Accounting first for the determinants of the flow demand for gold, economic theory suggests that the industrial demand for gold would be a function primarily of the real price of gold, world real income, and the real price of close substitutes. In accordance with theory, recent studies have found the own price elasticity to be negative and close to one, with the real income elasticity greater than one.[56]

On the supply side, gold production in market economies should

Table 8-2. Fundamentals of the World Gold Market, 1968-1980.

Year	Industrial Demand[a]	Asset Demand	Total Demand	World Production (in market economies)	Net Sales From Stocks	Total Supply	Price of Gold (London price)	Real Price of Gold[c]
1968	39.3	20.7	60.0	40.1	19.9	60.0	38.64	37.70
1969	38.6	3.4	42.0	40.3	1.7	42.0	41.12	38.61
1970	44.3	7.7	52.0	40.9	11.1	52.0	35.94	32.55
1971	44.7	—	44.7	39.7	5.0	44.7	40.81	35.83
1972	43.2	4.9	48.1	38.1	10.0	48.1	58.16	48.83
1973	27.2	17.2	45.1	36.0	9.1	45.1	97.32	72.25
1974	25.4	16.5	41.9	32.4	9.5	41.9	159.26	99.48
1975	31.6	4.1	35.7	30.7	5.0	35.7	160.90	92.00
1976	44.5	1.8	46.3	31.2	15.1	46.3	124.84	68.22
1977	45.6	7.1	52.7	31.2	21.5	52.7	148.11	76.27
1978	51.3	5.0	56.3	31.5	24.8	56.3	193.36	92.38
1979	42.3	12.5	54.8	30.9	23.9	54.8	307.82	130.65
1980	21.0	16.4	37.4	30.3	7.1	37.4	613.67	228.44

a. Millions of fine troy ounces.
b. Dollars per ounce.
c. London price of gold divided by U.S. WPI (1967 = 100).

Sources: See tables 4-1, 4-2, and Sc-16, *Report to the Congress of the Commission on the Role of Gold in the Domestic and International Monetary Systems* 1 (March 1982): 157-67, 219-25.

be a positive function of the real price, the price of key inputs and technology. However, recent studies have found the price elasticity of market economy gold production to be negative and quite low.[57] This result is largely explained by the behavior of South African gold production, which in 1980 accounted for 71 percent of total market economy production.[58]

In South Africa, the rapid increase in the real price of gold since 1968 has led to a considerable expansion in milling capacity, but the number of ounces produced has steadily declined, reflecting a decline in the average grade of ore milled.[59] This phenomenon largely reflects official South African policy to preserve its reserves of gold. The calculation of South African reserves depends critically on the concept of pay limit, which is the minimum quantity of metal in a ton of rock sufficient to yield the revenue to cover the costs of mining, processing, and marketing gold. The reserves usually include ore available for extraction within a year. All gold mines in South Africa lease mines from the state subject to the restriction that the company must mine to the average value of its published ore reserves. When the price of gold was fixed, the pay limit rose as mining costs increased; since the 1970s, the pay limit has declined when the price of gold has risen and vice versa.[60]

Thus, the determinants of flow supply and demand should be important in explaining movements in the real price of gold. Indeed, on the basis of a very simple model both of industrial demand as a function of the real price of gold, the real price of silver, and world real income, and of market economy production as a function of the real price of gold (current and lagged by one year) and a time trend as a proxy for technological progress, I found that the independent variables of the demand and supply functions explained 95 percent of the variation in real price in the 1969-80 period. The remainder of the movements in the real price must be explained by the net asset demand for gold and by sales by Western and Communist bloc official sources.[61]

The net asset demand for gold should be a function of, among other things, the opportunity cost of holding real financial assets, the expected rate of inflation, and variables reflecting world economic and political instability. Indeed, consistent with a number of other studies, I found proxies for these variables to explain much of the variation in the net asset demand for gold.[62] Moreover, accounting for these factors adds 3 percent further to the explanation of the variation in the real price of gold.

The final factors to be accounted for are the flows of gold to the market economies from the Communist bloc, which are believed to fluctuate with its real need for foreign exchange, and net official sales by Western monetary authorities, which would be explained by different factors in each instance.[63]

Putting all the information together suggests that choosing a "correct" official price may be a difficult task. Even accounting for the volatile factors affecting the net asset demand for gold as well as for net sales from the Communist bloc, we cannot be sure that these factors are sufficiently stable or predictable to maintain such a price for long.[64]

Is There Sufficient Gold to Maintain Long-run Price Stability? Even if we choose the "correct" price for establishing a gold standard, we still must ascertain whether gold production will be sufficient in the future to ensure a growth rate of the world's monetary gold stock, and hence the world money supply, sufficient to match the growth of real per capita output and population and to account for underlying trends in velocity.[65]

As background to the discussion, Figure 8-7 displays annual data on world gold production since 1800. Most of the world's gold has been produced since 1850; indeed, two-thirds of it has been produced in the past fifty years. In addition, there is evidence of a direct relationship between the real price of gold and gold production with a long lead—at least until World War II.[66] Thus, the large increase in production from the mid-1930s to the 1960s reflects the U.S. response to the rise in the official price of gold in 1934 from $20.67 to $35.00 per ounce. Subsequently, with a declining real price of gold in the 1960s in the face of worldwide inflation and a fixed gold price, production peaked in 1970 and has followed a declining trend since then.

Since South Africa currently accounts for over half of world production and is believed to possess at least half of the world's proven reserves of 1 billion ounces, the prospect for world production hinges largely on the South African industry.

A number of factors suggest that South African production will not increase in the near future. These include high capital costs—which deter both the expansion of existing mines mining lower grade ores and the reopening of mines that were uneconomical when the

Figure 8-7. World Gold Production, 1800-1980.

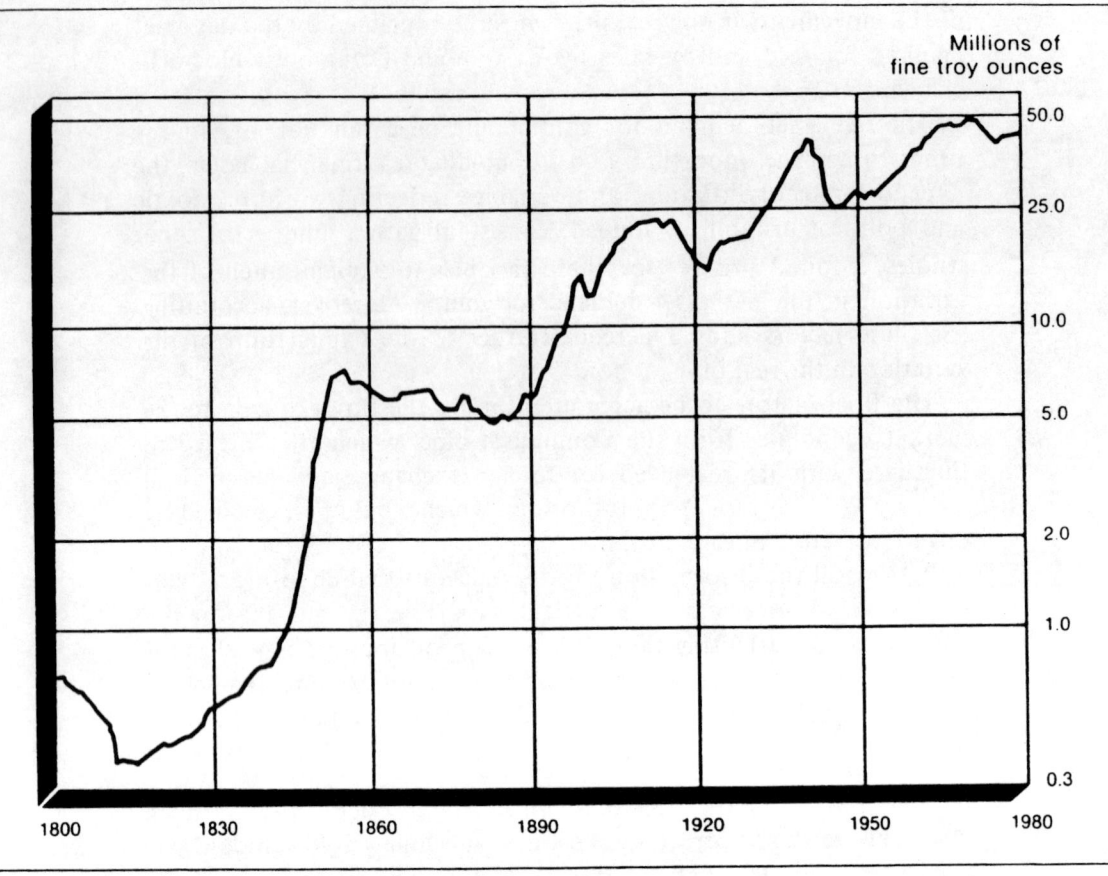

Millions of fine troy ounces

[Line graph showing world gold production from 1800 to 1980, with y-axis values 0.3, 1.0, 2.0, 5.0, 10.0, 25.0, 50.0 and x-axis years 1800, 1830, 1860, 1890, 1920, 1950, 1980]

Source: *Report to the Congress of the Commission on the Role of Gold in the Domestic and International Monetary Systems* 1 (March 1982): 170.

gold price was fixed—and rising labor costs.[67] In addition, gold mining in South Africa is a labor intensive industry: Mechanization of the gold fields is impractical because of the depth at which mining is carried out, the hardness of the rock that has to be excavated to develop access tunnels, the high temperature of the rock, and the narrowness of the ore body. The final factor is the government-mandated shift to lower grade ores when the average gold price rises.[68]

Indeed, Consolidated Gold Fields project that South Africa's annual gold output will total 22.5 million ounces until 1987 (in 1980 it was 21 billion ounces) and then gradually decline to 11.25 million ounces by 2000, assuming a current gold price of $450, rising to $554 in 1984 and then remaining constant in real terms until 2000.[69]

The country with the next largest share in world output and in proven reserves is the USSR. Its current output is estimated at between 8 and 11 million ounces and is not expected to increase dramatically in the future. Also, since it does not seem to gear its sales to production but rather to balance of payments needs, it is unclear how steady a source of supply it would be.[70]

Finally, gold production in the United States and Canada has displayed a negative postwar trend, although the recent rise in gold prices has encouraged a reopening of mines and exploration.[71]

Thus, barring a major gold discovery, it is doubtful whether rising gold production in Brazil and elsewhere would be sufficient to offset the declining trend. Since 1970, world gold production has decreased on average by 1.5 percent per year, whereas total world real output has increased in excess of 3 percent per year. Even if outstanding private gold hoards, estimated to be 662 million ounces, could be attracted to the existing world monetary gold stock of 1132.3 million ounces,[72] it is unlikely that they would be sufficient in the long run to offset the shortfall in production. This suggests that return to a gold standard would ultimately be associated with deflation.

A declining price trend may seem desirable after decades of rising prices, but deflation also imposes costs on the economy. These include the transition cost of moving from an inflationary to a deflationary environment in a world of long-term contracts as well as distribution effects, to the extent that the deflation is not fully anticipated—costs that may be as severe in their social consequence as those associated with inflation.

CONCLUSION: BENEFITS AND COSTS OF RETURNING TO A GOLD STANDARD

In assessing the case for a return by the United States and the rest of the world to a gold standard, we must weigh the benefits of such a policy against the costs.

The key benefit to a return to a gold standard would be a return to long-run price stability. This would create an environment where private market participants would have incentives to make long-term contracts, which are necessary for the efficient operation of a market economy. In addition, it would minimize the confusion between relative and absolute price level movements, reducing the incidence of false signals with regard to real economic decisions. An additional benefit would be a limited role of government intervention in the determination of the price level and overall economic activity.[73]

The costs, however, are not inconsiderable. These include the high resource costs of maintaining the standard; short-term instability in the price level, real output, and employment; and the subordination of monetary independence to international considerations. In addition, there is the risk of choosing the wrong fixed price of gold and the likelihood that in the long run instead of a stable price trend we would have deflation.

The question then remains, How can we attain the benefits of a gold standard without the costs? Irving Fisher offered one solution to the problem sixty years ago: that we adopt a tabular standard. By a tabular standard he meant varying the gold content of the dollar to keep the purchasing power constant. In the face of a rising price level, he recommended raising the gold content of the dollar—thus lowering the price of gold. In the face of a declining price level, he recommended lowering the gold content of the dollar—thus raising the price of gold.[74] Such a scheme could be applied to any type of gold standard.[75]

Another solution, advocated by many economists, is to follow a fiduciary money standard based on a monetary rule of a steady and known rate of monetary growth. The key problem, however, with such a standard is to ensure that the rule is maintained and that a commitment is made to the goal of long-run price stability.

1. See, e.g., Robert Bleiberg and James Grant, "For Real Money: the Dollar Should Be as Good as Gold," *Barron's*, 15 June 1981; Robert A. Mundell, "Gold Would Serve into the 21st Century," *Wall Street Journal*, 30 September 1981; and Arthur E. Laffer and Charles Kadlec, "The Point of Linking the Dollar to Gold," *Wall Street Journal*, 13 October 1981.

2. The Gold Commission, headed by Treasury Secretary Donald Regan and consisting of members of both houses of Congress as well as representatives from the Federal Reserve Board, the Council of Economic Advisers, the Treasury Department, and the private sector, submitted its report in two volumes on March 31, 1982. See *Report to the Congress of the Commission on the Role of Gold on the Domestic and International Monetary Systems. March 1982.* U.S. Treasury (processed). Also see Anna J. Schwartz, "Reflections on the Gold Committee Report," *Journal of Money, Credit and Banking* 14, no. 4 (March 1982), pp. 538-51.

3. Milton Friedman refers to type 1 as a "real" gold standard and to all the others as "pseudo" gold standards, in "Real and Pseudo Gold Standards," *Journal of Law and Economics* 14 (October 1961), pp. 66-79.

4. Over the history of the gold standard, numerous writers have proposed the use of commodity standards based on commodities other than gold, with convertibility for all holders of noncommodity money in the designated basket of commodities.

5. The recent proposal by Robert E. Weintraub, "Restoring the Gold Certificate Reserve," *Joint Economic Committee U.S. Congress Study* (1981), for the U.S. to tie its monetary base to the monetary gold stock valued initially at a price to be determined, and then to allow it to grow only in accordance with the value of the monetary gold stock, with growth in the latter determined by a rise in the price of gold equal to the growth of real economic activity, is not really a gold standard, since it does not allow convertibility of gold. It is rather a form of monetary rule based on gold. See also "The New Role for Gold in U.S. Monetary Policy," Weintraub's contribution to this volume (Chapter 9).

6. For a historical survey of the literature on the gold standard, see Michael David Bordo, "The Gold Standard: The Traditional Approach," in Michael D. Bordo and Anna J. Schwartz, eds., *A Retrospective on the Classical Gold Standard, 1821 to 1931* (Chicago: University of Chicago Press, 1984).

7. Of course, in earlier times governments manipulated gold by debasement, clipping, and so on. Such practices, however, were the exception. See Anna J. Schwartz, "Secular Price Change in Historical Perspective," *Journal of Money, Credit and Banking* 5 (February 1973): 243-69.

8. For a lucid discussion of the theory of commodity money, see Milton Friedman, "Commodity-Reserve Currency," in Milton Friedman, ed., *Essays in Positive Economics* (University of Chicago Press, 1953), pp. 204-50.

9. In actuality, the buying and selling prices will differ, reflecting the cost of certifying and minting coins. This difference is referred to as brassage.

10. The United States fixed the price of an ounce of gold at $20.67, and the United Kingdom set it at £3. 17s. 10½d. The U.K. definition of an ounce of gold was 11/12 of the U.S. definition.

11. It is important to note that a monetary standard such as the gold standard has two aspects: a domestic one and an international one. The domestic aspect applies to the arrangements regulating the quantity and growth rate of the domestic money supply, whereas the international aspect applies to the arrangement by which the external value of the currency is determined. Thus, it is possible to have a domestic gold standard where the monetary authorities of one country fix the weight of gold in domestic currency and allow free convertibility, but where other countries base their currencies on other commodities, such as silver, or on inconvertible paper. In that case the external value of the currency would be determined by the open-market price of the two currencies, and a flexible exchange rate would prevail.

12. Friedman estimated the cost of maintaining a full gold coin standard for the United States in 1960 to be in excess of 2½ percent of GNP. See Milton Friedman, *A Program for Monetary Stability* (New York: Fordham University Press, 1959), p. 105.

13. It also meant that changes in the composition of the money supply between the monetary base (gold coins and government paper) and bank-provided money (notes and deposits) could be a source of monetary instability.

14. See A. I. Bloomfield, *Short-Term Capital Movements Under the Pre-1914 Gold Standard*, Princeton Studies in International Finance no. 11 (Princeton: Princeton University Press, 1968).

15. See A. I. Bloomfield, *Patterns of Fluctuation in International Investment before 1914*, Princeton Studies in International Finance no. 21 (Princeton: Princeton University Press, 1968).

16. Noted examples are France and Belgium. See P. B. White, "The Working of the Pre-War Gold Standard," *Economica* (February 1937): 18-32; and A. I. Bloomfield, *Monetary Policy Under the International Gold Standard* (New York: Federal Reserve Bank of New York, 1959).

17. Usually gold outflows were offset by open-market purchases of domestic securities. For U.S. experience, see Milton Friedman and Anna J. Schwartz, *A Monetary History of the United States, 1867-1960* (Princeton: Princeton University Press, 1964). For other countries, see Bloomfield, *Monetary Policy*.

18. Much of this discussion derives from Peter H. Lindert, *Key Currencies and Gold, 1900-1913*, Princeton Studies in International Finance no. 24 (Princeton: Princeton University Press, 1969).

19. Indeed, Britain's total gold reserves in 1913 accounted for only 9.5 percent of the world's monetary gold stock, whereas the Bank of England's holdings accounted for 3.5 percent. See John Maynard Keynes, *A Treatise on Money: 2, The Applied Theory of Money*, vol. 6 of *The Collected Writings of John Maynard Keynes*, ed. Elizabeth Johnson and Donald Moggridge (London: Macmillan, Cambridge University Press for the Royal Economic Society, 1971).

20. It probably caused monetary crises in the United States in the 1837-43 period and again in 1873. See Peter Temin, *The Jacksonian Economy* (New York: Norton, 1969), and Friedman and Schwartz, *Monetary History*.

21. Also, the period after 1900 marked a growing trend toward earmarking gold holdings in major centers, rather than transporting gold between centers.

22. See Bloomfield, *Short-Term Capital Movements*, p. 44.

23. See Melchior Palyi, *The Twilight of Gold 1914 to 1936: Myths and Realities* (Chicago: Henry Regnery, 1972); and David Williams, "The Evolution of the Sterling System," in C. R. Whittlesey and J. S. G. Wilson, eds., *Essays in Money and Banking in Honour of R. S. Sayers* (Oxford: Clarendon Press, 1968).

24. Argentina and other Latin American countries did so, for example. See Alec George Ford, *The Gold Standard 1880-1914, Britain and Argentina* (Oxford: Clarendon Press, 1962).

25. Under a bimetallic standard, each of two precious metals, gold and silver, serves as legal tender, and the two metals are kept by the mint in a fixed proportion to each other. The relationship between the official exchange rate of gold for silver and the market rate determines whether either one or both metals are used as money. Thus, for example, in 1834, the United States raised the mint ratio of silver to gold from 15:1 to 16:1, hence valuing silver slightly lower relative to gold than the world market. As a result, little silver was offered for coinage, and the U.S. was in effect on the gold standard. See Leland B. Yeager, *International Monetary Relations: Theory, History and Policy*, 2d ed. (New York: Harper & Row, 1976), p. 296.

26. The switch from silver to gold reflected both changes in the relative supplies of the two precious metals, brought on by the gold discoveries of the 1840s and 1850s, and a growing preference for the more precious metal as world real income rose.

27. See Palyi, *Twilight of Gold*; and Yeager, *International Monetary Relations*, ch. 15.

28. The United States alone remained on the gold standard, except for a brief embargo on gold exports from 1917 to 1919.

29. See W. A. Brown, *The International Gold Standard Reinterpreted, 1914-1934* (New York: National Bureau of Economic Research, 1940); and Yeager, *International Monetary Relations*, ch. 17.

30. See H. G. Johnson, "Theoretical Problems of the International Monetary System," *Pakistan Development Review* 7: 1-28.

31. Managed fiduciary money is a monetary standard where the government is not committed to maintaining a fixed price of gold. The United States had such a standard from 1861 to 1879 and has been on one since 1971. Under such a standard, the monetary authorities have complete control over the domestic money supply. An alternative situation, often called managed money, occurs when the monetary authorities, though committed to maintaining a fixed price of gold, engage in a systematic policy of sterilizing (or neutralizing), using offsetting open-market operations, the influence of gold flows on the domestic money supply. Thus the period from 1914 to 1933 in U.S. monetary history can be viewed as a period of managed money because of the frequent sterilizing activity of the Federal Reserve System. See Friedman and Schwartz, *Monetary History*, pp. 462-92.

32. Also excluded from the gold standard are the turbulent years 1838-43, during part of which period specie payments were suspended.

33. The United Kingdom was chosen as representative of the pre-1914 world because it was a large, open economy with few trade restrictions; hence, its wholesale price index was dominated by internationally traded goods.

34. Indeed, this inverse relationship prevailed virtually until the late 1960s. Since the freeing of the price of gold in 1968, the purchasing power of gold has varied directly with the wholesale price index. This reflects primarily the rising demand for gold as a hedge against inflation and increasing world political and monetary instability.

35. The highest statistically significant negative correlation in the 1821 to 1914 period occurred when deviations from trend in the monetary gold stock led deviations from trend in the purchasing power of gold by two years. The correlation coefficient, -0.644, was statistically significant at the 1 percent level.

36. The highest statistically significant positive correlation in the 1821-1914 period occurred with deviations from trend in the purchasing power of gold leading deviations from trend in the world monetary gold stock by twenty-five years. The correlation was 0.436, statistically significant at the 1 percent level.

37. An important difference between the behavior of the U.S. monetary gold stock and that of the world as a whole is that short-run movements in the United States series reflect not only changes in gold production and shifts between monetary and nonmonetary uses of gold but also gold movements between the United States and other countries.

38. The highest statistically significant negative correlation from 1879 to 1914 occurred with the contemporaneous relationship between deviations from trend in the monetary gold stock and deviations from trend in the purchasing power of gold. The correlation coefficient, -0.656, was statistically significant at the 1 percent level.

39. The highest statistically significant positive correlation from 1879 to 1914 occurred when deviations from trend in the purchasing power of gold led deviations from trend in the monetary gold stock by fourteen years. The correlation coefficient was 0.793, statistically significant at the 1 percent level. The highest statistically significant positive correlation in this period occurred when deviations from trend in the *world* purchasing power of gold led deviations from trend in the *world* monetary gold stock by sixteen years. The correlation coefficient was 0.863, statistically significant at the 1 percent level. The considerably longer lead observed over the 1821-1914 period (see n. 36 above) likely reflects a longer adjustment period in the early part of the nineteenth century.

40. See Benjamin Klein, "Our New Monetary Standard: The Measurement and Effects of Price Uncertainty, 1880-1973," *Economic Inquiry* 13, no. 4 (December 1975): 461-84, for evidence of long-run price stability in the U.S. under the gold standard. His evidence that positive (or negative) autocorrelations of the price level are succeeded by negative (or positive) autocorrelations is consistent with the hypothesis that the price level reverted back to its mean level. As a consequence of this mean reversion phenomenon, year-to-year changes in the price level were substantial for each country. However, the standard deviations of year-to-year changes in the wholesale price index were still considerably lower in the pre-World War I gold standard era than in the post-World War I managed fiduciary money era. For the United Kingdom, the standard deviations are: 1821-1913, 6.20; 1919-79 (excluding 1939-45), 12.00. For the United States, the standard deviations are: 1834-1913 (excluding 1838-43 and 1861-79), 6.29; 1919-79 (excluding 1941-45), 9.28.

41. Indeed, evidence presented in Klein, "New Monetary Standard," shows a marked decline since 1960 in long-term price level predictability—the belief in long-term stability measured by a moving standard deviation of changes in the price level. At the same time, short-term price level predictability—the belief about price level behavior in the near future—has improved in the postwar period. See pp. 461-84.

42. See Friedrich August von Hayek, *A Tiger by the Tail*, Hobart Papers (London: Institute of Economic Affairs, 1972); Milton Friedman, "Nobel Lecture: Inflation and Unemployment," *Journal of Political Economy* 85 (June 1977): 451-72; Axel Leijonhufvud, "Costs and Consequences of Inflation," *Information and Co-Ordination: Essays in Macro Economic Theory* (London: Oxford University Press, 1981).

43. The standard deviations of year-to-year percentage changes in real per capita income for the United States were: 1879-1913, 5.79; 1919-79 (excluding 1941-45), 6.1. For the United Kingdom, they were: 1870-1913, 2.62; 1919-79 (excluding 1939-45), 3.24.

44. Both world wars are omitted from this comparison for two reasons. First, both wars were accompanied by rapid inflation in both countries, and in each case wartime government expenditures were largely financed by the issue of government fiat money. Hence, a comparison of the price-stabilizing characteristics of the two monetary standards that included two major wars in the case of the managed fiduciary money standard and none in the case of the gold standard would bias the case against the former. Second, measured real out-

put would tend to be higher than otherwise in wartime to the extent that resources (both employed and other unemployed) are devoted to nonproductive wartime use. Hence, including wartime real output would bias the case in favor of managed fiduciary money.

45. Comparing the two countries' unemployment rate with the measure of real output stability reveals an interesting difference. Real output was less stable in the United States, but unemployment was higher in the United Kingdom. The high and persistent unemployment in the United Kingdom in the interwar period is attributed by some to significant increases in the ratio of unemployment benefits to wages. See Daniel K. Benjamin and Levis A. Kochin, "Searching for an Explanation of Unemployment in Interwar Britain," *Journal of Political Economy* 87 (June 1979): 441-78.

46. See Milton Friedman, *A Theoretical Framework for Monetary Analysis*, Occasional Paper no. 112 (New York: National Bureau of Economic Research, 1971).

47. See John Maynard Keynes, *The Economic Consequences of Mr. Churchill*, vol. 9 of *Collected Works*.

48. See Friedman and Schwartz, *Monetary History*.

49. Friedman forcefully argued this point in his 1968 presidential address to the American Economic Association. See Milton Friedman, "The Role of Monetary Policy," *The American Economic Review* 58 (May 1968): 1-17.

50. The U.S. silver purchase program beginning December 21, 1933, trebled the market price of silver in two years, caused a massive silver outflow from China and severe deflationary pressure in that country, and ultimately forced China to abandon the silver standard in November 1935. See Friedman and Schwartz, *Monetary History*, pp. 489-91.

51. According to the second amendment to the IMF Charter, members are not obliged to maintain an official price of gold or to use gold in transactions with the fund. See Sir Joseph Gold, "Gold in International Monetary Law: Change, Uncertainty, and Ambiguity," *Journal of International Law and Economics* 15, no. 2 (1981): 323-69.

52. Thus Great Britain returned to gold at £3 17s. 10½d. after a period of wartime inflation in 1821 and again in 1925. In both cases, it underwent internal deflation. And in both cases, there was a major controversy over the choice between devaluation and deflation. The United States returned to gold in 1879 under similar circumstances.

53. With the adoption of the two-tier system in 1968, governments maintained the fixed price of $35.00 per ounce only for official transactions.

54. In this breakdown, medallions and coins are included under industrial demand; however, even if they had been included as part of asset demand, the behavior of the two components would not be much different.

55. See Leslie Lipschitz and Ichiro Otani, "A Simple Model of the Private Gold Market, 1968-1974: An Exploratory Econometric Exercise," *IMF Staff Papers* 24 (March 1977): 36-63.

56. In a recent study by the International Gold Corporation using annual data over the period 1970-80, the real price elasticity was found to be -1.2 and the real income elasticity, 2.9. See International Gold Corporation Limited, "A Gold Pricing Model" (August 1981), p. 6. (Mimeo.) Using quarterly data over the 1968-74 period, Lipschitz and Otani found a price elasticity of -0.7 and an income elasticity of 0.6; they also found an elasticity of -0.11 over the 1968-74 period ("Simple Model," p. 50). In a log linear regression of industrial demand for gold, using annual data over the period 1950-80, I found the price elasticity to be -0.8, the income elasticity to be 2.3, and the silver price coefficient to be insignificant. Similar results were produced using the world CPI over a similar period. By contrast, a similar regression run over the 1969-80 period yielded own price elasticities closer to 1 and a real income elasticity closer to 4.

57. Using annual data over the 1950-80 period, I found a current period elasticity of -0.07 based on a loglinear regression of market economy production as the real price and a time trend. Using the real price of gold lagged one year as an independent variable produced an elasticity of -0.10. Similar results were obtained for the 1969-80 period.

58. In 1980, South Africa accounted for 55.6 percent of the world's total output, with the USSR second at 21.3 percent, Canada third at 4.1 percent, Brazil fourth at 2.8 percent, and the United States fifth at 2.4 percent; see J. Aron, *Gold Statistics and Analysis* (New York: n.p., January 1981).

59. A similar phenomenon has been observed in Canada and the United States.

60. See Lipschitz and Otani, "Simple Model," p. 50; see also F. Hirsch, "Influences on Gold Production," *IMF Staff Papers* 15 (November 1968): 405-70. In addition, South Africa, like Canada, subsidizes gold mines that are no longer profitable, thus enabling marginal mines to remain in operation. If the price of gold should decline, the amount of state assistance, which has been negligible recently, could rise again.

61. Net asset demand for gold is defined as the sum of net private bullion purchases, coins, and medallions less net dishoarding of private bullion holdings.

62. Lipschitz and Otani found their hoarding demand for gold to be significant functions of Eurodollar and Euromark interest rates, expected inflation and wealth over the 1968–74 period ("Simple Model," p. 50). The International Gold Corporation study, using monthly data, found measures of the real rate of interest, lagged world money growth, and world political tension to explain most of the variation in the price of gold ("Gold Pricing Model," p. 15). Using annual data over the 1969–80 period, I found the net asset demand to be significantly related to the real rate of interest (measured by the ninety-day Eurodollar rate on an annual basis less the annual rate of change of the world CPI), the annual rate of change of the world CPI, and world real income. Similar results were found using the U.S. ninety-day T-bill rate and the U.S. CPI.

63. See S. W. Salant and D. W. Henderson, "Market Anticipation of Government Policies and the Price of Gold," *Journal of Political Economy* 86, no. 4 (August 1978): 627–48; they regard speculation on the timing of official sales as an important determinant of fluctuations in the price of gold in the 1970s.

64. Robert Aliber suggests an interesting method to arrive at an equilibrium gold price. He takes the price of $35 per ounce in 1961, a year when the United States had virtual price stability, as an initial equilibrium price. Assuming that no other factors affected the real price, the nominal price of gold should have increased to the same extent as the increase in the U.S. price level since 1961. Since the U.S. CPI tripled between 1961 and 1980, the nominal price of gold should have been $105 in 1980; using the increase in the world CPI (based on IMF data), it should have been $155. However, other factors would have affected the real price of gold in addition to the increase in the general price level. If the world real income elasticity is about 2 (based on the results discussed in n. 56) and the increase in world income about 80 percent (based on the IMF index of world real GNP), then the demand for gold would have increased by 160 percent over the period 1961–80. Over the same period, the total world gold stock increased by 35 percent (based on U.S. Bureau of the Mines data). Thus, the excess demand for gold amounted to about 125 percent since 1961. If we take the price elasticity of demand for gold to be –1 and the price elasticity of supply to be close to zero, then the real price would have increased (other things being equal) by about 120 percent since 1961. On this calculation, the equilibrium price of gold in 1980 would have been between $230 and $350. This exercise assumes that factors affecting the net asset demand for gold are transitory and would vanish once price stability is restored. See Robert Aliber, "Inflationary Expectations and the Price of Gold" (Paper for the World Conference on Gold, Rome, February 5, 1982).

65. The same question was asked by both G. Cassel and J. Kitchin in their contributions to the *Interim Report of the Gold Delegation of the League of Nations* (Geneva: League of Nations, 1931).

66. Over the period 1800–1913, the highest statistically significant positive correlation occurred with the real price of gold leading world gold production by fourteen years. The correlation coefficient was 0.724, significant at the 1 percent level. Over the period 1914–45, the highest statistically significant positive correlation occurred with the real price of gold leading world gold production by two years. The correlation coefficient was 0.924, significant at the 1 percent level. Finally, over the period 1946–80, correlations with the real price of gold leading world gold production were negative and significant, with the highest significant correlation of –0.917 reached after thirteen years. This undoubtedly reflects the South African government's gold policy, as outlined above.

67. Related to this is inelasticity in the supply of skilled labor, since most of the people employed in the industry are unskilled black migrant workers whose families must stay in the tribal "homelands" and whose movement into skilled work is opposed by white trade union members.

68. See Consolidated Gold Fields, Inc., *Gold 1981* (New York: 1981), app. 4, pp. 71–85.

69. Ibid., p. 77.

70. Ibid., p. 18–21.

71. J. Aron, *Gold Statistics and Analysis* (Precious Metals Research Department, J. Aron Commodities Corporation, January 1981).

72. Ibid., p. 14.

73. The history of the pre–World War I gold standard suggests that it worked because it was a "managed" international standard. In addition, the concentration of world capital and money markets in London and the use of sterling as a key currency enabled the system to function smoothly with very limited gold reserves and to withstand a number of severe external shocks. Perhaps of paramount importance for the successful operation of the managed gold standard was the tacit cooperation of the major participants in ultimately maintaining the gold standard link and its corrollary—long-run price stability as the primary goal of economic policy.

74. See Irving Fisher, *Stabilizing the Dollar* (New York: n.p., 1920), p. 498. He proposed changing the dollar value of gold by a simple formula: Every month, change the dollar price by 1 percent downward for each percent increase in the price level above a target, change the dollar price by 1 percent upward for each percent decrease in the price level below a target.

75. Such a standard could also be applied to a wider basket of commodities. See Robert E. Hall, "Explorations in the Gold Standard and Related Policies for Stabilizing the Dollar," in Robert E. Hall, ed., *Inflation: Causes and Effects* (Chicago: University of Chicago Press, 1982).

This paper was written while I was research staff member to Anna J. Schwartz, executive director of the Gold Commission. I would like to thank the following for helpful suggestions: Anna J. Schwartz, Anatole Balbach, and Daniel Landau. Parts of this paper are based on my article "The Classical Gold Standard: Some Lessons for Today," in the *Federal Reserve Bank of St. Louis Review* 63, no. 5 (May 1981), pp. 2-17. For able research assistance, I am indebted to Glen Vogt, Michael Hollihan, and Fernando Santos.

20. Choice in Currency: A Way to Stop Inflation
F.A. Hayek

Should governments get out of the money business? When F.A. Hayek first proposed the idea as "a way to stop inflation" in 1976, many took it as a cynical joke. Since then, however, numerous historical studies of past "free banking" episodes have shown that the issuance of currency by competing, private banks is perfectly feasible. —G.S., Ed.

****

I
MONEY, KEYNES AND HISTORY**

THE CHIEF ROOT of our present monetary troubles is, of course, the sanction of scientific authority which Lord Keynes and his disciples have given to the age-old superstition that by increasing the aggregate of money expenditure we can lastingly ensure prosperity and full employment. It is a superstition against which economists before Keynes had struggled with some success for at least two centuries.† It had governed most of earlier history. This history, indeed, has been largely a history of inflation; significantly, it was only during the rise of the prosperous modern industrial systems and during the rule of the gold standard, that over a period of about two hundred years (in Britain from about 1714 to 1914, and in the United States from about 1749 to 1939) prices were at the end about where they had been at the beginning. During this unique period of monetary stability the gold standard had imposed upon monetary authorities a discipline which prevented them from abusing their powers, as they have done at nearly all other times. Experience in other parts of the world does not seem to have been very different: I have been told that a Chinese law attempted to prohibit paper money for all times (of course, ineffectively), long before the Europeans ever invented it!

Keynesian rehabilitation
It was John Maynard Keynes, a man of great intellect but limited knowledge of economic theory, who ultimately succeeded in rehabilitating a view long the preserve of cranks with whom he openly sympathised. He had attempted by a succession of new theories to justify the same, superficially persuasive, intuitive belief that had been held by many practical men before, but that will not withstand rigorous analysis of the price mechanism: just as there cannot be a uniform price for all kinds of labour, an equality of demand and supply for labour in general cannot be secured by managing *aggregate* demand. The volume of employment depends on the correspondence of demand and supply *in each sector* of the economy, and therefore on the wage structure and the distribution of demand between the sectors. The consequence is that over a longer period the Keynesian remedy does not cure unemployment but makes it worse.

The claim of an eminent public figure and brilliant polemicist

---

** [The main section and sub-headings have been inserted to help readers, especially non-economists unfamiliar with Professor Hayek's writings, to follow the argument; they were not part of the original lecture. – ED.]

† [This observation is amplified by Professor Hayek in a note, 'A Comment on Keynes, Beveridge and Keynesian Economics', page 23. – ED.]

to provide a cheap and easy means of permanently preventing serious unemployment conquered public opinion and, after his death, professional opinion too. Sir John Hicks has even proposed that we call the third quarter of this century, 1950 to 1975, the age of Keynes, as the second quarter was the age of Hitler.[1] I do not feel that the harm Keynes did is really so much as to justify *that* description. But it is true that, so long as his prescriptions seemed to work, they operated as an orthodoxy which it appeared useless to oppose.

Personal confession

I have often blamed myself for having given up the struggle after I had spent much time and energy criticising the first version of Keynes's theoretical framework. Only after the second part of my critique had appeared did he tell me he had changed his mind and no longer believed what he had said in the *Treatise on Money* of 1930 (somewhat unjustly towards himself, as it seems to me, since I still believe that volume II of the *Treatise* contains some of the best work he ever did). At any rate, I felt it then to be useless to return to the charge, because he seemed so likely to change his views again. When it proved that this new version – the *General Theory* of 1936 – conquered most of the professional opinion, and when in the end even some of the colleagues I most respected supported the wholly Keynesian Bretton Woods agreement, I largely withdrew from the debate, since to proclaim my dissent from the near-unanimous views of the orthodox phalanx would merely have deprived me of a hearing on other matters about which I was more concerned at the time. (I believe, however, that, so far as some of the best British economists were concerned, their support of Bretton Woods was determined more by a misguided patriotism – the hope that it would benefit Britain in her post-war difficulties – than by a belief that it would provide a satisfactory international monetary order.)

II
THE MANUFACTURE OF UNEMPLOYMENT

I WROTE 36 years ago on the crucial point of difference:

'It may perhaps be pointed out that it has, of course, never been denied that employment can be rapidly increased, and a position of "full employment" achieved in the shortest possible time, by means of monetary expansion – least of all by those economists whose outlook has been influenced by the experience of a major inflation. All that has been contended is that the kind of full employment which can be created in this way is inherently unstable, and that to create employment by these means is to perpetuate fluctuations. There may be desperate situations in which it may indeed be necessary to increase employment at all costs, even if it be only for a short period – perhaps the situation in which Dr Brüning found himself in Germany in 1932 was such a situation in which desperate means would have been justified. But the economist

[1] John Hicks, *The Crisis in Keynesian Economics*, Oxford University Press, 1974, p. 1.

should not conceal the fact that to aim at the maximum of employment which can be achieved in the short run by means of monetary policy is essentially the policy of the desperado who has nothing to lose and everything to gain from a short breathing space.'[1]

To this I would now like to add, in reply to the constant deliberate misrepresentation of my views by politicians, who like to picture me as a sort of bogey whose influence makes conservative parties dangerous, what I regularly emphasise and stated nine months ago in my Nobel Memorial Prize Lecture at Stockholm in the following words:

'The truth is that by a mistaken theoretical view we have been led into a precarious position in which we cannot prevent substantial unemployment from re-appearing: not because, as my view is sometimes misrepresented, this unemployment is deliberately brought about as a means to combat inflation, but because it is now bound to appear as a deeply regrettable but *inescapable* consequence of the mistaken policies of the past as soon as inflation ceases to accelerate.'[2]

Unemployment via 'full employment policies'
This manufacture of unemployment by what are called 'full employment policies' is a complex process. In essence it operates by temporary changes in the distribution of demand, drawing both unemployed and already employed workers into jobs which will disappear with the end of inflation. In the periodically recurrent crises of the pre-1914 years the expansion of credit during the preceding boom served largely to finance industrial investment, and the over-development and subsequent unemployment occurred mainly in the industries producing capital equipment. In the engineered inflation of the last decades things were more complex.

What will happen during a major inflation is illustrated by an observation from the early 1920s which many of my Viennese contemporaries will confirm: in the city many of the famous coffee houses were driven from the best corner sites by new bank offices and returned after the 'stabilisation crisis', when the banks had contracted or collapsed and thousands of bank clerks swelled the ranks of the unemployed.

The lost generation
The whole theory underlying the full employment policies has by now of course been thoroughly discredited by the experience of the last few years. In consequence the economists are also beginning to discover its fatal intellectual defects which they ought to have seen all along. Yet I fear the theory will still give us a lot of trouble: it has left us with a lost generation of economists who have learnt nothing else. One of our chief problems will be to protect our money against those economists

[1] F. A. Hayek, *Profits, Interest and Investment*, Routlege & Kegan Paul, London, 1939, p. 63n.
[2] F. A. Hayek, 'The Pretence of Knowledge', Nobel Memorial Prize Lecture 1974, reprinted in *Full Employment at Any Price?*, Occasional Paper 45, IEA, 1975, p. 37.

who will continue to offer their quack remedies, the short-term effectiveness of which will continue to ensure them popularity. It will survive among blind doctrinaires who have always been convinced that they have the key to salvation.

The 1863 penny
In consequence, though the rapid descent of Keynesian doctrine from intellectual respectability can be denied no longer, it still gravely threatens the chances of a sensible monetary policy. Nor have people yet fully realised how much irreparable damage it has already done, particularly in Britain, the country of its origin. The sense of financial respectability which once guided British monetary policy has rapidly disappeared. From a model to be imitated Britain has in a few years descended to be a warning example for the rest of the world. This decay was recently brought home to me by a curious incident: I found in a drawer of my desk a British penny dated 1863 which a short 12 years ago, that is, when it was exactly a hundred years old, I had received as change from a London bus conductor and had taken back to Germany to show to my students what long-run monetary stability meant. I believe they were duly impressed. But they would laugh in my face if I now mentioned Britain as an instance of monetary stability.

III

THE WEAKNESS OF POLITICAL CONTROL OF MONEY

A WISE MAN should perhaps have foreseen that less than 30 years after the nationalisation of the Bank of England the purchasing power of the pound sterling would have been reduced to less than one-quarter of what it had been at that date. As has sooner or later happened everywhere, government control of the quantity of money has once again proved fatal. I do not want to question that a very intelligent and wholly independent national or international monetary authority *might* do better than an international gold standard, or any other sort of automatic system. But I see not the slightest hope that any government, or any institution subject to political pressure, will ever be able to act in such a manner.

Group interests harmful
I never had much illusion in this respect, but I must confess that in the course of a long life my opinion of governments has steadily worsened: the more intelligently they try to act (as distinguished from simply following an established rule), the more harm they seem to do – because once they are known to aim at particular goals (rather than merely maintaining a self-correcting spontaneous order) the less they can avoid serving sectional interests. And the demands of all organised group interests are almost invariably harmful – except only when they protest against restrictions imposed upon them for the benefit of other group interests. I am by no means re-assured by the fact that, at least in some countries, the civil servants who run affairs are mostly intelligent, well-meaning, and honest men. The point

is that, if governments are to remain in office in the prevailing political order, they have no choice but to use their powers for the benefit of particular groups – and one strong interest is always to get additional money for extra expenditure. However harmful inflation is in general seen to be, there are always substantial groups of people, including some for whose support collectivist-inclined governments primarily look, which in the short run greatly gain by it – even if only by staving off for some time the loss of an income which it is human nature to believe will be only temporary if they can tide over the emergency.

Rebuilding the resistances to inflation
The pressure for more and cheaper money is an ever-present political force which monetary authorities have never been able to resist, unless they were in a position credibly to point to an absolute obstacle which made it impossible for them to meet such demands. And it will become even more irresistible when these interests can appeal to an increasingly unrecognisable image of St Maynard. There will be no more urgent need than to erect new defences against the onslaughts of popular forms of Keynesianism, that is, to replace or restore those restraints which, under the influence of his theory, have been systematically dismantled. It was the main function of the gold standard, of balanced budgets, of the necessity for deficit countries to contract their circulation, and of the limitation of the supply of 'international liquidity', to make it impossible for the monetary authorities to capitulate to the pressure for more money. And it was exactly for that reason that all these safeguards against inflation, which had made it possible for representative governments to resist the demands of powerful pressure groups for more money, have been removed at the instigation of economists who imagined that, if governments were released from the shackles of mechanical rules, they would be able to act wisely for the general benefit.

I do not believe we can now remedy this position by *constructing* some new international monetary order, whether a new international monetary authority or institution, or even an international agreement to adopt a particular mechanism or system of policy, such as the classical gold standard. I am fairly convinced that any attempt now to re-instate the gold standard by international agreement would break down within a short time and merely discredit the ideal of an international gold standard for even longer. Without the conviction of the public at large that certain immediately painful measures are occasionally necessary to preserve reasonable stability, we cannot hope that any authority which has power to determine the quantity of money will long resist the pressure for, or the seduction of, cheap money.

Protecting money from politics
The politician, acting on a modified Keynesian maxim that in the long run we are all out of office, does not care if his successful cure of unemployment is bound to produce more unemployment in the future. The politicians who will be blamed for it will not be those who created the inflation but those who stopped it.

No worse trap could have been set for a democratic system in which the government is forced to act on the beliefs that the people think to be true. Our only hope for a stable money is indeed now to find a way to protect money from politics.

With the exception only of the 200-year period of the gold standard, practically all governments of history have used their exclusive power to issue money in order to defraud and plunder the people. There is less ground than ever for hoping that, so long as the people have no choice but to use the money their government provides, governments will become more trustworthy. Under the prevailing systems of government, which are supposed to be guided by the opinion of the majority but under which in practice any sizeable group may create a 'political necessity' for the government by threatening to withhold the votes it needs to claim majority support, we cannot entrust dangerous instruments to it. Fortunately we need not yet fear, I hope, that governments will start a war to please some indispensable group of supporters, but money is certainly too dangerous an instrument to leave to the fortuitous expediency of politicians – or, it seems, economists.

A dangerous monopoly
What is so dangerous and ought to be done away with is not governments' right to issue money but the *exclusive* right to do so and their power to force people to use it and to accept it at a particular price. This monopoly of government, like the postal monopoly, has its origin not in any benefit it secures for the people but solely in the desire to enhance the coercive powers of government. I doubt whether it has ever done any good except to the rulers and their favourites. All history contradicts the belief that governments have given us a safer money than we would have had without their claiming an exclusive right to issue it.

IV

Choice of Money for Payment in Contracts

But why should we not let people choose freely what money they want to use? By 'people' I mean the individuals who ought to have the right to decide whether they want to buy or sell for francs, pounds, dollars, D-marks, or ounces of gold. I have no objection to governments issuing money, but I believe their claim to a *monopoly,* or their power to *limit* the kinds of money in which contracts may be concluded within their territory, or to determine the *rates* at which monies can be exchanged, to be wholly harmful.

At this moment it seems that the best thing we could wish governments to do is for, say, all the members of the European Economic Community, or, better still, all the governments of the Atlantic Community, to bind themselves mutually not to place any restrictions on the free use within their territories of one another's – or any other – currencies, including their purchase and sale at any price the parties decide upon, or on their use as accounting units in which to keep books. This, and not a utopian European Monetary Unit, seems to me now both the practicable and the desirable arrangement to aim at. To make the scheme effective it would be important, for reasons I state later, also to provide that banks in one country be free to establish branches in any of the others.

Government and legal tender

This suggestion may at first seem absurd to all brought up on the concept of 'legal tender'. Is it not essential that the law designate one kind of money as the legal money? This is, however, true only to the extent that, *if* the government does issue money, it must also say what must be accepted in discharge of debts incurred in that money. And it must also determine in what manner certain non-contractual legal obligations, such as taxes or liabilities for damage or torts, are to be discharged. But there is no reason whatever why people should not be free to make contracts, including ordinary purchases and sales, in any kind of money they choose, or why they should be obliged to sell against any particular kind of money.

There could be no more effective check against the abuse of money by the government than if people were free to refuse any money they distrusted and to prefer money in which they had confidence. Nor could there be a stronger inducement to governments to ensure the stability of their money than the knowledge that, so long as they kept the supply below the demand for it, that demand would tend to grow. Therefore, let us deprive governments (or their monetary authorities) of all power to protect their money against competition: if they can no longer conceal that their money is becoming bad, they will have to restrict the issue.

The first reaction of many readers may be to ask whether the effect of such a system would not according to an old rule be that the bad money would drive out the good. But this would be a misunderstanding of what is called Gresham's Law. This indeed is one of the oldest insights into the mechanism of money, so old that 2,400 years ago Aristophanes, in one of his comedies, could say that it was with politicians as it is with coins, because the bad ones drive out the good.[1] But the truth which apparently even today is not generally understood is that Gresham's Law operates *only* if the two kinds of money have to be accepted at a prescribed rate of exchange. Exactly the opposite will happen when people are free to exchange the different kinds of money at whatever rate they can agree upon. This was observed many

---

[1] Aristophanes, *Frogs*, 891–898, in Frere's translation:
Oftentimes we have reflected on a similar abuse
In the choice of men for office, and of coins for common use,
For our old and standard pieces, valued and approved and tried,
Here among the Grecian nations, and in all the world besides,
Recognised in every realm for trusty stamp and pure assay,
Are rejected and abandoned for the trash of yesterday,
For a vile adulterated issue, drossy, counterfeit and base,
Which the traffic of the city passes current in their place.
About the same time, the philosopher Diogenes called money 'the legislators' game of dice'!

times during the great inflations when even the most severe penalties threatened by governments could not prevent people from using other kinds of money – even commodities like cigarettes and bottles of brandy rather than the government money – which clearly meant that the good money was driving out the bad.[1]

Benefits of free currency system
Make it merely legal and people will be very quick indeed to refuse to use the national currency once it depreciates noticeably, and they will make their dealings in a currency they trust. Employers, in particular, would find it in their interest to offer, in collective agreements, not wages anticipating a foreseen rise of prices but wages in a currency they trusted and could make the basis of rational calculation. This would deprive government of the power to counteract excessive wage increases, and the unemployment they would cause, by depreciating their currency. It would also prevent employers from conceding such wages in the expectation that the national monetary authority would bail them out if they promised more than they could pay.

There is no reason to be concerned about the effects of such an arrangement on ordinary men who know neither how to handle nor how to obtain strange kinds of money. So long as the shopkeepers knew that they could turn it instantly at the current rate of exchange into whatever money they preferred, they would be only too ready to sell their wares at an appropriate price for any currency. But the malpractices of government would show themselves much more rapidly if prices rose only in terms of the money issued by it, and people would soon learn to hold the government responsible for the value of the money in which they were paid. Electronic calculators, which in seconds would give the equivalent of any price in any currency at the current rate, would soon be used everywhere. But, unless the national government all too badly mismanaged the currency it issued, it would probably be continued to be used in everyday retail transactions. What would be affected mostly would be not so much the use of money in daily payments as the willingness to *hold* different kinds of money. It would mainly be the tendency of all business and capital transactions rapidly to switch to a more reliable standard (and to base calculations and accounting on it) which would keep national monetary policy on the right path.

V
LONG-RUN MONETARY STABILITY

THE UPSHOT would probably be that the currencies of those countries trusted to pursue a responsible monetary policy would tend to displace gradually those of a less reliable character. The reputation of financial righteousness would become a jealously guarded asset of all issuers of money, since they would know that even the slightest deviation from the path of honesty would reduce the demand for their product.

[1] During the German inflation after the First World War, when people began to use dollars and other solid currencies in the place of marks, a Dutch financier (if I rightly remember, Mr Vissering) asserted that Gresham's Law was false and the opposite true.

I do not believe there is any reason to fear that in such a competition for the most general acceptance of a currency there would arise a tendency to deflation or an increasing value of money. People will be quite as reluctant to borrow or incur debts in a currency expected to appreciate as they will hesitate to lend in a currency expected to depreciate. The convenience of use is decidedly in favour of a currency which can be expected to retain an approximately stable value. If governments and other issuers of money have to compete in inducing people to *hold* their money, and make long-term contracts in it, they will have to create confidence in its long-run stability.

'The universal prize'
Where I am not sure is whether in such a competition for reliability any government-issued currency would prevail, or whether the predominant preference would not be in favour of some such units as ounces of gold. It seems not unlikely that gold would ultimately re-assert its place as 'the universal prize in all countries, in all cultures, in all ages', as Jacob Bronowski has recently called it in his brilliant book on *The Ascent of Man*,[1] if people were given complete freedom to decide what to use as their standard and general medium of exchange – more likely, at any rate, than as the result of any organised attempt to restore the gold standard.

The reason why, in order to be fully effective, the free international market in currencies should extend also to the services of banks is, of course, that bank deposits subject to cheque represent today much the largest part of the liquid assets of most people. Even during the last hundred years or so of the gold standard this circumstance increasingly prevented it from operating as a fully international currency, because any inflow or outflow in or out of a country required a proportionate expansion or contraction of the much larger super-structure of the national credit money, the effect of which falls indiscriminately on the whole economy instead of merely increasing or decreasing the demand for the particular goods which was required to bring about a new balance between imports and exports. With a truly international banking system money could be transferred directly without producing the harmful process of secondary contractions or expansions of the credit structure.

It would probably also impose the most effective discipline on governments if they felt immediately the effects of their policies on the attractiveness of investment in their country. I have just read in an English Whig tract more than 250 years old: 'Who would establish a Bank in an arbitrary country, or trust his money constantly there?'[2] The tract, incidentally, tells us that yet another 50 years earlier a great French banker, Jean Baptist Tavernier, invested all the riches he had amassed in his long rambles over the world in what the authors described as 'the barren rocks of Switzerland'; when asked why by Louis XIV, he had the courage to tell him that 'he was willing to have some-

---

[1] Jacob Bronowski, *The Ascent of Man*, BBC Publications, London, 1973.

[2] Thomas Gordon and John Trenchard, *The Cato Letters*, letters dated 12 May, 1722 and 3 February, 1721 respectively, published in collected editions, London, 1724, and later.

thing which he could call his own!' Switzerland, apparently, laid the foundations of her prosperity earlier than most people realise.

Free dealings in money better than monetary unions
I prefer the freeing of all dealings in money to any sort of monetary union also because the latter would demand an international monetary authority which I believe is neither practicable nor even desirable – and hardly to be more trusted than a national authority. It seems to me that there is a very sound element in the widespread disinclination to confer sovereign powers, or at least powers to command, on any international authority. What we need are not international authorities possessing powers of direction, but merely international bodies (or, rather, international treaties which are effectively enforced) which can prohibit certain actions of governments that will harm other people. Effectively to prohibit all restrictions on dealings in (and the possession of) different kinds of money (or claims for money) would at last make it possible that the absence of tariffs, or other obstacles to the movement of goods and men, will secure a genuine free trade area or common market – and do more than anything else to create confidence in the countries committing themselves to it. It is now urgently needed to counter that monetary nationalism which I first criticised almost 40 years ago[1] and which is becoming even more dangerous when, as a consequence of the close kinship between the two views, it is turning into monetary socialism. I hope it will not be too long before complete freedom to deal in any money one likes will be regarded as the essential mark of a free country.[2]

You may feel that my proposal amounts to no less than the abolition of monetary policy; and you would not be quite wrong. As in other connections, I have come to the conclusion that the best the state can do with respect to money is to provide a framework of legal rules within which the people can develop the monetary institutions that best suit them. It seems to me that if we could prevent governments from meddling with money, we would do more good than any government has ever done in this regard. And private enterprise would probably have done better than the best they have ever done.

[1] *Monetary Nationalism and International Stability*, Longmans, London, 1937.

[2] It may at first seem as if this suggestion were in conflict with my general support of fixed exchange rates under the present system. But this is not so. Fixed exchange rates seem to me to be necessary so long as national governments have a monopoly of issuing money in their territory in order to place them under a very necessary discipline. But this is of course no longer necessary when they have to submit to the discipline of competition with other issuers of money equally current within their territory.

21. Free Banking and Monetary Reform
George Selgin

Historical free banking systems were based upon the gold standard, whereas modern banking systems are based upon fiat monies issued by central banks. Must a free-banking reform therefore involve the restoration of a gold standard with all the attendant transition costs that would involve? In the following essay, the editor argues that a free banking system can also function on a fiat standard. His suggestion for reform involves freezing the monetary base (as some past Monetarists have recommended) while concurrently allowing private banks to fill changing demands for currency with their own, unregulated issues of bank notes that are freely redeemable in fiat money. —G.S., Ed.

****

Rules, Authority, or Freedom?

So LONG AS the money supply is centrally controlled, the central authority must either actively manipulate the money supply or it must adhere to a predetermined monetary rule.[1] That these are the *only* options for monetary policy is the view that has been handed down by several generations of economists. Implicitly or explicitly theorists have rejected the alternative of free banking. This is also true of many Chicago-School economists—the best-known proponents of monetary rules and opponents of monetary discretion—who otherwise argue for a free society based upon free markets.[2] For the cause of free banking the last fact is especially significant, because it means that a large and highly respected body of theorists, who might most readily have concurred with the arguments for free banking, have instead aligned themselves with advocates of monetary centralization.

Why have Chicago economists denied the efficacy of the free market in the realm of money and banking? To begin, they have doubted the very desirability of commercial banks issuing fiduciary media. Lloyd Mints (1950, 5 and 7) saw no benefits at all in such institutions; and although Simons (1951) and Friedman (1959, 8; 1953, 216–20) may not have shared this extreme position, they at least considered fractional-reserve banking to be "inherently unstable." Such a perspective does not incline its holders toward the view that banking should be entirely unregulated, except in peculiar cases (such as Mises's) where it is believed that free banking will somehow lead to the suppression of fractionally-based inside monies.

It has already been argued (in chapter 2) that fractional reserve banking is beneficial, contrary to Mints's position. It was also argued, in chapters 8 and 9, that there is no "inherent instability" in free banking. In fact, the particular sort of instability emphasized by Mints and Friedman—changes in the volume of money due to changes in the *form* in which the public wishes to hold its money—arises only in systems lacking freedom of note issue.[3] The problem is indeed inherent in systems with central banking and monopolized currency supply, but it is not inherent to all fractional-reserve banking.

Elsewhere various Chicago economists—especially Milton Friedman (1959, 4–9)—have criticized free banking on the grounds that it leads to unlimited inflation, involves excessive commodity-money resource costs, and encourages fraud. For these and other reasons they have claimed that the issue of currency is a technical monopoly which must be subject to government control. Each of these arguments has been critically examined and found wanting. The Chicago

School's dismissal of free banking was, in short, premature.

We are today in a much better position than the Chicago economists once were to consider free banking as an alternative monetary policy, distinct from reliance upon either rules or authorities. The best way to appreciate the advantages of this alternative is to view it in light of arguments on both sides of the rules-versus-authorities debate. Jacob Viner (1962, 244–74) provides an excellent summary of these arguments. According to him, the Chicago pro-rules position is that rules provide "protection . . . against arbitrary, malicious, capricious, stupid, clumsy, or other manipulation . . . by an 'authority' " and that they guarantee a monetary policy that is "certain" and "predictable" (ibid., 246).[4]

The principal argument for discretion is, on the other hand, the *ipso facto* deficiency of regulatory policies that "attempt to deal by simple rules with complex phenomena" (ibid.). A monetary rule necessarily precludes "the possibility of adaptation of regulation by well-intentioned, wise and skillful exercise of discretionary authority to the relevant differences in circumstances" (ibid.). Viner lists four considerations that stand in the way of the successful use of any monetary rule. They are (a) the existence of a multiplicity of policy ends, which no simple rule can fulfill; (b) the presence of more than one monetary authority or regulatory agency (which makes it difficult to assign responsibility for enforcement of a rule); (c) the existence of several instruments of monetary control (which complicates execution and enforcement of a rule even when there is a single monetary authority); and (d) the possibility that a satisfactory rule may not exist even if policy is aimed at a single end and is implemented by a single authority using a single instrument of control.

Although all these considerations are relevant, let us abstract from (a), (b), and (c) by assuming, first, that the sole end of monetary policy is to maintain monetary equilibrium (i.e., to adjust the nominal quantity of money in response to changes in demand); second, that responsibility for control of the money supply is vested with a single authority, namely, the "well-intentioned" directors of a central bank; and third, that open-market operations are the sole means for centrally administered changes in the money supply. This limits the problem to one of finding a satisfactory monetary rule. The difficulty here is that even a clearly defined policy end may involve "a quantity of some kind which is a function of several variables, all of which are important and are in unstable relation to each other" (ibid.). When this is true "there will be no fixed rule available which will be both practicable and appropriate to its objective" (ibid.).

Suppose the desired end is the accommodation of the demand for money, which is indeed "a quantity . . . of several variables . . . in unstable relation to each other." No simple monetary rule such as stabilization of a price index or a fixed percent money growth rate can fully satisfy this end. In fact the constant growth rate rule, which is now most popular, abandons any effort to accommodate seasonal and cyclical changes: it regards only secular changes in demand as predictable enough to be the basis for a steadfast formula.

And yet, as far as the desires of some advocates of monetary rules are concerned, the fixed money growth-rate proposal—especially when it is defined in terms of some monetary aggregate—is *not strict enough*. It still permits the monetary authority actively to conduct open-market operations to meet the prescribed growth rate. A pre-set schedule of open-market bond purchases cannot always be carried out, because the relevant money multipliers (which determine the effect of a given change in the supply of base money upon the supply of broader money aggregates) are not constant or fully predictable.[5] There will, therefore, always be occasions under such a rule when some discretion will have to be tolerated so that open-market purchases do not miss their target. On the other hand, if such discretion is permitted, it can be abused, and so, to state once more the warning of Henry Simons, it would make the supposed rule "a folly."

It is apparent, then, that if we must have a central monetary authority we must choose between the dangers of an imperfect and perhaps ill-maintained rule and the dangers of discretion and its possible abuse. This choice has been made somewhat less difficult in recent years, because the authorities' abuse of their discretionary powers has been such as to overshadow the potential damage that might result from blind adherence to some pre-set formula. In the United States the loss of faith in authority has given rise to a new proposal that is the ultimate expression of Simons's anti-discretion position. The proposal is that the supply of base money should be permanently *frozen*—that is, that the Federal Reserve System should cease open-market operations entirely.[6] Here at last is a rule calculated to prevent mischief: all that needs to be done to guarantee its strict observation is to close the Fed! Milton Friedman, who for years advocated a constant M–1 growth-rate rule, is now the most prominent champion of this frozen monetary base proposal.

Thus monetary policy has reached an impasse. Under a strict monetary rule, and especially in the case of the base-freeze proposal, the really desirable end of monetary policy—achieving monetary equilibrium—has to be sacrificed to the much lower, cruder end of merely preventing the authorities from introducing *more* instability into the system than might exist in the absence of any intervention, capricious or otherwise. Is such an inflexible arrangement the best that can be hoped for? So long as one clings to the assumption of centralized control and centralized currency supply, there is reason to believe that it is. We have seen, in chapter 7, why discretion, even in its best guise, is likely to hurt more than it helps.

But centralized control need not be taken for granted. The supply of currency could instead be placed on a competitive basis. This solution, unlike solutions based on centralized control, can achieve monetary stability while simultaneously eliminating government interference. Free note issue combines all the virtues of Friedman's proposal—which completely eliminates the danger of capricious manipulation of the money supply—with those of a system capable of meeting changing demands for money. Freedom of note issue resolves the "inherent instability" that afflicts centralized systems of fractional-reserve banking. By supplying an alternative form of pocket and till money—competitively issued bank notes—to accommodate changing public demands, free banking reduces the public's reliance upon base money as currency for use in everyday payments. In this way base money is allowed to remain in bank reserves to settle clearing balances. Fiat base money can thus be made to play a role similar to the one played by commodity money in the "typical" free banking system which has been given prominence through most of this study. Base money never has to move from bank reserves to circulation or vice-versa, so that, in such a system, there is no question of any need for reserve compensation to offset the ebb and flow of currency demand.

Free banking on a fiat standard may seem far from the sort of free banking discussed in previous chapters, but the difference is not really so great. True, the preceding pages discussed mainly a commodity standard, because this is the type that would most probably have evolved had banking been free all along; but events have been otherwise. For better or worse our monetary system is at present based on a fiat-dollar standard, and the momentum behind any existing standard is an argument for its retention. Existence of a fiat standard is, however, no barrier to the adoption of free banking. As far as banks today are concerned, fiat dollars are base money, which it is their business to receive and to lend and to issue claims upon. For most of the 20th century the only claims allowed (we are as usual considering ones redeemable on demand only) have been checkable deposits. What is proposed, therefore, is that commercial banks be given the right to issue their own notes, redeemable on demand for Federal Reserve Dollars, on the same assets that presently support checkable deposit liabilities.[7] Once the public becomes accustomed to using bank notes as currency, the stock of high-powered money can be permanently frozen according to a plan such as Friedman's without negative repercussions due to changes in the relative demand for currency.

This simple proposal does not involve any interference whatsoever with the dollar as the national monetary unit. Yet, it would make it possible for Federal Reserve high-powered money to be used exclusively as bank reserves, for settling interbank clearings, while allowing bank notes to take the place of Federal Reserve Dollars in fulfilling the currency needs of the public.[8]

A Practical Proposal for Reform

How can this proposal be implemented, and how can it be combined with a plan for freezing the monetary base? A reasonable starting point would be to remove archaic and obviously unnecessary regulations such as statutory reserve requirements and restrictions on regional and nationwide branch banking. The majority of nations with developed banking industries have not suffered from their lack of such regulations, evidence that their elimination in the United States would not have grave consequences. In fact, branch banking has significant micro- and macroeconomic advantages over unit banking, and its absence is probably the most important single cause of the relatively frequent failure of U. S. banks.[9] As for statutory reserve requirements, it has already been shown (in chapter 8) that they are impractical as instruments for reserve compensation. Apart from this, they serve no purpose other than to act as a kind of tax on bank liabilities. Furthermore, their existence interferes with banks' ability to accommodate changes in the demand for inside money. If the monetary base is frozen this restrictive effect is absolute. On the other hand, elimination of statutory reserve requirements, unless it proceeds in very small steps, could open the door to a serious bout of inflation. A solution would be to sterilize existing required reserves the moment the requirements are removed. This could be done as follows: suppose the statutory reserve requirement is 20 percent. Presumably banks operate with reserves of, say, 25 percent—only the excess 5 percent are an actual source of liquidity to the banks. It could then be announced that after a certain date there will be no further rediscounts by the Federal Reserve Banks (thus encouraging banks to acquire adequate excess reserves). Then when the deadline arrives reserves held for statutory purposes could be converted to Treasury bills—a non-high-powered money obligation—and the statutory reserve requirements could at the same moment be eliminated.[10]

In addition to reserve requirements and restrictions on branch banking, restrictions on bank diversification such as the Glass-Steagall Act should also be repealed. This would allow banks to set up equity accounts, reducing their exposure to runs by depositors, and opening the way to the replacement of government deposit insurance by private alternatives.

While these deregulations are in progress, Congress can proceed to restore to every commercial bank (whether national or state chartered) the right to issue its own redeemable demand notes (which might also bear an option-clause) unrestricted by bond-deposit requirements or by any tax not applicable to demand deposits. This reform would not in any way complicate the task facing the still operating Federal Reserve Board; indeed, it would reduce the Fed's need to take account of fluctuations in the public's currency needs when adjusting the money supply. The multiplier would become more stable and predictable to the extent that bank notes were employed to satisfy temporary changes in currency demand.[11] Over time banks would establish the reliability of their issues, which need not be considered any less trustworthy by the public than traveler's checks.

For competitively issued notes to displace base money from circulation entirely the public must feel comfortable using them as currency. This might be a problem: the situation differs from the case of a metallic base money, which is obviously a less convenient currency medium for most purposes than bank notes redeemable in it. There is no obvious advantage in using paper bank notes instead of equally handy paper base dollars. Nevertheless, imaginative innovations could probably induce the public to prefer bank notes. The existing base-money medium could as a deliberate policy be replaced by paper instruments of somewhat larger physical size, fitting less easily into wallets and tills. Bank notes, on the other hand, could be made the size of present Federal Reserve notes. The appearance of base dollars could also be altered in other ways, for instance, by having them engraved in red ink. In this form they might seem even less familiar to currency users than the newly available bank notes. Finally, base dollars could be made available only in less convenient denominations. Two-dollar bills would work, since they already have an established reputation for not being wanted by the public, but larger bills would be most convenient for settling interbank clearings. Banks, of course, should be allowed to issue whatever note denominations they discovered to be most desired by their customers.[12]

Other innovations need not be a matter of public policy but can be left to the private incentive of banks. Banks could stock their automatic teller machines with their own notes, and bank tellers could be instructed to give notes to depositors who desire currency, unless base dollars were specifically requested. Banks might also conduct weekly lottery drawings and offer prize money to persons possessing notes with winning serial numbers.[13] The drawings would be like similar lotteries now held by several daily newspapers. They would make notes more appealing to the public, as they would constitute an indirect way of paying interest to note holders, just as interest is now paid on some checkable deposits.

A combination of measures such as these would almost certainly lead to near-complete displacement of base dollars from circulation.

Once this stage was reached—say, once 5 percent or less of the total of checkable deposits and currency in circulation consists of base dollars[14]—a date could be chosen upon which the supply of base money would be permanently frozen. When this date arrived, outstanding Federal Reserve deposit credits would be converted into paper base dollars, and banks that held deposits with the Fed would receive their balances in cash. Banks could then exercise their option to convert some of this cash into specially created Treasury obligations (see note 12). At this point the Federal Reserve Board and Federal Open-Market Committee could be disbanded. This would end the Fed's money creating activities. The System's clearing operations could be privatized by having the twelve Federal Reserve Banks and their branches placed into the hands of their member-bank stockholders.[15] The frozen stock of base dollars could then be warehoused by the newly privatized clearinghouse associations. Dollar "certificates" or clearinghouse account entries could be used to settle interbank clearings, thereby saving the dollar supply from wear and tear. Only a small amount of base dollars would actually have to be kept on hand by individual banks to satisfy rare requests for them by customers. In the unlikely event of a redemption run, a single bank in distress could be assisted by some of its more liquid branches or by other banks acting unilaterally or through the clearinghouse associations; some banks might also have recourse to option clauses written on their notes. Finally, bank liabilities might continue to be insured (by private firms), although there might not be any demand for such insurance under the more stable and less failure-prone circumstances that free banking would foster.

The above discussion assumes that base money dollars will continue to command a saleability premium and that they will therefore continue to be used to settle clearing balances among banks absent any legal restrictions compelling their use. Such need not be the case, however. Indeed, it should be emphasized that, although the above reform is designed so that a continuation of the present paper-dollar standard is possible under it, the reform is not meant to guarantee the permanence of that standard. Some other asset might replace paper dollars as the most saleable asset in the economic system and hence as the ultimate means of settling debts. This would drive the value of paper dollars to zero (since there is no nonmonetary demand for them), rendering the dollar useless as a unit of account. In this event a new unit of account, linked to the most saleable asset in the system, would evolve, thus bringing the dollar standard to an end. As Vaubel (1986) emphasizes, one aim of a complete free-banking reform should be the elimination of any barriers standing in the way of the adoption of a new monetary standard. Fiat currencies issued by other governments or even by private firms (including composite currencies like the ECU), if they were judged more advantageous by the public, could then replace the present dollar standard. Also, the way would be opened for the restoration of some kind of commodity standard, such as a gold standard. This does not mean that a change of standard would be likely; however, *if* many people desired it, it could occur. A well-working free banking system can grow on the foundation of any sort of base money that the public is likely to select, and competition in the supply of base money is no less desirable than competition in the supply of bank liabilities, including bank notes, redeemable in base money.

Of course this reform is radical, and it is not likely to be adopted in the near future. Nevertheless, there are no great logistic or material barriers standing in the way of the adoption of free banking; the transition costs of a well-framed free banking reform are negligible—with benefits as great as the potential for undesirable fluctuations in the dollar supply if it is not undertaken. Therefore, although political reality renders such reform unlikely in the near future, it would be unfortunate if this were made the excuse for avoiding the vigorous discussion that might minimize the waiting time for its implementation. The present banking system is likely to generate a need for drastic change sooner or later, and if reform is delayed until a time of crisis, there can be no question of any smooth, costless transition to a **well-working, deregulated system. On the contrary, an occasion of panic is likely to breed the sort of "temporary" makeshift measures that end in *more* regulation and centralization, leaving the banking system in an even less satisfactory state, and still further removed from the practical and theoretical ideal of perfect freedom.**

22. The Lender of Last Resort: Alternative Views and Historical Experience

Michael David Bordo

Advocates of free banking want to get the government out of the money business, and so propose that private banks should be allowed to issue notes and that central banks should be abolished. The conventional view, however, is that private banks depend upon the presence of a central bank serving as a "lender of last resort." Is a "lender of last resort" really necessary or not, and if it is, must it also be a central bank? In "The Lender of Last Resort: Alternative Views and Historical Experience," Michael D. Bordo explores these and related questions. —G.S., Ed.

****

I. INTRODUCTION

Recent liquidity assistance to failing savings and loans and banks (some insolvent and some large) in the U.S. and similar rescues abroad have prompted renewed interest in the topic of the lender of last resort. Under the classical doctrine, the need for a lender of last resort arises in a fractional reserve banking system when a banking panic, defined as a massive scramble for high-powered money, threatens the money stock and, hence, the level of economic activity. The lender of last resort can allay an incipient panic by timely assurance that it will provide whatever high-powered money is required to satisfy the demand, either by offering liberal access to the discount window at a penalty rate or by open market purchases.

Henry Thornton (1802) and Walter Bagehot (1873) developed the key elements of the classical doctrine of the lender of last resort (LLR) in England. This doctrine holds that monetary authorities in the face of panic should lend unsparingly but at a penalty rate to illiquid but solvent banks. Monetarist writers in recent years have reiterated and extended the classical notion of the LLR. By contrast, Charles Goodhart and others have recently posited an alternative view, broadening the power of LLR to include aid to insolvent financial institutions. Finally, modern proponents of free banking have made the case against a need for any public LLR.

The remainder of this paper is organized as follows:

II. The LLR's role in preventing banking panics

III. Four views of the LLR: central propositions

IV. Historical evidence:
  Incidence of banking panics and LLR actions, U.S. and elsewhere
  Alternative LLR arrangements in the U.S., Scotland, and Canada
  Record of assistance to insolvent banks

V. Lessons from history in the context of the four views of the LLR

II. BANKING PANICS AND THE LENDER OF LAST RESORT

The need for a monetary authority to act as LLR arises in the case of a banking panic—a widespread attempt by the public to convert deposits into currency and, in response, an attempt by commercial banks to raise their desired reserve-deposit ratios. Banking panics can occur in a fractional reserve banking system when a bank failure or series of failures produces bank runs which in turn become contagious, threatening the solvency of otherwise sound banks.

Two sets of factors, some internal and some external to banks, can lead to bank failures. Internal factors, which affect both financial and nonfinancial enterprises, include poor management, poor judgment, and dishonesty. External factors include adverse changes in relative prices (e.g., land or oil prices) and in the overall price level.

Of the external factors, changes in relative prices can drastically alter the value of a bank's portfolio and render it insolvent. Banking structure can mitigate the effects of relative price changes. A nationwide branch banking system that permits portfolio diversification across regions enables a bank to absorb the effects of relative price changes. A unit banking system, even with correspondents, is considerably less effective. The nearly 6000 bank failures that occurred during the decade of the 1920s in the U.S. were mostly small unit banks in agricultural regions. Canada, in contrast, had nationwide branch banking. Consequently, many bank branches in those regions closed, but no banks failed (with the exception of one, in 1923, due to fraud).

A second external factor that can lead to bank failures is changes in the overall price level (Schwartz, 1988). Price level instability (in a nonindexed system) can produce unexpected changes in banks' net worth and convert *ex ante* sound investments into *ex post* mistakes. Instability means sharp changes from rising to falling prices or from inflation to disinflation. It was caused by gold movements under the pre-1914 gold standard, and, more recently, by the discretionary actions of monetary authorities.

Given that bank liabilities are convertible on demand, a run on an insolvent bank is a rational response by depositors concerned about their ability to convert their own deposits into currency. In normal circumstances, according to one writer, bank runs serve as a form of market discipline, reallocating funds from weak to strong banks and constraining bank managers from adopting risky portfolio strategies (Kaufman, 1988). Bank runs can also lead to a "flight to quality" (Benston and Kaufman et al., 1986). Instead of shifting funds from weak banks to those they regard to be sound, depositors may convert their deposits into high-quality securities. The seller of the securities, however, ultimately will deposit his receipts at other banks, leaving bank reserves unchanged.

When there is an external shock to the banking system, incomplete and costly information may sometimes make it difficult for depositors to distinguish sound from unsound banks. In that case, runs on insolvent banks can produce contagious runs on solvent banks, leading to panic. A panic, in turn, can lead to massive bank failures. Sound banks are rendered insolvent by the fall in the value of their assets resulting from a scramble for liquidity. By intervening at the point when the liquidity of solvent banks is threatened—that is, by supplying whatever funds are needed to meet the demand for cash—the monetary authority can allay the panic.

Private arrangements can also reduce the likelihood of panics. Branch banking allows funds to be transferred from branches with surplus funds to those in need of cash (e.g., from branches in a prosperous region to those in a depressed region). By pooling the resources of its members, commercial bank clearing houses, in the past, provided emergency reserves to meet the heightened liquidity demand. A clearing house also represented a signal to the public that help would be available to member banks in time of panic. Neither branch banking nor clearing houses, however, can stem a nationwide demand for currency occasioned by a major aggregate shock, like a world war. Only the monetary authority—the ultimate supplies of high-powered money—could succeed. Of course, government deposit insurance can prevent panics by removing the reason for the public to run to currency.[1] Ultimately, however, a LLR is required to back up any deposit scheme.

III. ALTERNATIVE VIEWS ON THE LLR FUNCTION

Four alternative views on the lender of last resort function are outlined below, including:

- The Classical View: the LLR should provide whatever funds are needed to allay a panic;
- Goodfriend and King: an open market operation is the only policy required to stem a liquidity crisis;
- Goodhart (and others): the LLR should assist illiquid and insolvent banks;
- Free Banking: no government authority is needed to serve as LLR.

The Classical Position

Both Henry Thornton's *An Enquiry into the Effects of the Paper Credit of Great Britain* (1802) and Walter Bagehot's *Lombard Street* (1873) were concerned with the role of the Bank of England in stemming periodic banking panics. In Thornton's time, the Bank of England—a private institution which served as the government's bank—had a monopoly of the note issue within a 26-mile radius of London, and Bank of England notes served as high-powered money for the English banking system.[2] For Thornton, the Bank's responsibility in time of panic was to serve as LLR, providing liquidity to the market and discounting freely the paper of all solvent banks, but denying aid to insolvent banks no matter how large or important (Humphrey, 1975, 1989).

Bagehot accepted and broadened Thornton's view. Writing at a time when the Bank had considerably enhanced its power in the British financial system, he stated four principles for the Bank to observe as lender of last resort to the monetary system:

- Lend, but at a penalty rate[3]: "Very large loans at very high rates are the best remedy for the worst malady of the money market when a foreign drain is added to a domestic drain." (Bagehot, 1873, p.56);
- Make clear in advance the Bank's readiness to lend freely;

- Accomodate anyone with good collateral (valued at pre-panic prices);
- Prevent illiquid but solvent banks from failing.[4,5]

Recent monetarist economists have restated the classical position. Friedman and Schwartz (1963), in *A Monetary History*, devote considerable attention to the role of banking panics in producing monetary stability in the United States (also see Cagan, 1965). According to them, the peculiarities of the nineteenth century U.S. banking system (unit banks, fractional reserves, and pyramiding of reserves in New York) made it highly susceptible to banking panics. Federal deposit insurance in 1934 provided a remedy to this vulnerability. It served to assure the public that their insured deposits would not be lost, but would remain readily available.

Friedman and Schwartz highlight the importance in the pre-FDIC system of timely judgment by strong and responsible leadership in intervening to allay the public's fear. Before the advent of the Fed, the New York Clearing House issued clearing house certificates and suspended convertibility, and, on occasion, the Treasury conducted open market operations. In two episodes, these interventions were successful; in three others, they were not effective in preventing severe monetary contraction. The Federal Reserve System, established in part to provide such leadership, failed dismally in the 1929-33 contraction. According to Friedman and Schwartz, had the Fed conducted open market operations in 1930 and 1931 to provide the reserves needed by the banking system, the series of bank failures that produced the unprecedented decline in the money stock could have been prevented.

Schwartz (1986) argues that all the important financial crises in the United Kingdom and the United States occurred when the monetary authorities failed to demonstrate at the beginning of a disturbance their readiness to meet all demands of sound debtors for loans and of depositors for cash. Finally, she views deposit insurance as not necessary to prevent banking panics. It was successful after 1934 in the U.S. because the lender of last resort was undependable. Had the Fed acted on Bagehot's principles, federal deposit insurance would not have been necessary, as the record of other countries with stable banking systems but no federal deposit insurance attests.

Meltzer (1986) argues that a central bank should allow insolvent banks to fail, for not to do so would encourage financial institutions to take greater risks. Following such an approach would "separate the risk of individual financial failures from aggregate risk by establishing principles that prevent banks' liquidity problems from generating an epidemic of insolvencies" (p. 85). The worst cases of financial panics, according to Meltzer, "arose because the central bank did not follow Bagehotian principles."[6]

Goodfriend-King and the Case for Open Market Operations

Goodfriend and King (1988) argue strongly for the exercise of the LLR function solely by the use of open market operations to augment the stock of high-powered money; they define this as monetary policy. Sterilized discount window lending to particular banks, which they refer to as banking policy, does not involve a change in high-powered money. They regard banking policy as redundant because they see sterilized discount window lending as similar to private provision of line-of-credit services; both require monitoring and supervision, and neither affects the stock of high-powered money.[7] Moreover, they argue that it is not clear that the Fed can provide such services at a lower cost than can the private sector. Goodfriend (1989) suggests that one reason the Fed may currently be able to extend credit at a lower cost is that it can make fully collateralized loans to banks, whereas private lenders cannot do so under current regulations. On the other hand, the availability of these fully collateralized discount window loans to offset funds withdrawals by uninsured depositors and others may on occasion permit delays in the closing of insolvent banks.[8] Goodfriend regards government-provided deposit insurance as basically a substitute for the portfolio diversification of a nationwide branch banking system. By itself, however, deposit insurance without a LLR commitment to provide high-powered money in times of stress is insufficient to protect the banking system as a whole from aggregate shock.

The Case for Central Bank Assistance to Insolvent Banks

Charles Goodhart (1985, 1987) advocates temporary central bank assistance to insolvent banks. He argues that the distinction between illiquidity and insolvency is a myth, since banks requiring LLR support because of "illiquidity will in most cases already be under suspicion about . . . solvency." Furthermore "because of the difficulty of valuing [the distressed bank's] assets, a Central Bank will usually have to take a decision on last resort support to meet an immediate liquidity problem when it knows that there is a doubt about solvency, but does not know just how bad the latter position actually is" (Goodhart, 1985, p. 35).

He also argues that by withdrawing deposits from an insolvent bank in a flight to quality, a borrower severs the valuable relationship with his banker. Loss of this relationship, based both on trust and agent-specific information, adds to the cost of flight, making it less likely to occur. Replacing such a connection requires costly search, a process which imposes losses (and possible bankruptcy) on the borrowers. To protect borrowers, Goodhart would have the central bank recycle funds back to the troubled bank.

Solow (1982) also is sympathetic to assisting insolvent banks. According to him, the Fed is responsible for the stability of the whole financial system. He argues that any bank failure, especially a large one, reduces confidence in the whole system. To prevent a loss of confidence caused by a major bank failure from spreading to the rest of the banking system, the central bank should provide assistance to insolvent banks. However, such a policy creates a moral hazard, as banks respond with greater risk-taking and the public loses its incentive to monitor them.

Free Banking: The Case against Any Public LLR

Proponents of free banking have denied the need for any government authority to serve as lender of last resort. They argue that the only reason for banking panics is legal restrictions on the banking system. In the absence of such restrictions, the free market would produce a panic-proof banking system.

According to Selgin (1988, 1990) two of the most important restrictions are the prohibition of nationwide branch banking in the U.S. and the prohibition everywhere of free currency issue by the commercial banking system. Nationwide branch banking would allow sufficient portfolio diversification to prevent relative price shocks from causing banks to fail. Free note issue would allow banks to supply whatever currency individuals may demand.

Free banking proponents also contend that contagious runs because of incomplete information would not occur because secondary markets in bank notes (note brokers, note detectors) would provide adequate information to note holders about the condition of all banks. True, such markets do not arise for demand deposits because of the agent-specific information involved in the demand deposit contract—it is costly to verify whether the depositor has funds backing his check. But, free banking advocates insist that clearing house associations can offset the information asymmetry involved in deposit banking.

According to Gorton (1985), and Gorton and Mullineaux (1987), clearing houses in the nineteenth century, by quickly organizing all member banks into a cartel-like structure, established a coinsurance scheme that made it difficult for the public to discern the weakness of an individual member bank. The clearing house could also allay a panic by issuing loan certificates which served as a close substitute for gold (assuming that the clearing house itself was financially sound). Finally, a restriction on convertibility of deposits into currency could end a panic. Dowd (1984) regards restrictions as a form of option clause.[9] In an alternative option (used in pre-1765 Scotland) banks had the legal right to defer redemption till a later date, with interest paid to compensate for the delay.

For Selgin and Dowd, the public LLR evolved because of a monopoly in the issue of currency. The Bank of England's currency monopoly within a 26-mile radius of London until 1826 and its extension to the whole country in 1844 made it more difficult than otherwise for depositors to satisfy their demand for currency in times of stress. This, in turn, created a need for the Bank, as sole provider of high-powered money, to serve as LLR.[10] In the U.S., bond-collateral restrictions on state banks before 1863 and on the national banks thereafter were responsible for the well-known problem of currency inelasticity. Selgin and Dowd do not discuss the case of a major aggregate shock that produces a widespread demand for high-powered money. In that situation, only the monetary authority will suffice.

In sum, the four views—classical, Goodfriend/King, Goodhart, and free banking—have considerably different implications for the role of a LLR. With these views as backdrop, the remaining paragraphs now examine evidence on banking panics and their resolution in the past.

IV. THE HISTORICAL RECORD

In this section, I present historical evidence for a

number of countries on the incidence of banking panics, their likely causes, and the role of a LLR in their resolution. I then consider alternative institutional arrangements that served as surrogate LLRs in diverse countries at different times. Finally, I compare the historical experience with the more recent assistance to insolvent banks in the U.S., Great Britain, and Canada. This evidence is then used to shed light on the alternative views of the lender of last resort discussed in section III.

Banking Panics and Their Resolution

The record for the past 200 years for at least 17 countries shows a large number of bank failures, fewer bank runs (but still a considerable number) and a relatively small number of banking panics. According to a chronology compiled by Anna Schwartz (1988), for the U.S. between 1790 and 1930, bank panics occurred in 14 years; Great Britain had the next highest number with panics occurring in 8 years between 1790 and 1866. France and Italy followed with 4 each.

An alternative chronology that I prepared (Bordo, 1986, Table 1) for 6 countries (the U.S., Great Britain, France, Germany, Sweden, and Canada) over the period 1870-1933 lists 16 banking crises (defined as bank runs and/or failures), and 4 banking panics (runs, failures, and suspensions of payments), all of which occurred in the U.S. It also lists 30 such crises, based on Kindleberger's definition of financial crises as comprising manias, panics, and crashes and 71 stock market crises, based on Morgenstern's (1959) definition.

The similar failure rates for banks and nonfinancial firms in many countries largely reflect that individual banks, like other firms, are susceptible to market vagaries and to mismanagement. Internal factors were important, as were the external factors of relative price changes, banking structure, and changes in the overall price level. The relatively few instances of banking panics in the past two centuries suggests that either (1) monetary authorities in time developed the procedures and expertise to supply the funds needed to meet depositors' demands for cash or (2) the problem of banking panics is exaggerated.

A comparison of the performances of Great Britain and the U.S. in the past century serves to illustrate the importance of the lender of last resort in preventing banking panics. In the first half of the nineteenth century, Great Britain experienced banking panics when the insolvency of an important financial institution precipitated runs on other banks, and a scramble for high-powered money ensued. In a number of instances, the reaction of the Bank of England to protect its own gold reserves worsened the panic. Eventually, the Bank supplied funds to the market, but often too late to prevent many unnecessary bank failures. The last such panic followed the failure of the Overend Gurney Company in 1866. Thereafter, the Bank accepted its responsibility as lender of last resort, observing Bagehot's Rule "to lend freely but at a penalty rate". It prevented incipient financial crises in 1878, 1890, and 1914 from developing into full-blown panics by timely announcements and action.

The United States in the antebellum period experienced 11 banking panics (according to Schwartz's chronology) of which the panics of 1837, 1839, and 1857 were most notable.[11] The First and Second Banks of the United States possessed some central banking powers in part of the period; some states developed early deposit insurance schemes (see Benston, 1983; Calomiris, 1989), and the New York Clearing House Association began issuing clearing house loan certificates in 1857. None of these arrangements sufficed to prevent the panics.

In the national banking era, the U.S. experienced three serious banking panics — 1873, 1893, and 1907-08. In these episodes, the Clearing Houses of New York, Chicago, and other central reserve cities issued emergency reserve currency in the form of clearing house loan certificates collateralized by member banks' assets and even issued small denomination hand-to-hand currency. But these lender of last resort actions were ineffective. In contrast to successful intervention in 1884 and 1890, the issue of emergency currency was too little and too late to prevent panic from spreading. The panics ended upon the suspension of convertibility of deposits into currency. During suspension, both currency and deposits circulated freely at flexible exchange rates, thereby relieving the pressure on bank reserves. The panics of 1893 and especially 1907 precipitated a movement to establish an agency to satisfy the public's demand for currency in times of distrust of deposit convertibility. The interim Aldrich-Vreeland Act of 1908 allowed ten or more national banks to form national currency associations and issue emergency currency; it was successful in preventing a panic in 1914.

The Federal Reserve System was created in 1914

to serve as a lender of last resort. The U.S. did not experience a banking panic until 1930, but as Friedman and Schwartz point out, during the ensuing three years, a succession of nationwide banking panics accounted for the destruction of one-third of the money stock and the permanent closing of 40 percent of the nation's banks. Only with the establishment of federal deposit insurance in 1934 did the threat of banking panics recede.

Table I compares American and British evidence on factors commonly believed to be related to banking panics, as well as a chronology of banking panics and banking crises for severe NBER business cycle recessions (peak to trough) in the period 1870-1933.[12] The variables isolated include: deviations from trend of the average annual growth rate of real output; the absolute difference of the average annual rate of change in the price level during the preceding trough to peak and the current peak to trough as a measure of the effect of changes in the overall price level; deviations from trend of the average annual rate of monetary growth; and the percentage change in the money stock due to changes in the deposit-currency ratio.[13]

The table reveals some striking similarities in the behavior of variables often related to panics but a remarkable difference between the two countries in the incidence of panics. Virtually all six business cycle downturns designated by the NBER as severe were marked in both countries by significant declines in output, large price level reversals, and large declines in money-growth. Also, in both countries, falls in the deposit-currency ratio produced declines in the money stock in the three most severe downturns: 1893-94 (U.S.); 1890-1894 (G.B.); 1907-08; and 1929-32.

However, the difference in the incidence of panics is striking—the U.S. had four while Britain had none. Both countries experienced frequent stock market crashes (see Bordo, 1986, Table 6.1). They were buffeted by the same international financial crises. Although Britain faced threats to the banking system in 1878, 1890, and 1914, the key difference between the two countries (see the last three columns of Table I) was successful LLR action by the British authorities in defusing incipient crises.

Similar evidence over the 1870-1933 period for France, Germany, Sweden, and Canada is available

Table I
Banking Panics (1870-1933): Related Factors, Incidence, and Resolution

	Reference Cycle Peak	Trough	Deviations from Trend of Average Annual Real Output Growth[a] (peak to trough)**	Absolute Difference of Average Annual Rate of Price Level Change (trough to peak minus peak to trough)*	Deviations from Trend of Average Annual Monetary Growth[b] (specific cycle peak to trough)**	Change in Money due to Change in Deposit-Currency Ratio (specific cycle peak to trough)**	Banking Crisis[c]**	Banking Panic[d]**	Existence of Clear and Credible LLR Policy***	Resolution***	Agency***
United States	1873	1879	0.5%	-7.1%	-4.7%	2.7%		8/73	No	Restriction of Payments	Clearing Houses/Treasury
	1882	1885	-3.2%	-12.2%	2.6%	5.2%	5/84		Yes	Successful LLR	Clearing Houses/Treasury
	1893	1894	-9.5%	-9.0%	-9.3%	-4.3%		7/93	No	Restriction of Payments	Clearing Houses/Treasury
	1907	1908	-14.7%	-6.1%	-1.7%	-2.7%		10/07	No	Restriction of Payments	Clearing Houses/Treasury
	1920	1921	-7.6%	-56.7%	-2.5%	2.8%			(?)		
	1929	1932	-16.7%	-12.5%	-11.7%	-27.4%	1930,1931,1932	1933	No	Unsuccessful LLR	Federal Reserve
Great Britain	1873	1879	0.9%	-7.1%	-3.1%	5.2%			Yes		
	1883	1886	-1.2%	-5.4%	-2.8%	2.3%			Yes		
	1890	1894	-0.2%	-4.4%	-2.5%	-2.2%	Baring Crisis 11/90		Yes	Successful	Bank of England
	1907	1908	-4.7%	-13.6%	-1.6%	-1.0%			Yes		
	1920	1921	-6.9%	-68.0%	-5.1%	4.5%			Yes		
	1929	1932	-3.7%	-7.9%	-4.3%	-1.3%			Yes		

Data Sources: * See Data Appendix in Bordo (1981).
  ** See Data Appendix in Bordo (1986).
  *** Judgmental, based on this paper and other research.

Notes: (a) The trend growth rates of real output were 3.22% for the U.S. (1870-1941) and 1.48% for Great Britain (1870-1939). Each was calculated as the difference between the natural logs of real output in terminal and initial years divided by the number of years.
  (b) The trend monetary growth rates were 5.40% for the U.S. (1870-1941) and 2.71% for Great Britain (1870-1939). Each was calculated as in footnote (a).
  (c) Banking crisis—runs and/or failures. Source Bordo (1986).
  (d) Banking panic—runs, failures, suspension of payments. Ibid.

in Bordo (1986). In all four countries, the quantitative variables move similarly during severe recessions to those displayed here for the U.S. and Great Britain, yet there were no banking panics. In France, appropriate actions by the Bank of France in 1882, 1889, and 1930 prevented incipient banking crises from developing into panics. Similar behavior occurred in Germany in 1901 and 1931 and in Canada in 1907 and 1914.

One other key difference was that all five countries had nationwide branch banking whereas the U.S. had unit banking. That difference likely goes a long way to explain the larger number of bank failures in the U.S.

Alternative LLR Arrangements

In the traditional view, the LLR role is synonymous with that of a central bank. Goodhart's explanation for the evolution of central banking in England and other European countries is that the first central banks evolved from commercial banks which had the special privilege of being their governments' banks. Because of its sound reputation, position as holder of its nation's gold reserves, ability to obtain economies by pooling reserves through a correspondent banking system, and ability to provide extra cash by rediscounting, such a bank would evolve into a bankers' bank and lender of last resort in liquidity crises. Once such banks began to act as lenders of last resort, "moral hazard" on the part of member banks (following riskier strategies than they would otherwise) provided a rationale for some form of supervision or legislation. Further, Goodhart argues that the conflict between the public duties of such an institution and its responsibilities to its shareholders made the transition from a competitive bank to a central bank lengthy and painful.

Though Goodhart (1985 Annex B) demonstrates that a number of central banks evolved in this fashion, the experiences of other countries suggests that alternative arrangements were possible. In the U.S. before the advent of the Fed, a variety of institutional arrangements were used on occasion in hopes of allaying banking panics, including:

- Deposit insurance schemes: relatively successful in a number of states before the Civil War (Benston, 1983; Calomiris, 1989);
- A variety of early twentieth century deposit insurance arrangements which were not successful (White, 1981);
- Clearing houses and the issue of clearing house loan certificates (Timberlake, 1984; Gorton, 1985);
- Restriction of convertibility of deposits into currency by the clearing house associations in the national banking era;
- Various U.S. Treasury operations between 1890 and 1907 (Timberlake, 1978);
- The Aldrich-Vreeland Act of 1908.

Two countries which managed successfully for long periods without central banks were Scotland and Canada. Scotland had a system of free banking from 1727 to 1844. The key features of this system were a) free entry into banking and free issue of bank notes, b) bank notes that were fully convertible into full-bodied coin, and c) unlimited liability of bank shareholders.

Scotland's record under such a system was one of remarkable monetary stability. That country experienced very few bank failures and very few financial crises. One reason, according to White (1984), was the unlimited liability of bank stockholders and strict bankruptcy laws that instilled a sense of confidence in noteholders.[14] Indeed, the Scottish banks would take over at par the issue of failed banks (e.g., the Ayr bank, 1772) to increase their own business. A second reason was the absence of restrictions on bank capital and of other impediments to the development of extensive branching systems that allowed banks to diversify risk and withstand shocks.[15] Faced with a nationwide scramble for liquidity, however, Scottish banks were always able to turn to the Bank of England as a lender of last resort (Goodhart 1985).

Although Canada had a competitive fractional reserve banking system throughout the nineteenth century, no central bank evolved (Bordo and Redish, 1987). By the beginning of the twentieth century, though, virtually all the elements of traditional central banking were being undertaken either by private institutions or directly by the government.

By 1890, the chartered banks, with the compliance of the Government, had established an effective self-policing agency, the Canadian Bankers Association. Acting in the absence of a central bank, it succeeded in insulating the Canadian banks from the deleterious effects of the U.S. banking panics of 1893 and 1907. It did so by quickly arranging mergers between sound and failing banks, by encouraging cooperation between strong and weaker banks in times of stringency, and by establishing a reserve fund to be used to compensate note holders in the event of failure.

In addition, the nationwide branch system overcame the problem of seasonal liquidity crises that characterized the United States after the Civil War, thus lessening the need for a lender of last resort. However, the Bank of Montreal (founded in 1817) very early became the government's bank and performed many central bank functions.

Because Canadian banks kept most of their reserves on "call" in the New York money market, they were able in this way to satisfy the public's demand for liquidity, again precluding the need for a central bank. On two occasions, 1907 and 1914, however, these reserves proved inadequate to prevent a liquidity crisis and the Government of Canada had to step in to supplement the reserves.

The Finance Act, passed in 1914 to facilitate wartime finance, provided the chartered banks with a liberal rediscounting facility. By pledging appropriate collateral (this was broadly defined) banks could borrow Dominion notes from the Treasury Board. The Finance Act clause, which was extended after the wartime emergency by the Amendment of 1923, provided a discount window/lender of last resort for the Canadian banking system.

In sum, though Canada, Scotland, and several other countries did not have formal central banks serving as LLRs, all had access to a governmental authority which could provide high-powered money in the event of such a crisis.

LLR Assistance to Insolvent Banks

The classical prescription for LLR action is to lend freely but at a penalty rate to illiquid but solvent banks. Both Thornton and Bagehot advised strongly against assistance to insolvent financial institutions. They opposed them because they would encourage future risk-taking without even eradicating the threat of runs on other sound financial institutions. Bagehot also advocated lending at a penalty rate to discourage all but those truly in need from applying and to limit the expansion in liquidity to the minimum necessary to end the panic.

Between 1870 and 1970, European countries generally observed the classical strictures. In the Baring Crisis of 1890, the Bank of England successfully prevented panic. It arranged (with the Bank of France and the leading Clearing Banks) to advance the necessary sums to meet the Barings' immediate maturing liability. These other institutions effectively became part of a joint LLR by guaranteeing to cover losses sustained by the Bank of England in the process (Schwartz, 1986, p. 19). The German Reichsbank in 1901 prevented panic by purchasing prime bills on the open market and expanding its excess note issue, but it did not intervene to prevent the failure of the Leipziger and other banks (Goodhart, 1985, p. 96). The Bank of France also followed classical precepts in crises in 1881 and 1889.

The Austrian National Bank, however, ignored the classical advice during the Credit Anstalt crisis of 1931 by providing liberal assistance to the Credit Anstalt at low interest rates (Schubert, 1987). Then, a run on the Credit Anstalt and other Viennese banks in May 1931 followed the disclosure of the Credit Anstalt's insolvency and a government financial rescue package. The run degenerated into a speculative attack on the fixed price of gold of the Austrian Schilling.

The U.S. record over the same period is less favorable than that of the major European countries. Before the advent of the Federal Reserve System and during the banking panics of the early 1930s, LLR action was insufficient to prevent panics. By contrast, over the past two decades, panics may have been prevented, but LLR assistance has been provided on a temporary basis to insolvent banks and, prior to the Continental Illinois crisis in 1984, no penalty rate was charged. In the U.S. on three notable occasions, the Fed (along with the FDIC) provided liberal assistance to major banks whose solvency was doubtful at the time of the assistance: Franklin National in 1974, First Pennsylvania in 1980, and Continental Illinois in 1984. Further, in the first case, loans were advanced at below-market rates (Garcia and Plautz, 1988). This Federal Reserve policy toward large banks of doubtful solvency differs significantly from the classical doctrine.

The Bank of England followed similar policies in the 1974 Fringe Bank rescue and the 1982 Johnson Matthey affair. In 1985, the Bank of Canada arranged for the major chartered banks to purchase the assets of two small insolvent Alberta banks and fully compensate all depositors. In contrast to the Anglo-Saxon experience, the German Bundesbank allowed the Herstatt Bank to be liquidated in 1974 but provided LLR assistance to the market. Thus, although the classical doctrine has been long understood and successfully applied, recent experience suggests that its basic message is no longer always adhered to.

V. CONCLUSION: SOME LESSONS FROM HISTORY

One can draw a number of conclusions from the historical record.

(1) Banking panics are rare events. They occurred more often in the U.S. than in other countries. They usually occurred during serious recessions associated with declines in the money supply and sharp price level reversals. The likelihood of their occurrence would be greatly diminished in a diversified nationwide branch banking system.

(2) Successful LLR actions prevented panics on numerous occasions. On those occasions when panics were not prevented, either the requisite institutions did not exist or the authorities did not understand the proper actions to take. Most countries developed an effective LLR mechanism by the last one-third of the nineteenth century. The U.S. was the principal exception.

(3) Some public authority must provide the lender of last resort function. The incidence of major international financial crises in 1837, 1857, 1873, 1890-93, 1907, 1914, 1930-33 suggests that in such episodes aggregate shocks can set in train a series of events leading to a nationwide scramble for high-powered money.

(4) Such an authority does not have to be a central bank. This is evident from the experience of Canada and other countries (including the U.S. experience under the Aldrich-Vreeland Act in 1914). In these cases, lender of last resort functions were provided by other forms of monetary authority, including the U.S. Treasury, Canadian Department of Finance, and foreign monetary authorities.

(5) The advent of federal deposit insurance in 1934 solved the problem of banking panics in the U.S. The absence of government deposit insurance in other countries that were panic-free before the 1960s and 1970s, however, suggests that such insurance is not required to prevent banking panics.

(6) Assistance to insolvent banks was the exception rather than the rule until the 1970s.[16] The monetary authorities in earlier times erred on the side of deficiency rather than excess. Goodhart's view is certainly not a description of past practice. The recent experience with assistance to insolvent banks is inconsistent with the classical prescription. Liberal assistance to insolvent banks, combined with deposit insurance which is not priced according to risk, encourages excessive risk-taking, creating the conditions for even greater assistance to insolvent banks in the future.

In sum, the historical record for a number of countries suggests that monetary authorities following the classical precepts of Thornton and Bagehot can prevent banking panics. Against the free banking view, the record suggests that such a role must be provided by a public authority. Moreover, contrary to Goodhart's view, successful LLR actions in the past did not require assistance to insolvent banks. Finally, the record suggests that the monetary authority's task would be eased considerably by allowing nationwide branch banking and by following a policy geared towards price level stability. Under such a regime, as Goodfriend and King argue, open market operations would be sufficient to offset unexpected scrambles for liquidity.

NOTES

[1] In theory private deposit insurance could also be used. In practice, to succeed in the U.S., such arrangements would require the private authority to have the power, currently possessed by the FDIC, to monitor, supervise, and declare insolvent its members. Also the capacity of the private insurance industry is too limited to underwrite the stock of government-insured deposits. (Benston et al., 1986, ch. 3). Alternatives to deposit insurance include requiring banks to hold safe assets (treasury bills), charging fees for service, and one hundred percent reserves.

[2] Bank of England notes served as currency and reserves for the London banks. Country banks issued bank notes but kept correspondent balances in the London banks. From 1797 to 1821, Bank of England notes were inconvertible into gold.

[3] Bagehot distinguished between the response to an external gold drain induced by a balance of payment deficit (raising the Bank rate) and the response to an internal drain (lending freely).

[4] Bagehot has been criticized for not stating clearly when the central bank should intervene (Rockoff, 1986), for not giving specific guidelines to distinguish between sound and unsound banks (Humphrey, 1975), and for not realizing that provision of the LLR facility to individual banks would encourage them to take greater risks than otherwise (Hirsch, 1977).

[5] In part, Humphrey's summary of the Classical position is:

". . . The lender of last resort's responsibility is to the entire financial system and not to specific institutions."

"The lender of last resort exists not to prevent the occurrence but rather to neutralize the impact of financial shocks."

"The lender's duty is a twofold one consisting first, of lending without stint during actual panics and second, of acknowledging beforehand its duty to lend freely in all future panics."

"The lender should be willing to advance indiscriminately to any and all sound borrowing on all sound assets no matter what the type."

"In no case should the central bank accommodate unsound borrowers. The lender's duty lay in preventing panics from spreading to the sound institutions, and not in rescuing unsound ones."

"All accommodations would occur at a penalty rate, i.e., the central bank should rely on price rather than non-price mechanisms to ration use of its last resort lending facility."

"The overriding objective of the lender of last resort was to prevent panic-induced declines in the money stock...." (Humphrey, 1975 p.9)

[6] Meltzer (1986) succinctly restates Bagehot's four principles:

"The central bank is the only lender of last resort in a monetary system such as ours."

"To prevent illiquid banks from closing, the central bank should lend on any collateral that is marketable in the ordinary course of business when there is a panic..."

"Central bank loans, or advances, should be made in large amounts, on demand, at a rate of interest above the market rate."

"The above three principles of central bank behavior should be stated in advance and followed in a crisis." (Meltzer, 1986, p. 83)

[7] Like Goodfriend and King, Friedman (1960) earlier argued for use of open market operations exclusively and against the use of the discount window as an unnecessary form of discretion which "involves special governmental assistance to a particular group of financial institutions" (p. 38). Also see Hirsch (1977) and Goodhart (1988) for the argument that Bagehot's rule was really designed for a closely knit/cartelized banking system such as the London clearing banks.

[8] Cagan (1988) in his comment on Goodfriend and King makes the case for retention of discount window lending in the case of "a flight to quality". In that case, the discount window can be used to provide support to particular sectors of the economy which have had banking services temporarily curtailed.

[9] A restriction of convertibility itself could exacerbate a panic because the public, in anticipating such restriction, demands currency sooner.

[10] Selgin (1990) argues that the Bank Charter Act of 1844 exacerbated the problem of panics because it imposed tight constraints on the issue of bank notes by the Issue Department. However, the Banking Department surely could have discounted commercial paper from correspondent banks without requiring further note issue. That is one of Bagehot's main points in *Lombard Street*.

[11] Selgin (1990), based on evidence by Rolnick and Weber (1986), argues that the episodes designated as panics in the antebellum Free Banking era are not comparable to these in the National Banking era because they did not involve contagion effects. Evidence to the contrary, however, is presented by Hasan and Dwyer (1988).

[12] For similar evidence for the remaining cyclical downturns in this period, see Bordo (1986, Table 6, 1A).

[13] In relating the changes in the money stock to changes in the deposit-currency ratio, we hold constant the influence of the other two proximate determinants of the money supply: the deposit-reserve ratio and the stock of high-powered money. It is calculated using the formula developed in Friedman and Schwartz (1963), Appendix B.

[14] Sweden from 1830 to 1902 had a system of competitive note issue and unlimited liability. According to Jonung (1985), there is evidence neither of overissue nor of bank runs.

[15] Switzerland also had a successful experience with free banks 1826-1850 (Weber, 1988) but like Scotland's dependence on the Bank of England, she depended on the Bank of France as lender of last resort (Goodhart, 1985).

[16] Although in the U.S., the policy of purchase and assumption carried out by the FDIC and FSLIC before that date incorporated elements of public subsidy.

REFERENCES

Bagehot, W. (1873). *Lombard Street: A Description of the Money Market*. London: H.S. King.

Benston, G. J. (1983). "Deposit Insurance and Bank Failures." Federal Reserve Bank of Atlanta *Economic Review*. (March), pp. 4-17.

Benston, G. J., et al. (1986). *Perspectives on Safe and Sound Banking: Past, Present, and Future*. Cambridge: MIT Press.

Bordo, M. D. (1981). "The Classical Gold Standard: Some Lessons for Today." Federal Reserve Bank of St. Louis *Review*. (May), 63: 2-17.

_____ (1986). "Financial Crises, Banking Crises, Stock Market Crashes and the Money Supply: Some International Evidence, 1870-1933." In F. Capie and G. E. Wood (eds.), *Financial Crises and the World Banking System*. London: MacMillan.

Bordo, M. D. and A. Redish (1987). "Why did the Bank of Canada Emerge in 1935?" *Journal of Economic History*. (June), 47(2): 401-17.

Cagan, P. (1965). *Determinants and Effects of Changes in the Stock of Money, 1875-1960*. New York: Columbia University Press.

_____ (1988). "Commentary." In W. S. Haraf and R. M. Kushmeider, (eds.) *Restructuring Banking and Financial Services in America*. Washington: American Enterprise Institute.

Calomiris, C. (1989). "Deposit Insurance: Lessons from the Record." Federal Reserve Bank of Chicago *Economic Perspectives*. (May-June), pp. 10-30.

Cowen, T. and R. Kroszner (1989). "Scottish Banking Before 1845: A Model for Laissez-Faire." *Journal of Money, Credit and Banking*. (May), 21(2): 221-31.

Dowd, K. (1988). *Private Money: The Path to Monetary Stability*. Institute of Economic Affairs Hobart Paper 112. London.

Friedman, M. (1960). *A Program for Monetary Stability*. New York: Fordham University Press.

Friedman, M. and A. J. Schwartz (1963). *A Monetary History of the United States*. Princeton: Princeton University Press.

Garcia, G. and E. Plautz (1988). *The Federal Reserve: Lender of Last Resort*. Cambridge: Ballinger Publishing Company.

Goodfriend, M. (1989). "Money, Credit, Banking, and Payments System Policy." In D. B. Humphrey (ed.), *The U.S. Payments Systems: Efficiency, Risk and the Role of the Federal Reserve*. Boston: Kluwer Academic Publishers.

Goodfriend, M. and R. A. King, (1988). "Financial Deregulation, Monetary Policy, and Central Banking." In W. S. Haraf and R. M. Kushmeider (eds.), *Restructuring Banking and Financial Services in America*. Washington: American Enterprise Institute.

Goodhart, C. A. E. (1985). *The Evolution of Central Banks*. London: London School of Economics and Political Science.

_____ (1987). "Why Do Banks Need a Central

Bank?" *Oxford Economic Papers.* (March), 39:75-89.

Gorton, G. (1985). "Clearing houses and the Origins of Central Banking in the U.S." *Journal of Economic History.* (June), 45: 277-84.

Gorton, G. and D. J. Mullineaux (1987). "Joint Production of Confidence: Endogenous Regulation and 19th Century Commercial Bank Clearinghouses." *Journal of Money, Credit and Banking.* (November), 19(4): 457-68.

Hasan, I. and G. P. Dwyer, Jr. (1988). "Contagious Bank Runs in the Free Banking Period." (mimeo). Cliometrics Conference, Oxford, Ohio.

Hirsch, F. (1977). "The Bagehot Problem." *Manchester School of Economics and Social Studies.* (September), 45(3): 241-57.

Humphrey, T. (1975). "The Classical Concept of the Lender of Last Resort." Federal Reserve Bank of Richmond *Economic Review.* (January/February), 61:2-9.

_____ (1989). "Lender of Last Resort: The Concept in History." Federal Reserve Bank of Richmond *Economic Review.* (March/April), 75: 8-16.

Jonung, L. (1985). "The Economics of Private Money: the Experience of Private Notes in Sweden, 1831-1902." (mimeo) Lund University.

Kaufman, G. G. (1988). "The Truth about Bank Runs." In C. England and T. Huertas (eds.), *The Financial Services Revolution.* Boston: Kluwer Academic Publishers.

Kindleberger, C. (1978). *Manias, Panics and Crashes.* London: MacMillan.

Meltzer, A. (1986). "Financial Failures and Financial Policies." In G. G. Kaufman and R. C. Kormendi (eds.), *Deregulating Financial Service: Public Policy in Flux.* Cambridge: Ballinger Publishing Company.

Morgenstern, O. (1959). *International Financial Transactions and Business Cycles.* Princeton: Princeton University Press.

Rockoff, H. (1986). "Walter Bagehot and the Theory of Central Banking." In F. Capie and G. E. Wood (eds.), *Financial Crises and the World Banking System.* London: MacMillan.

Rolnick, A. and W. Weber. (1985). "Inherent Instability in Banking: The Free Banking Experience." *Cato Journal*, May.

Schubert, A. (1987). "The Creditanstalt Crisis of 1931—A Financial Crisis Revisited." *Journal of Economic History.* (June), 47(2).

Schwartz, A. J. (1988). "Financial Stability and the Federal Safety Act." In W. S. Haraf and R. M. Kushmeider (eds.), *Restructuring Banking and Financial Services in America.* Washington: American Enterprise Institute.

_____ (1986). "Real and Pseudo—Financial Crises." In F. Capie and G. E. Wood (eds.), *Financial Crises and the World Banking System.* London: MacMillan.

Selgin, G. A. (1988). *The Theory of Free Banking: Money Supply Under Competitive Note Issue.* Totowa, N. J.: Rowman and Littlefield.

_____ (1990). "Legal Restrictions, Financial Weakening, and the Lender of Last Resort." *Cato Journal*. forthcoming.

Research for this article began while the author was a Visiting Scholar at the Federal Reserve Bank of Richmond in Summer, 1988. Thanks go to the following for help on this paper and on an earlier draft: George Benston, Marvin Goodfriend, Bob Hetzel, Tom Humphrey, Allan Meltzer, Anna Schwartz, and Bob Graboyes. Paulino Texeira provided valuable research assistance. The views expressed are those of the author and not necessarily those of the Federal Reserve Bank of Richmond or the Federal Reserve System.